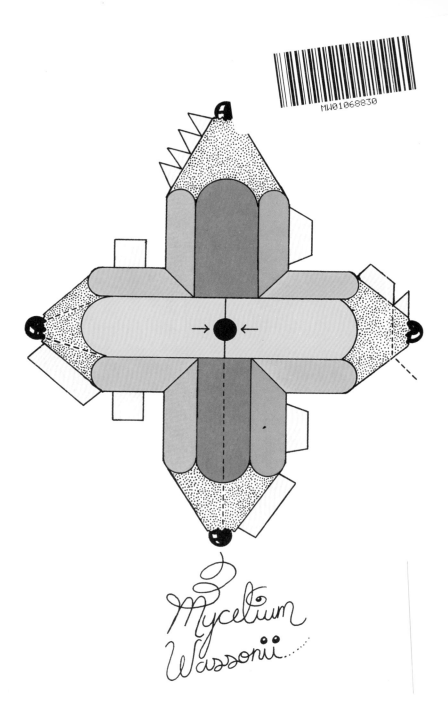

Mycelium Wassonii

First published in the United States of America in 2021 by Anthology Editions, LLC • 87 Guernsey St., Brooklyn, NY 11222 • anthologyeditions.com • Copyright © 2021 by Anthology Editions, LLC • Artwork © 2021 by Brian Blomerth • Introduction © 2021 by Paul Stamets • All rights reserved under Pan American and International Copyright Conventions. No part of this publication may be reproduced, stored in a retrieval system, or transmitted in any form or by any means, electronic, mechanical, photocopying, recording, or otherwise, without prior consent of the publishers. • Editor: Mark Iosifescu • Design: Brian Blomerth and Bryan Cipolla • First Edition • Second Printing • ARC 096 • Printed in China • ISBN: 978-1-944860-41-7 • Library of Congress Control Number: 2021939776

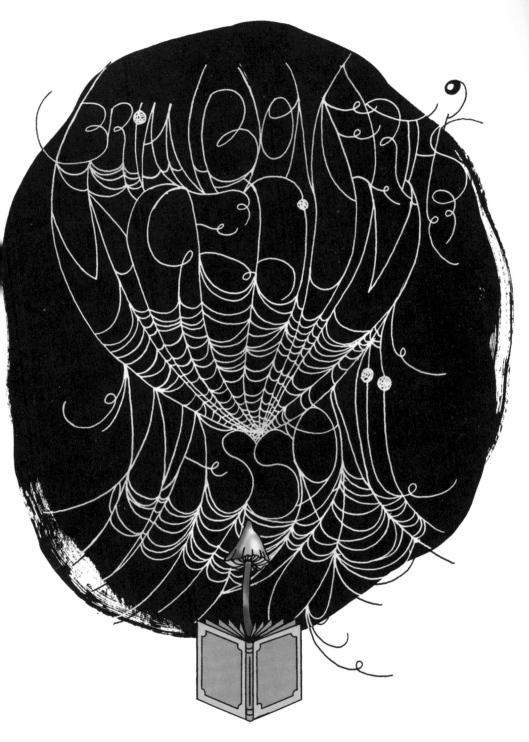

Anthology Editions
New York

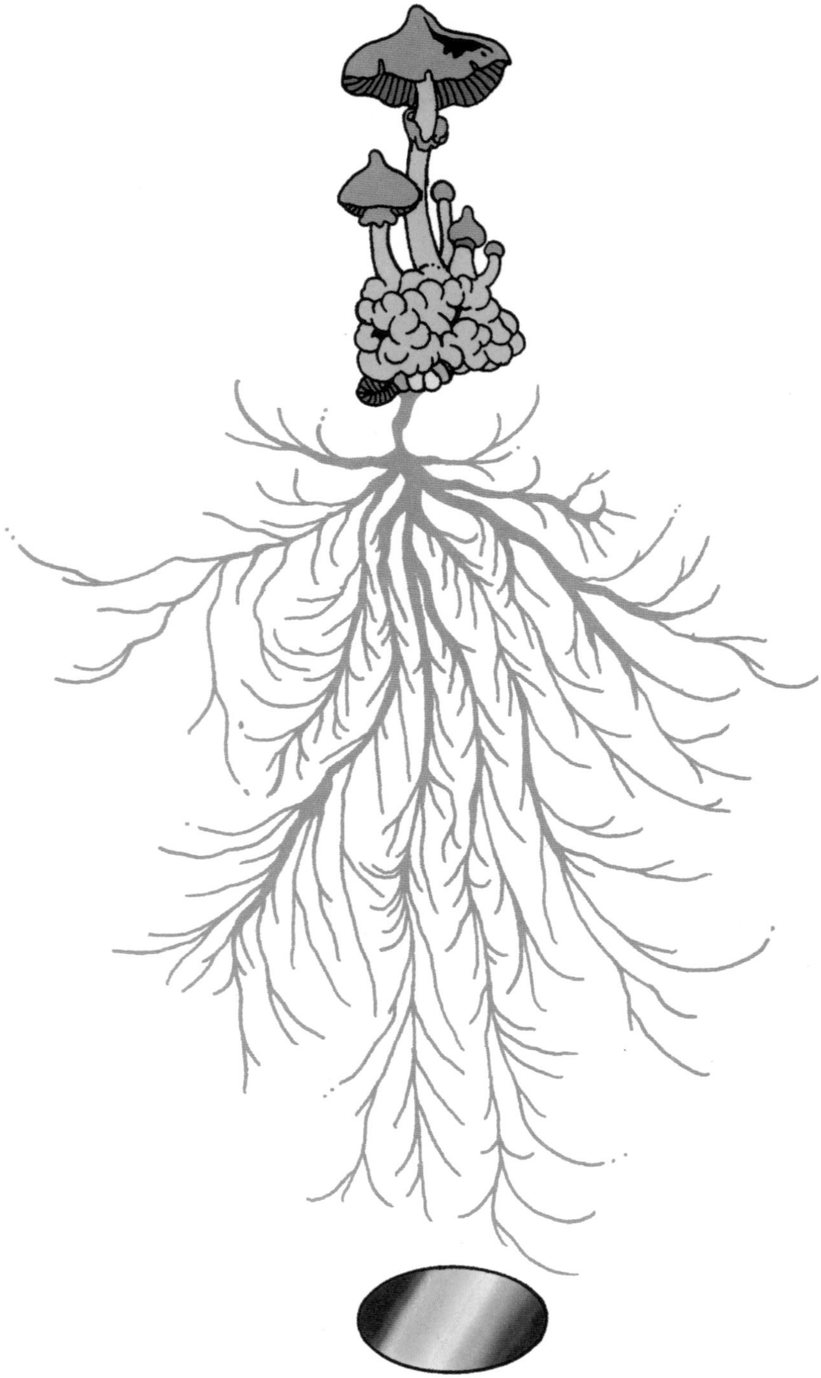

THIS BOOK BELONGS TO:

FOR...

VALENTINA PAVLOVNA WASSON

B. GORDON WASSON

MARIA SABINA

ROGER HEIM

AND

KATE LEVITT ◆◆◆

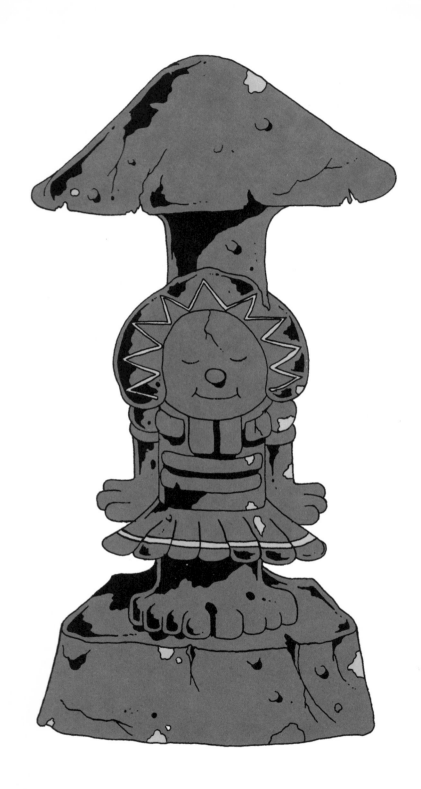

Introduction

— Paul Stamets —

I met R. Gordon Wasson several times in the late 1970s. Although most readers know of Gordon's massive contribution to bettering our understanding of the importance of psilocybin and amanita mushrooms throughout history, few understand that none of these achievements would have occurred without Valentina Pavlovna Wasson, his wife and an accomplished pediatrician, who was the true inspiration for their collective journey.

Tina Pavlovna hailed from Russia, a country with a history of "mycophilia," whereas Gordon Wasson, an American, had been instilled since childhood with "mycophobia." In fact, these terms were invented by the couple to describe their respective mushroom upbringings. Tina had collected, studied, and consumed wild mushrooms from an early age. Gordon, on the other hand, was initially appalled by Tina's enthusiasm for fungi; he associated mushrooms with death, decomposition, and the dark, dank, dangerous underground.

Gordon and Tina's first joint encounter with the mushroom, which famously came while they hiked the Catskill Mountains of New York State on their honeymoon, underscored their cultural biases. After comparing their reactions, the pair embarked on a collective lifelong journey studying ethnomycology—the cultural use and history of mushroom lore among a variety of cultures, from Russian to Mesoamerican, North American to Indian.

Gordon, schooled and inspired by Tina, came to an appreciation of mushrooms late in life. History must give Tina proper credit: she was the mycologist in their relationship, not to mention an early pioneer in noting that psilocybin could be helpful in treating psychiatric health challenges. Tina led Gordon literally by the hand into a deep field of study he would not otherwise have explored. Sadly she died prematurely, from cancer, at the age of fifty-seven in 1958, the same

year that the first monograph of Roger Heim and Gordon's epic two-volume set *Les champignons hallucinogènes du Mexique* was published. In that treatise, a new species name, "Psilocybe wassonii," was proposed in honor of the Wassons' work. Unfortunately, a few weeks before publication, another name for the same species had been published, usurping the hard-earned honoring of Roger Heim and the Wassons' multiyear effort in the taxonomy of Mexican psilocybes. "Psilocybe wassonii" was subjugated to another taxon. For this reason, *Mycelium Wassonii*, the title of this book, has an especially deep meaning to me, and hopefully will to you. It honors the collective work and partnership of this dynamic duo.

Tina's inspiration was not lost on Gordon. During the three lectures I attended, Gordon spoke effusively and passionately about his undying love for Tina. I witnessed him cry when remembering the love and adventures they had shared. I think they both would be honored to know that this book, wonderfully written and illustrated by Brian Blomerth, elevates Tina's role in the now popular psilocybin mushroom movement.

So here is a nod and a bow to Tina Wasson, a catalyst and leader. Along with other greats, such as María Sabina, the Mazatec shaman curandera who so graciously shared indigenous traditions with the Wassons and many others, Tina's example has served to carry the torch of knowledge forward through the millennia, sharing the stage in history.

We are here today because of great mycologists like María Sabina and Valentina Wasson. Respect.

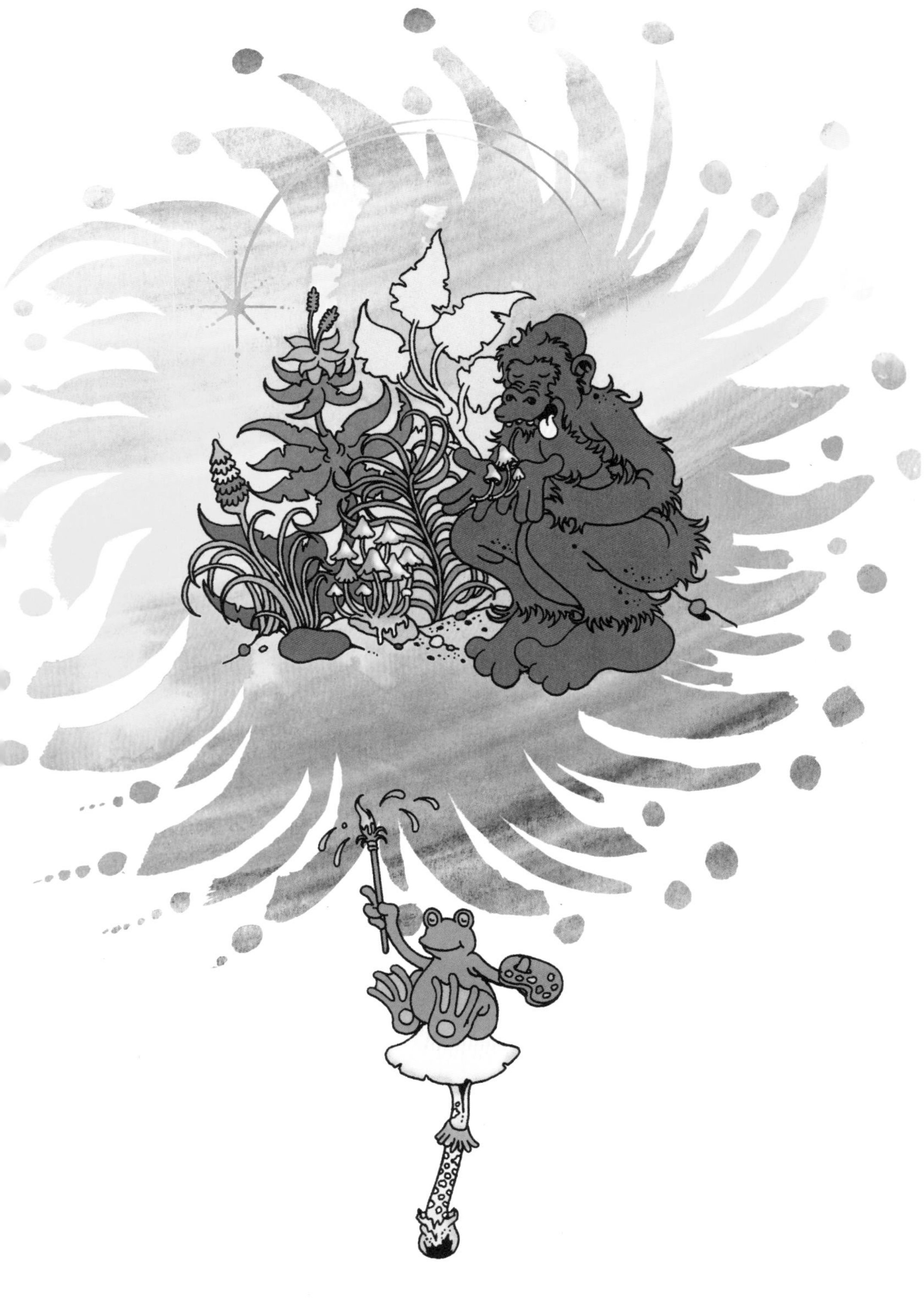

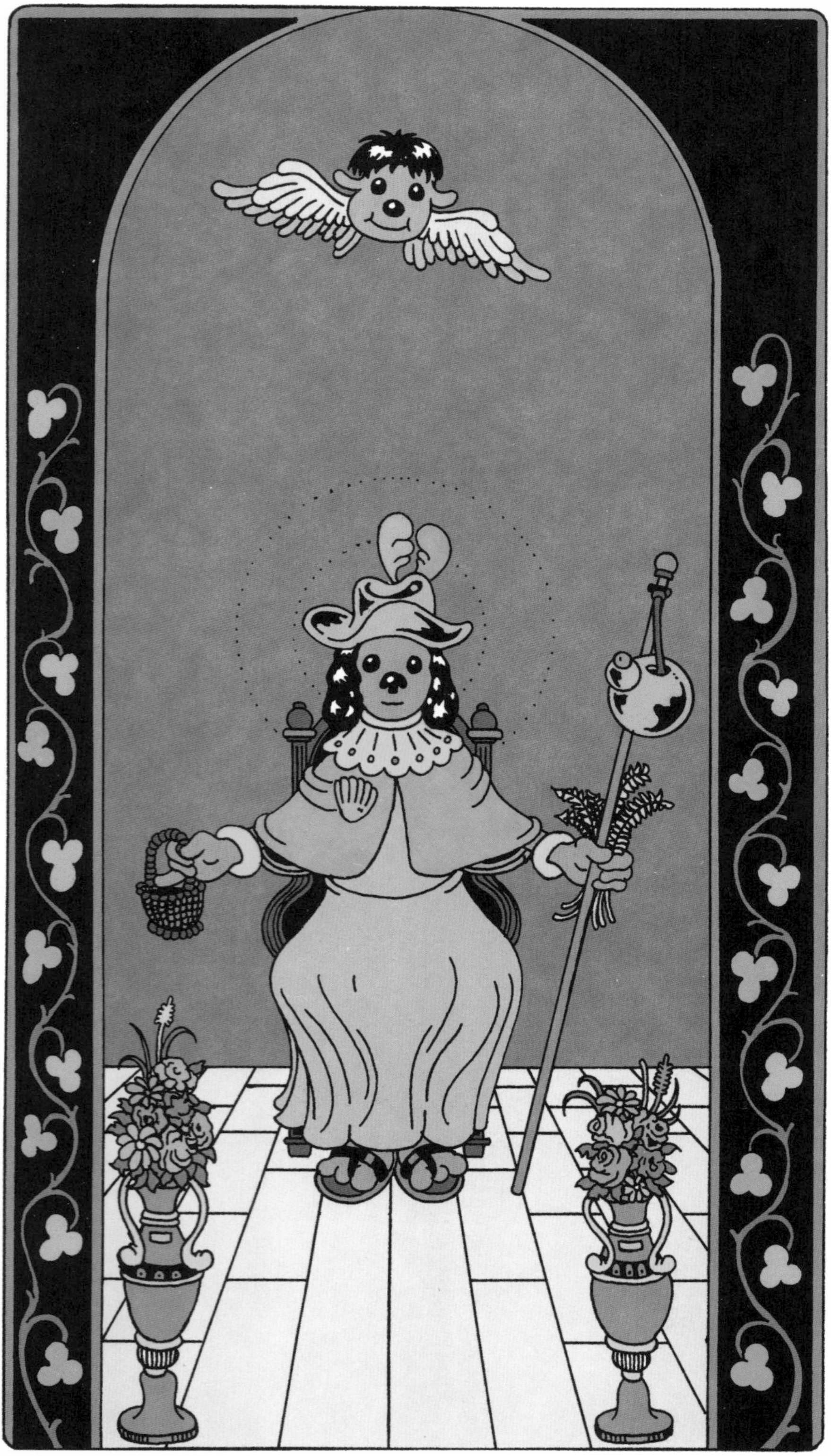

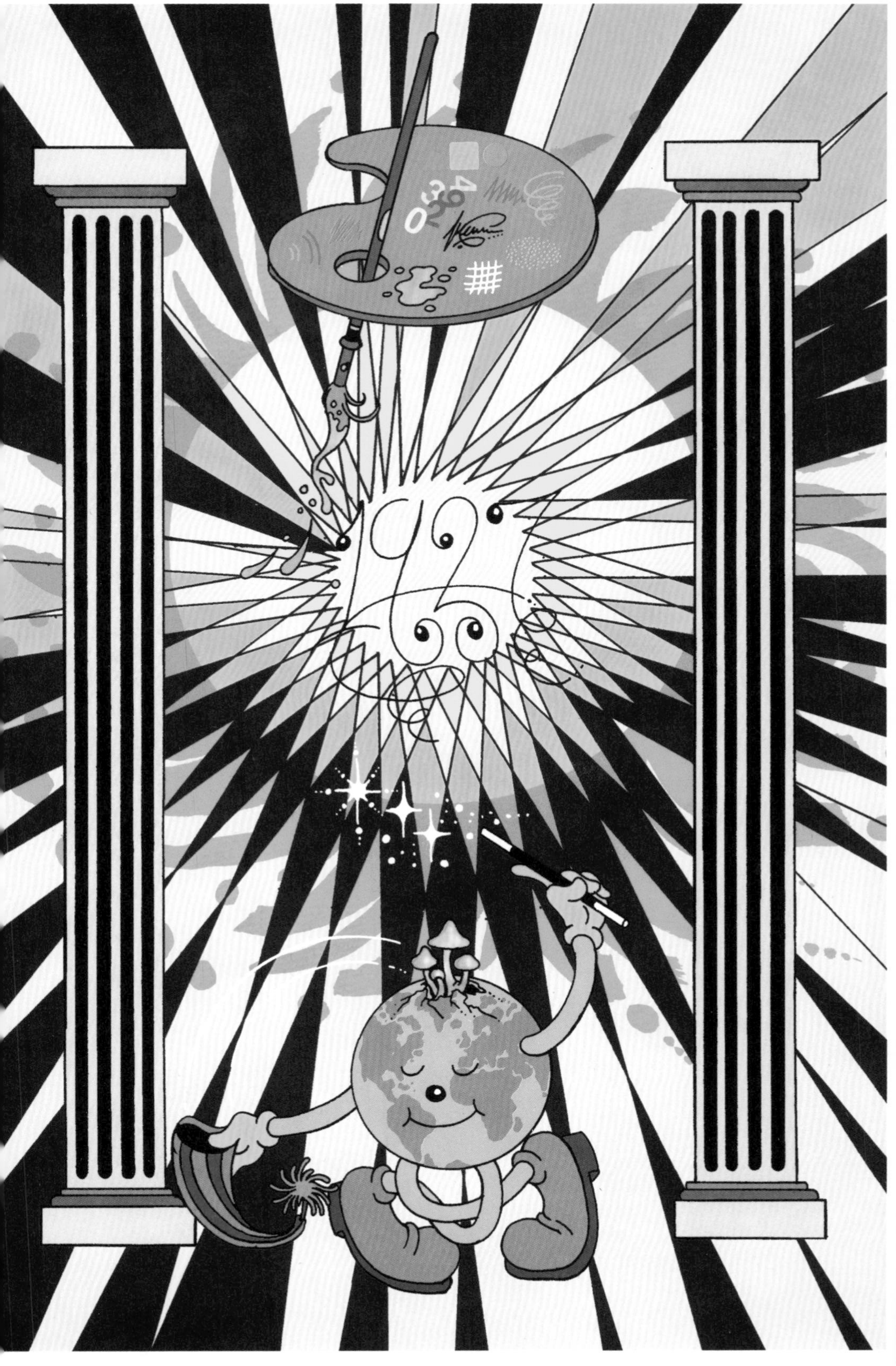

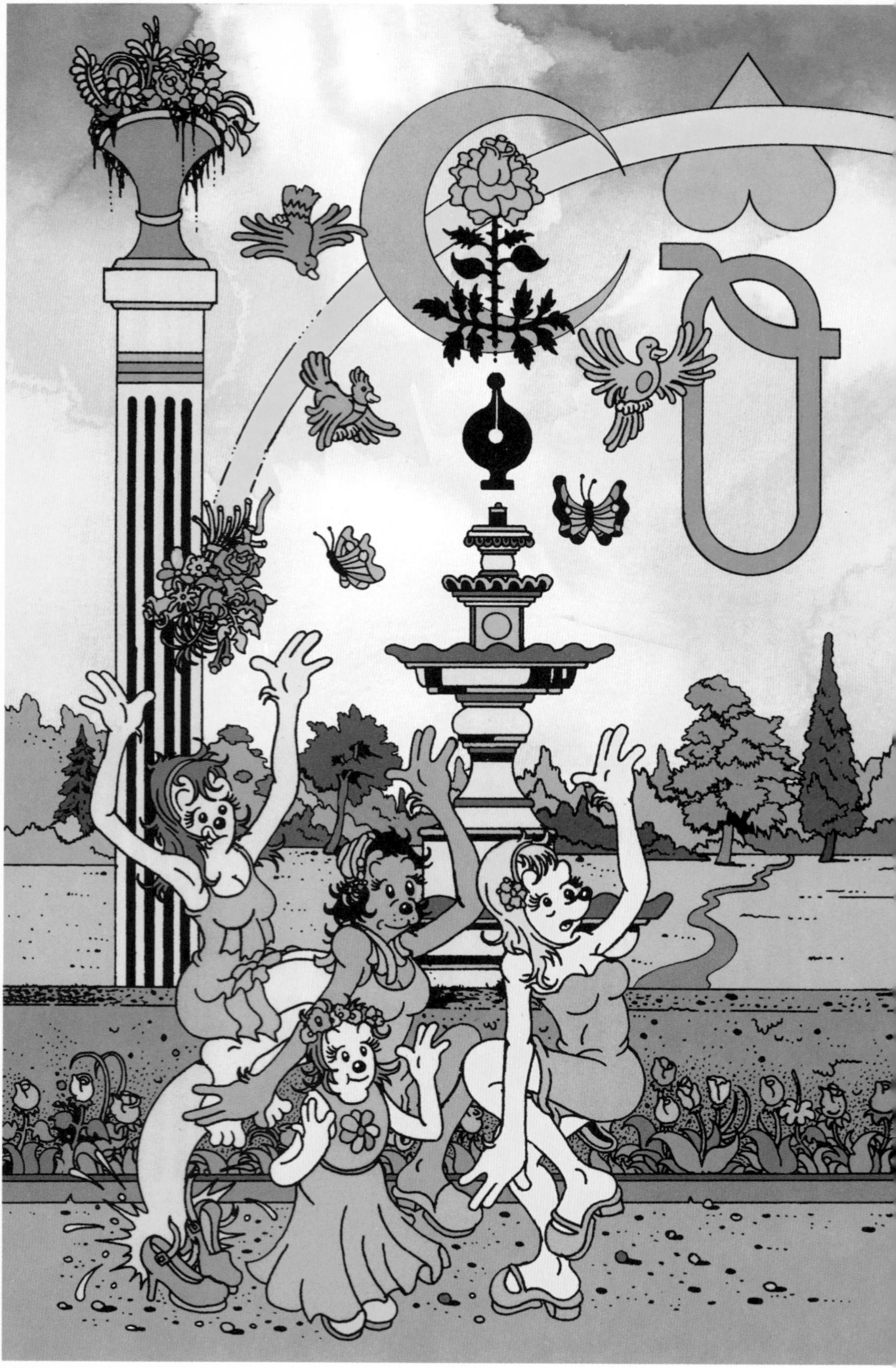

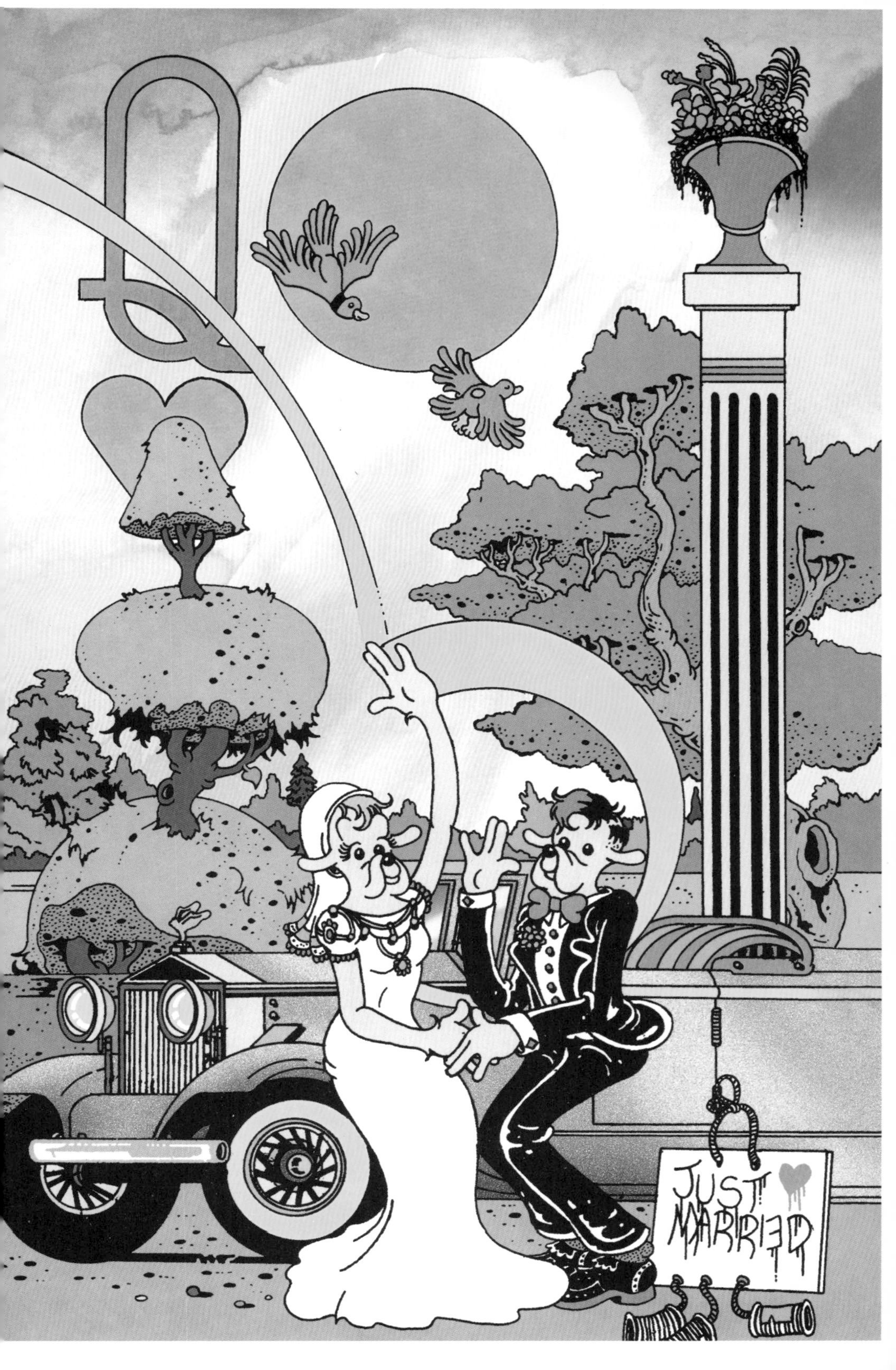
JUST MARRIED

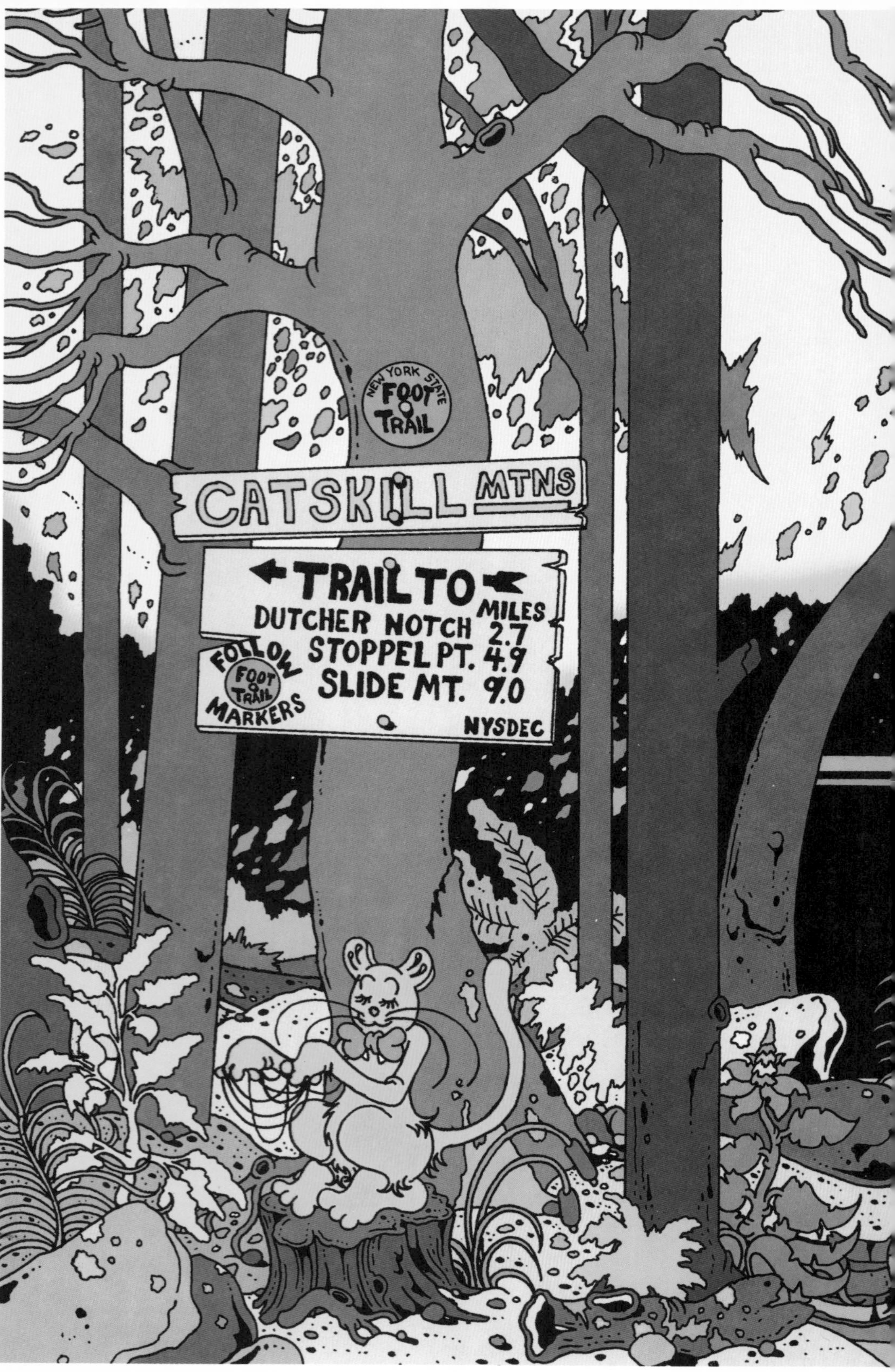

NEW YORK STATE FOOT TRAIL
CATSKILL MTNS
TRAIL TO
MILES
DUTCHER NOTCH 2.7
STOPPEL PT. 4.9
SLIDE MT. 9.0
FOLLOW FOOT TRAIL MARKERS
NYSDEC

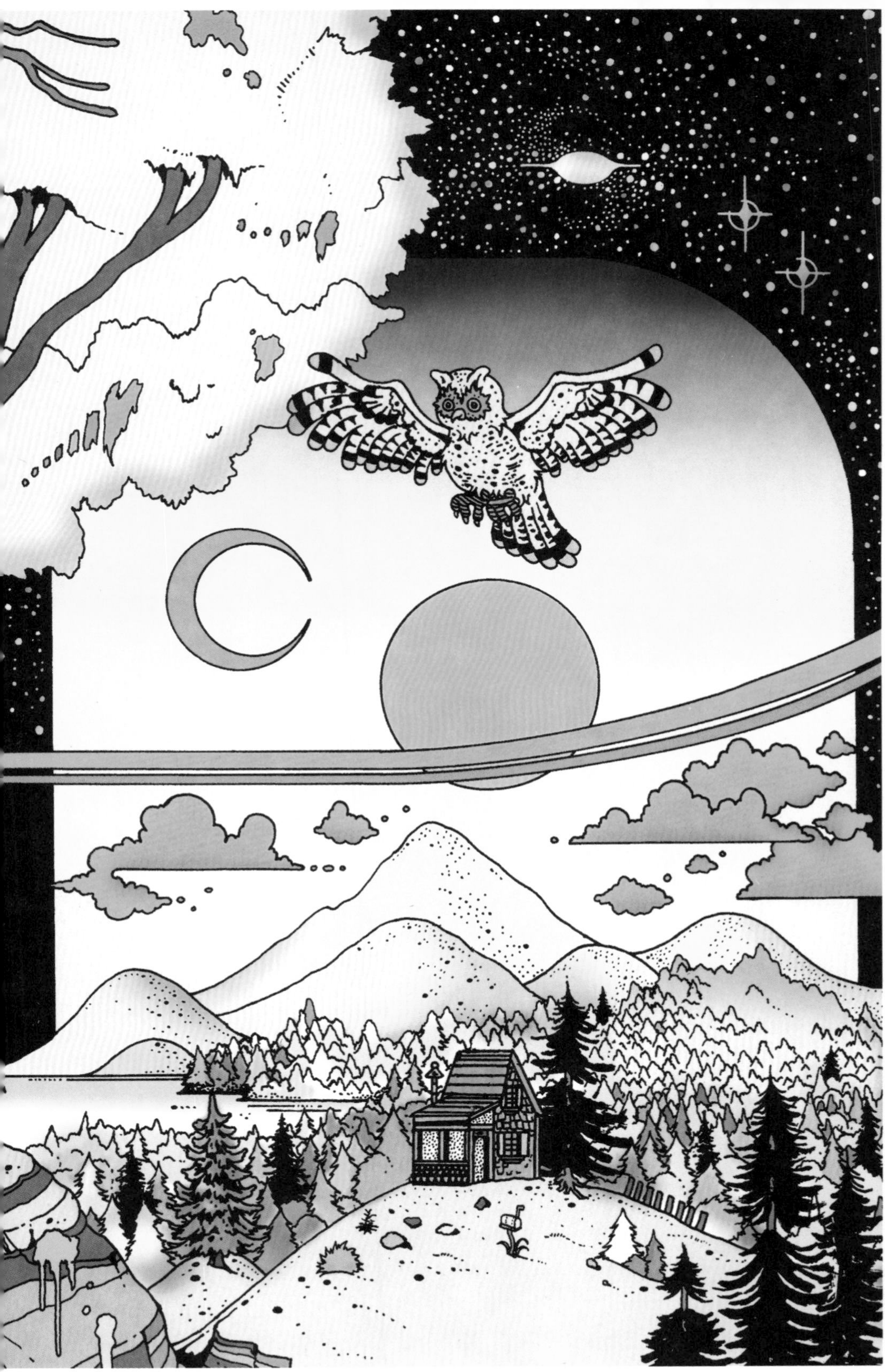

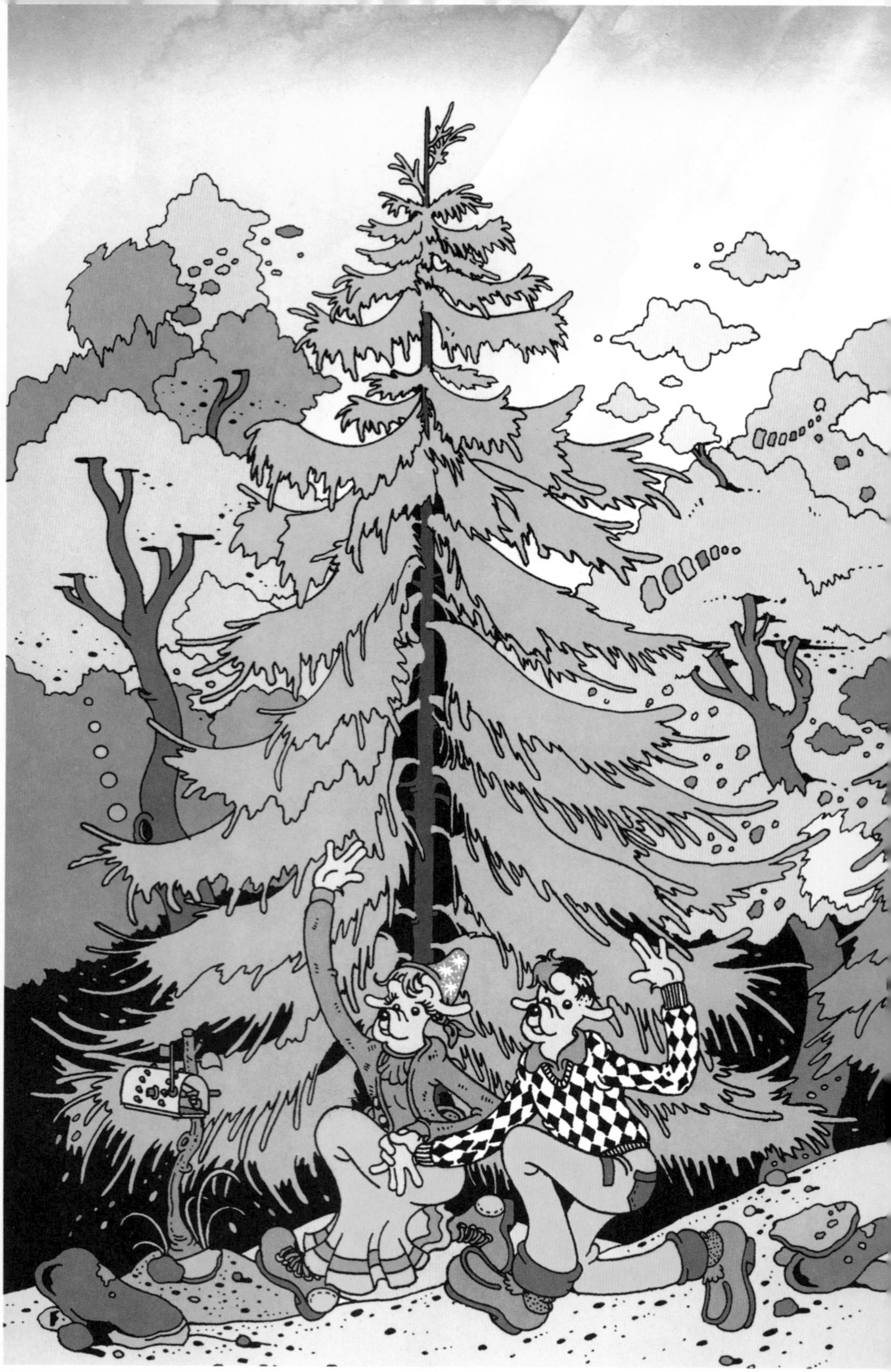

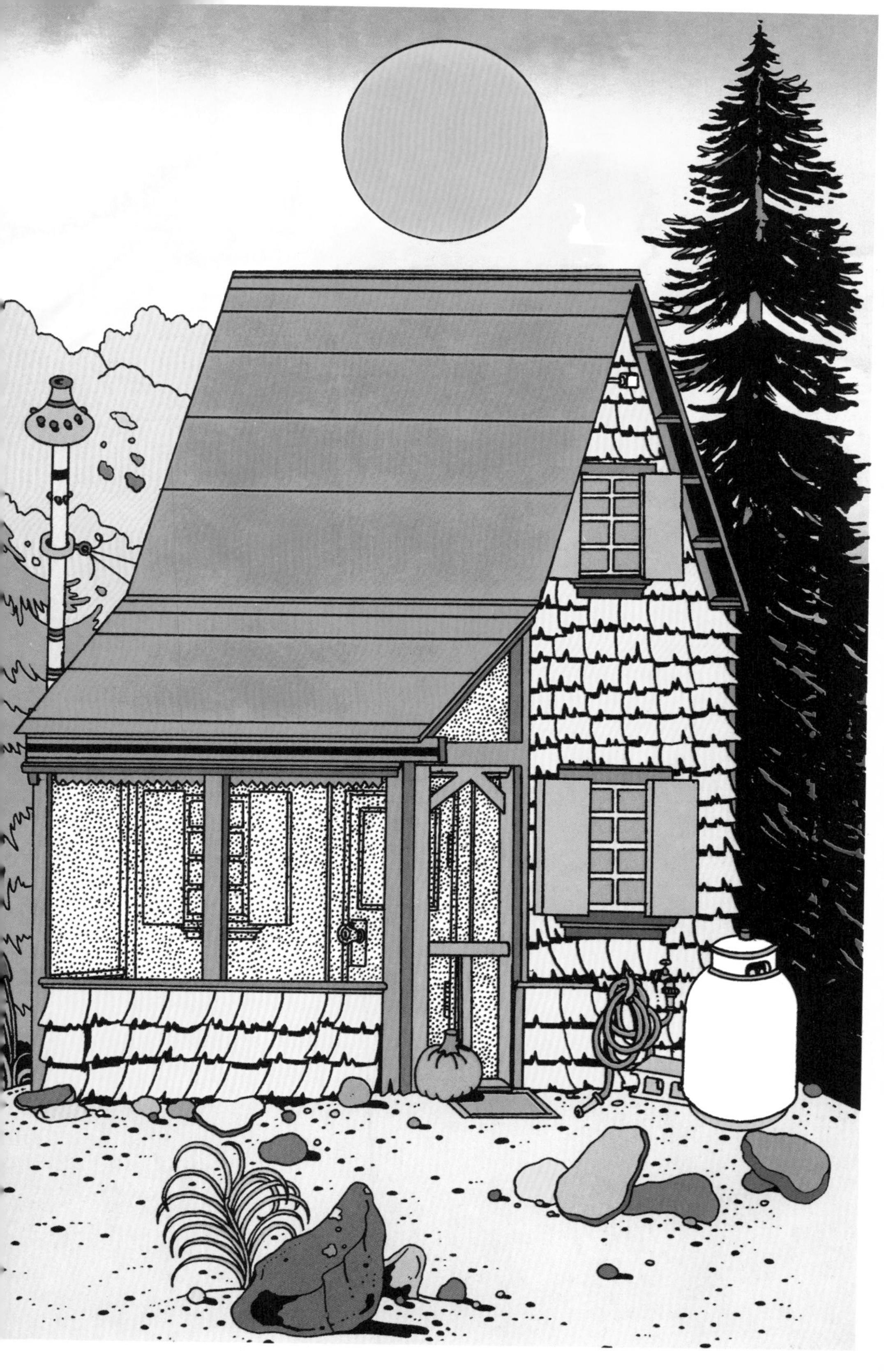

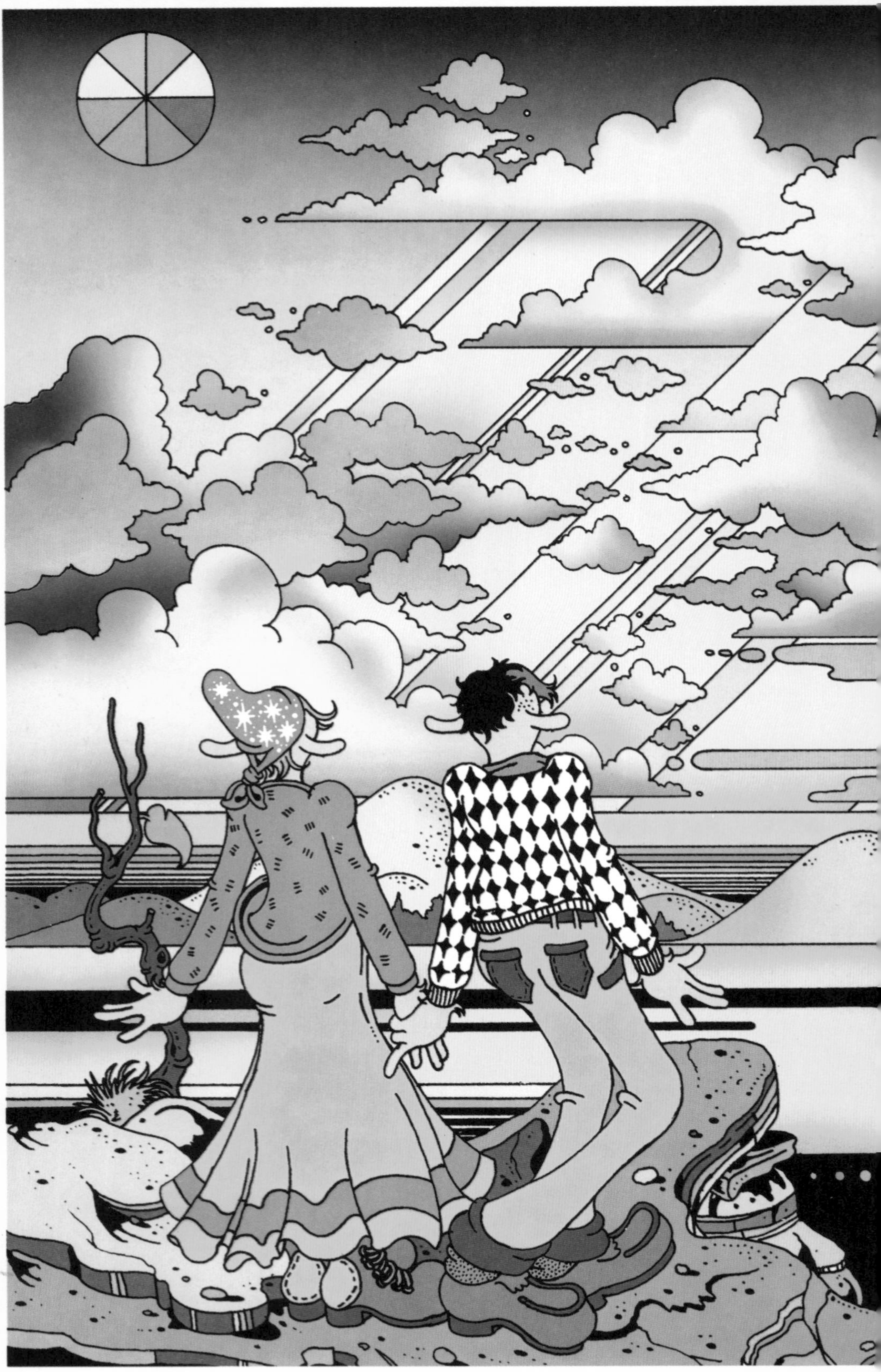

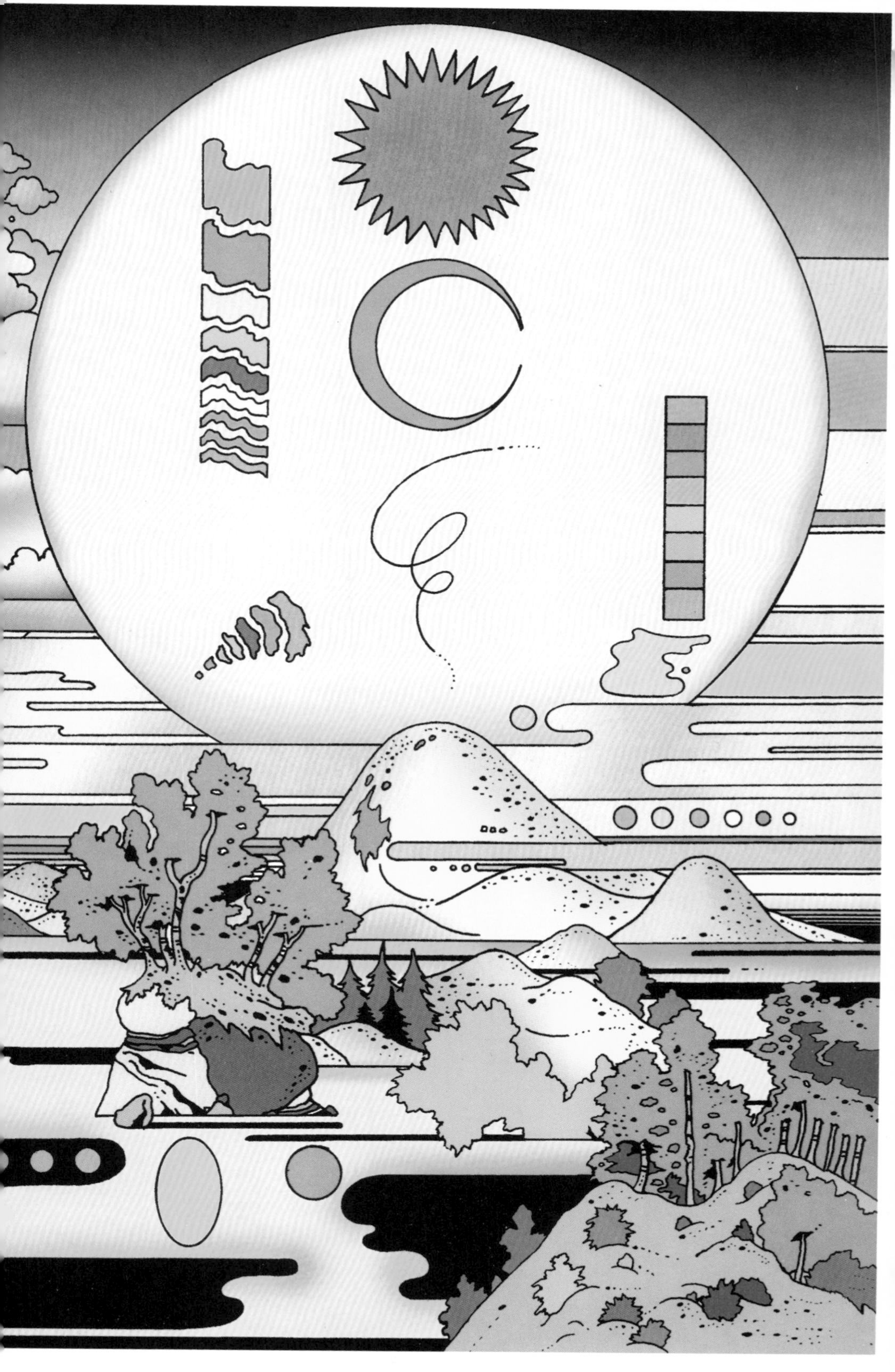

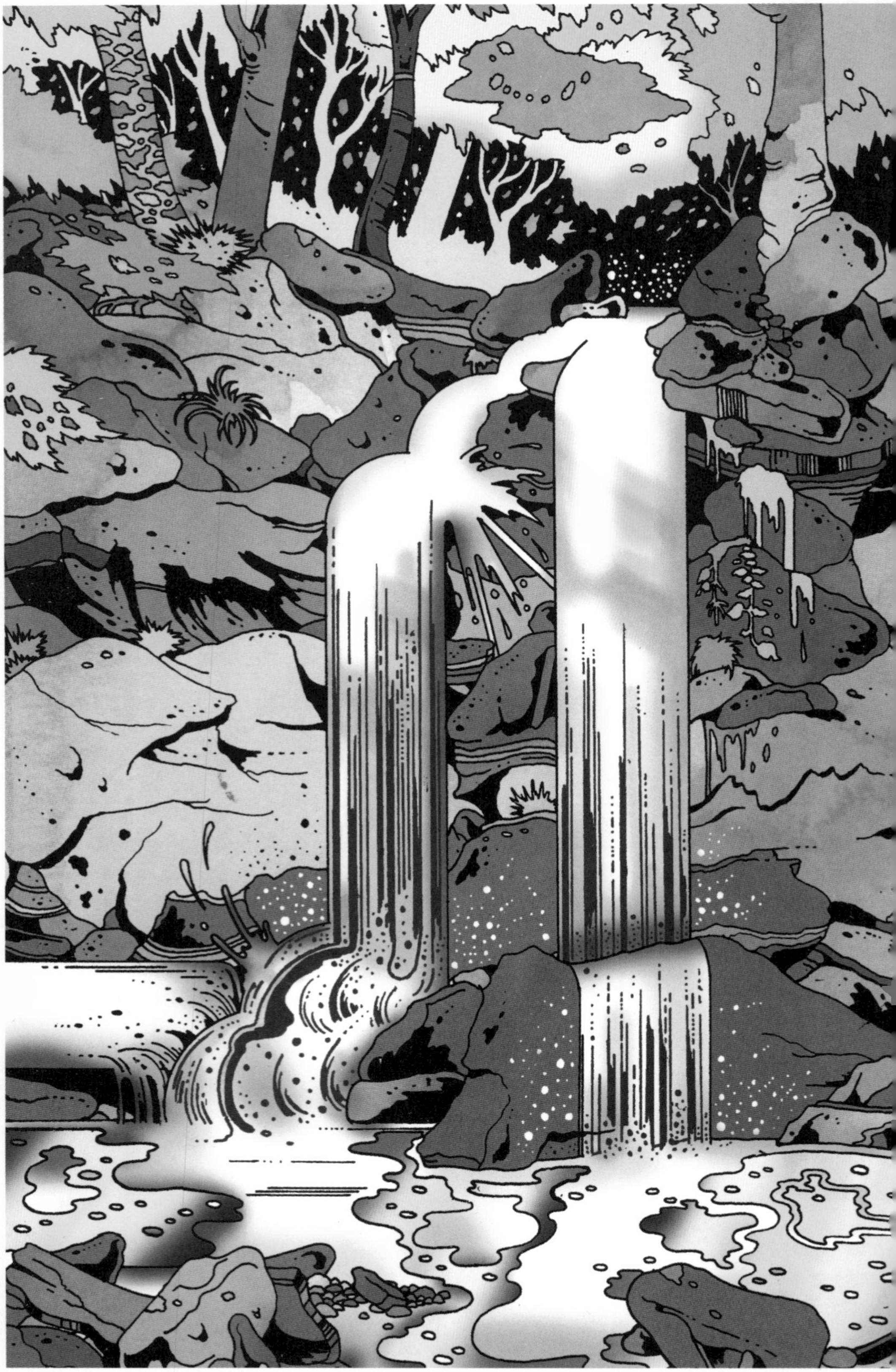

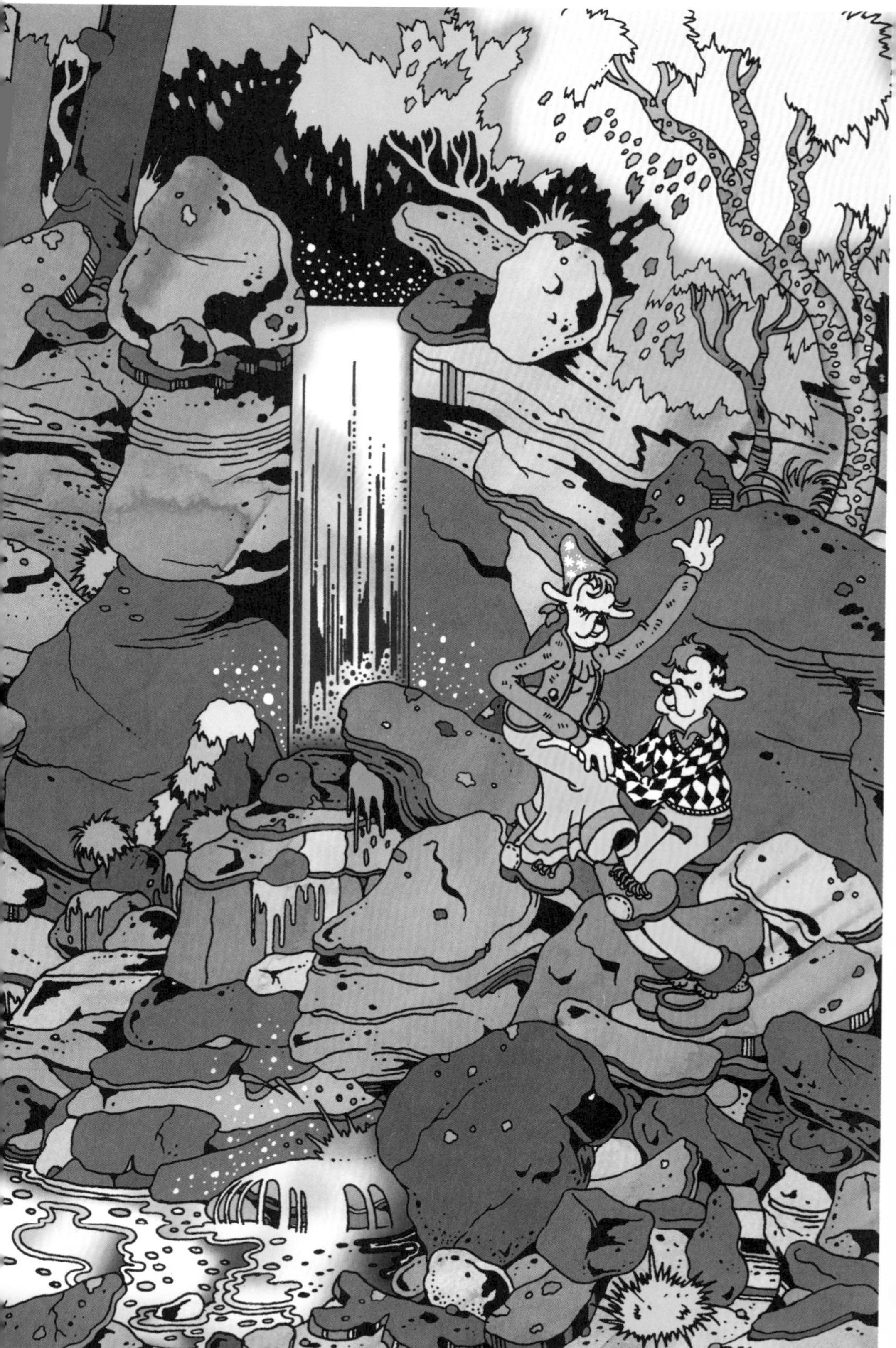

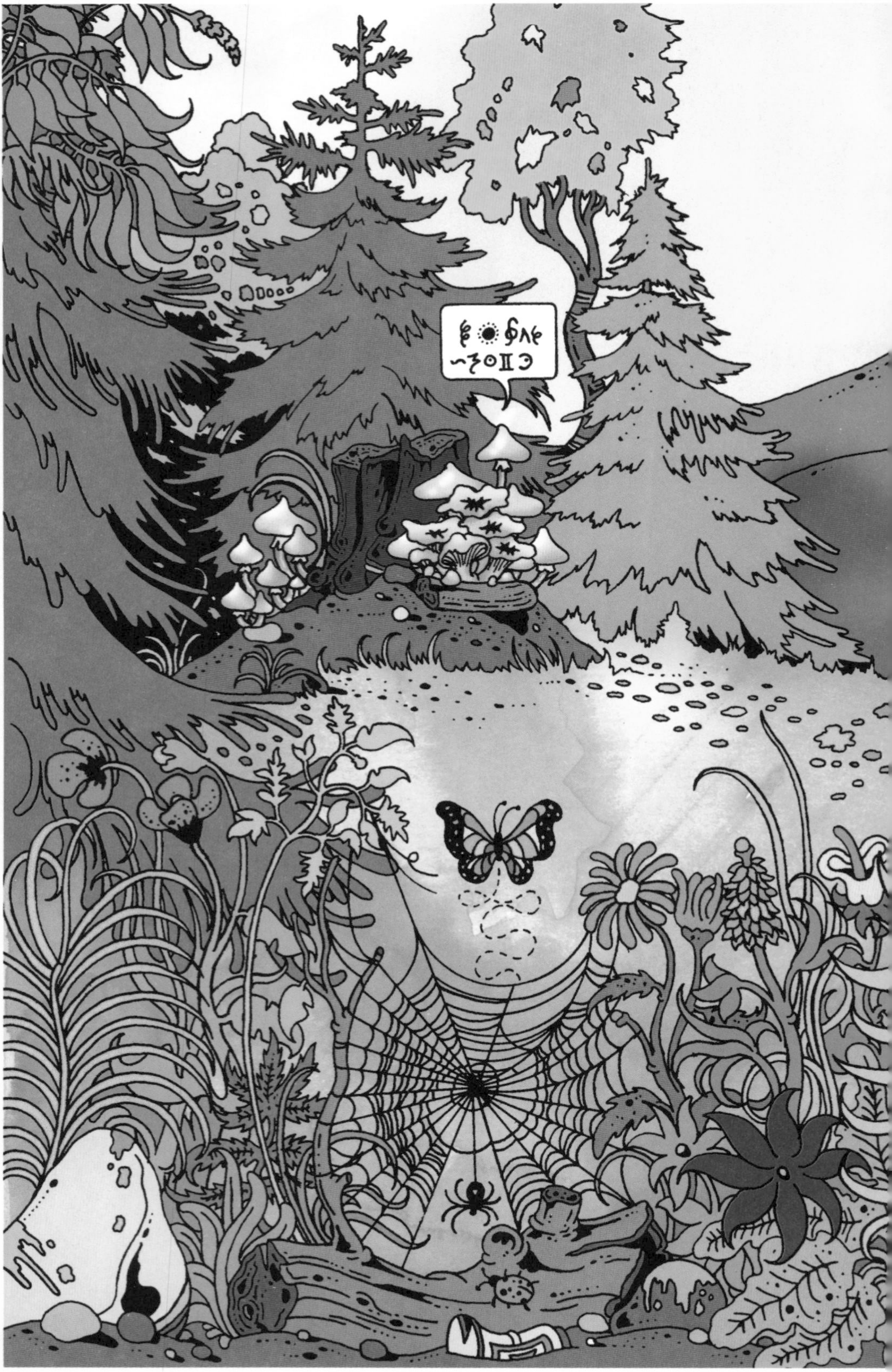

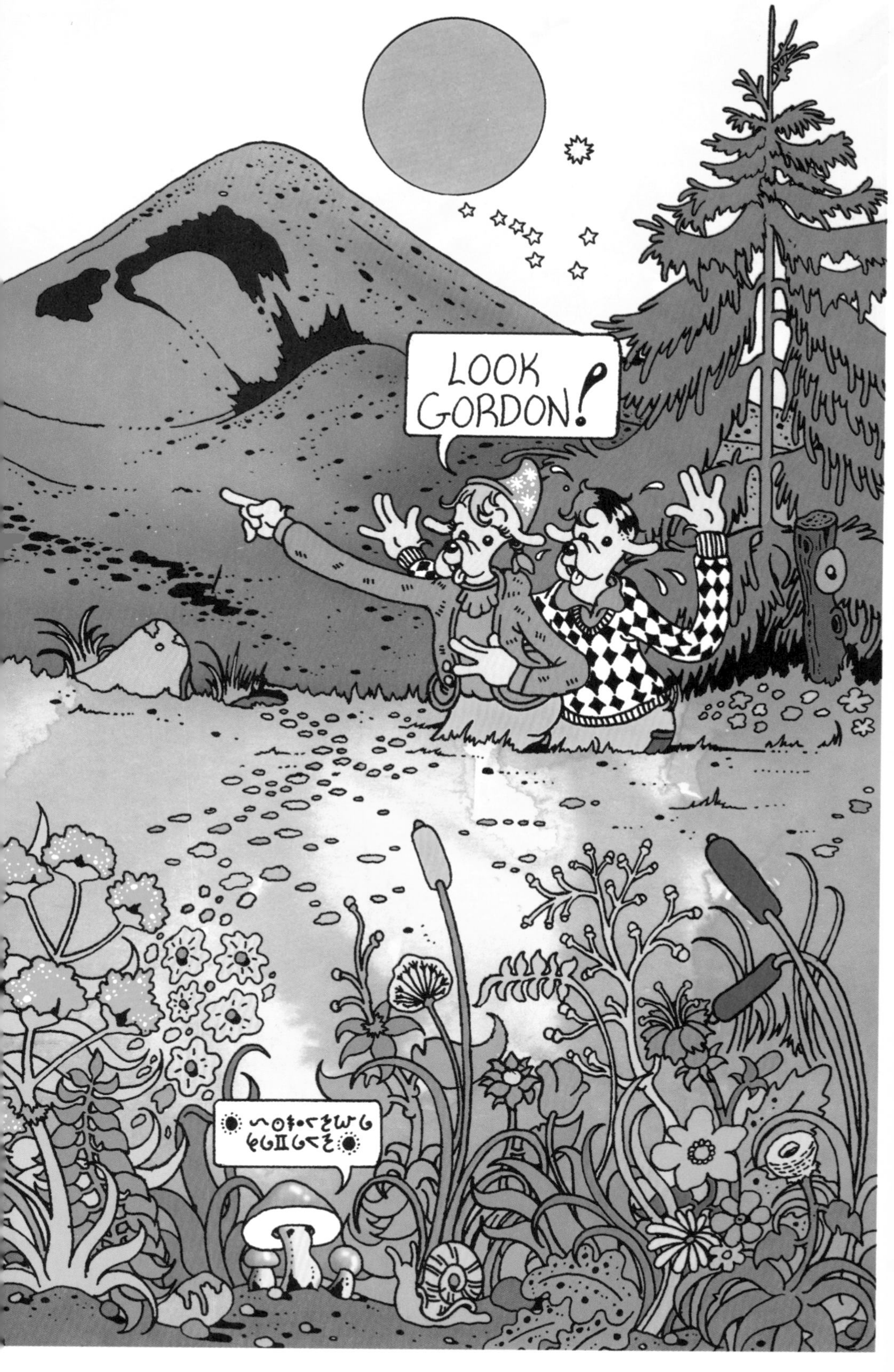
LOOK GORDON!

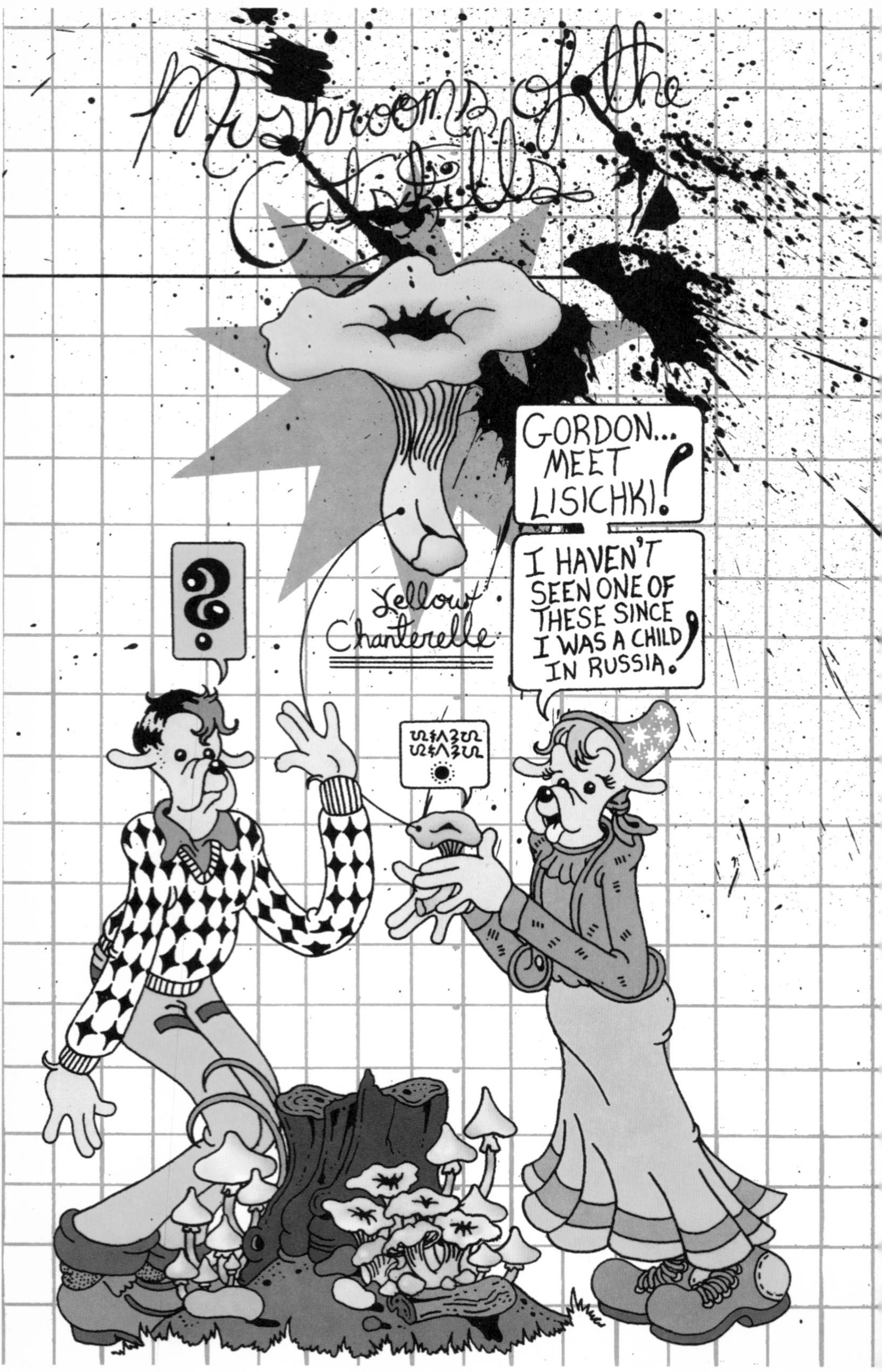

Mushrooms of the Catskills
Yellow Chanterelle
GORDON... MEET LISICHKI!
?
I HAVEN'T SEEN ONE OF THESE SINCE I WAS A CHILD IN RUSSIA!

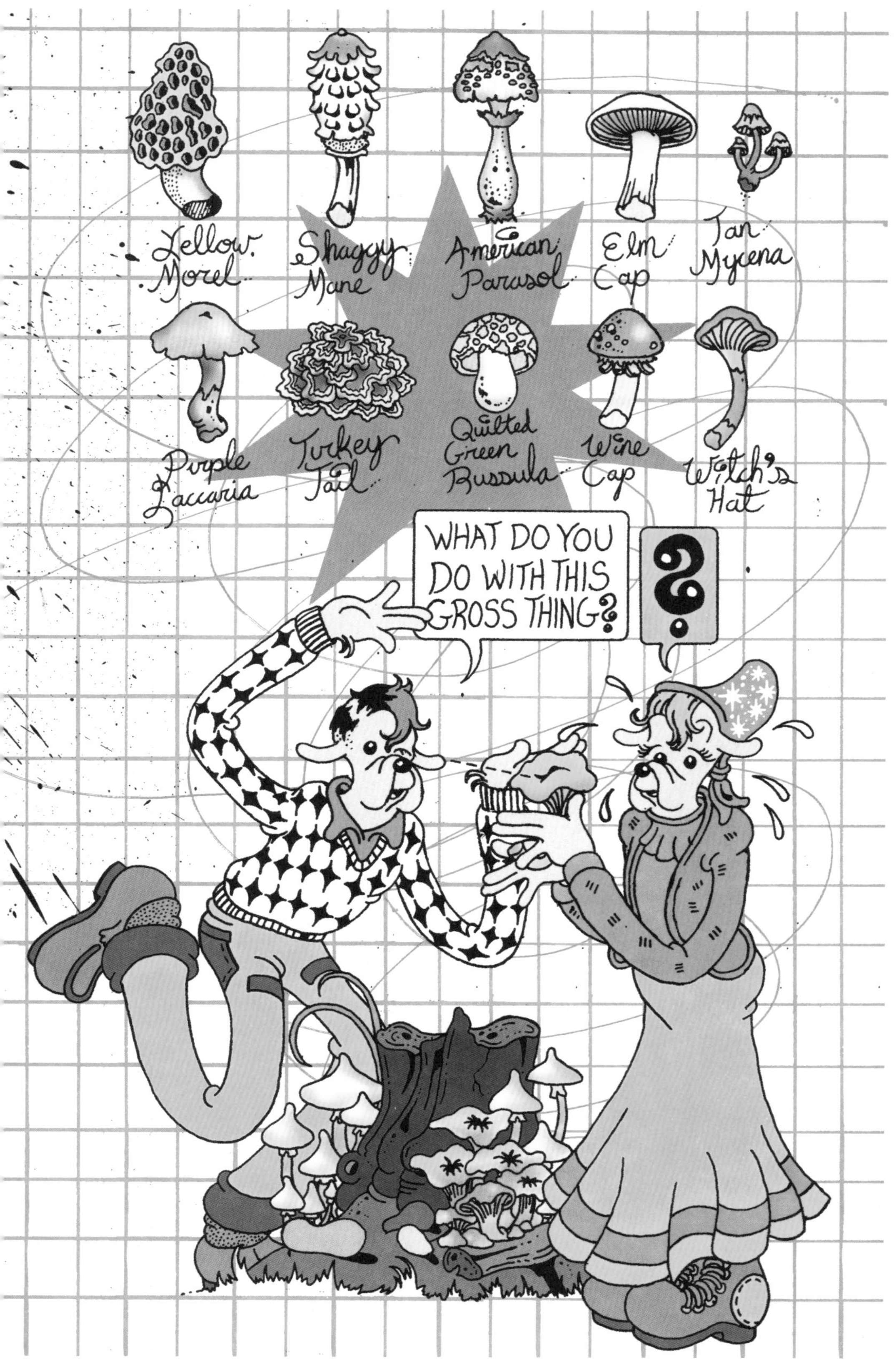

Yellow Morel
Shaggy Mane
American Parasol
Elm Cap
Tan Mycena
Purple Laccaria
Turkey Tail
Quilted Green Russula
Wine Cap
Witch's Hat
WHAT DO YOU DO WITH THIS GROSS THING?
?

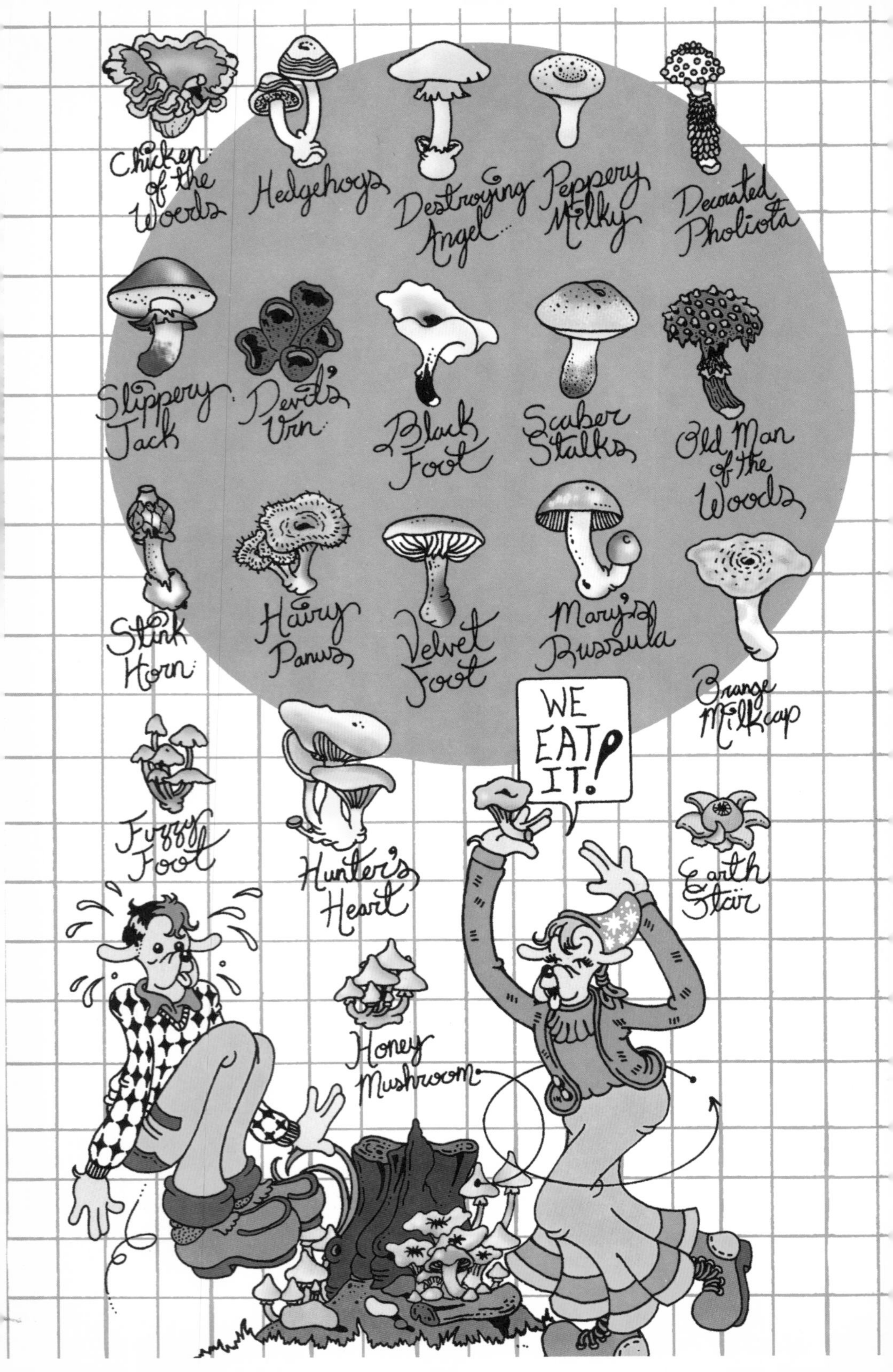
Chicken of the Woods
Hedgehogs
Destroying Angel...
Peppery Milky
Decorated Pholiota
Slippery Jack
Devil's Urn
Black Foot
Scaber Stalks
Old Man of the Woods
Stink Horn
Hairy Panus
Velvet Foot
Mary's Russula
Orange Milkcap
WE EAT IT!
Fuzzy Foot
Hunter's Heart
Earth Star
Honey Mushroom

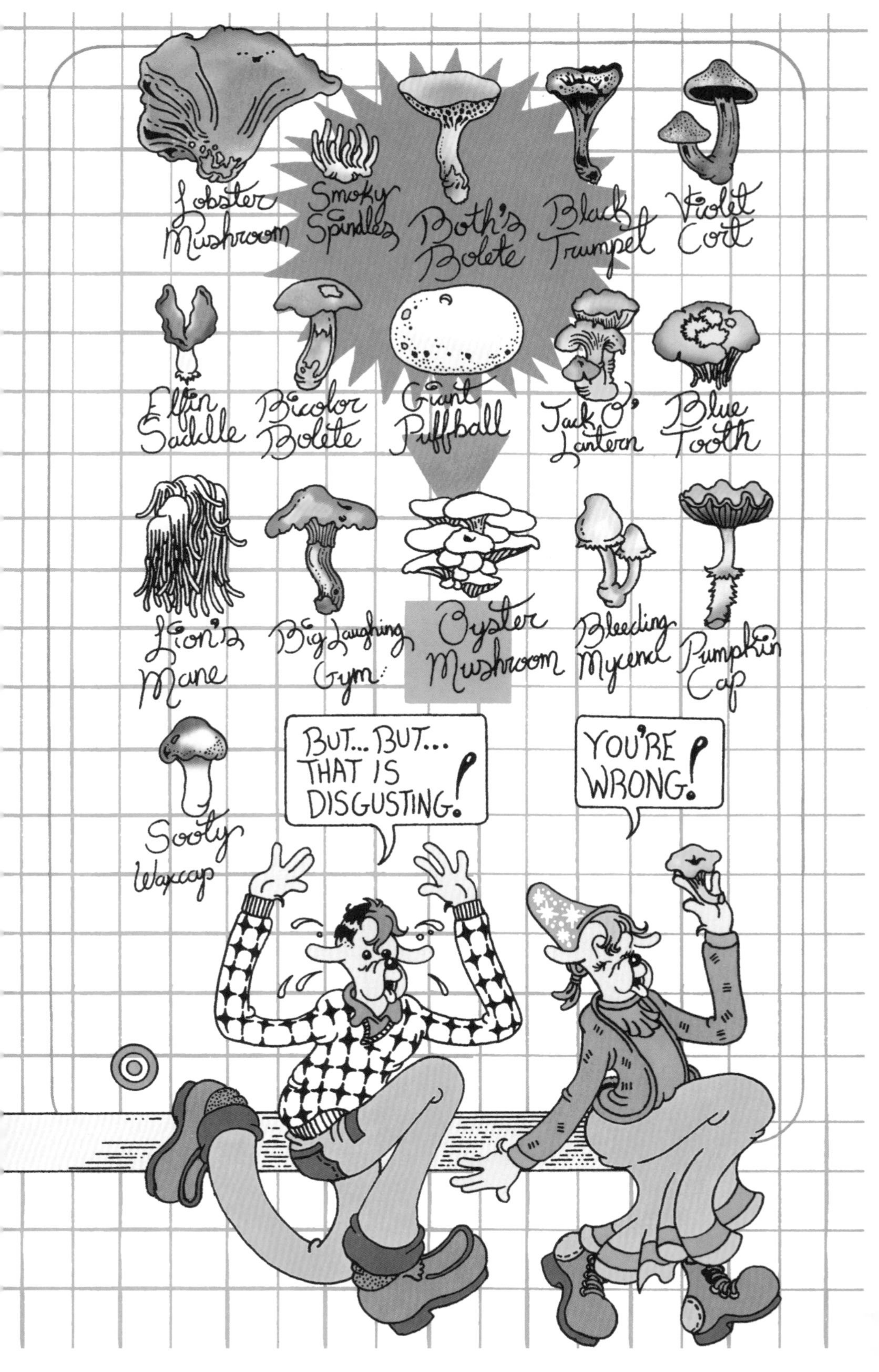

Lobster Mushroom
Smoky Spindles
Both's Bolete
Black Trumpet
Violet Cort
Elfin Saddle
Bicolor Bolete
Giant Puffball
Jack O' Lantern
Blue Tooth
Lion's Mane
Big Laughing Gym
Oyster Mushroom
Bleeding Mycena
Pumpkin Cap
Sooty Waxcap
BUT... BUT... THAT IS DISGUSTING!
YOU'RE WRONG!

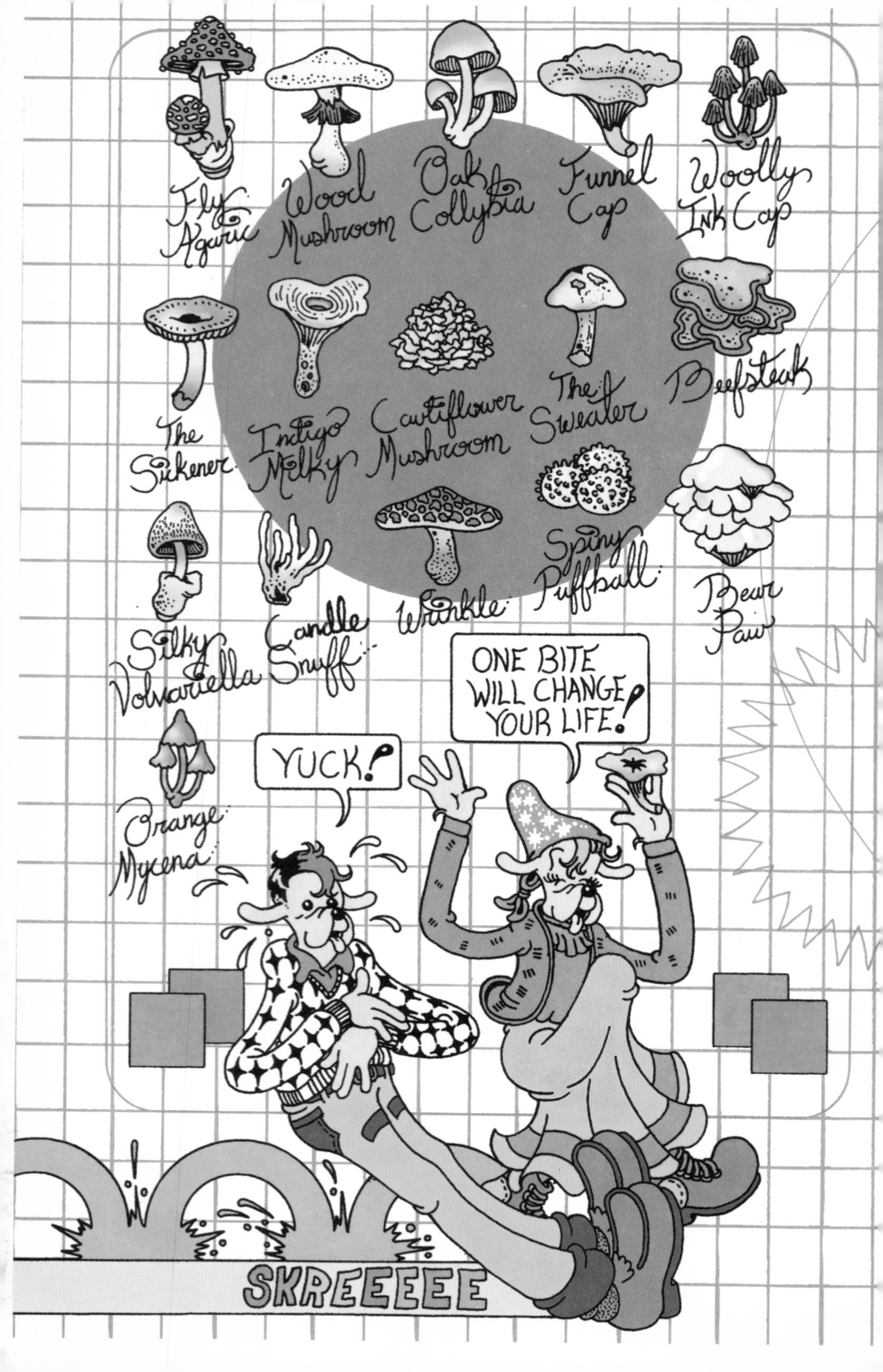

Fly Agaric
Wood Mushroom
Oak Collybia
Funnel Cap
Woolly Ink Cap
The Sickener
Indigo Milky
Cauliflower Mushroom
The Sweater
Beefsteak
Silky Volvariella
Candle Snuff
Wrinkle
Spiny Puffball
Bear Paw
Orange Mycena
YUCK!
ONE BITE WILL CHANGE YOUR LIFE!
SKREEEEEE

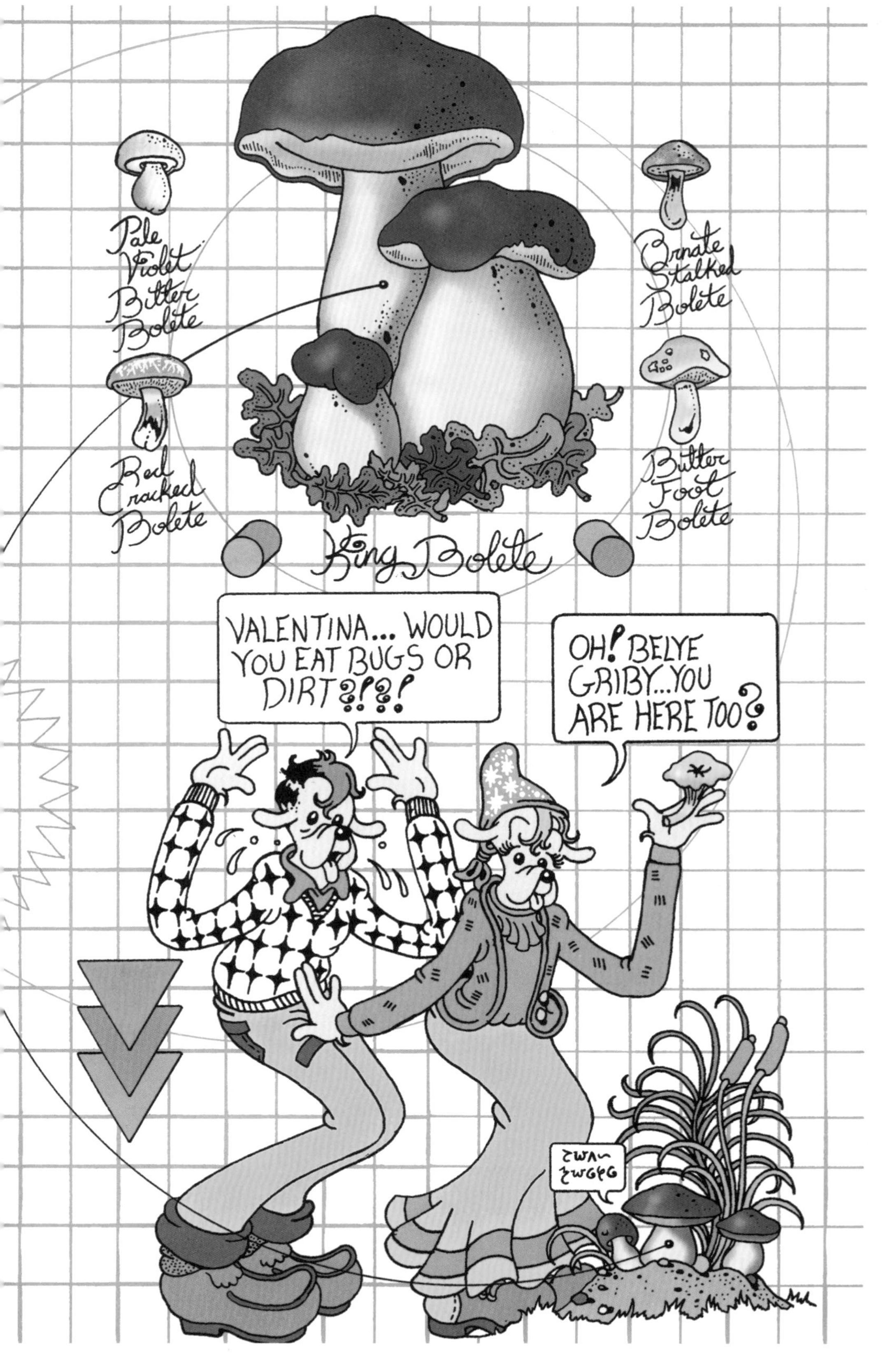
Pale Violet Bitter Bolete
Red Cracked Bolete
Ornate Stalked Bolete
Butter Foot Bolete
King Bolete
VALENTINA... WOULD YOU EAT BUGS OR DIRT?!?!
OH! BELYE GRIBY...YOU ARE HERE TOO?

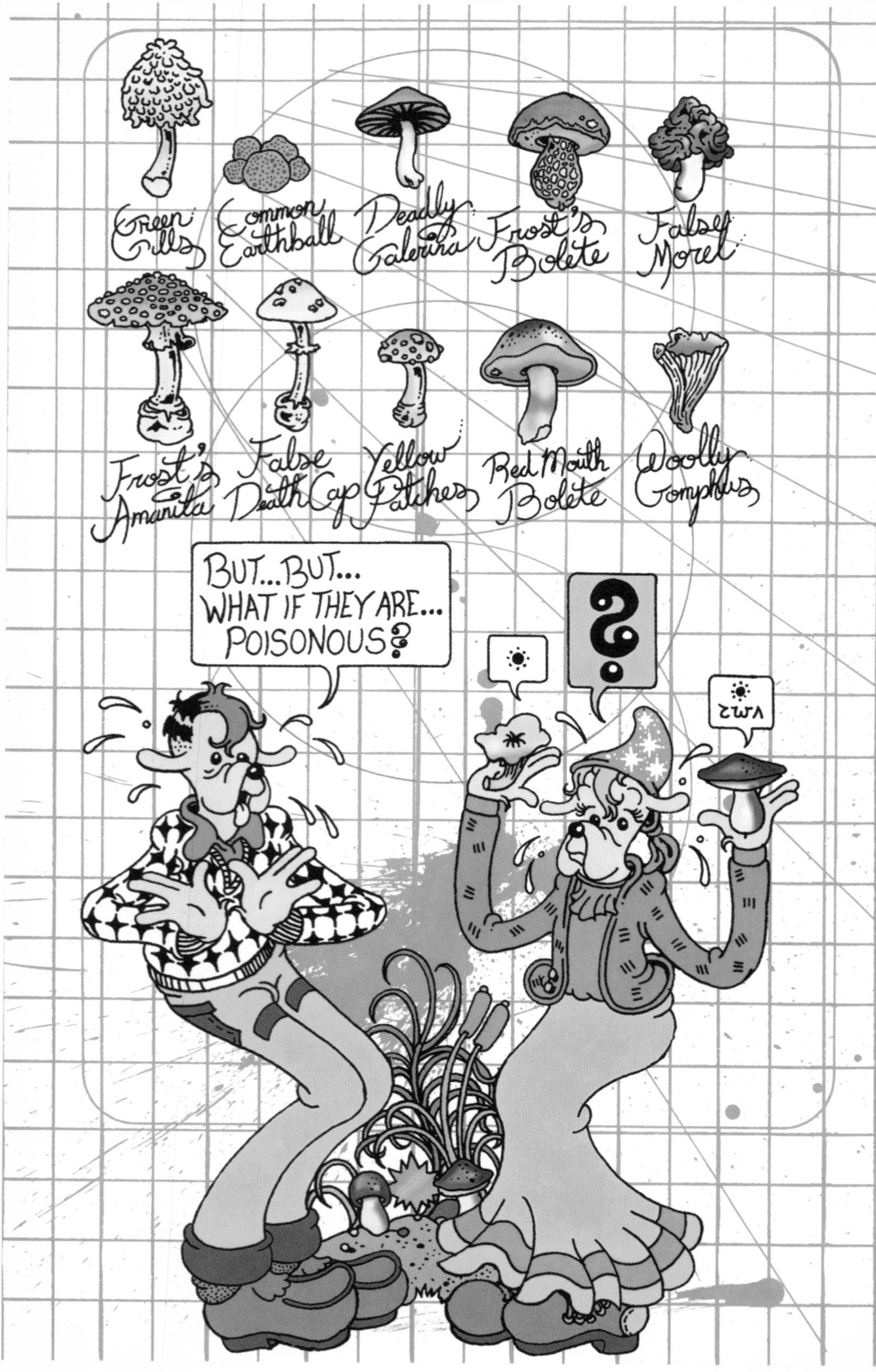
Green Gills
Common Earthball
Deadly Galerina
Frost's Bolete
False Morel
Frost's Amanita
False Death Cap
Yellow Patches
Red Mouth Bolete
Woolly Gomphus
BUT...BUT... WHAT IF THEY ARE... POISONOUS?

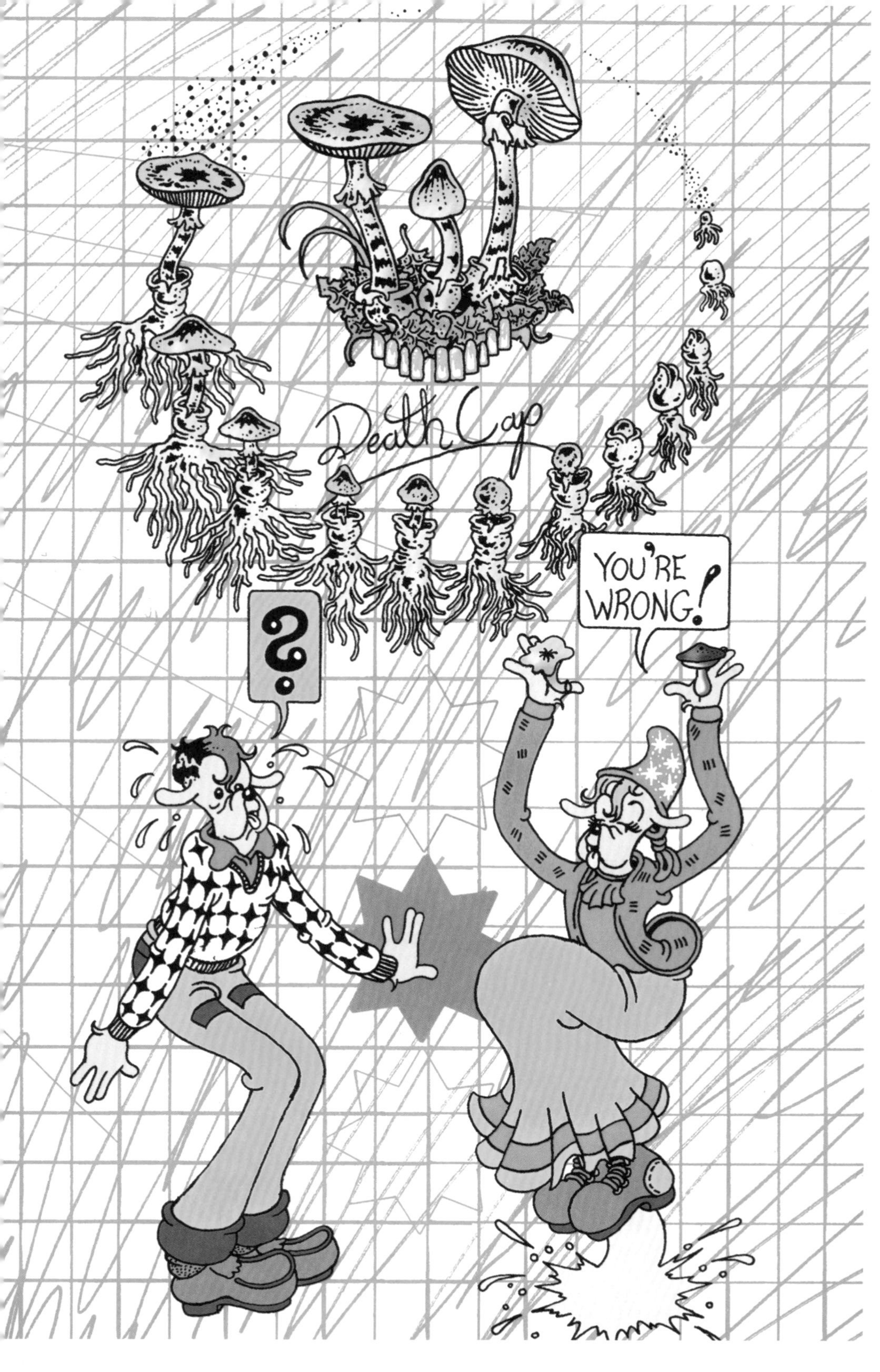
Death Cap
?
YOU'RE WRONG!

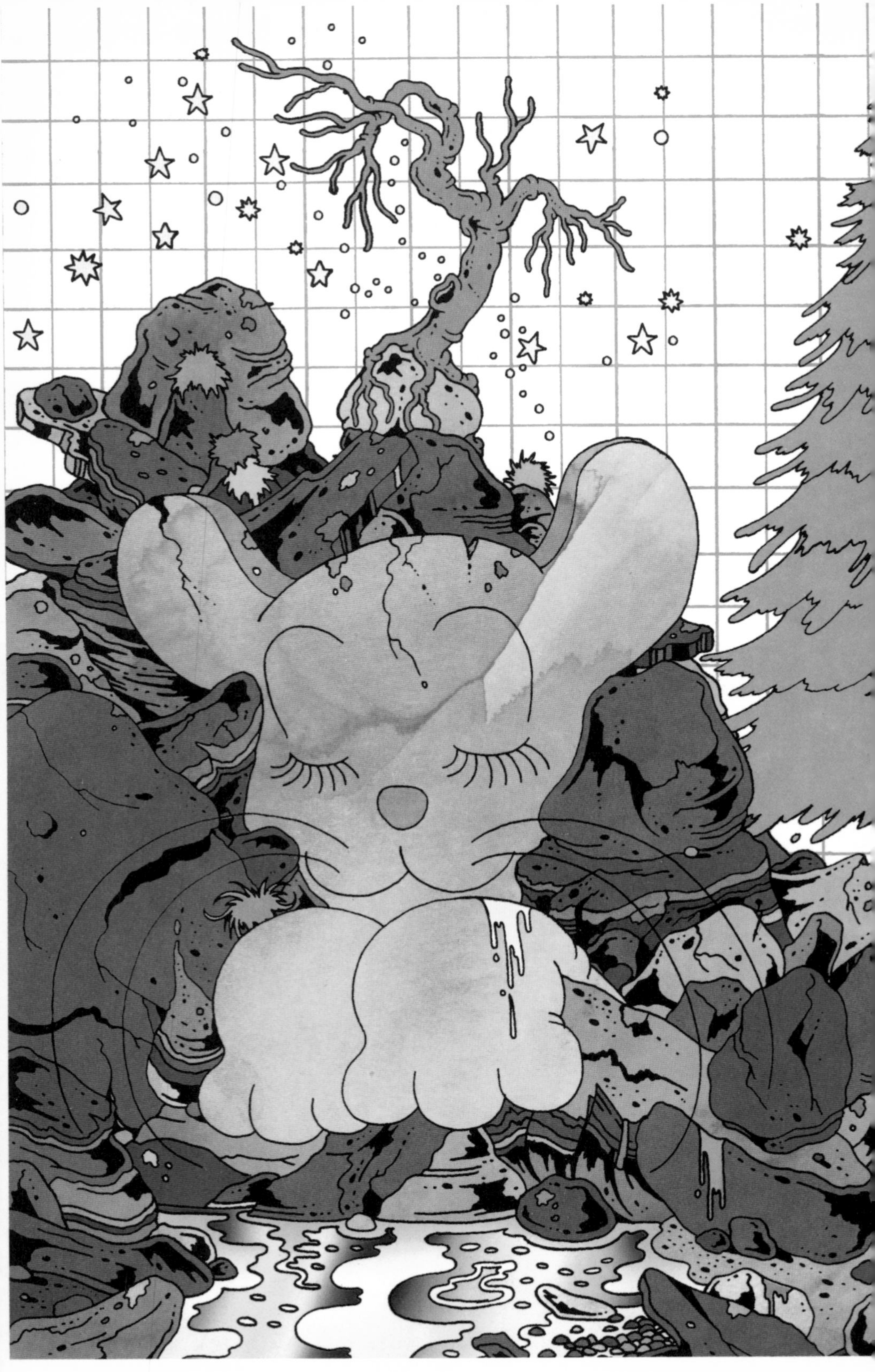

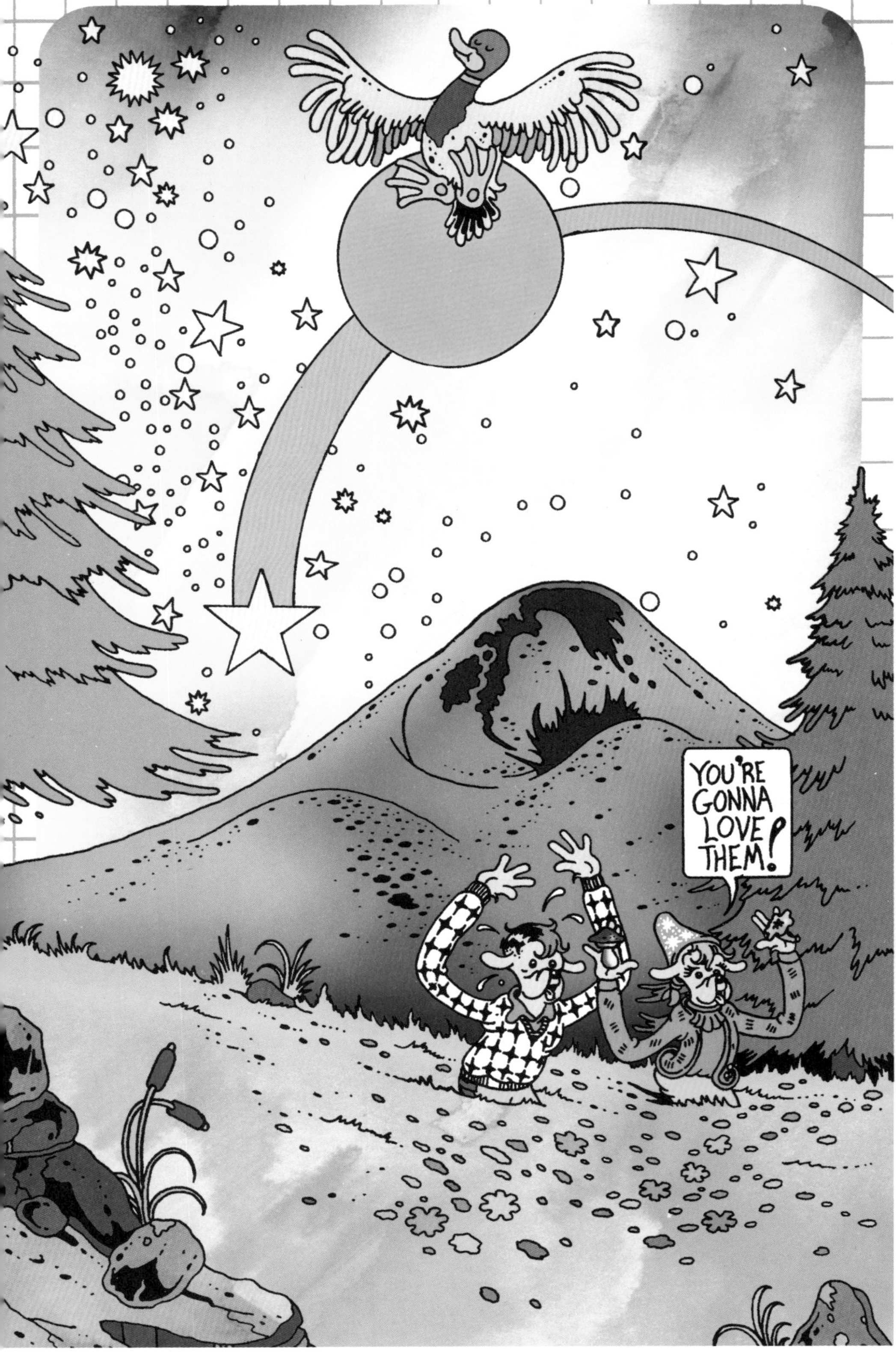
YOU'RE GONNA LOVE THEM!

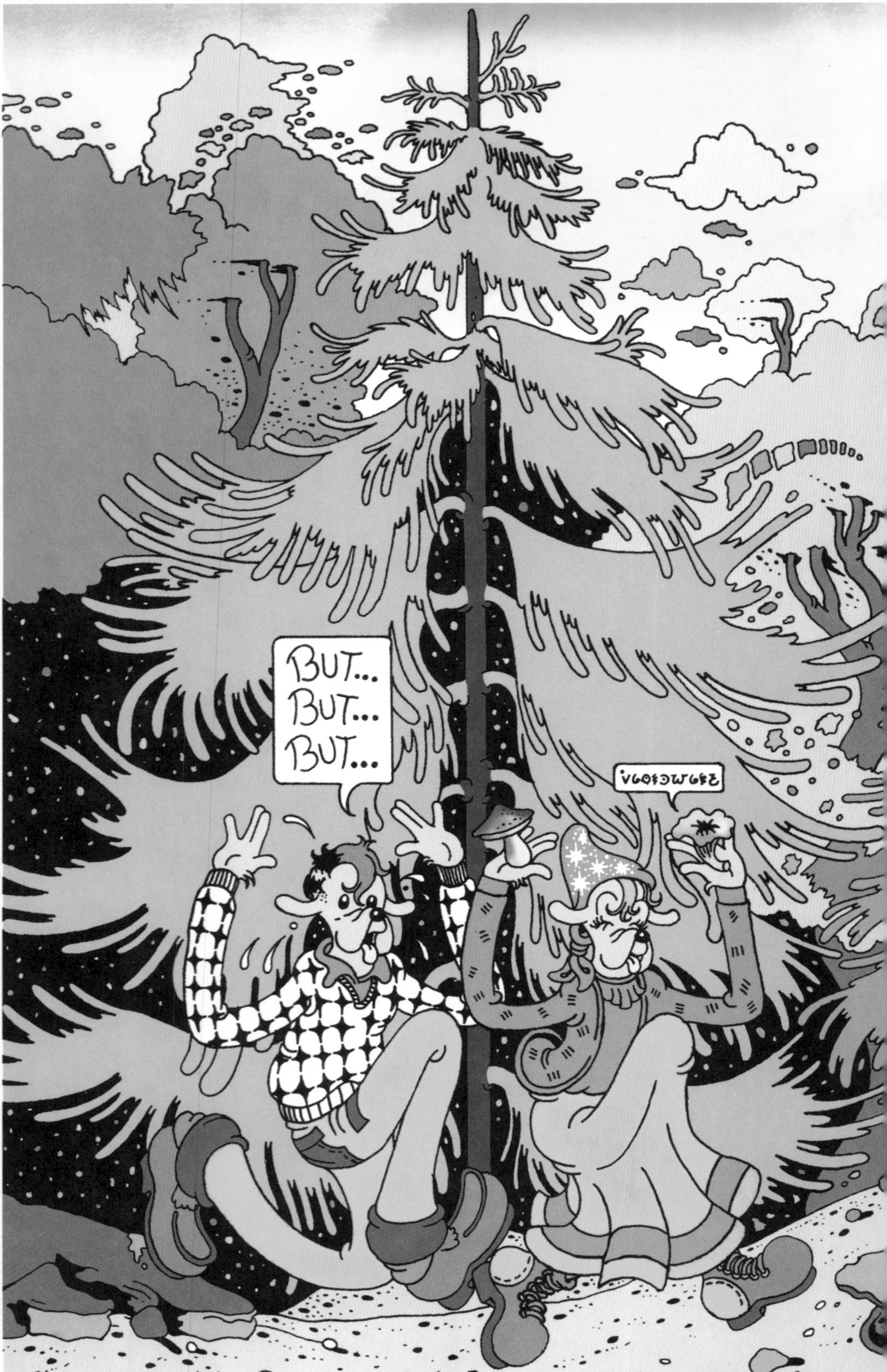
BUT... BUT... BUT...

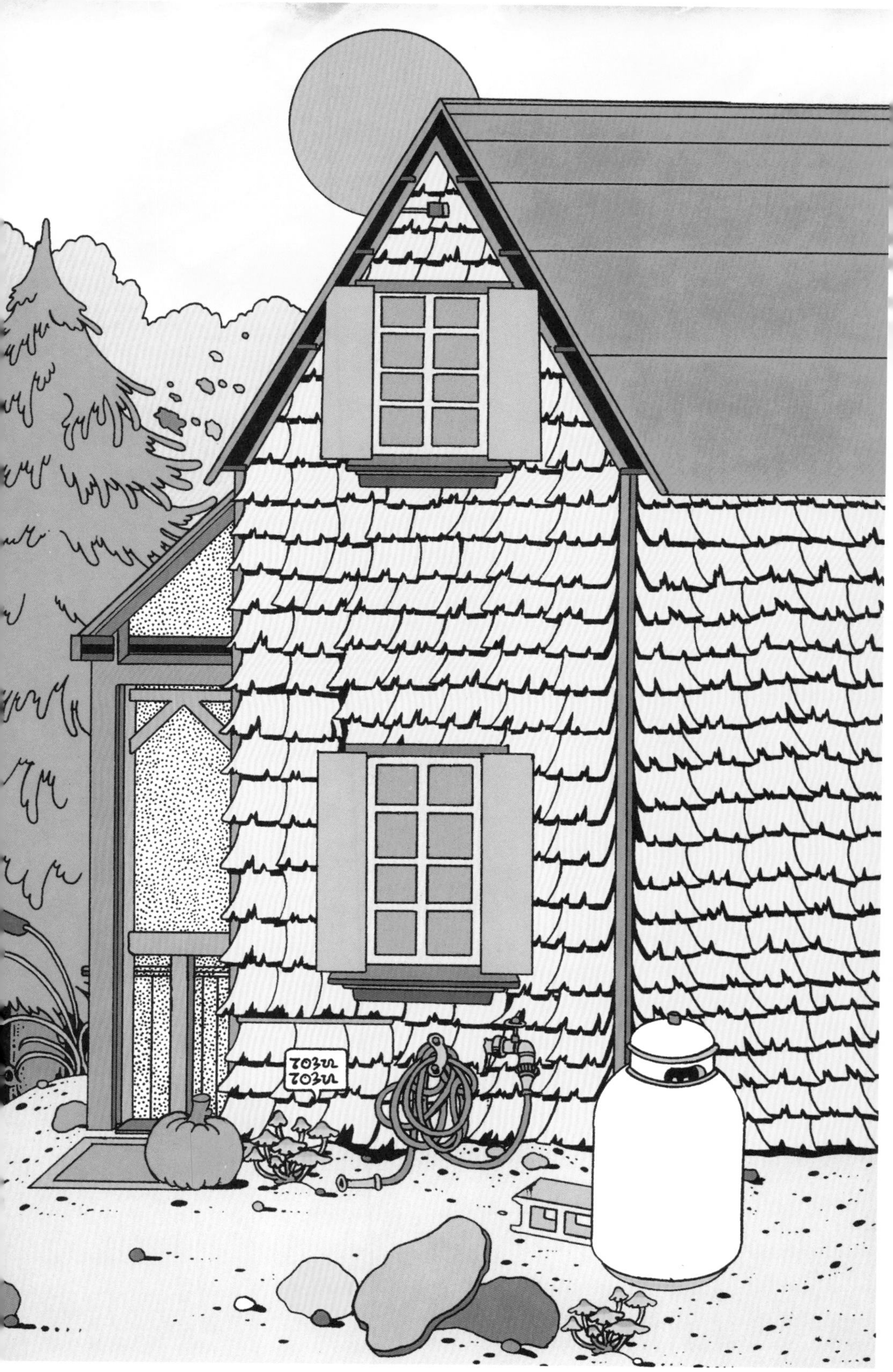

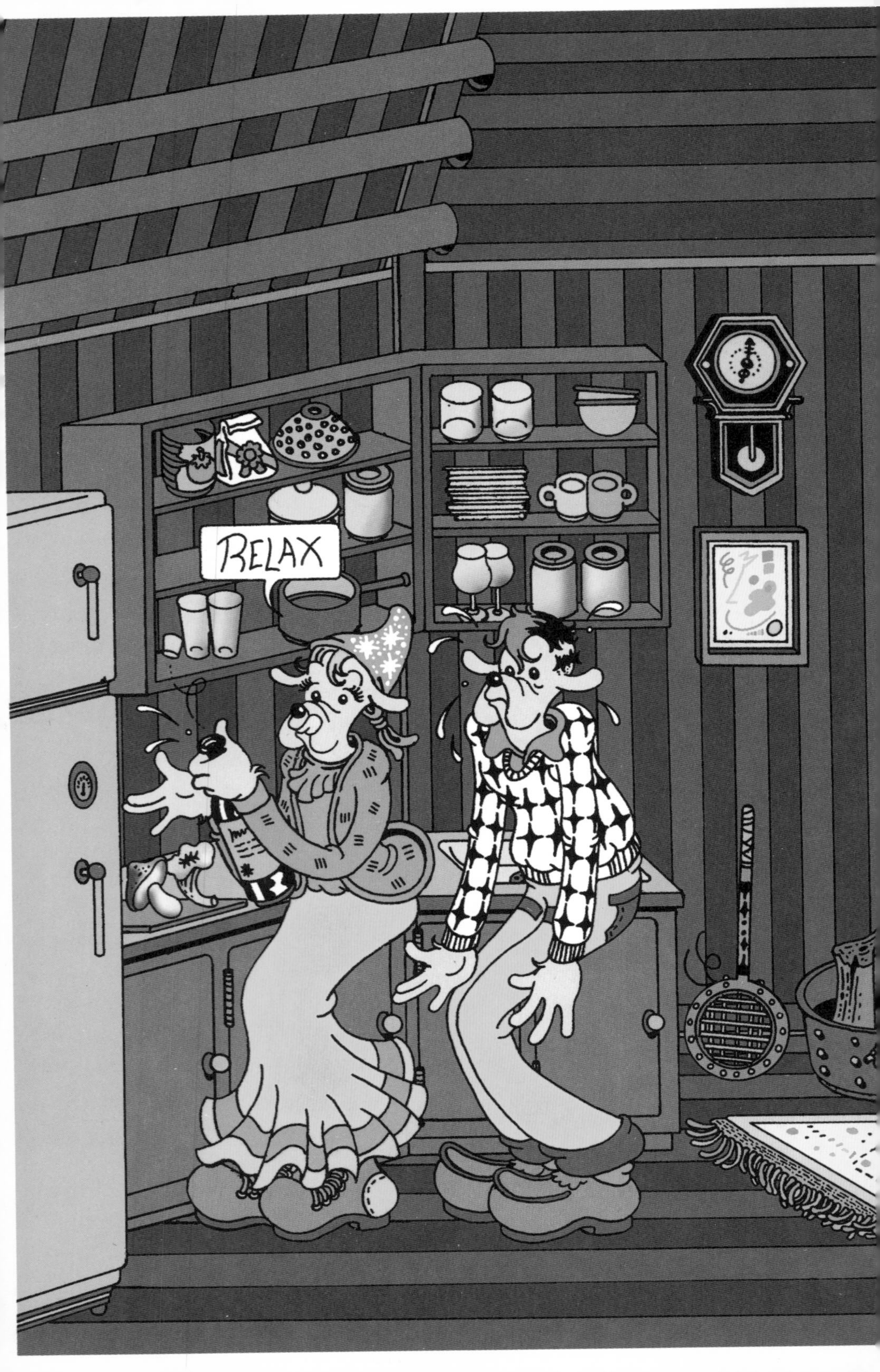
RELAX

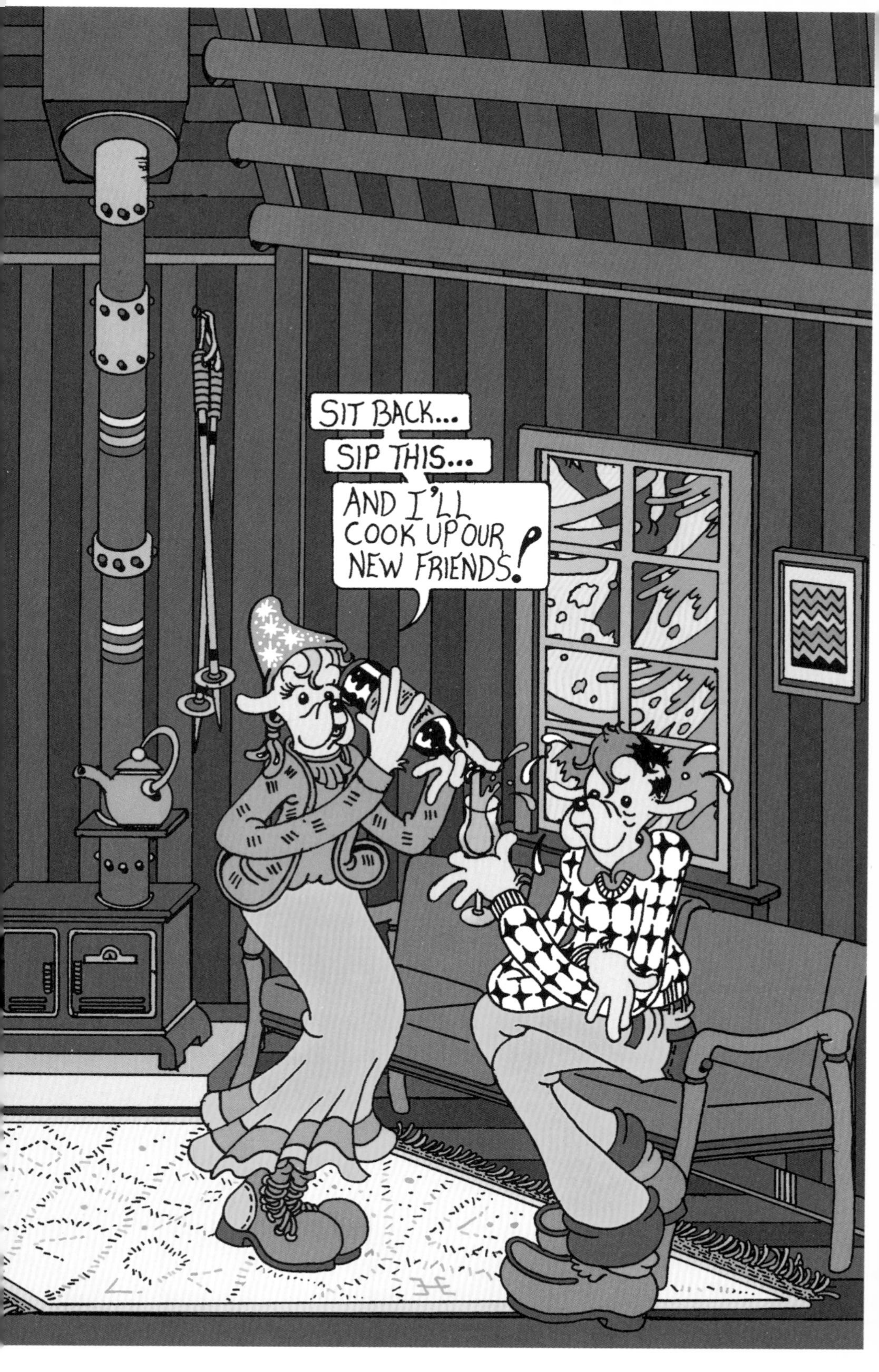
SIT BACK...
SIP THIS...
AND I'LL COOK UP OUR NEW FRIENDS!

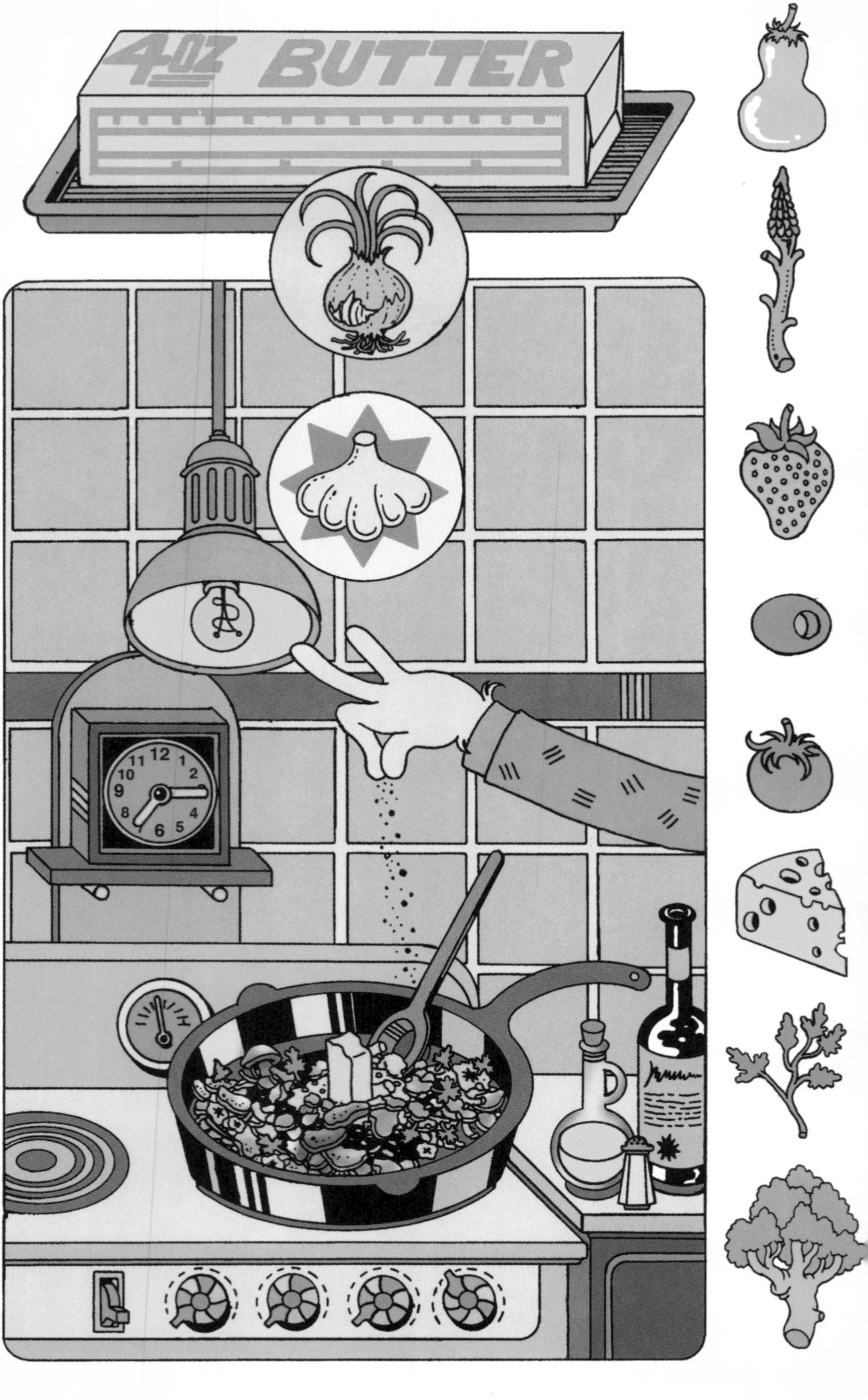
4OZ
BUTTER

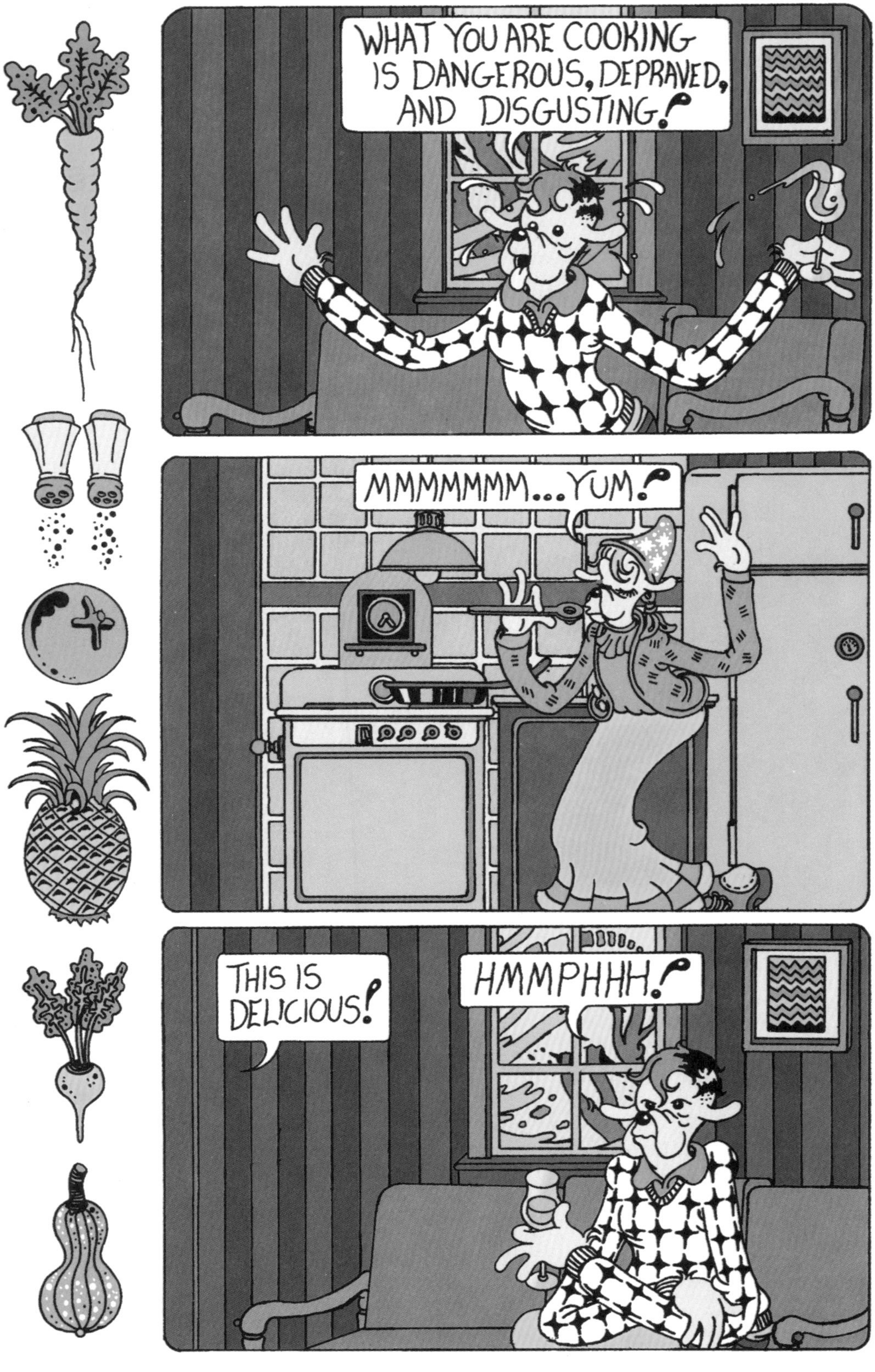
WHAT YOU ARE COOKING IS DANGEROUS, DEPRAVED, AND DISGUSTING!
MMMMMMM...YUM!
THIS IS DELICIOUS!
HMMPHHH!

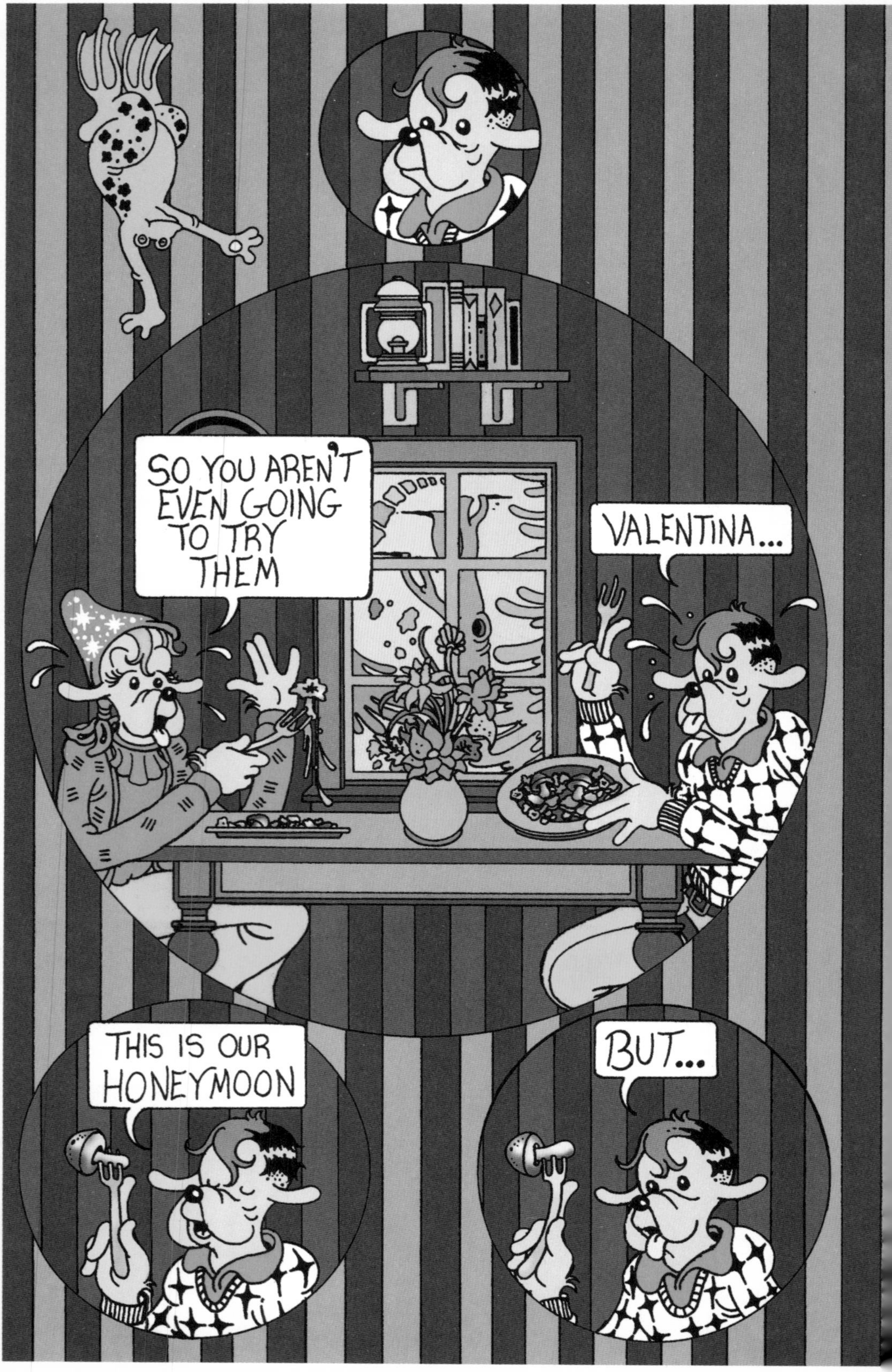

SO YOU AREN'T EVEN GOING TO TRY THEM
VALENTINA...
THIS IS OUR HONEYMOON
BUT...

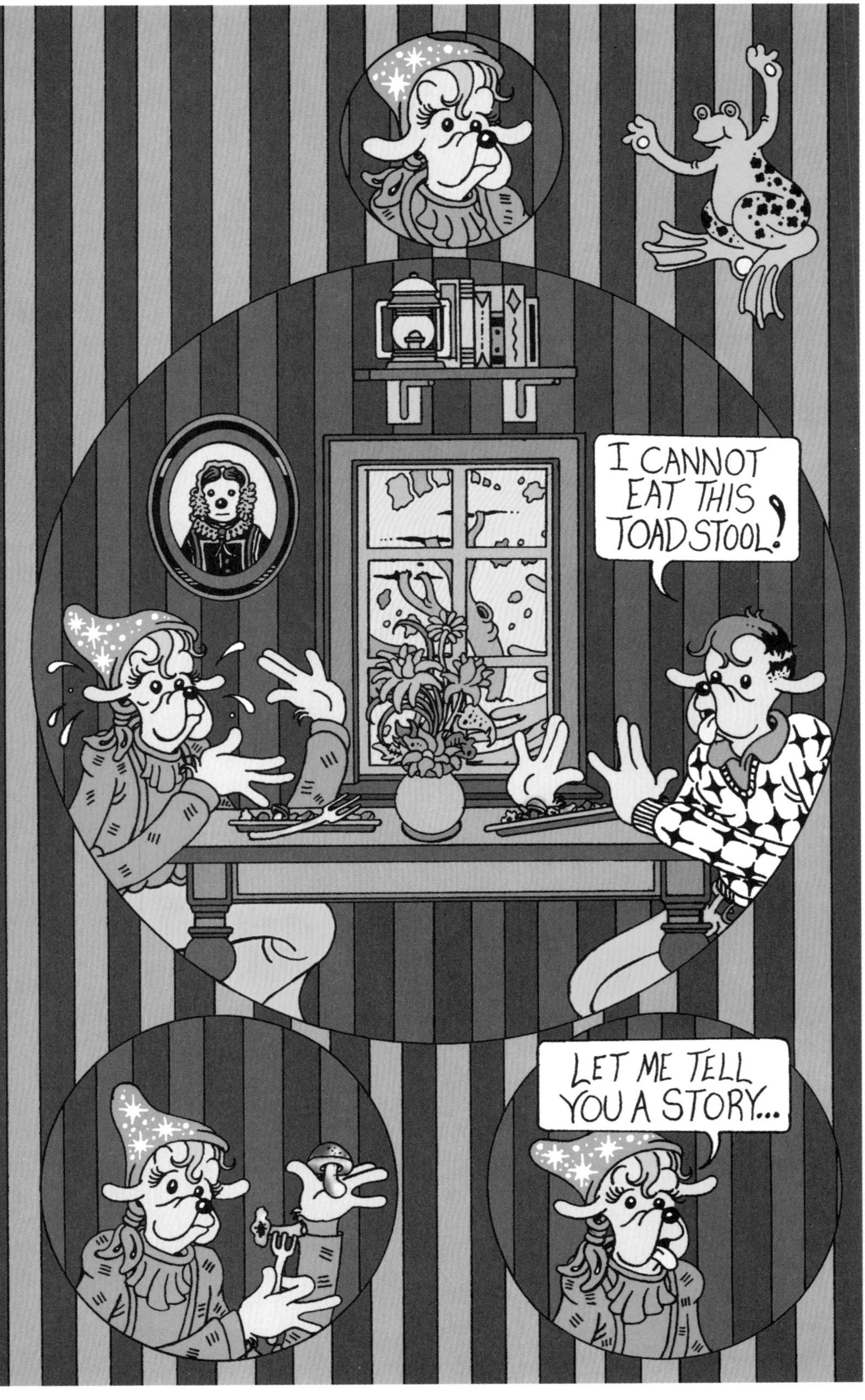
I CANNOT EAT THIS TOADSTOOL!
LET ME TELL YOU A STORY...

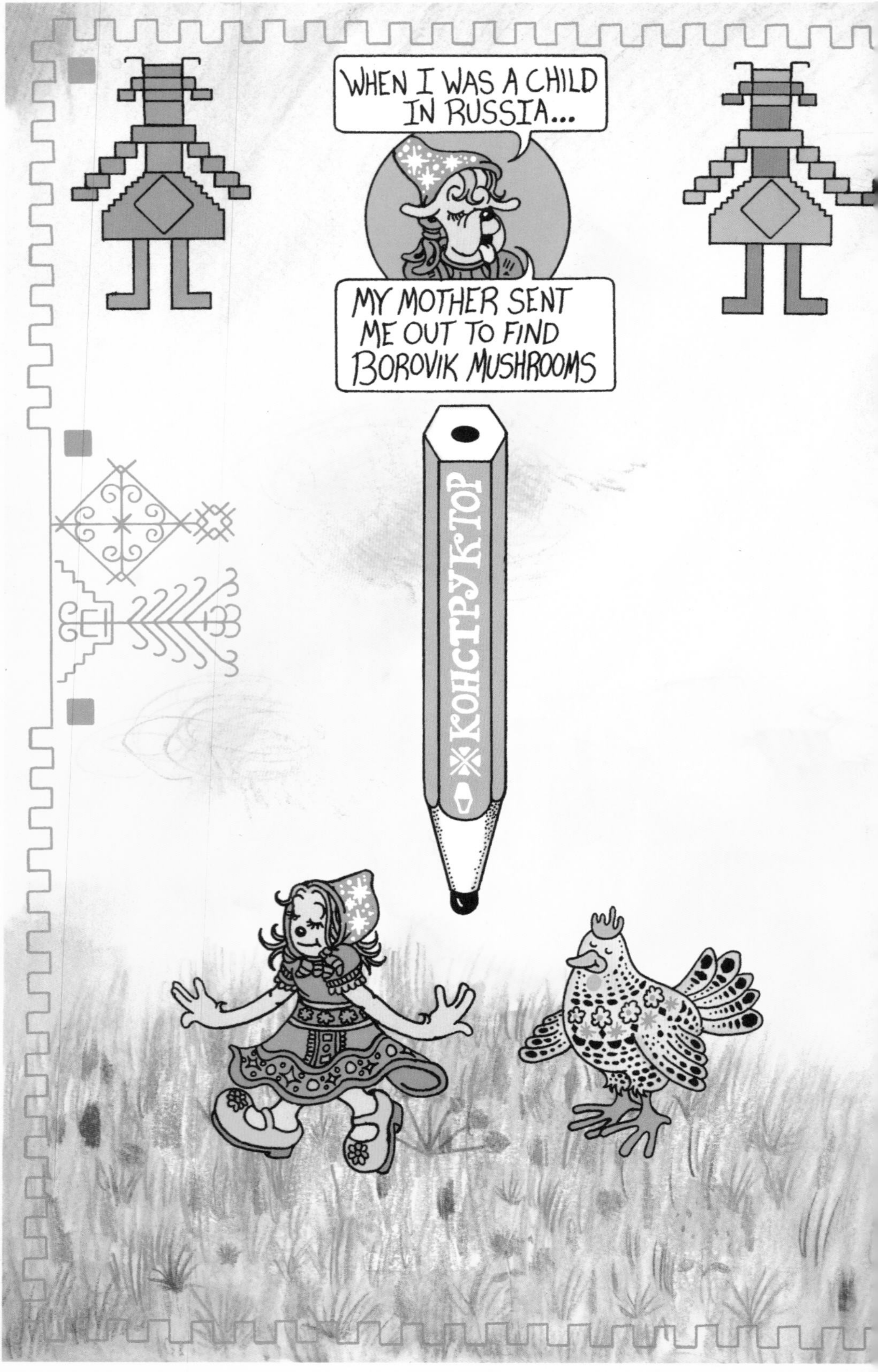
WHEN I WAS A CHILD IN RUSSIA...
MY MOTHER SENT ME OUT TO FIND BOROVIK MUSHROOMS
КОНСТРУКТОР

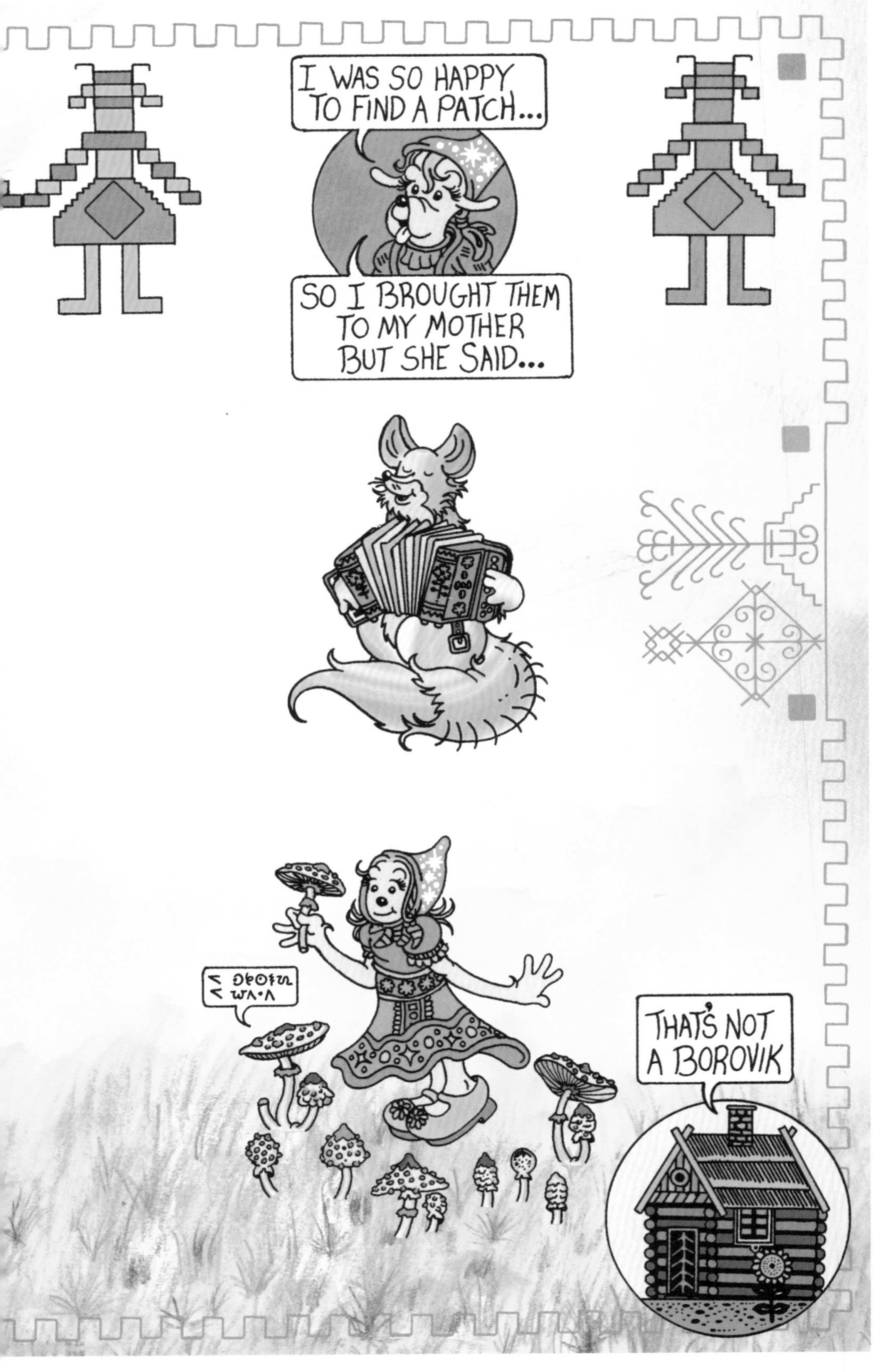
I WAS SO HAPPY TO FIND A PATCH...
SO I BROUGHT THEM TO MY MOTHER BUT SHE SAID...
THAT'S NOT A BOROVIK

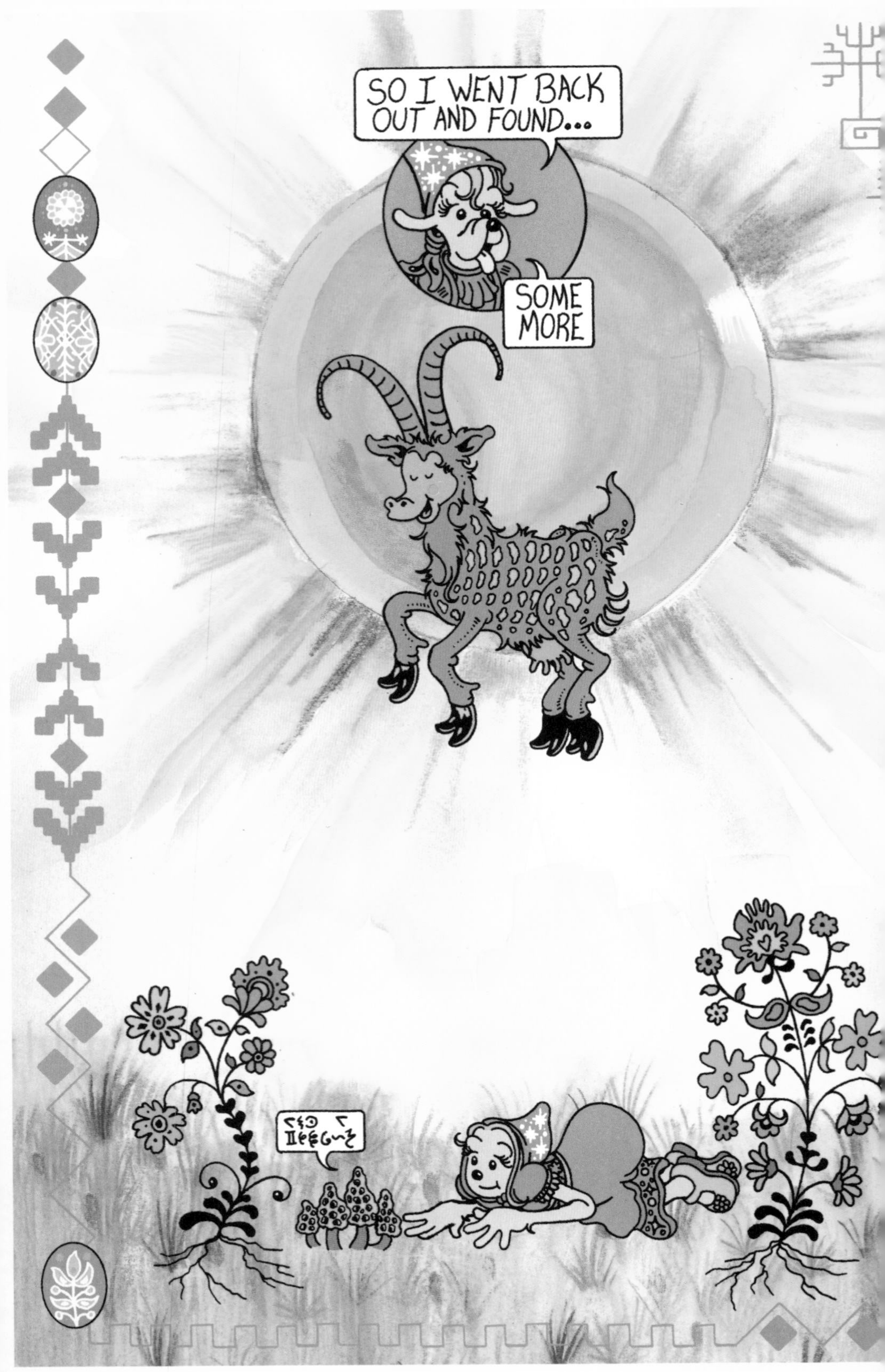
SO I WENT BACK OUT AND FOUND...
SOME MORE

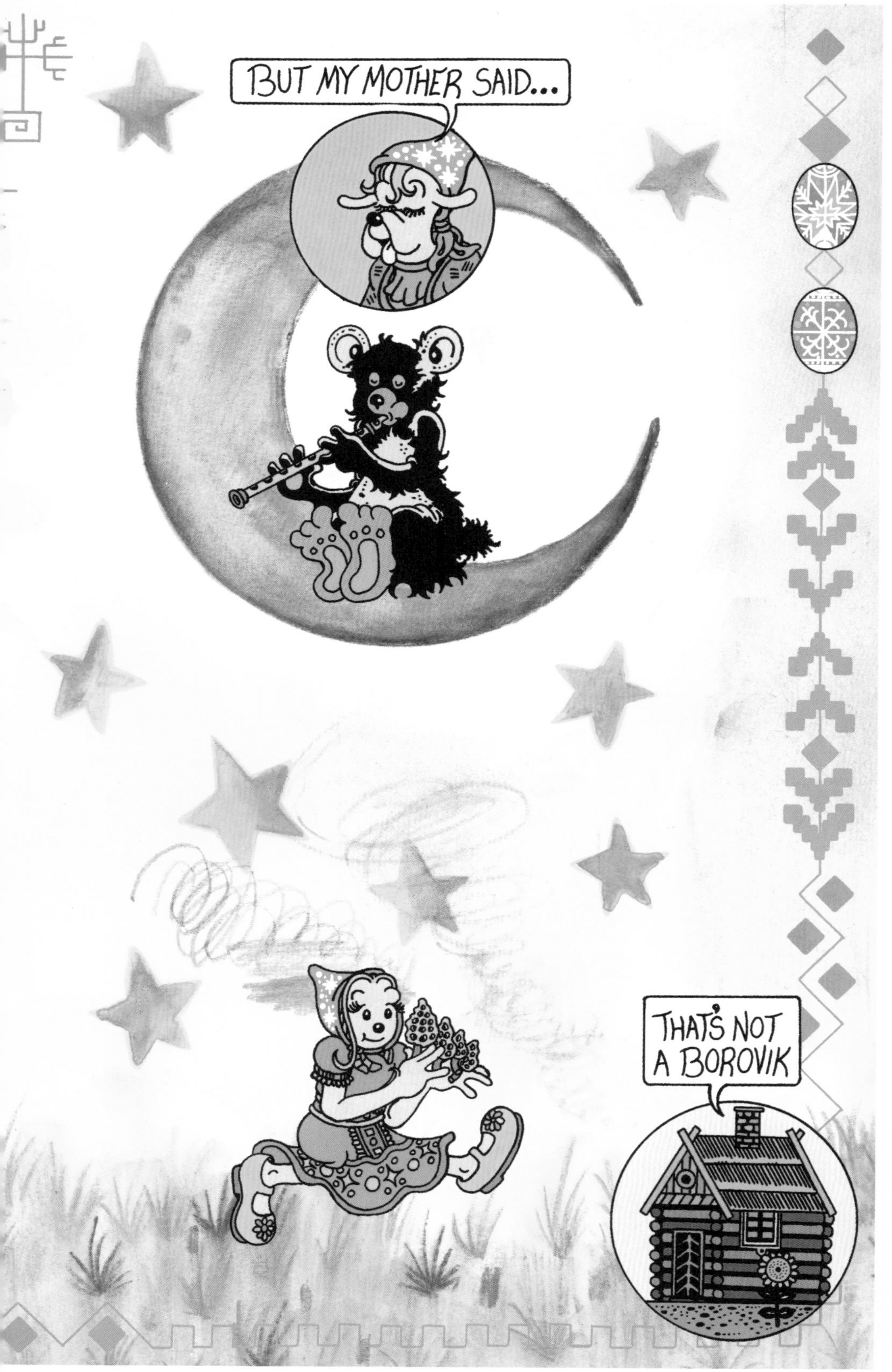
BUT MY MOTHER SAID...
THAT'S NOT A BOROVIK

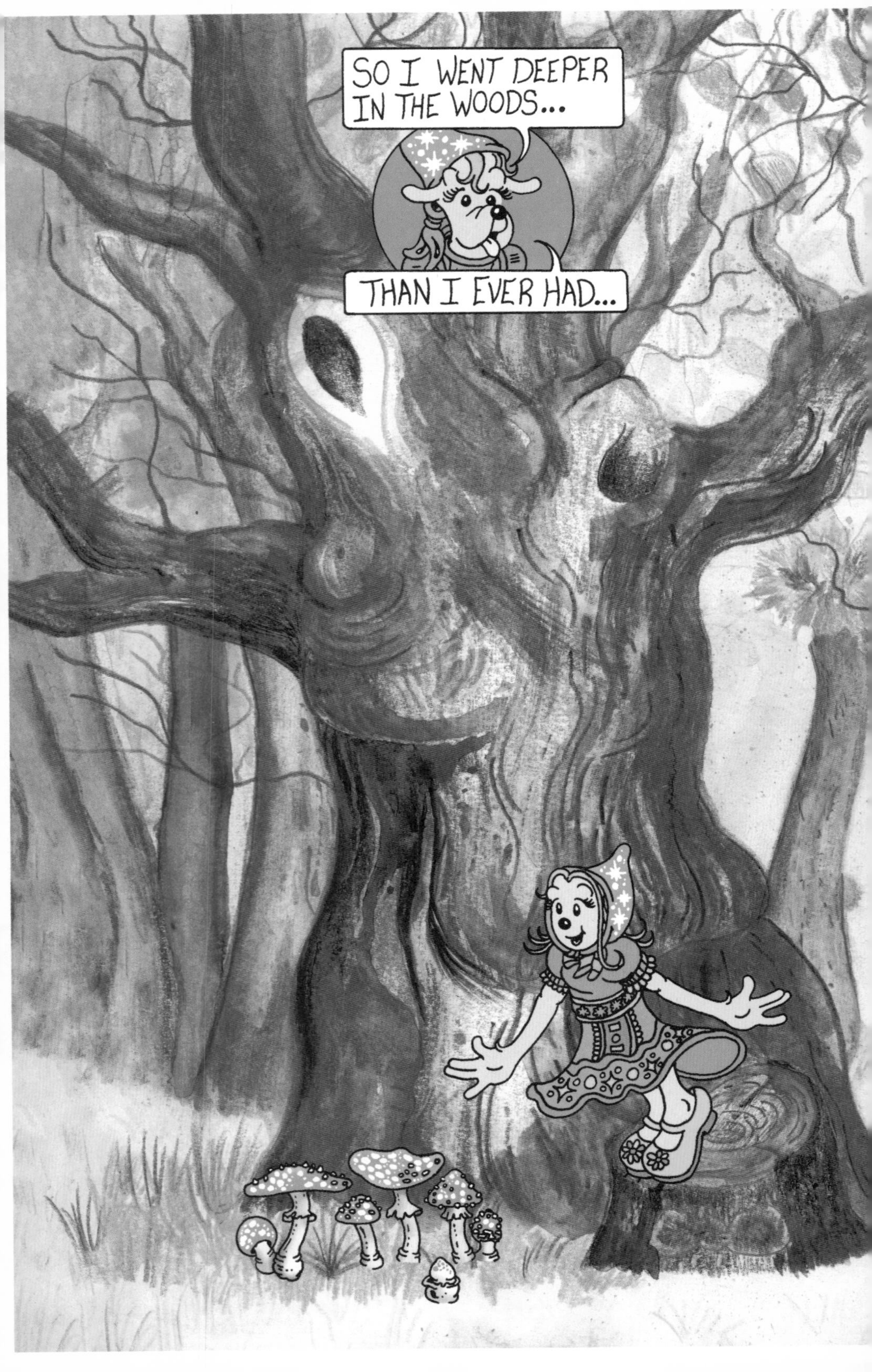
SO I WENT DEEPER IN THE WOODS...
THAN I EVER HAD...

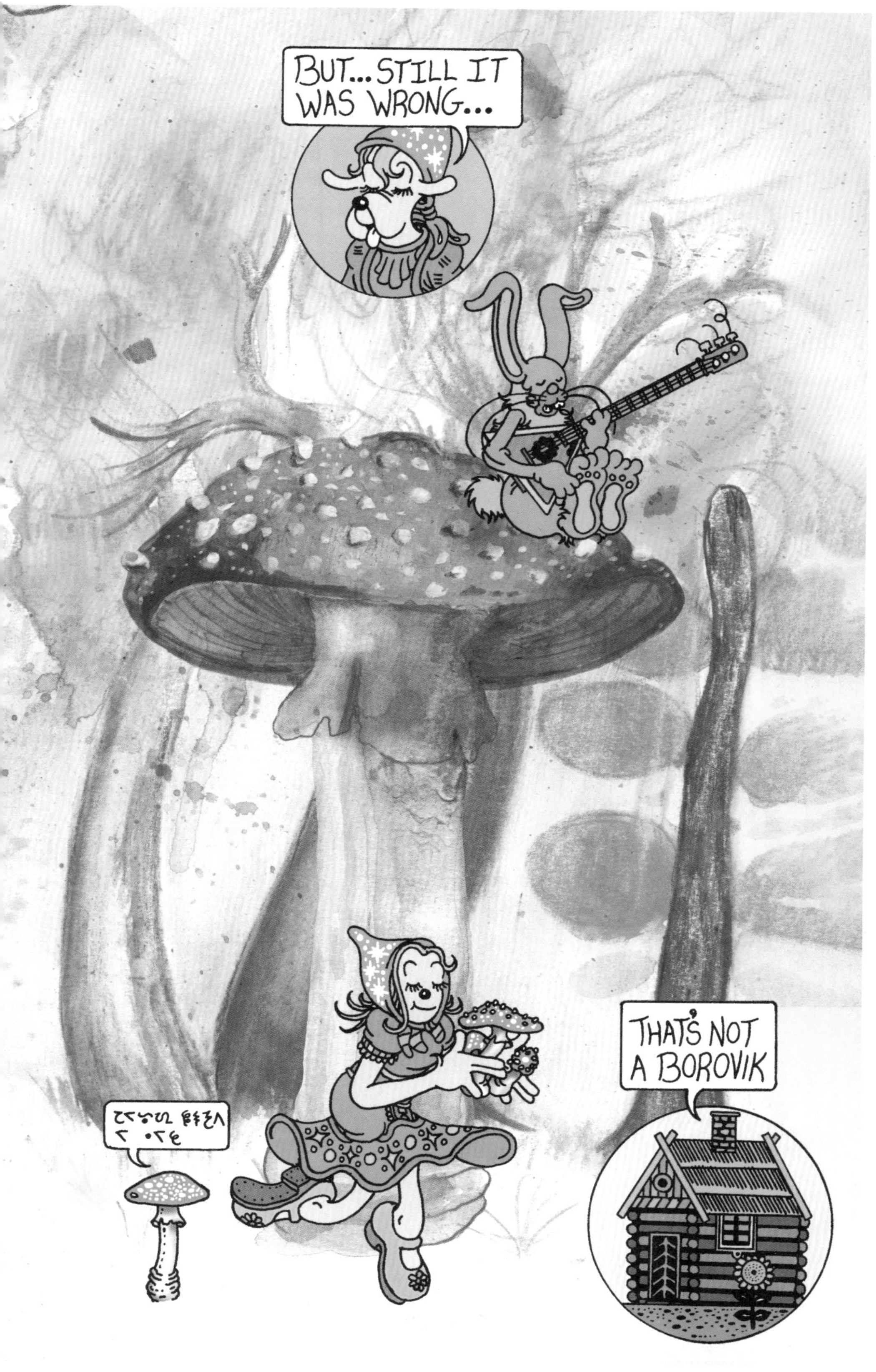
BUT... STILL IT WAS WRONG...
THAT'S NOT A BOROVIK

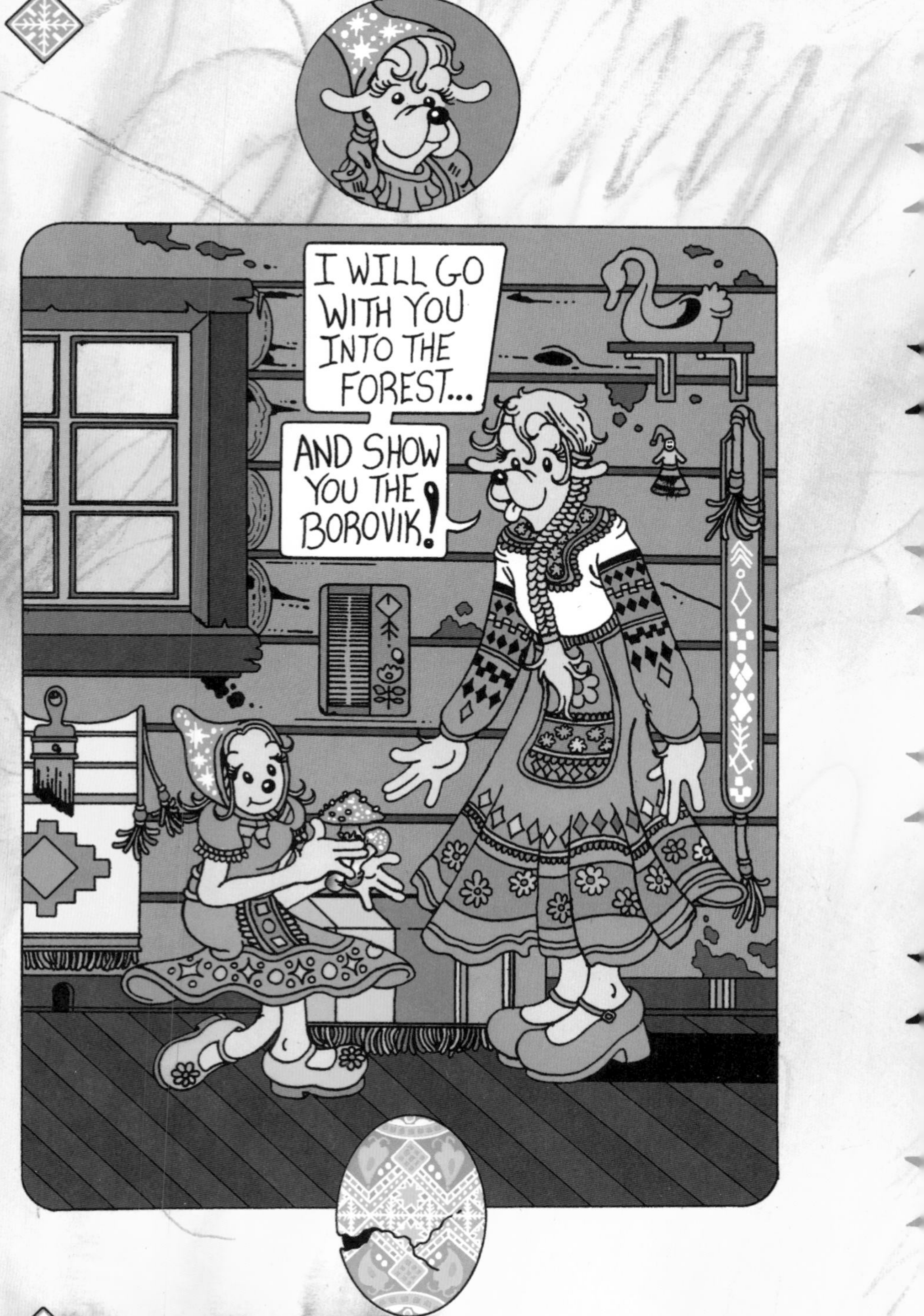
I WILL GO WITH YOU INTO THE FOREST...
AND SHOW YOU THE BOROVIK!

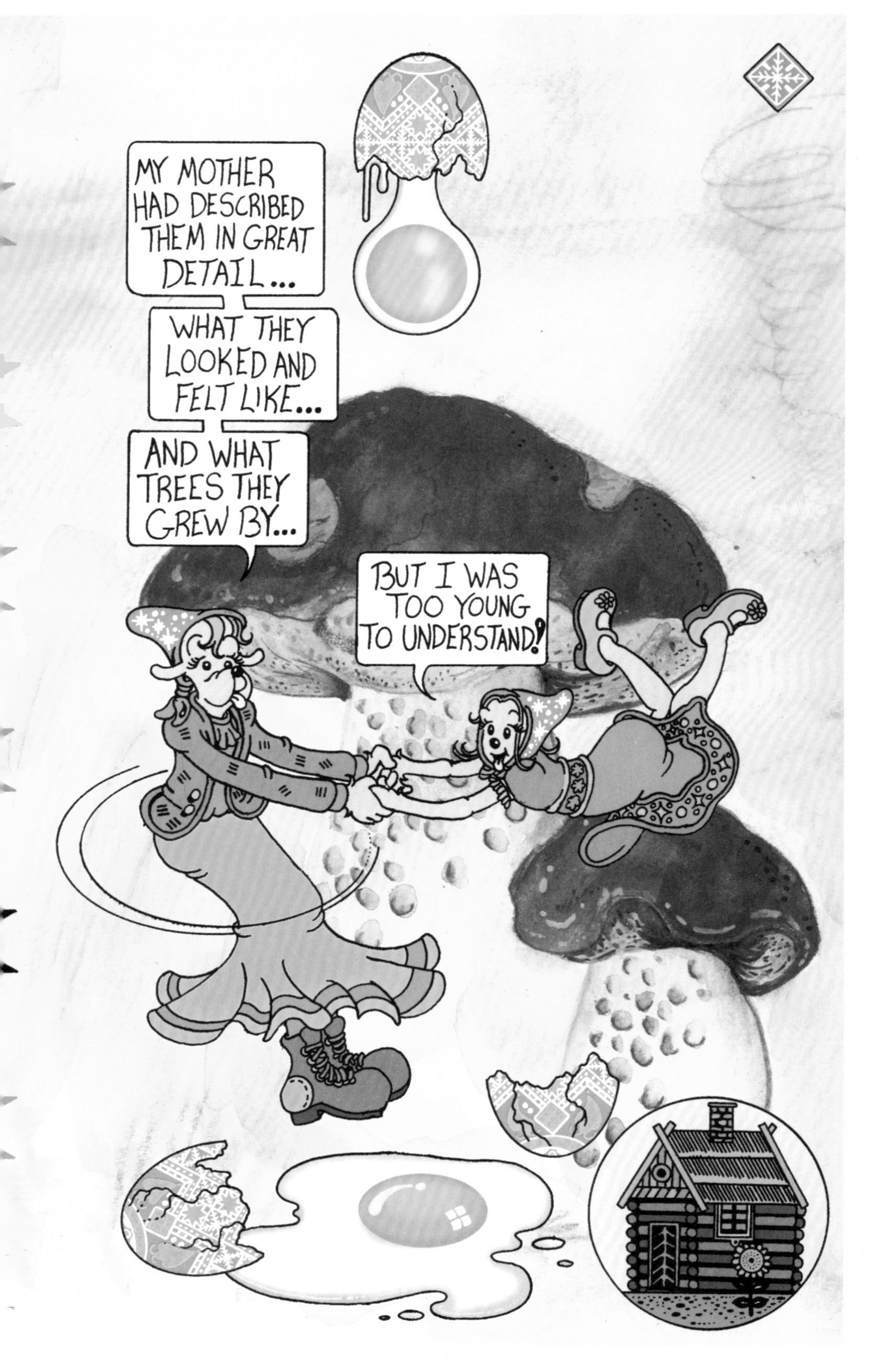
MY MOTHER HAD DESCRIBED THEM IN GREAT DETAIL...
WHAT THEY LOOKED AND FELT LIKE...
AND WHAT TREES THEY GREW BY...
BUT I WAS TOO YOUNG TO UNDERSTAND!

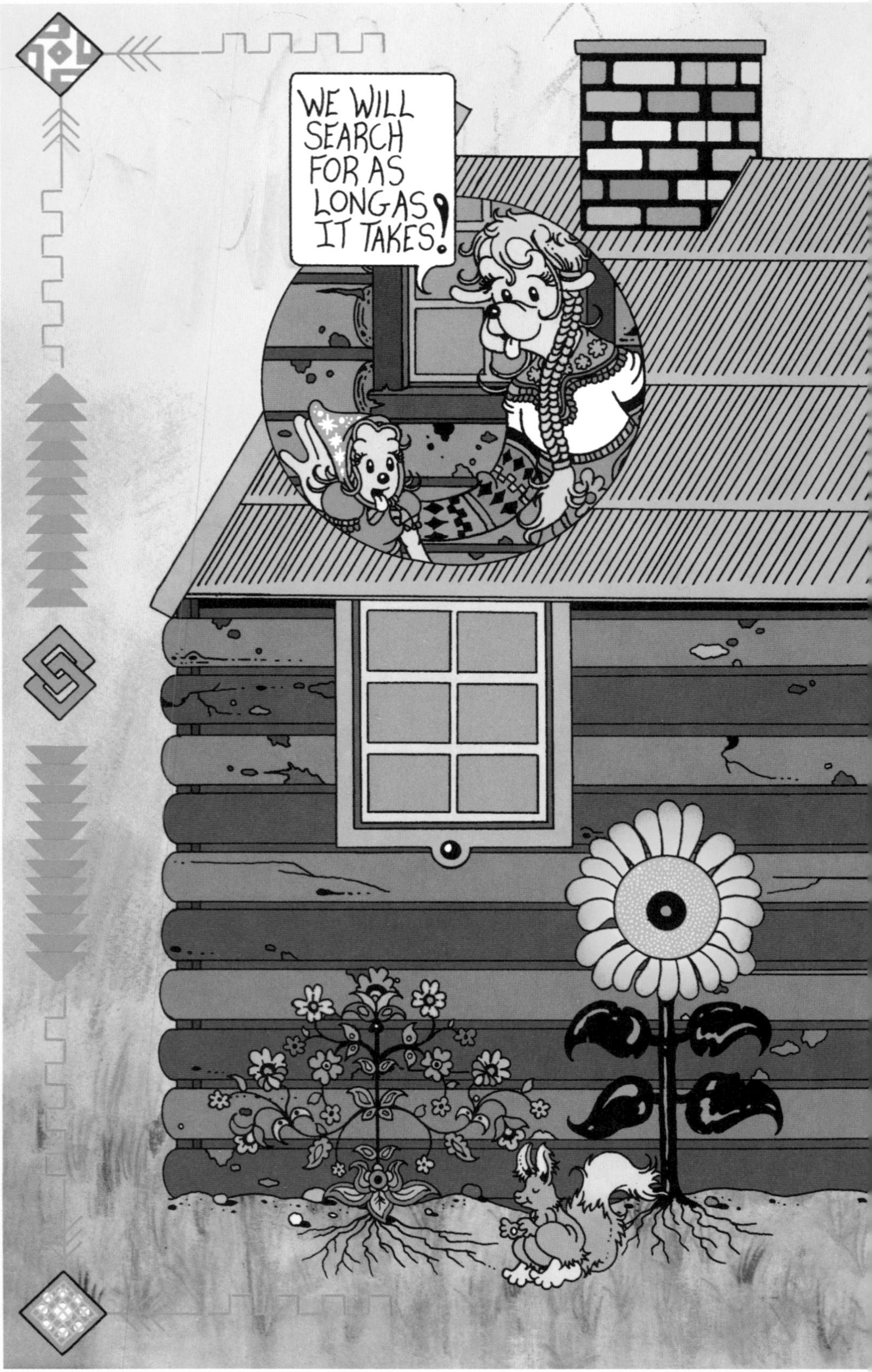
WE WILL SEARCH FOR AS LONG AS IT TAKES!

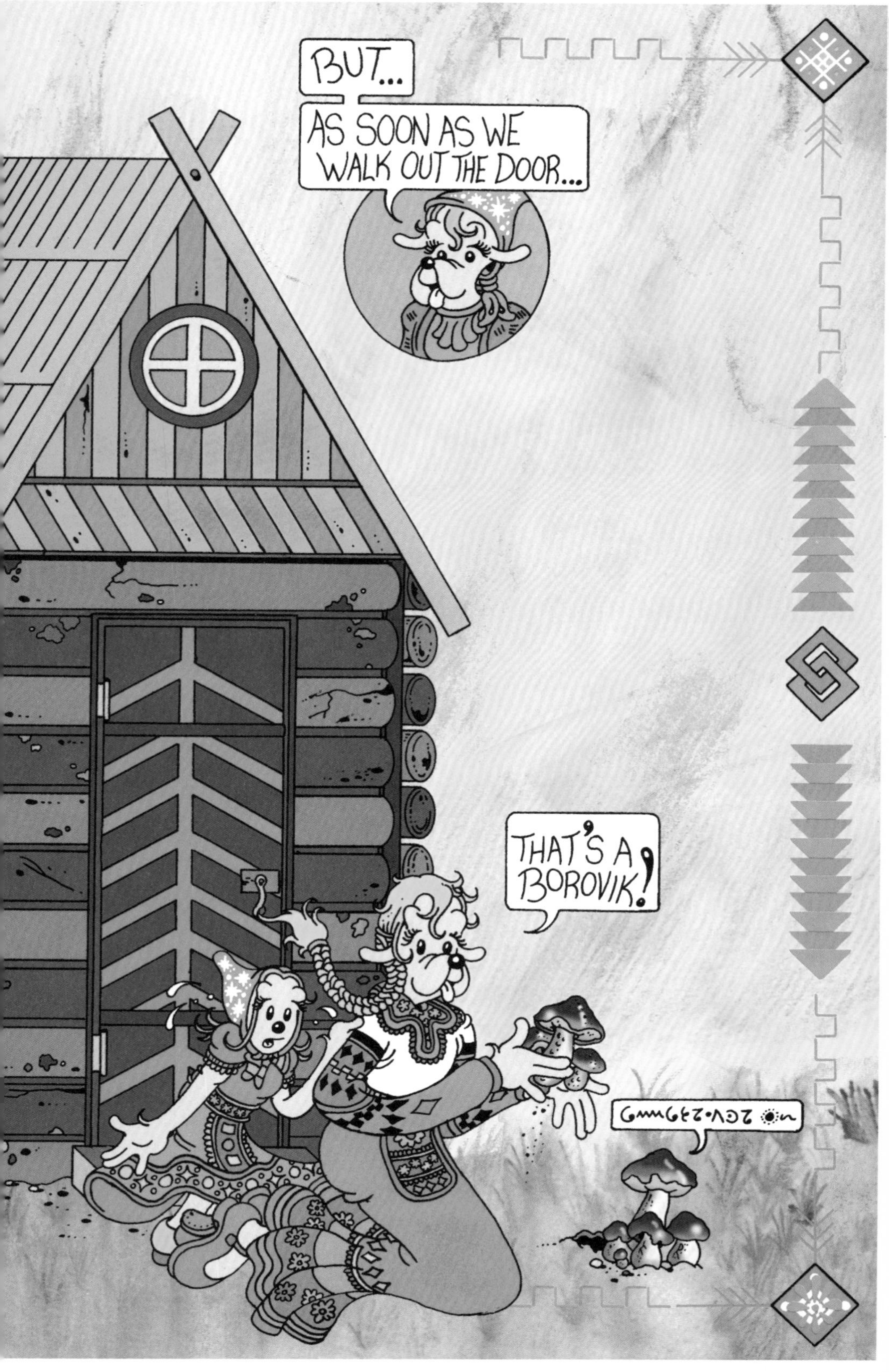
BUT...
AS SOON AS WE WALK OUT THE DOOR...
THAT'S A BOROVIK!

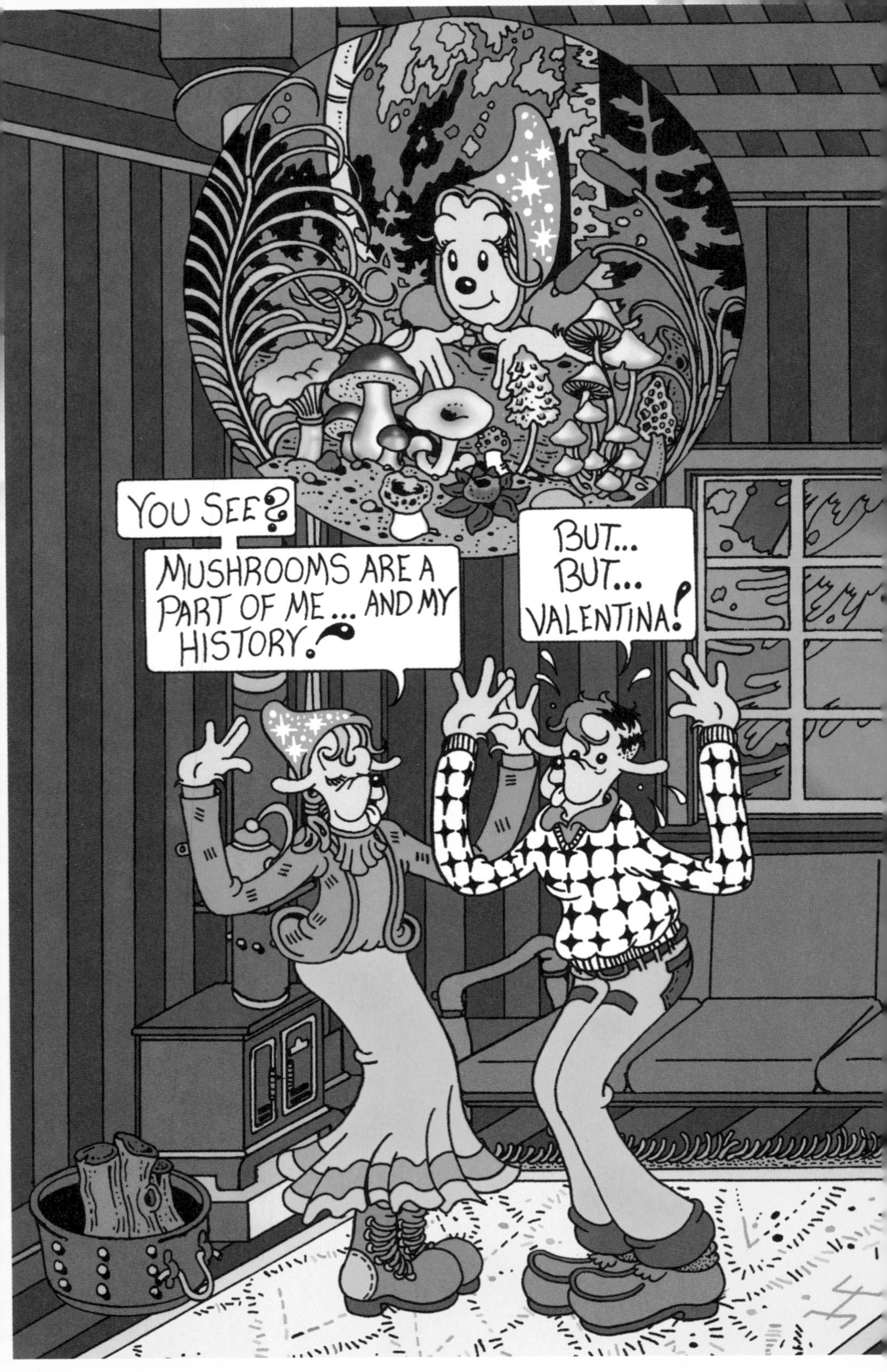
YOU SEE?
MUSHROOMS ARE A PART OF ME... AND MY HISTORY!
BUT... BUT... VALENTINA!

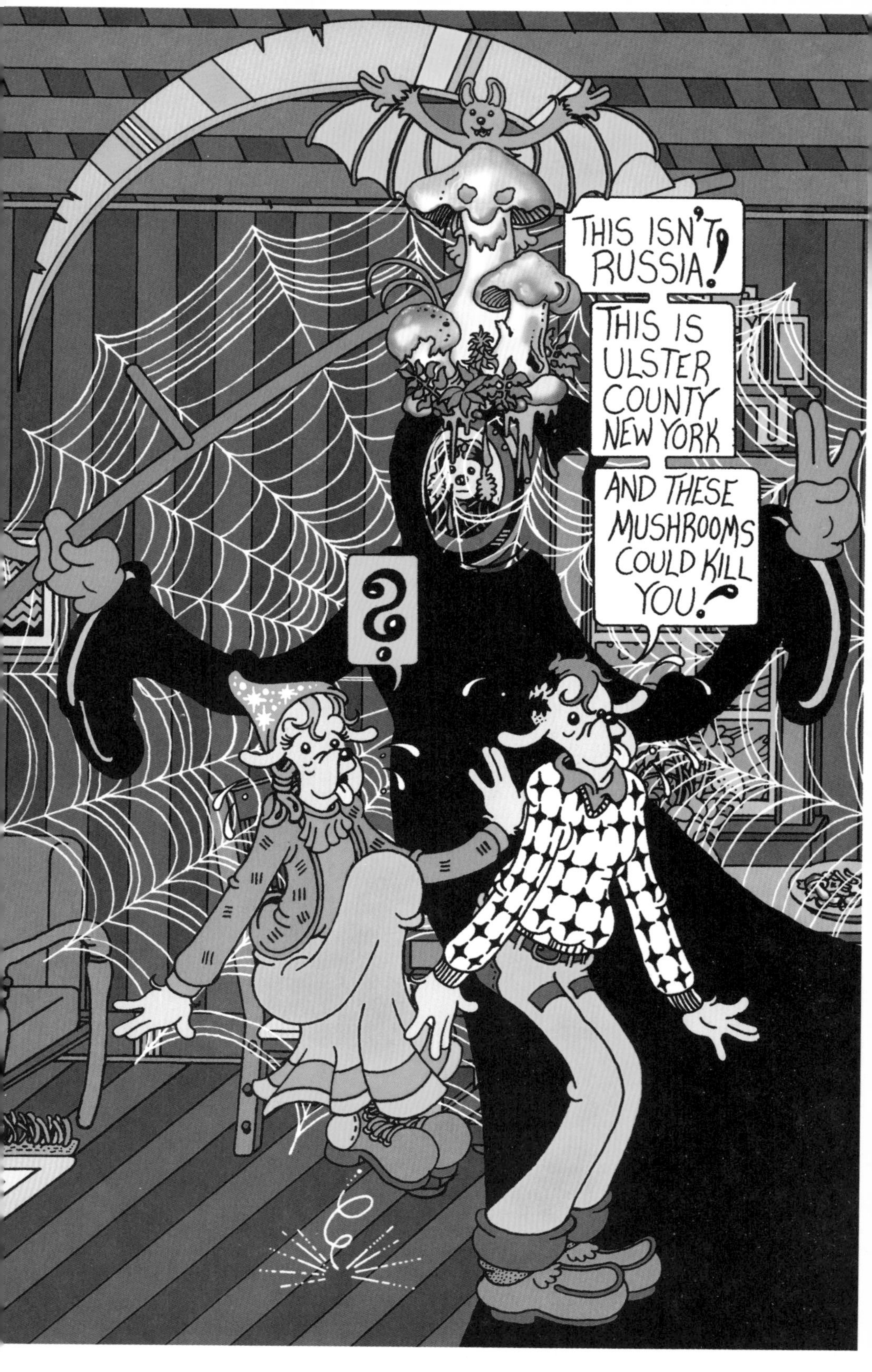
THIS ISN'T RUSSIA!
THIS IS ULSTER COUNTY NEW YORK
AND THESE MUSHROOMS COULD KILL YOU!
?

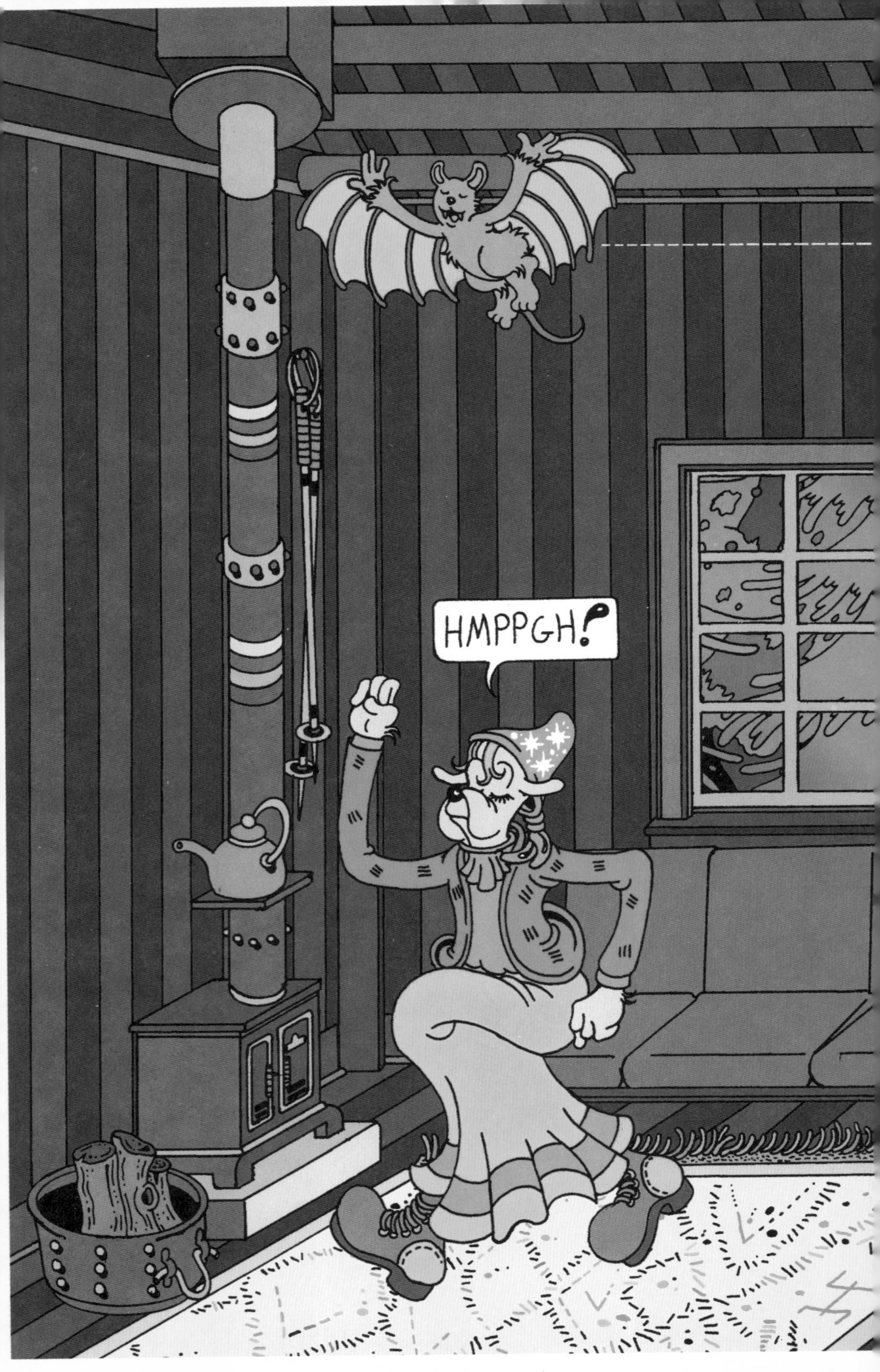
HMPPGH!

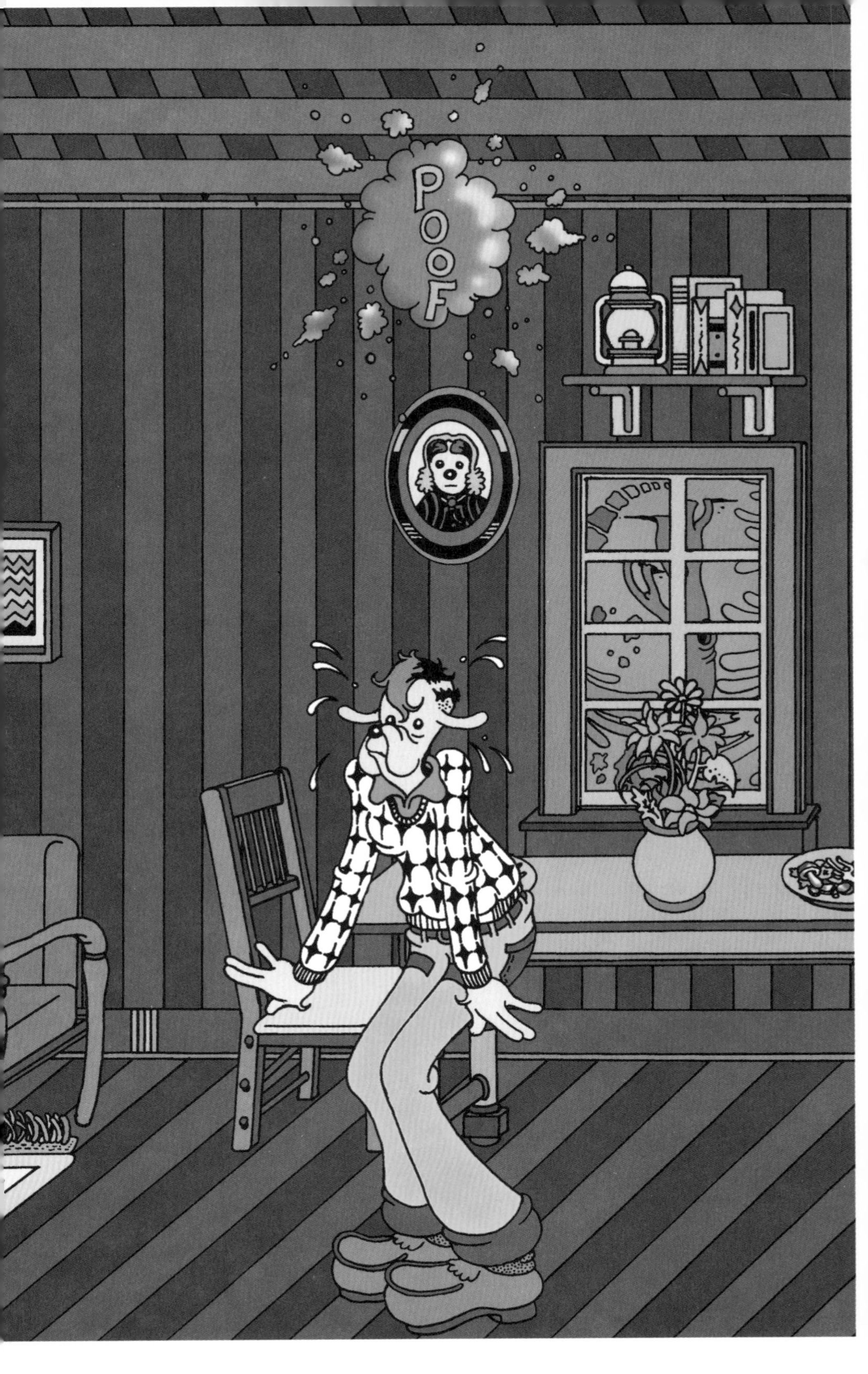
POOF

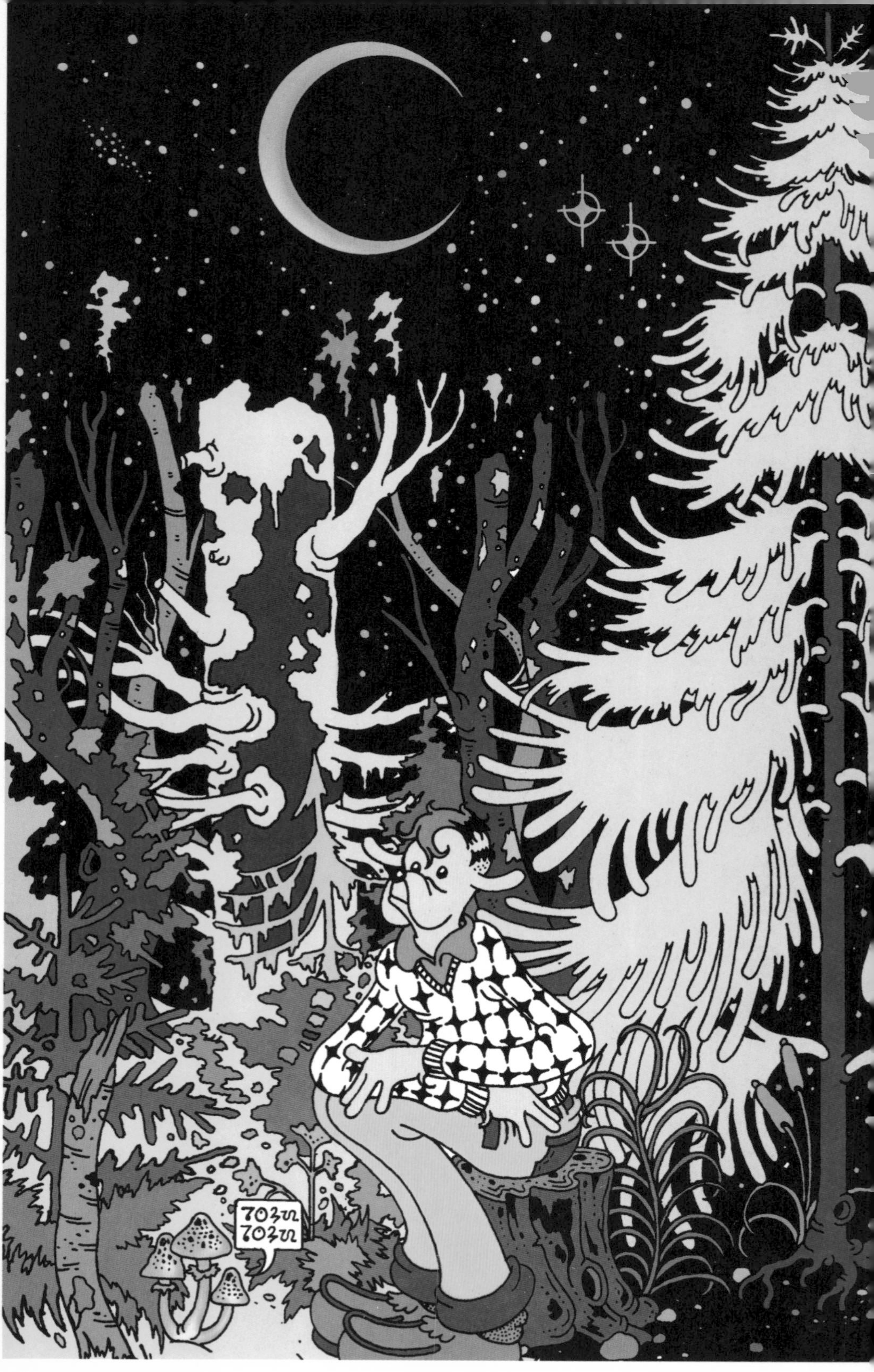

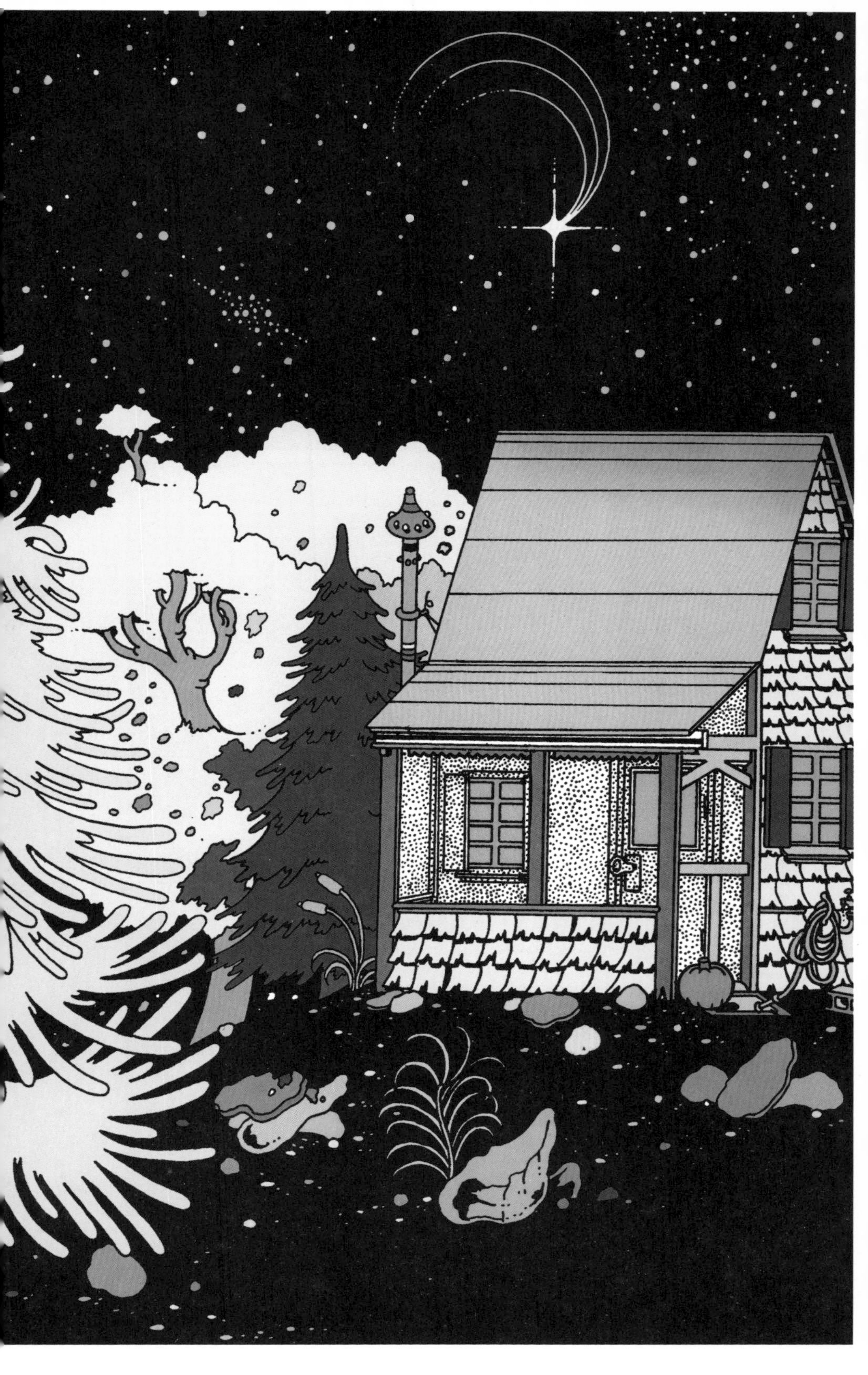

VALENTINA... I'M SORRY!
ZZ
I KNOW I'VE MADE A MESS OF OUR HONEYMOON...
ZZZZZZZ
BUT I DON'T WANT TO WAKE UP A WIDOWER...

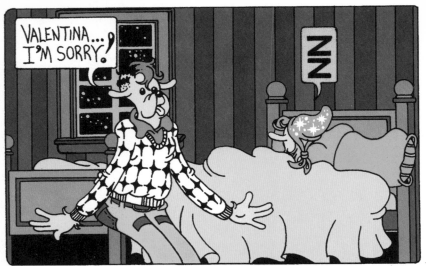

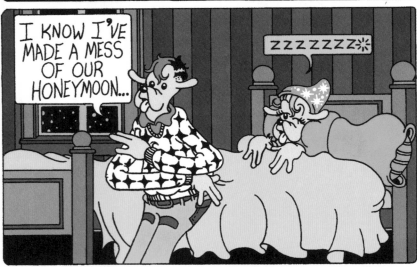

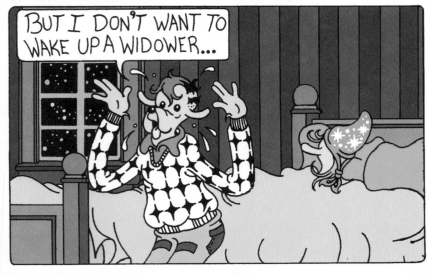

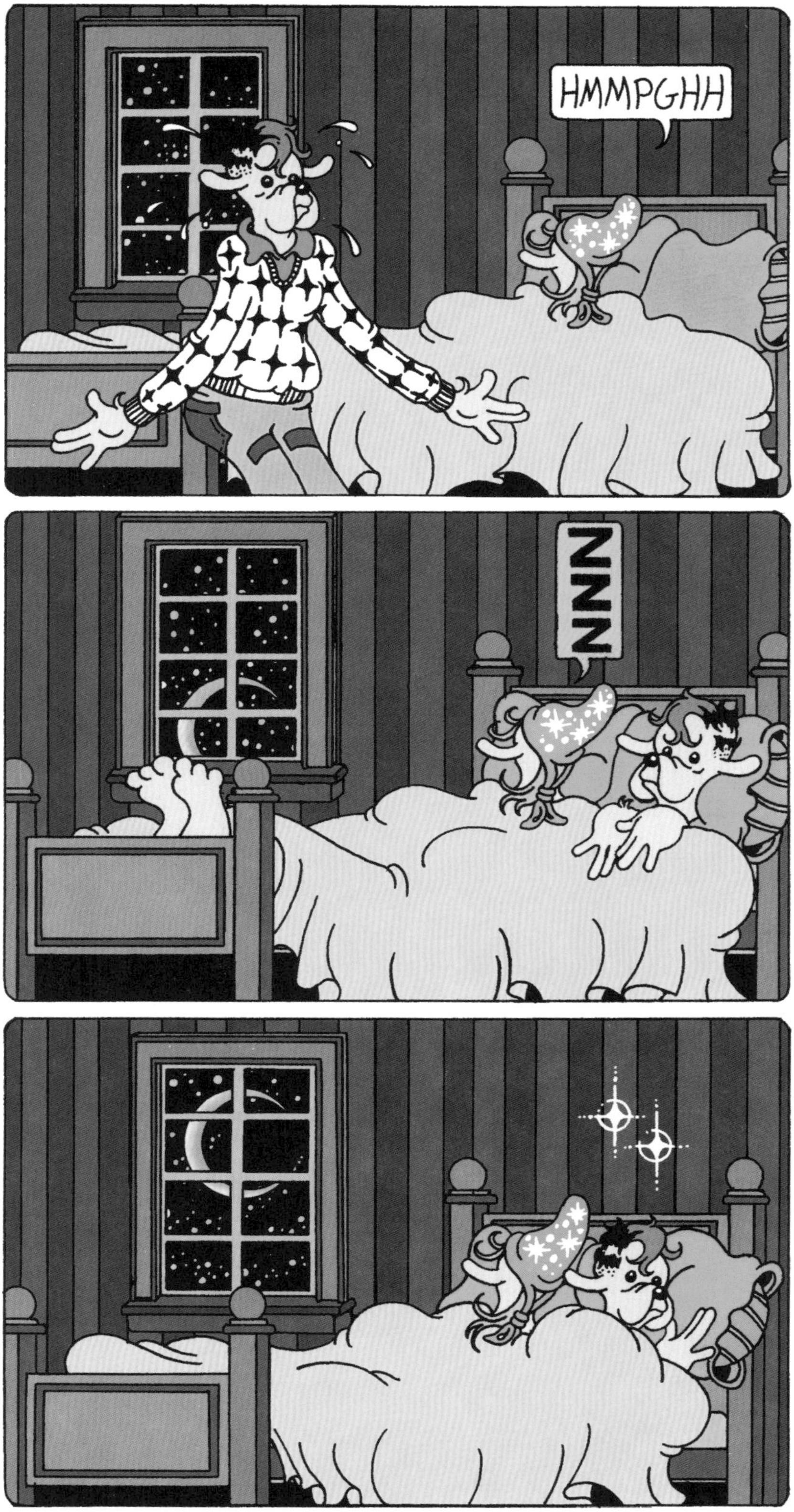
HMMPGHH
ZZZ

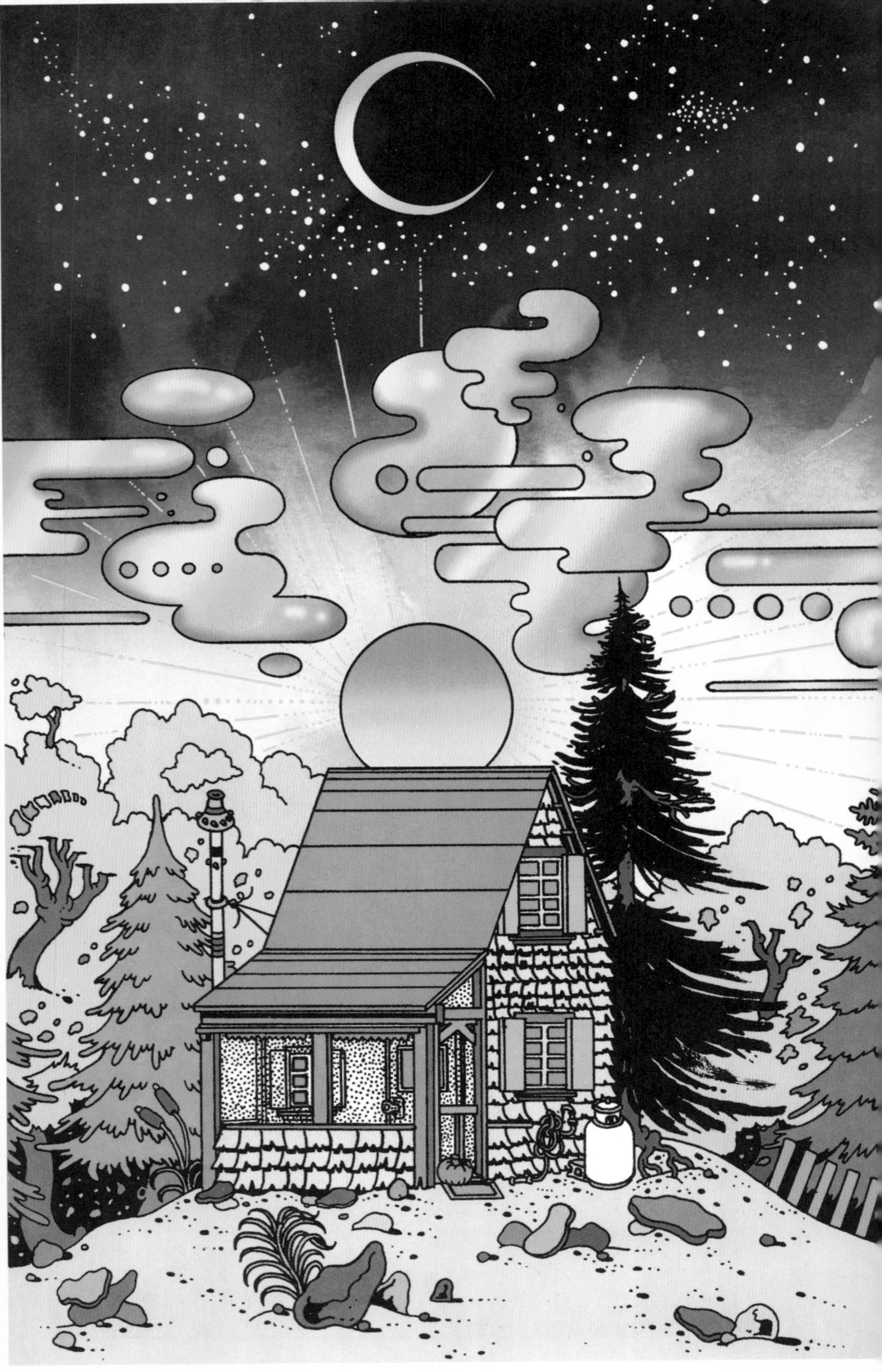

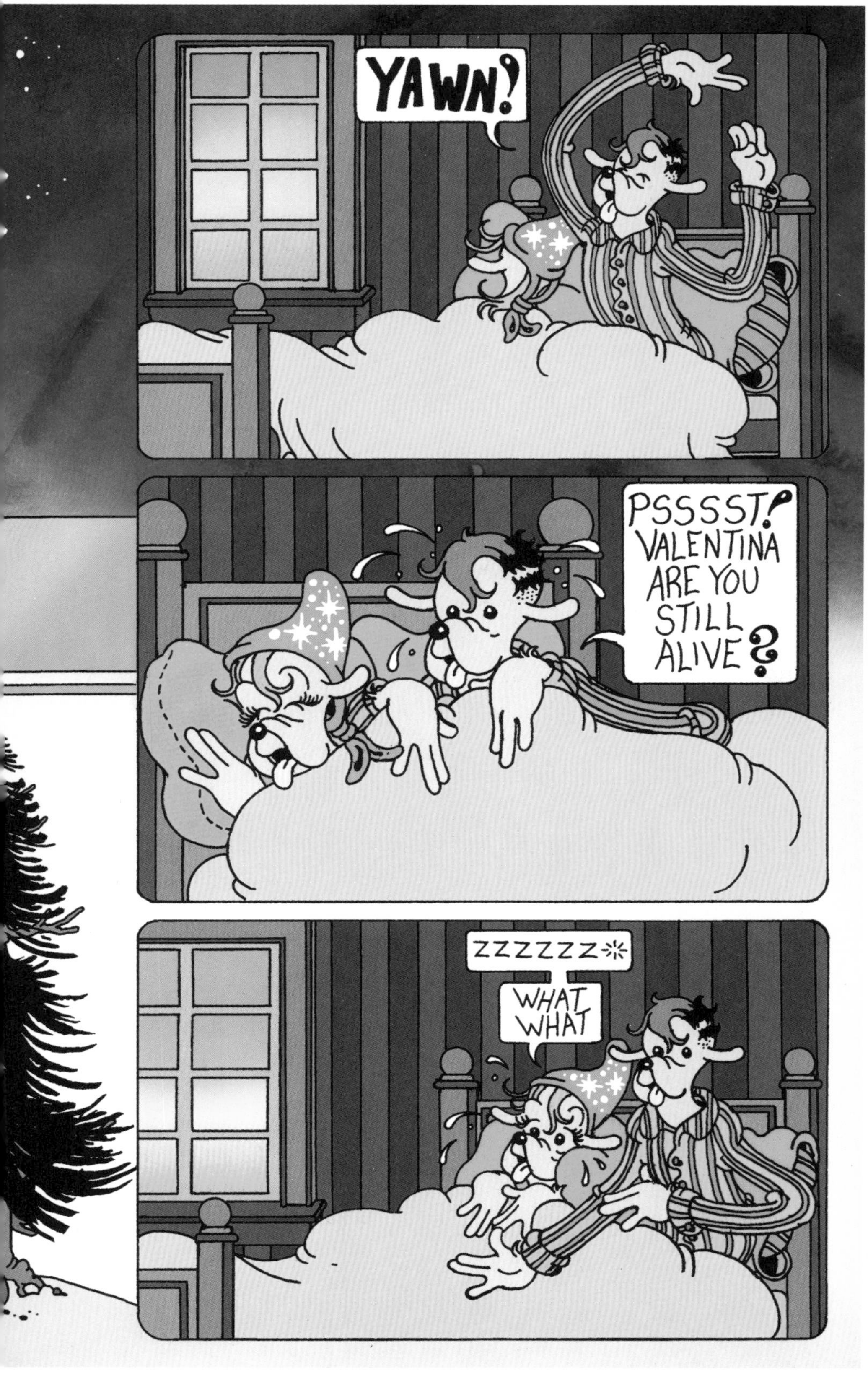
YAWN!
PSSSST! VALENTINA ARE YOU STILL ALIVE?
ZZZZZZ
WHAT WHAT

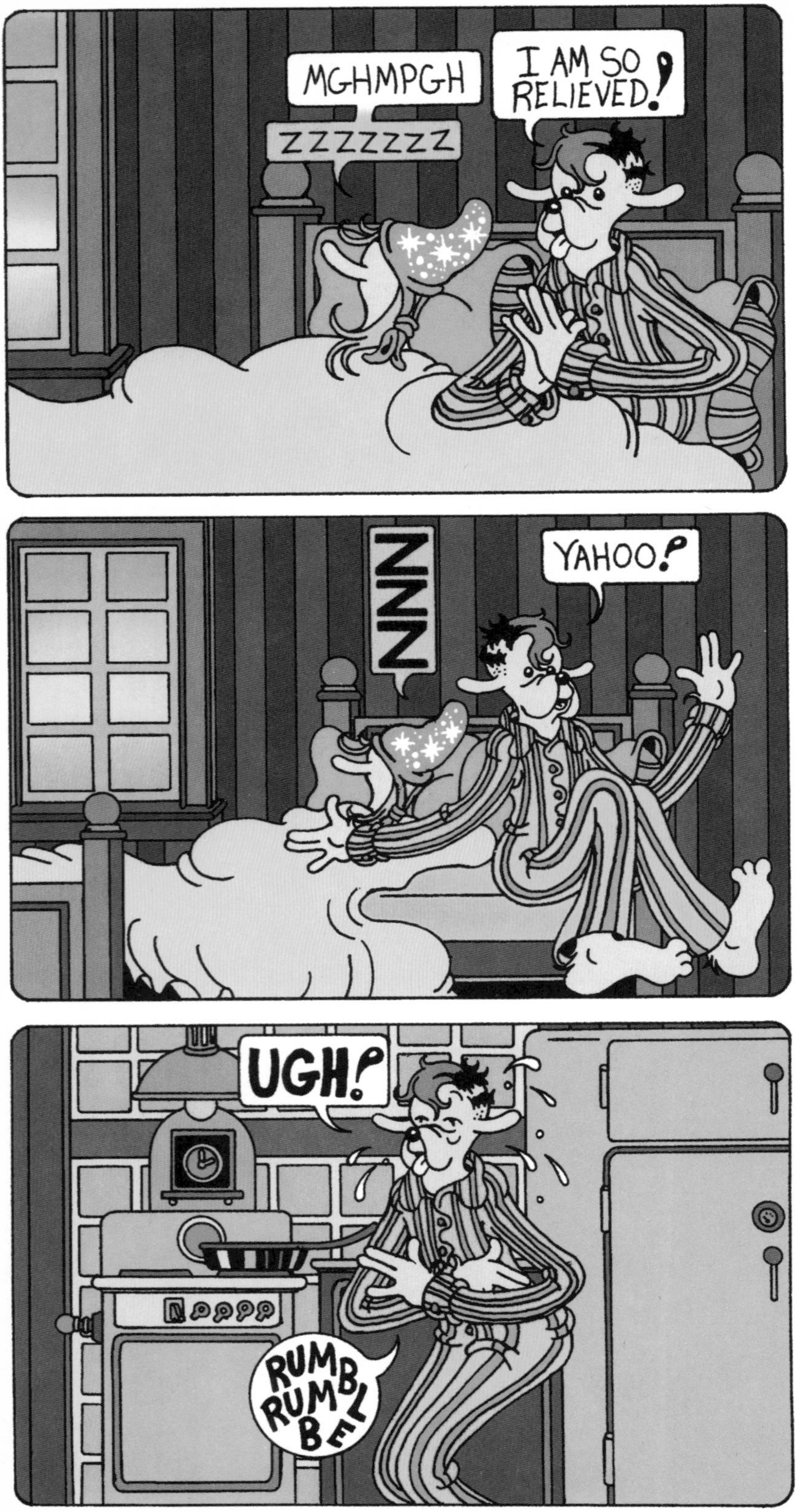

MGHMPGH
ZZZZZZZ
I AM SO RELIEVED!
ZZZ
YAHOO!
UGH!
RUMB
RUMBL
BE

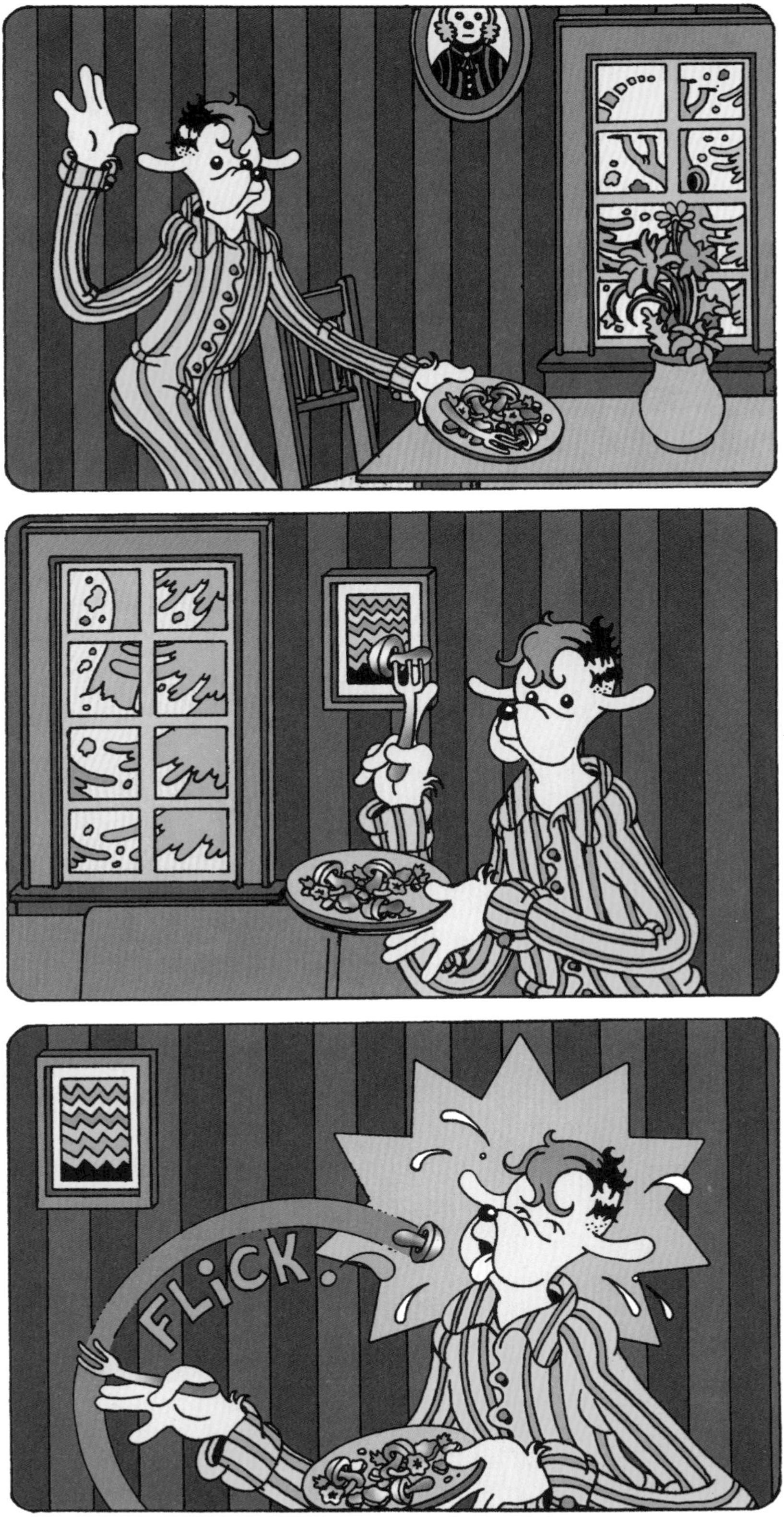
FLiCK.

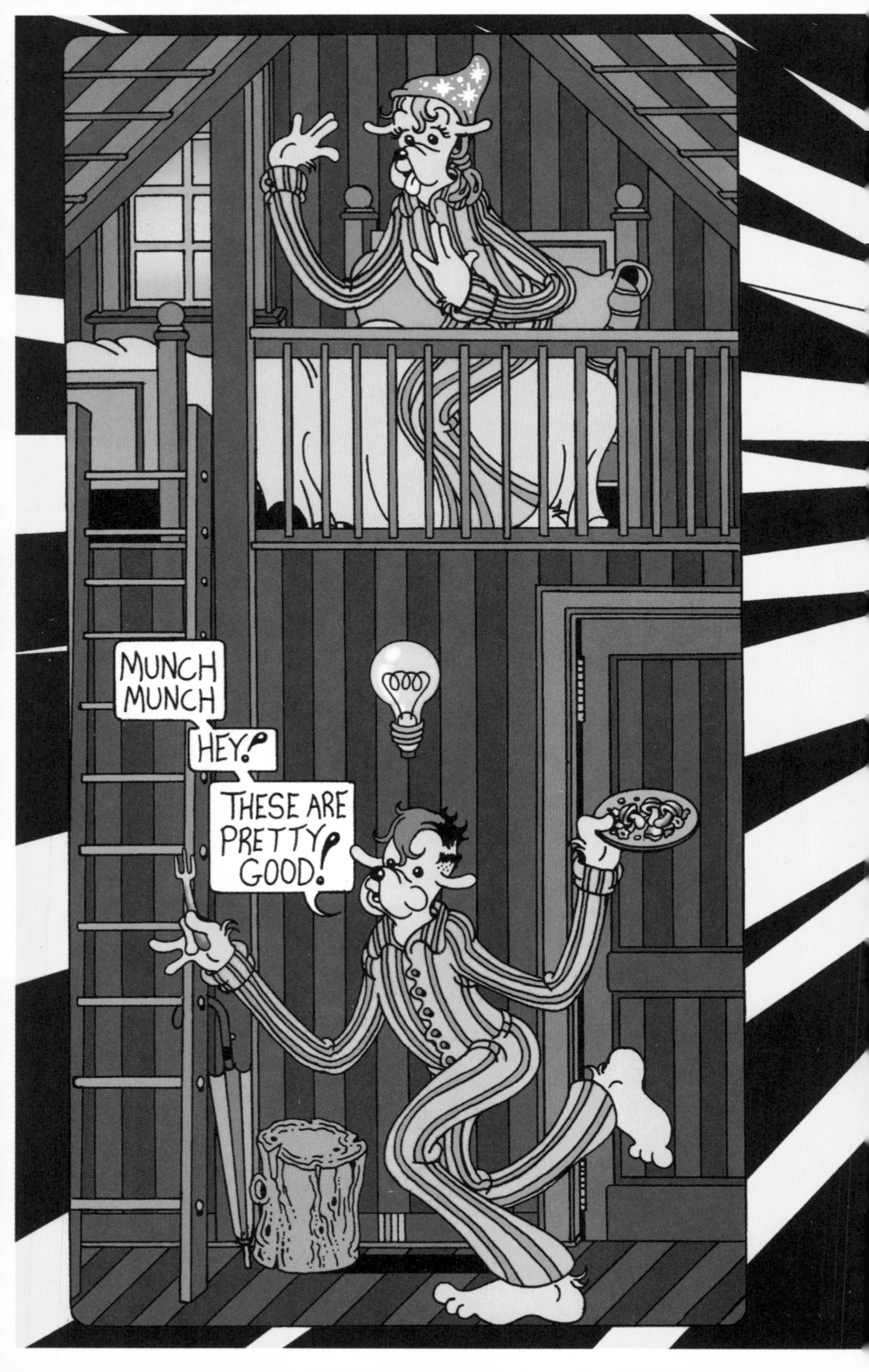
MUNCH
MUNCH
HEY!
THESE ARE PRETTY GOOD!

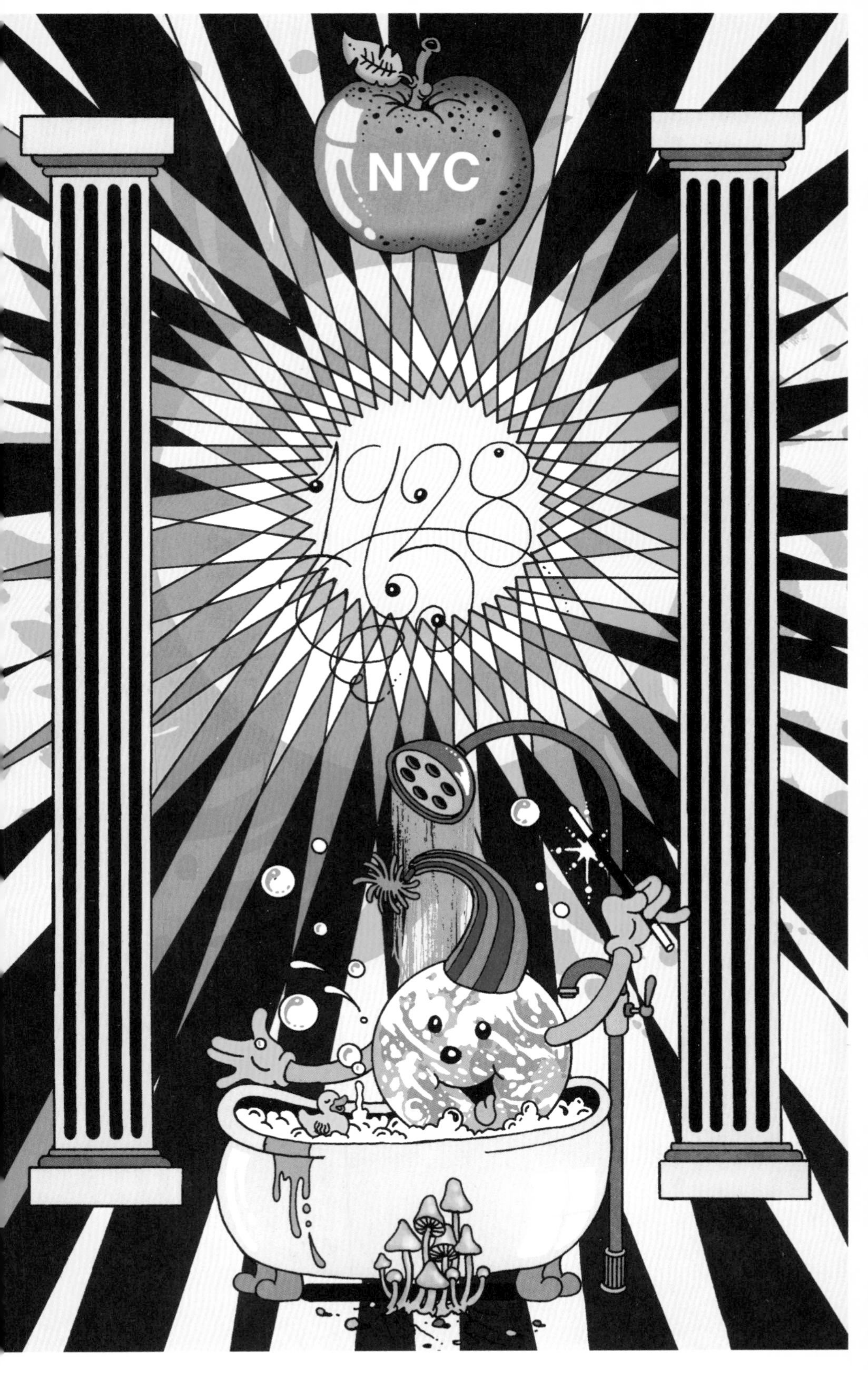
NYC

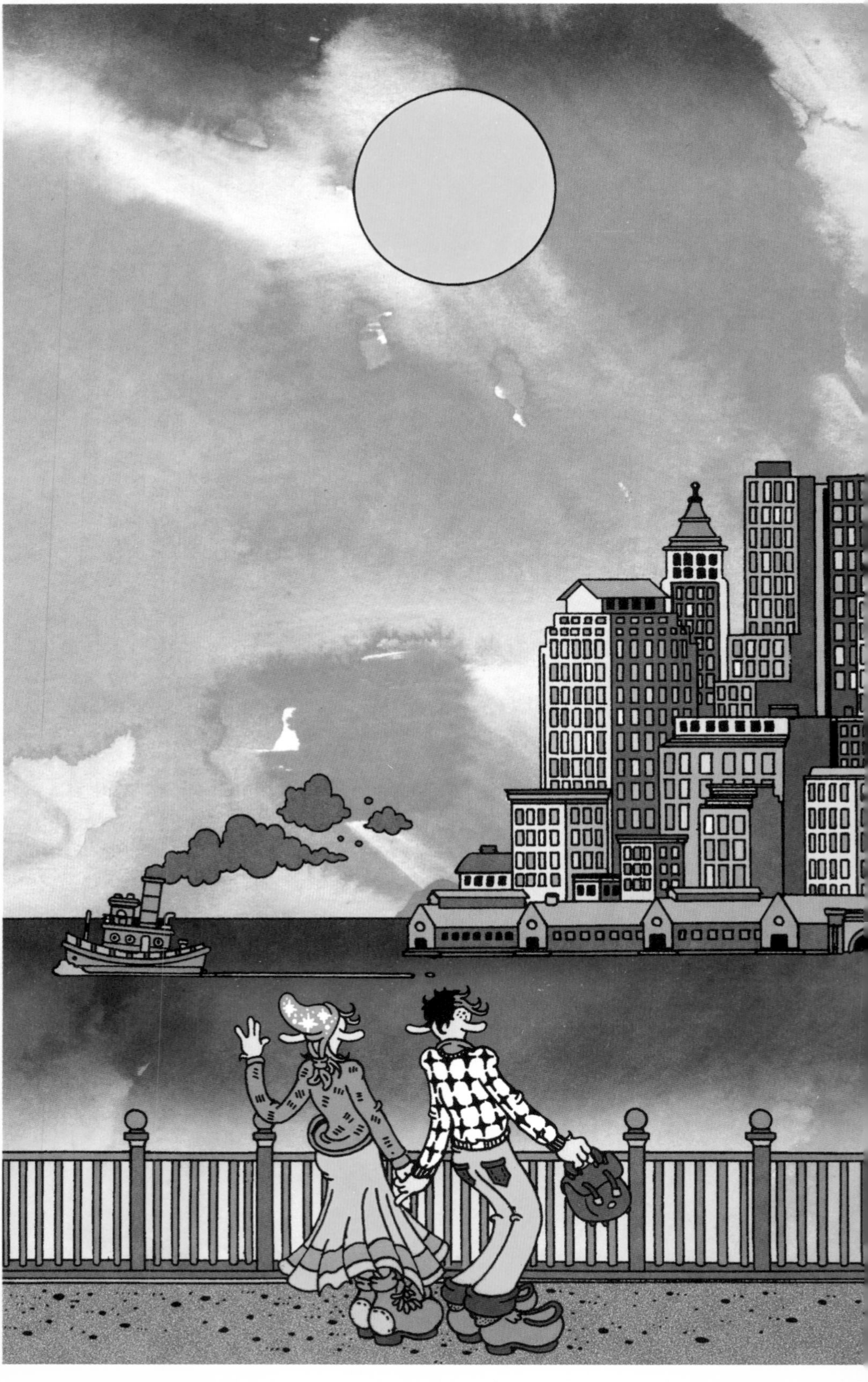

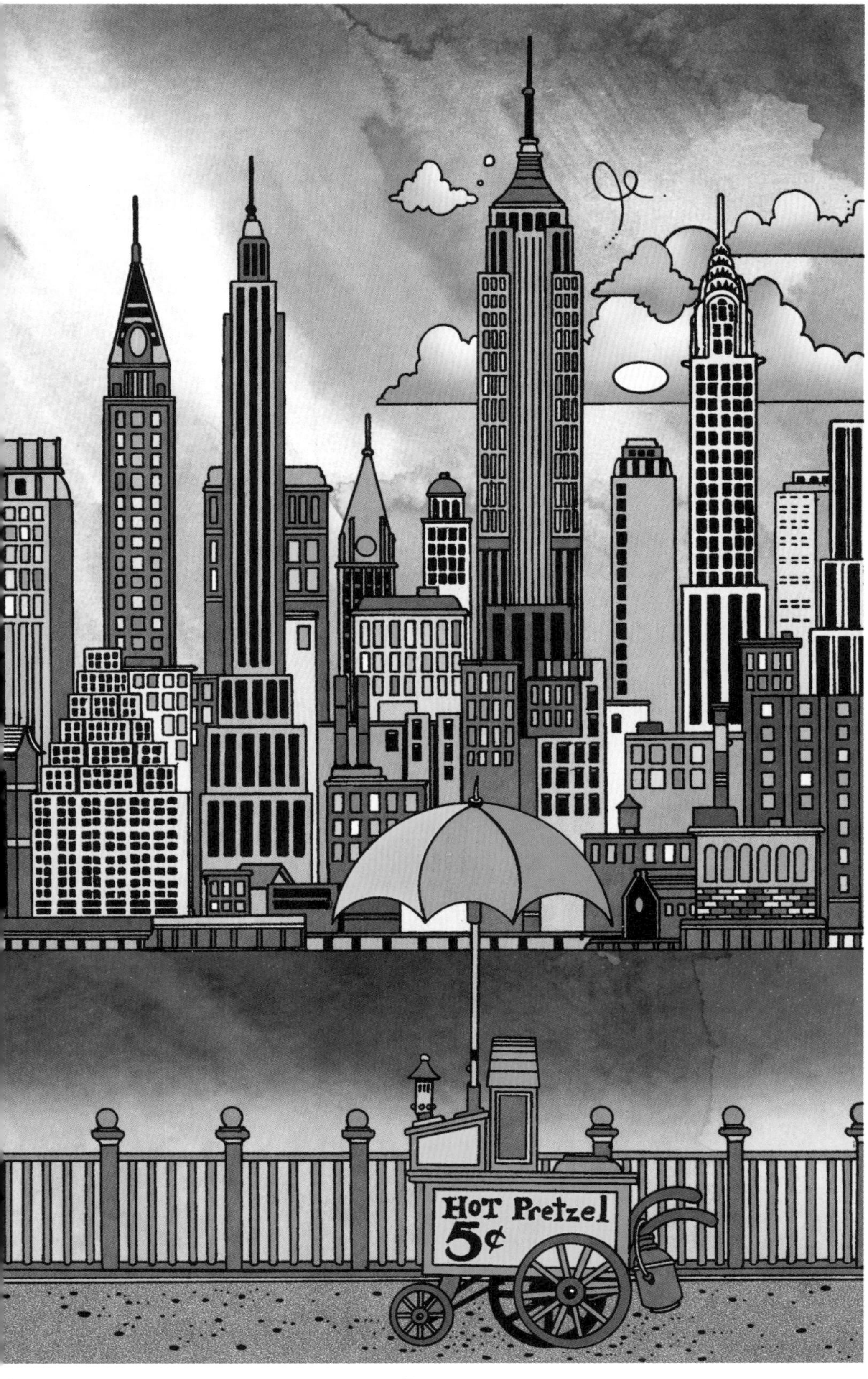
HOT Pretzel
5¢

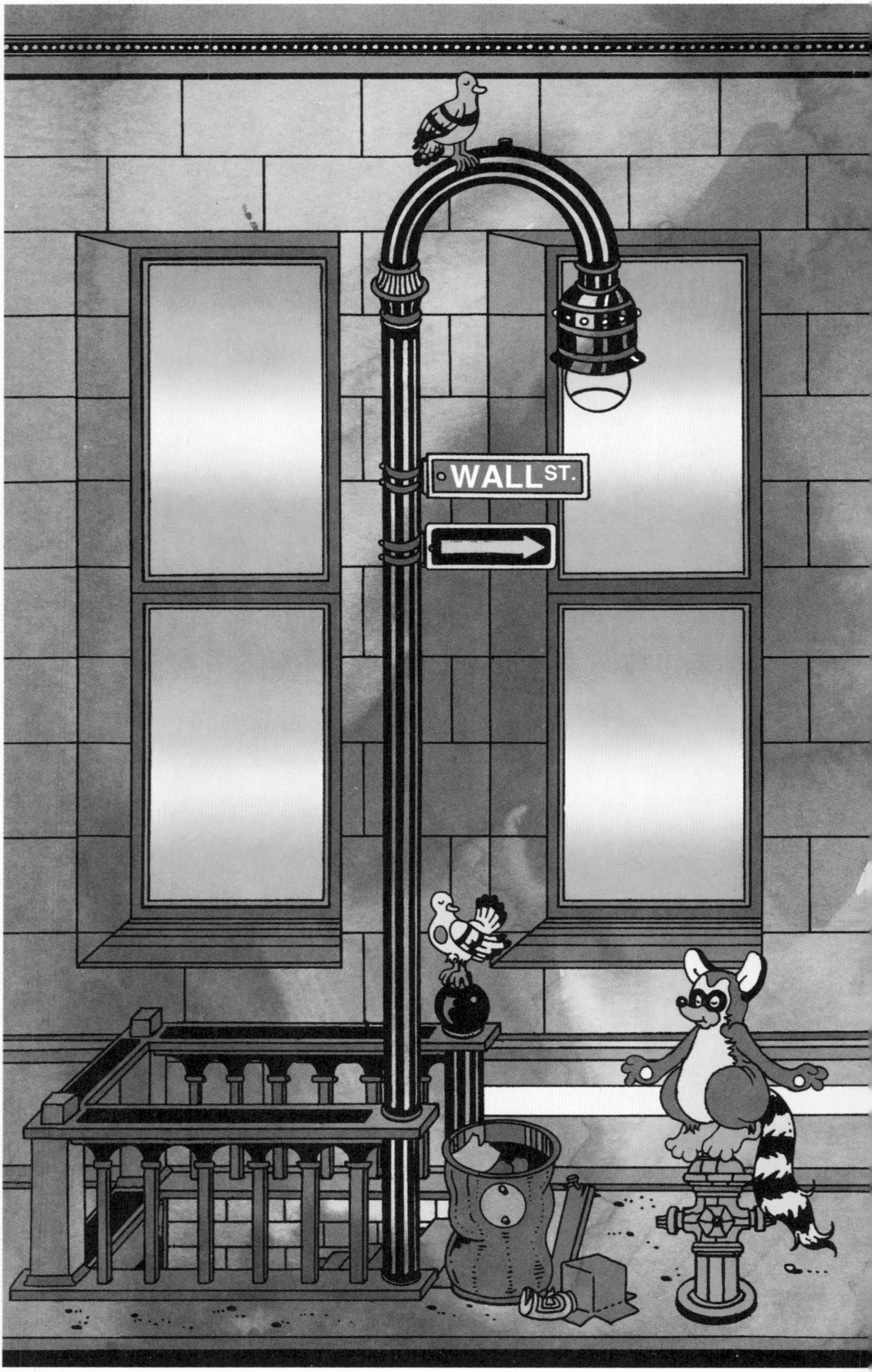
WALL ST.

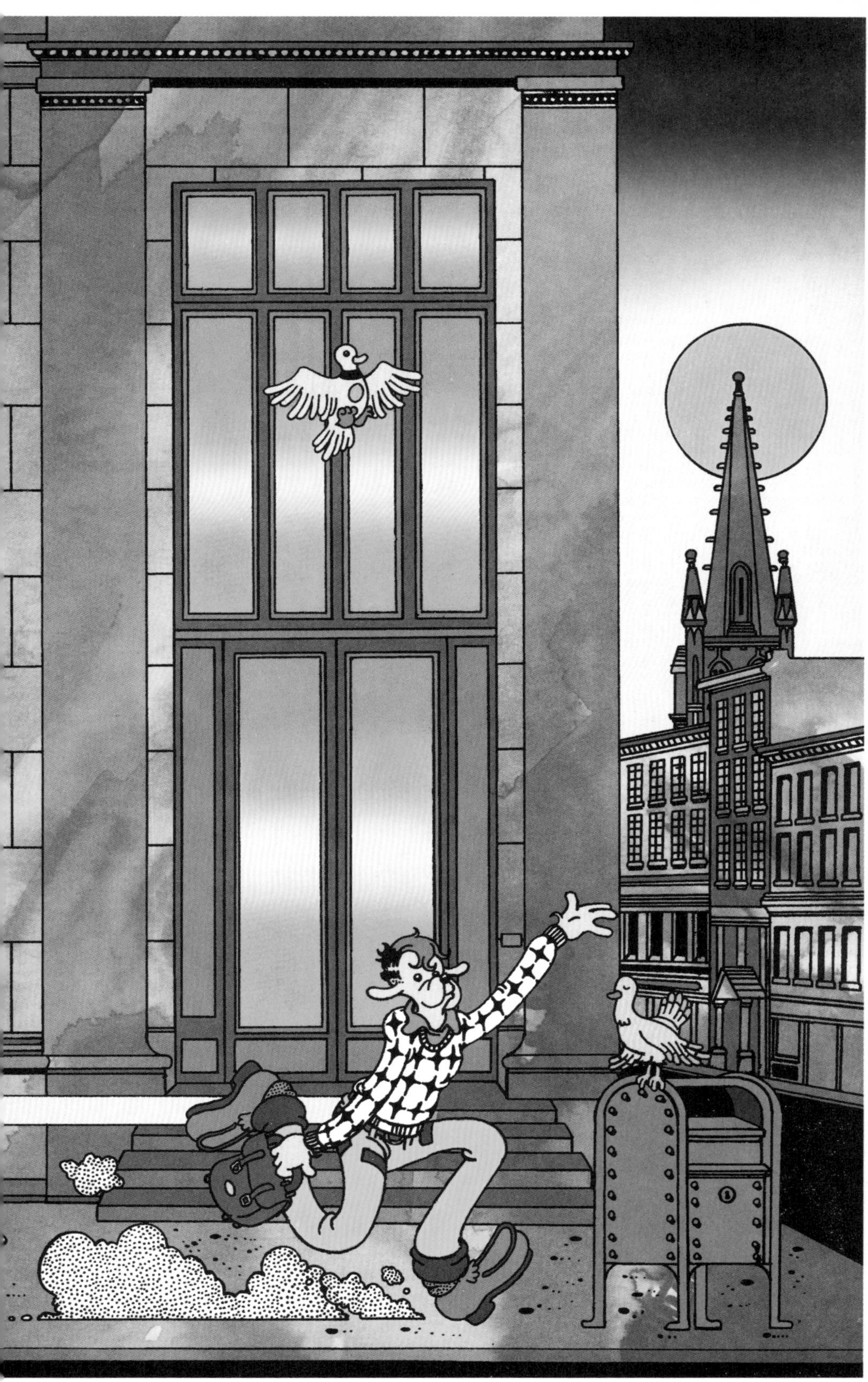

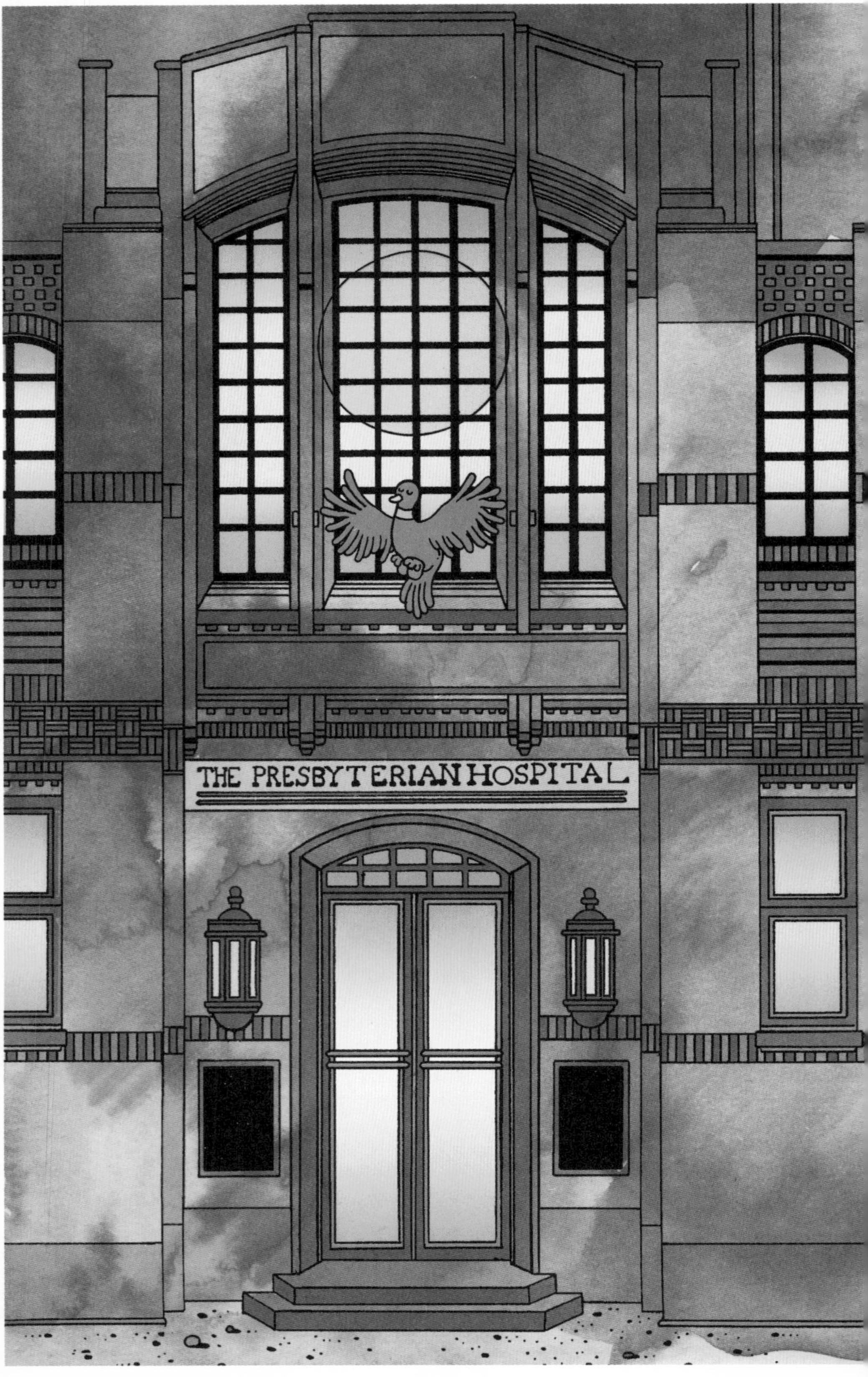
THE PRESBYTERIAN HOSPITAL

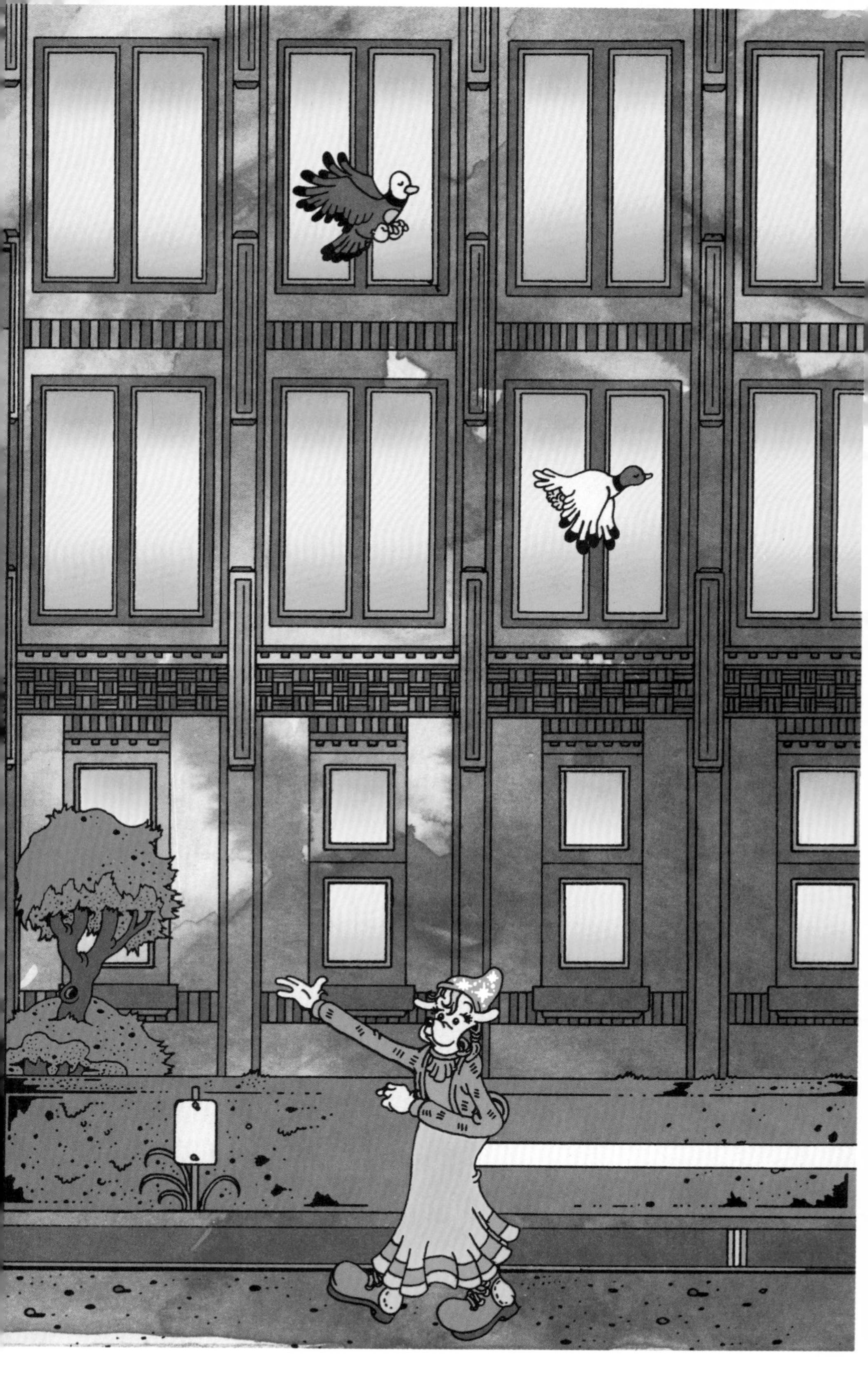

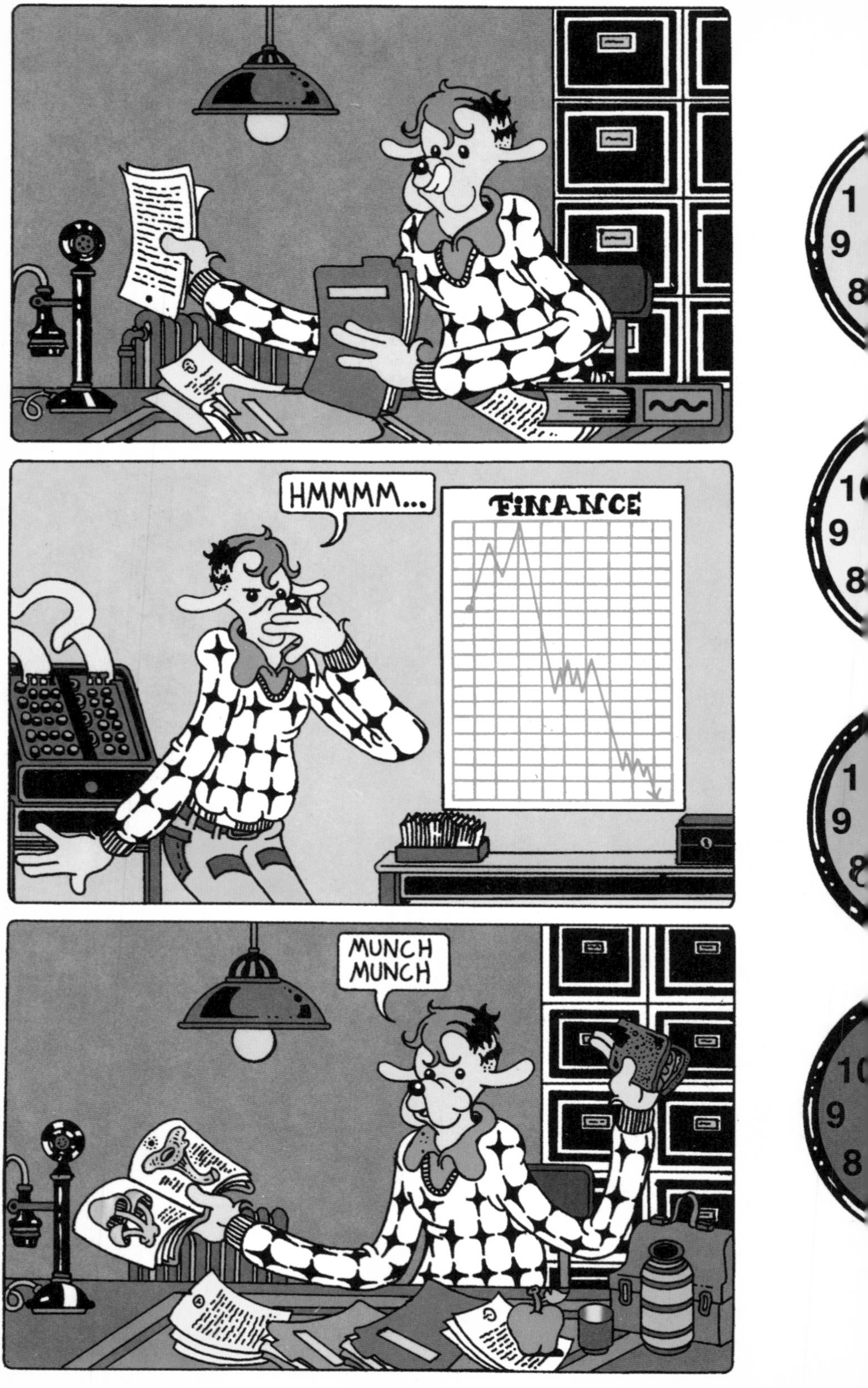
HMMMM...
FINANCE
MUNCH
MUNCH

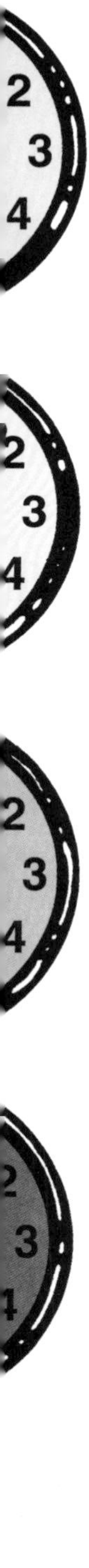
2
3
4

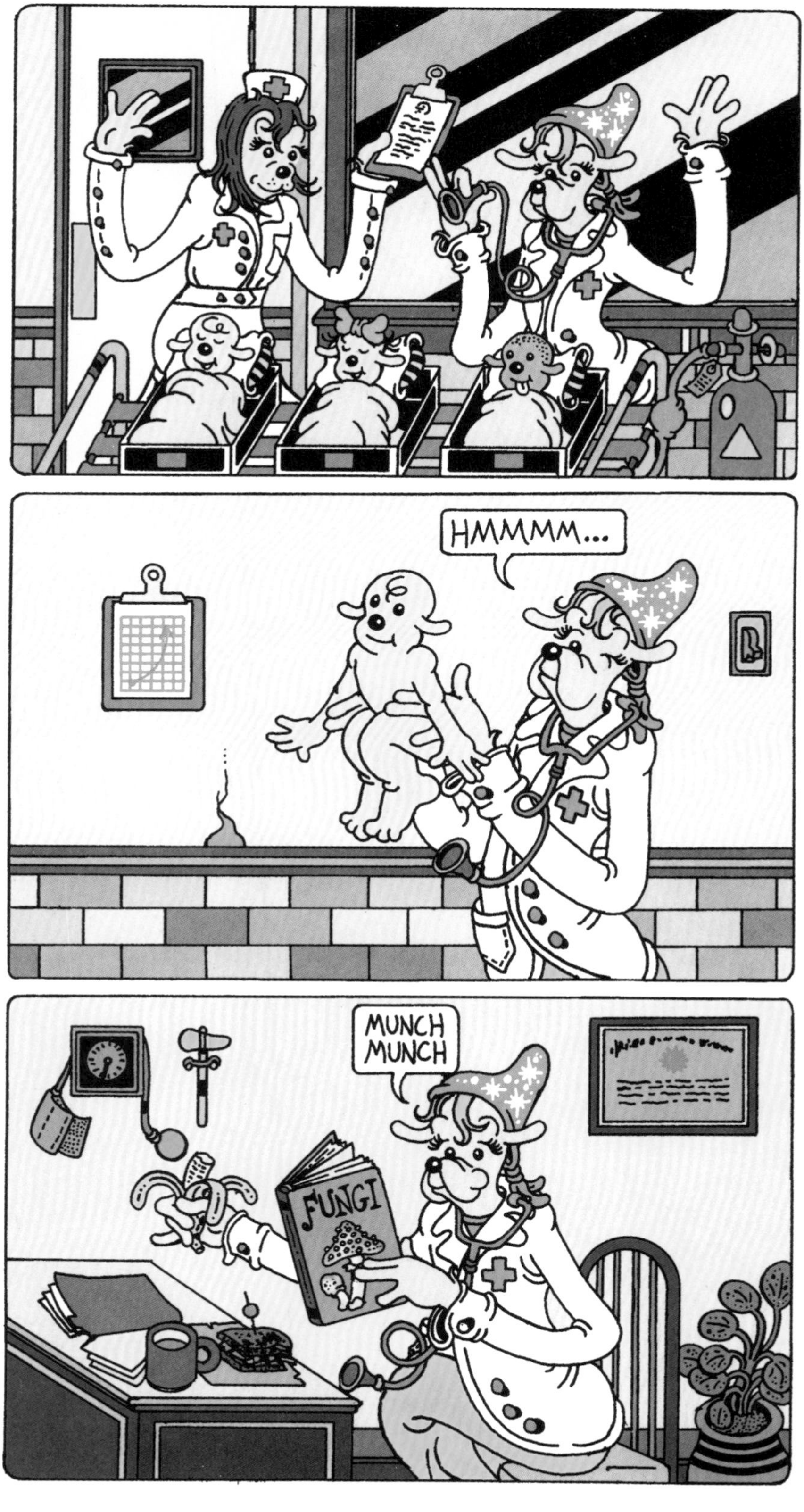
HMMMM...
MUNCH MUNCH
FUNGI

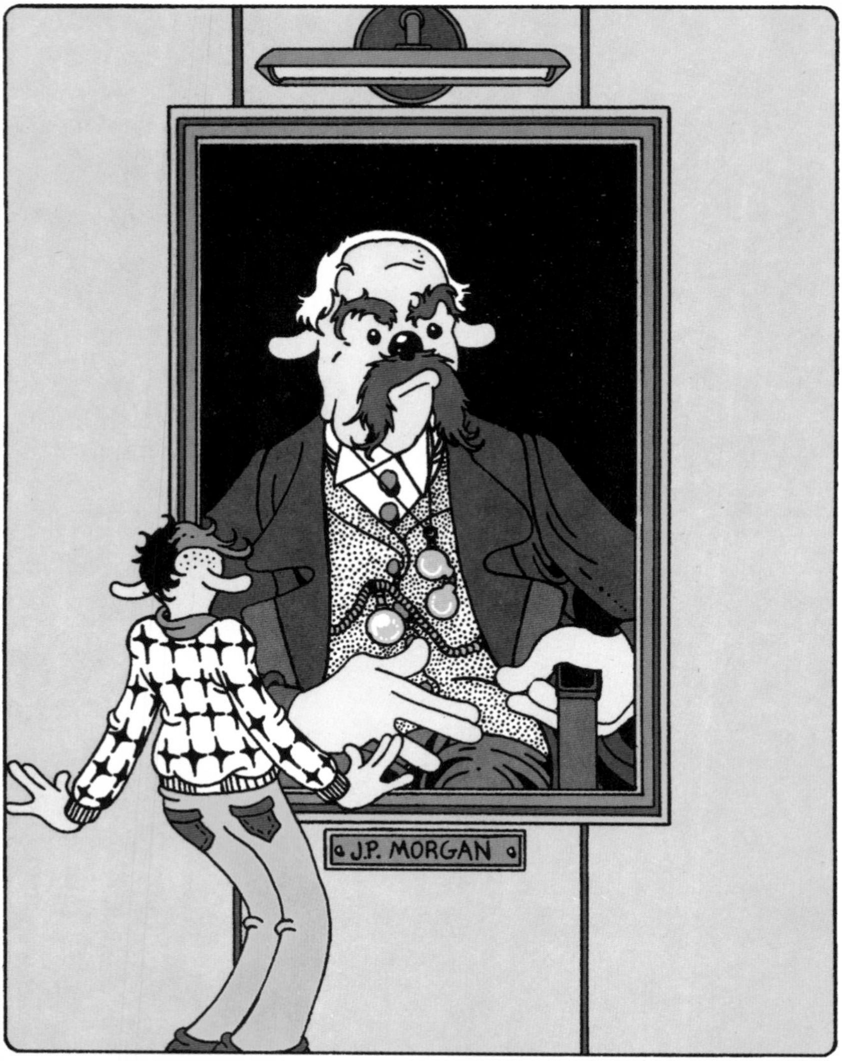
J.P. MORGAN

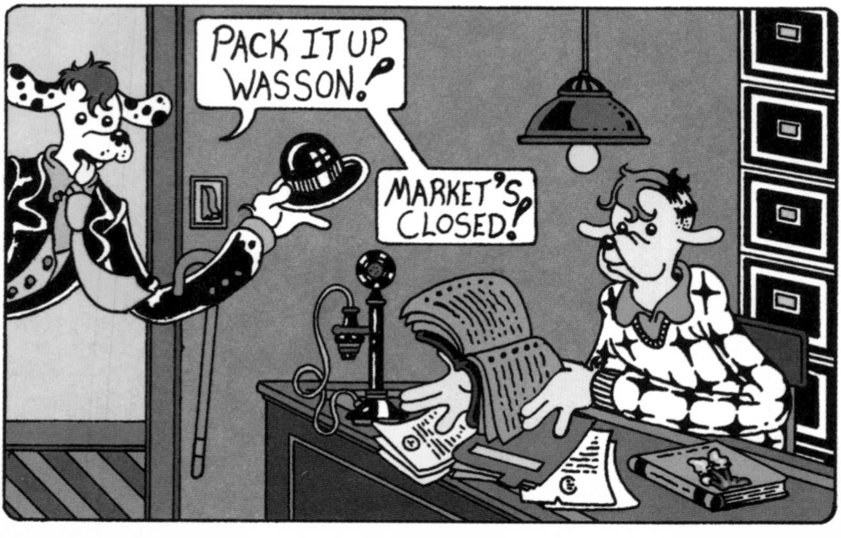
PACK IT UP WASSON!
MARKET'S CLOSED!

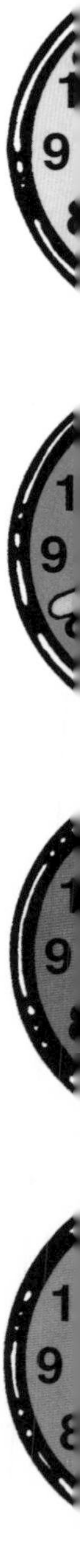

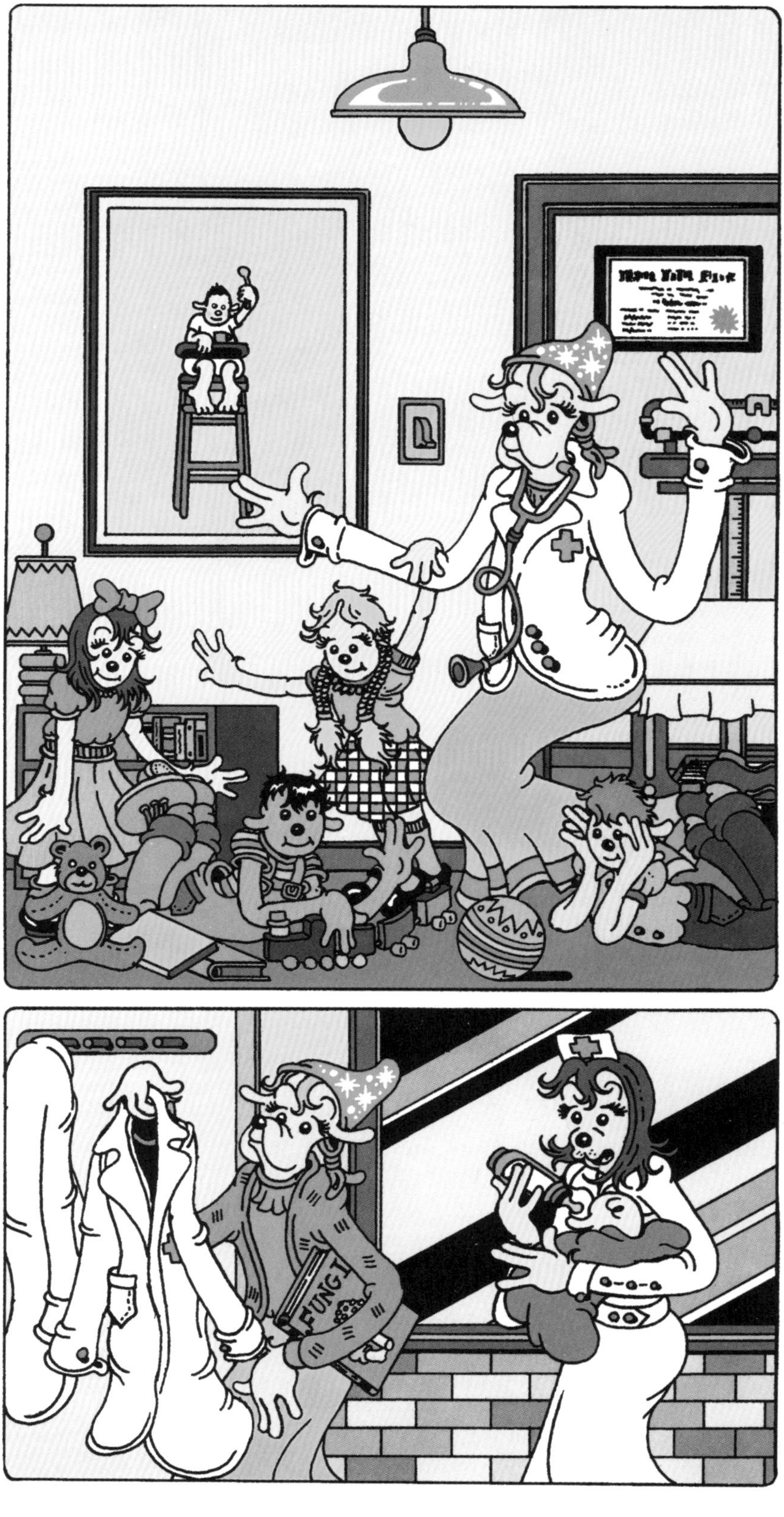
FUNGI

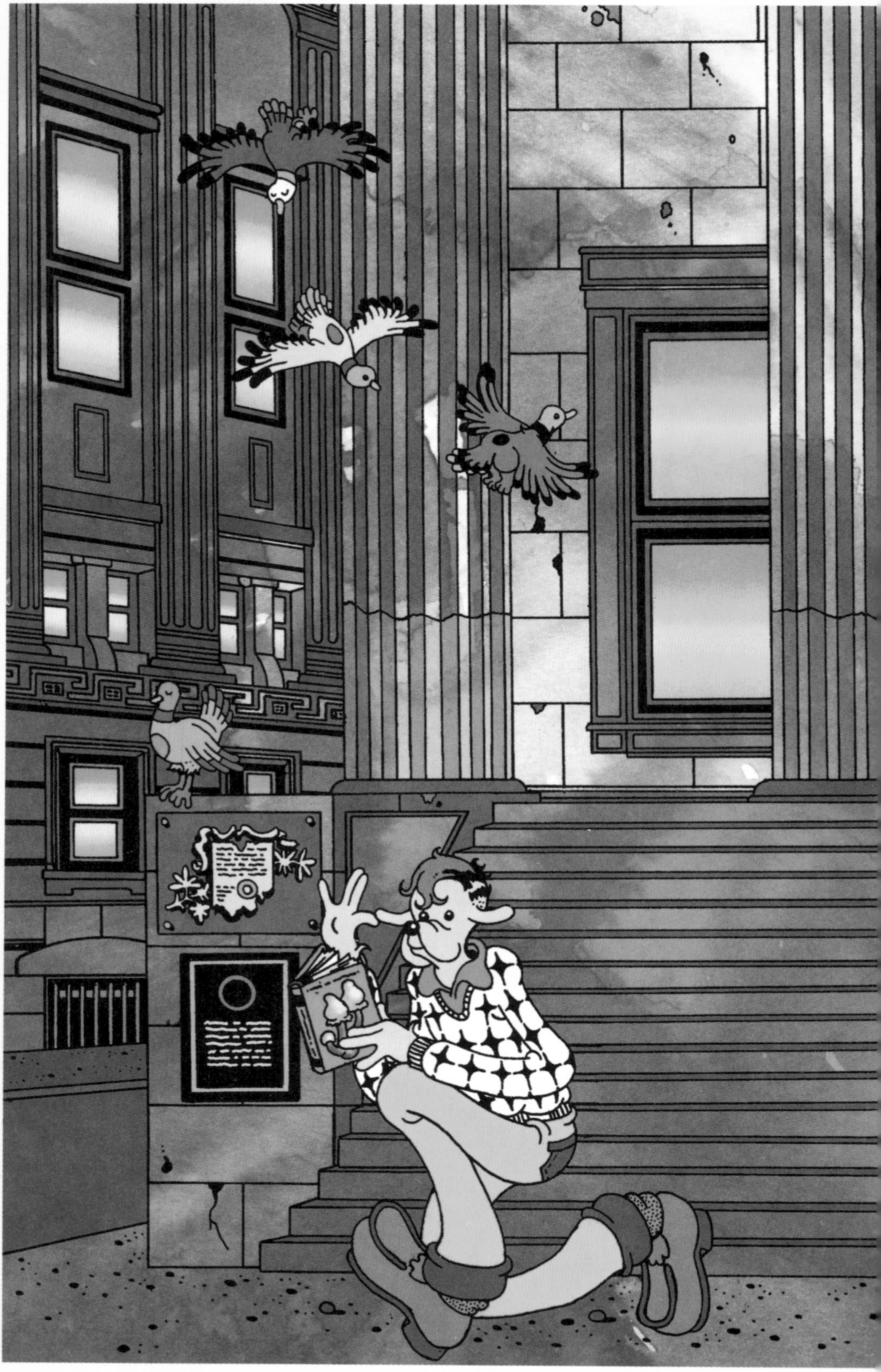

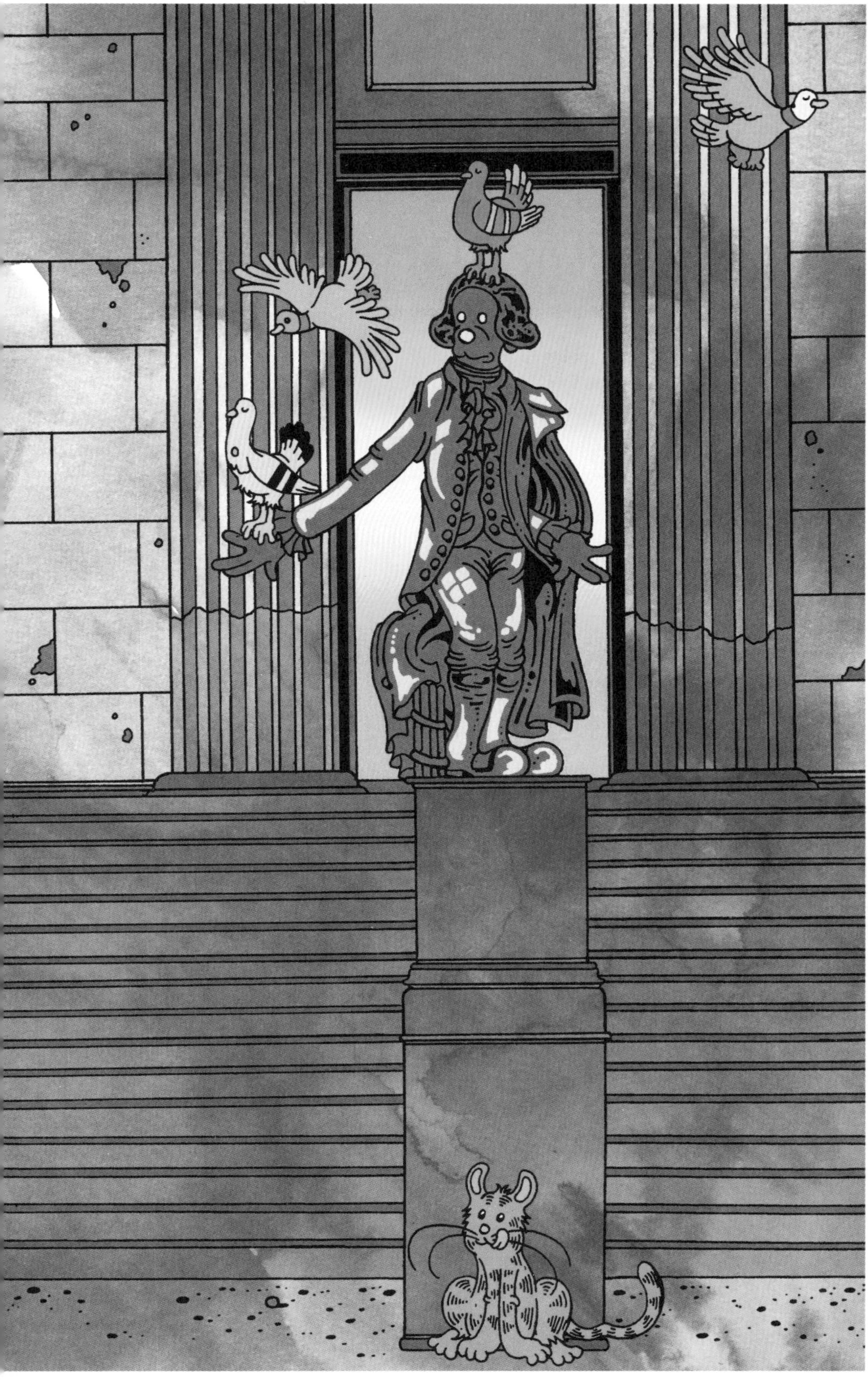

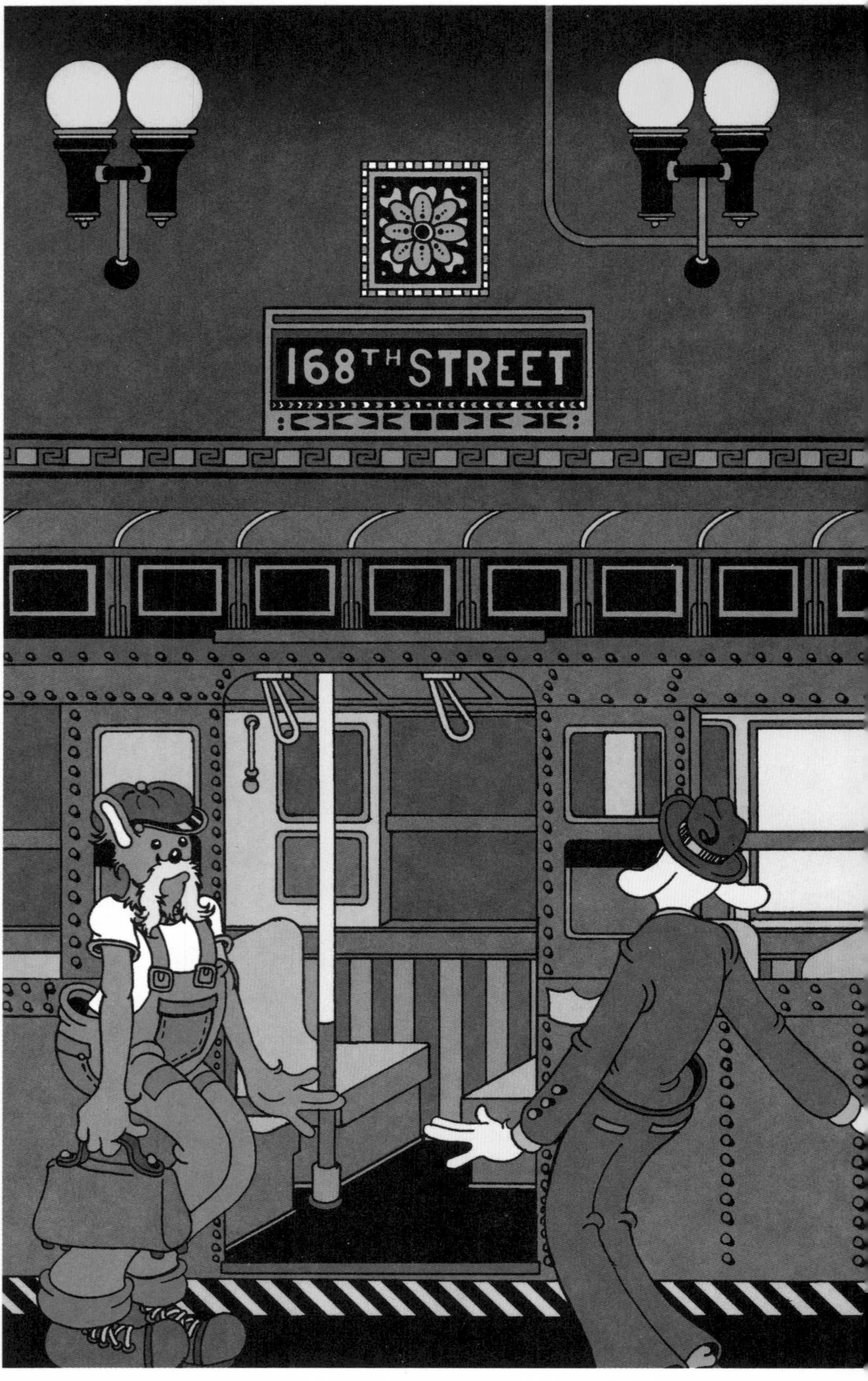
168TH STREET

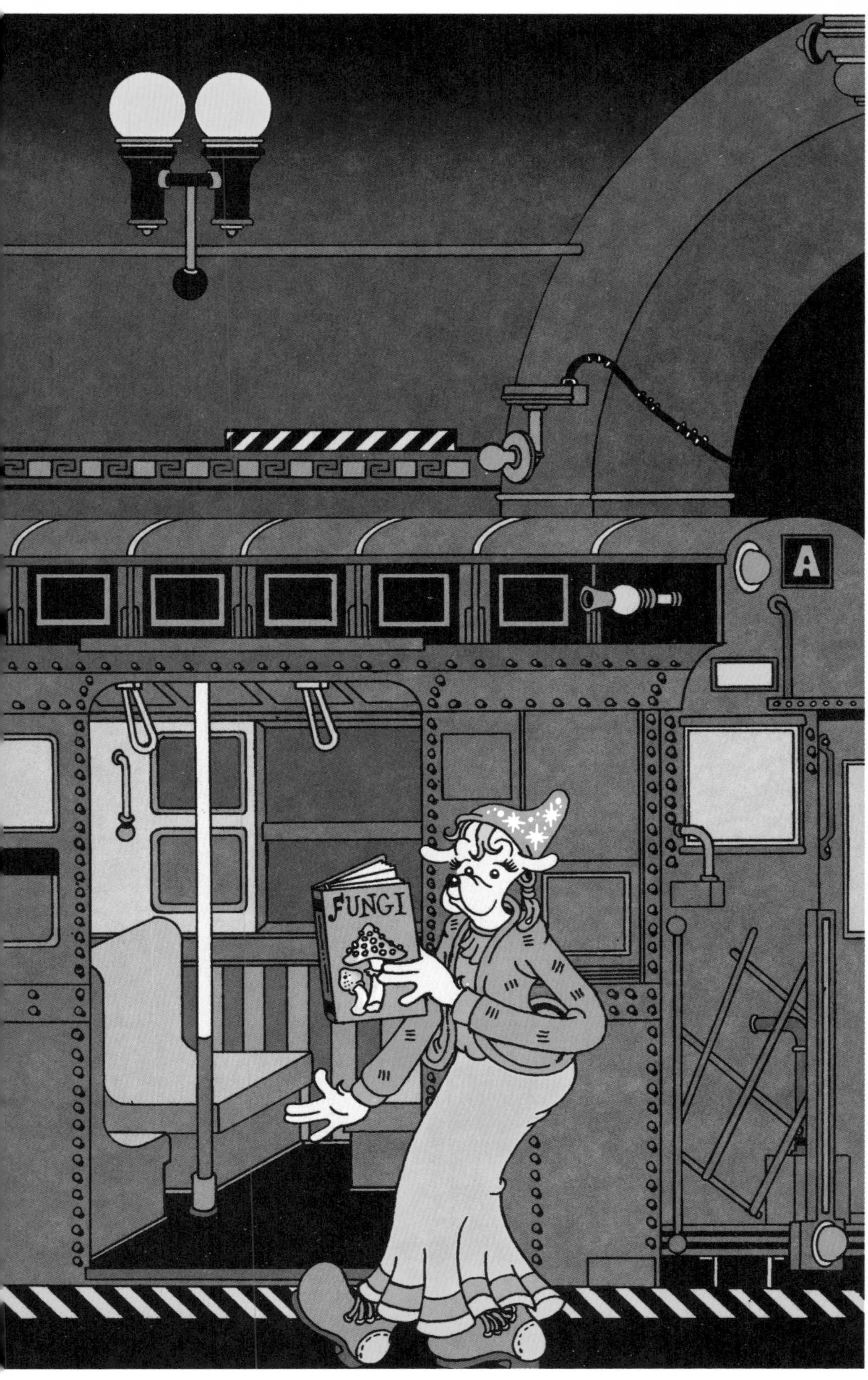
A
FUNGI

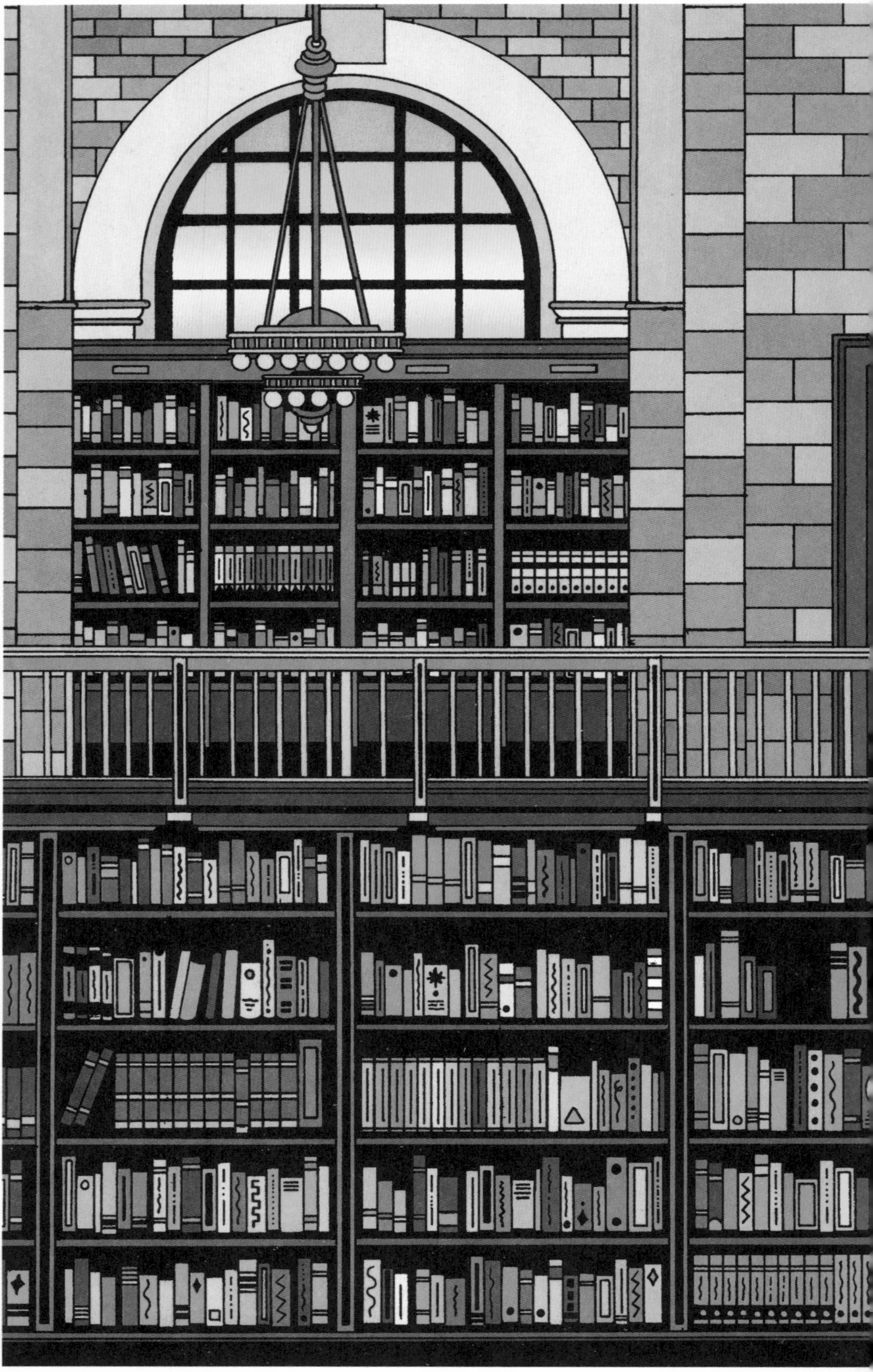

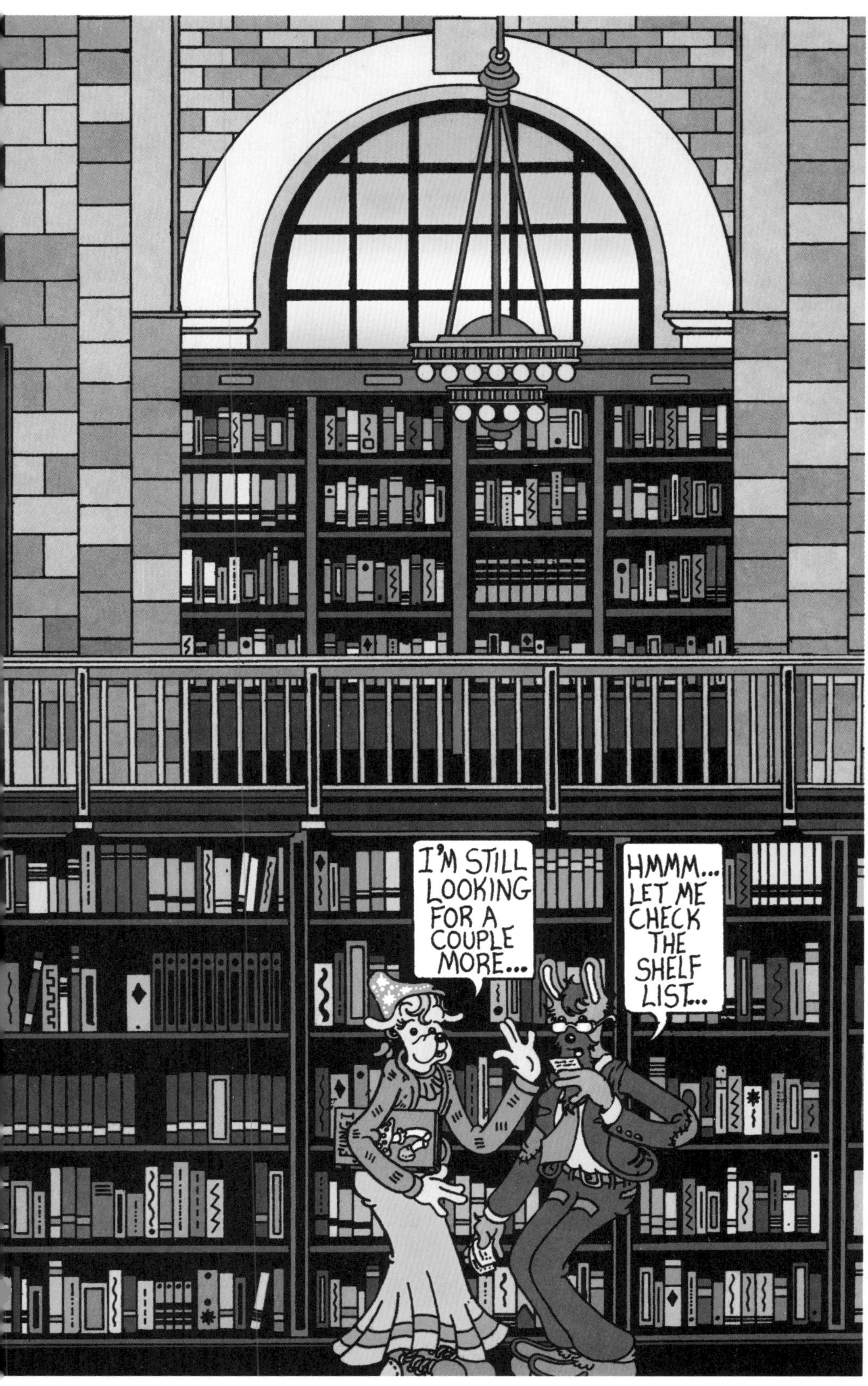
I'M STILL LOOKING FOR A COUPLE MORE...
HMMM... LET ME CHECK THE SHELF LIST...

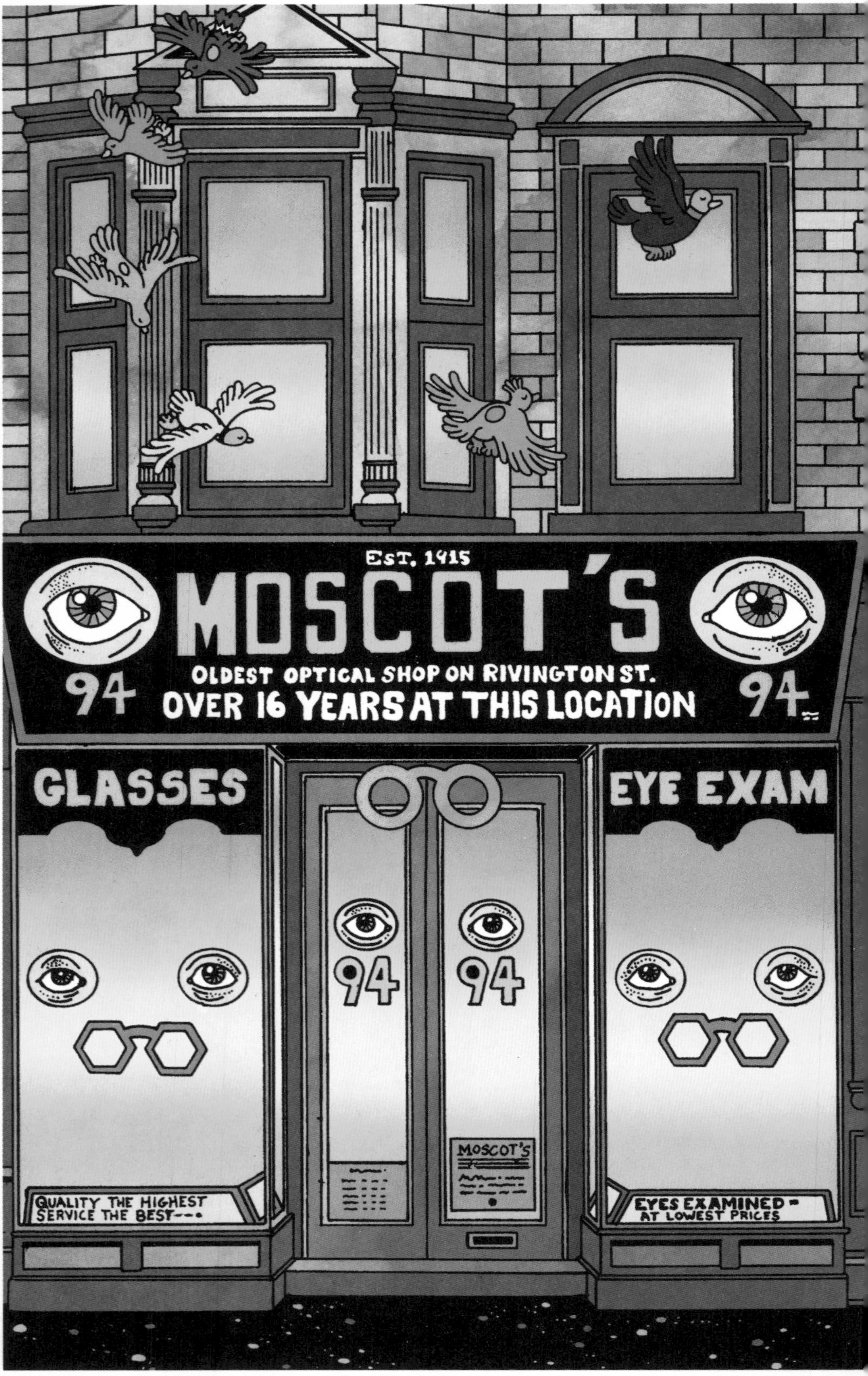
EST. 1915
MOSCOT'S
OLDEST OPTICAL SHOP ON RIVINGTON ST.
OVER 16 YEARS AT THIS LOCATION
94
94
GLASSES
EYE EXAM
94
94
MOSCOT'S
QUALITY THE HIGHEST
SERVICE THE BEST
EYES EXAMINED
AT LOWEST PRICES

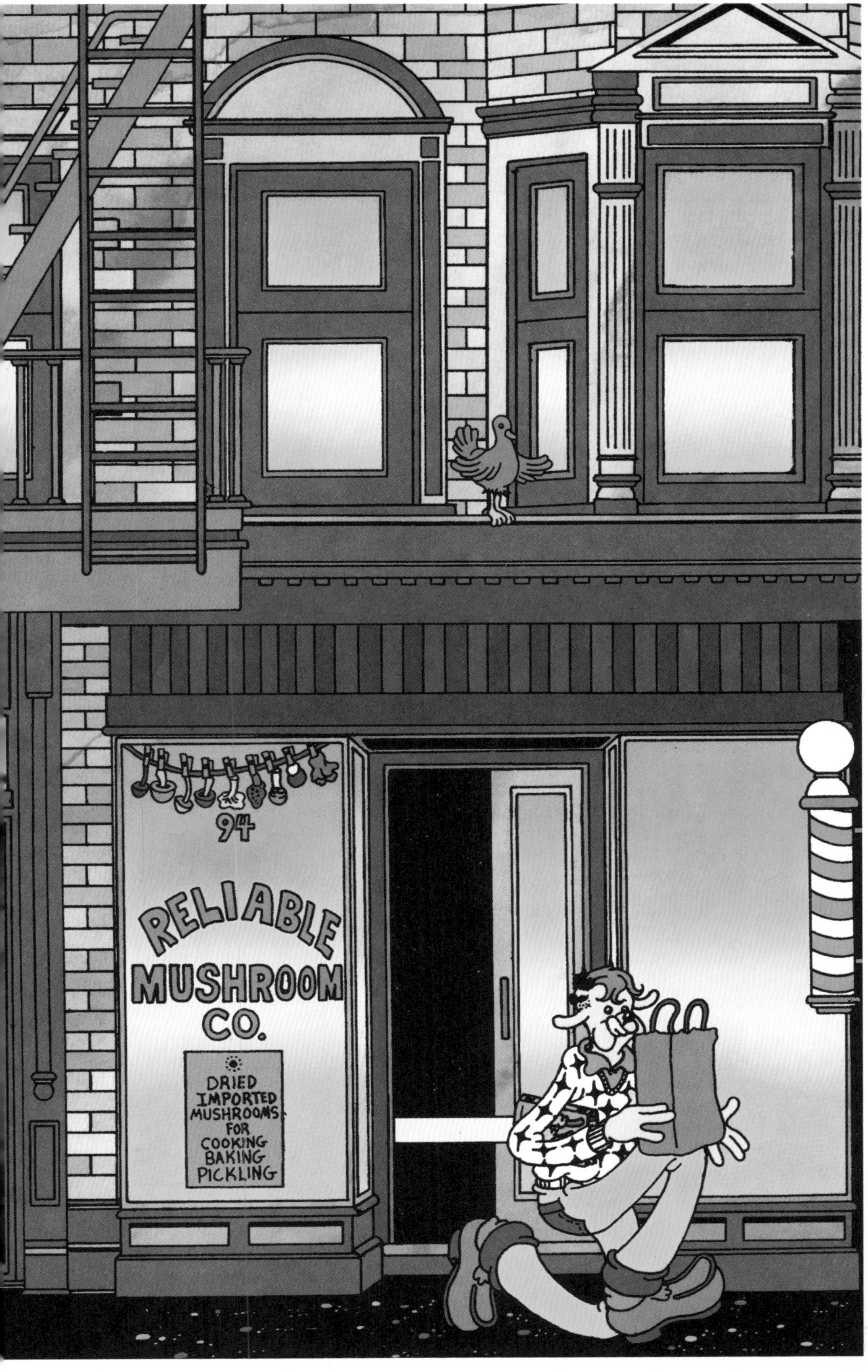
94
RELIABLE
MUSHROOM
CO.
DRIED
IMPORTED
MUSHROOMS
FOR
COOKING
BAKING
PICKLING

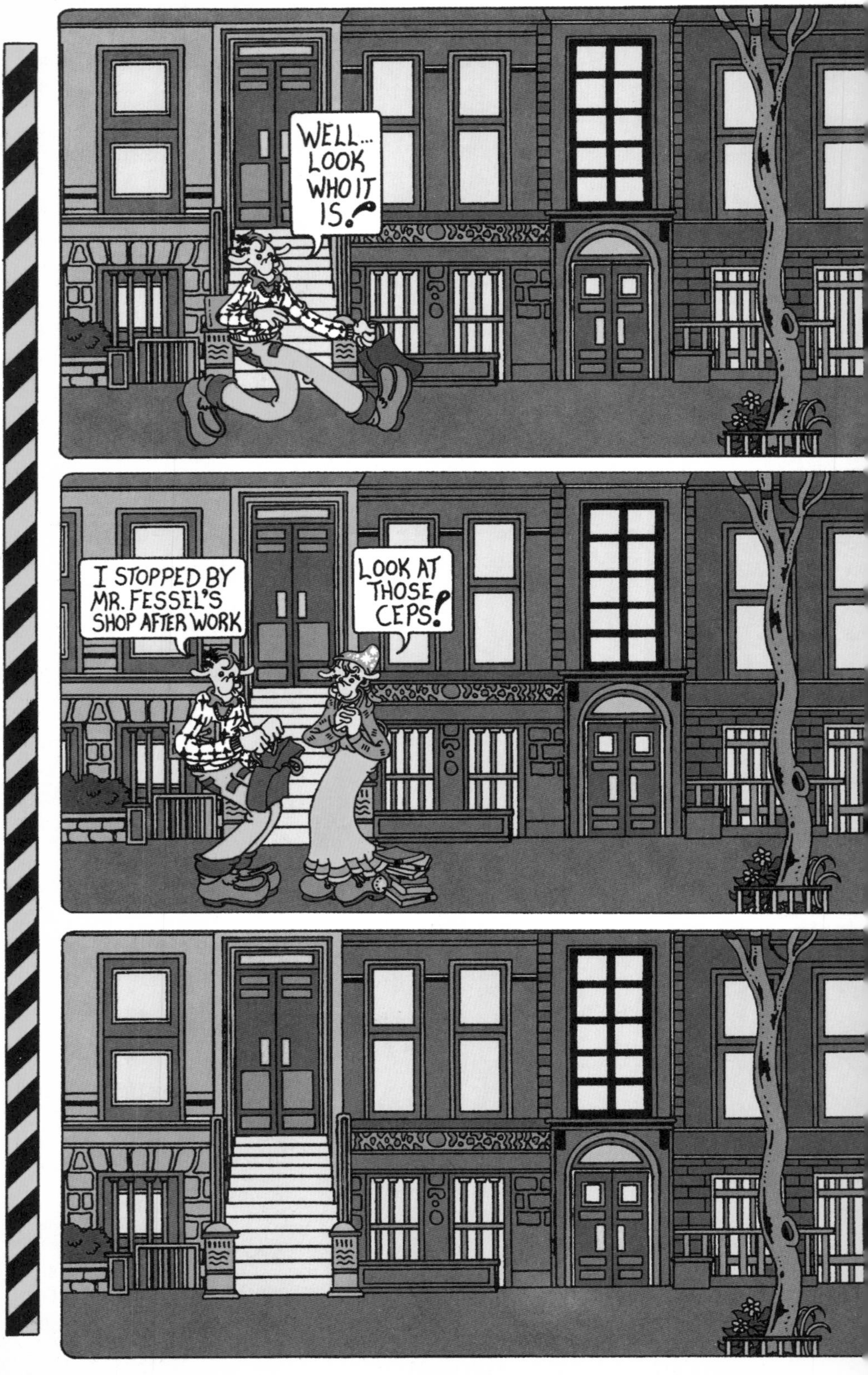

WELL... LOOK WHO IT IS?
I STOPPED BY MR. FESSEL'S SHOP AFTER WORK
LOOK AT THOSE CEPS!

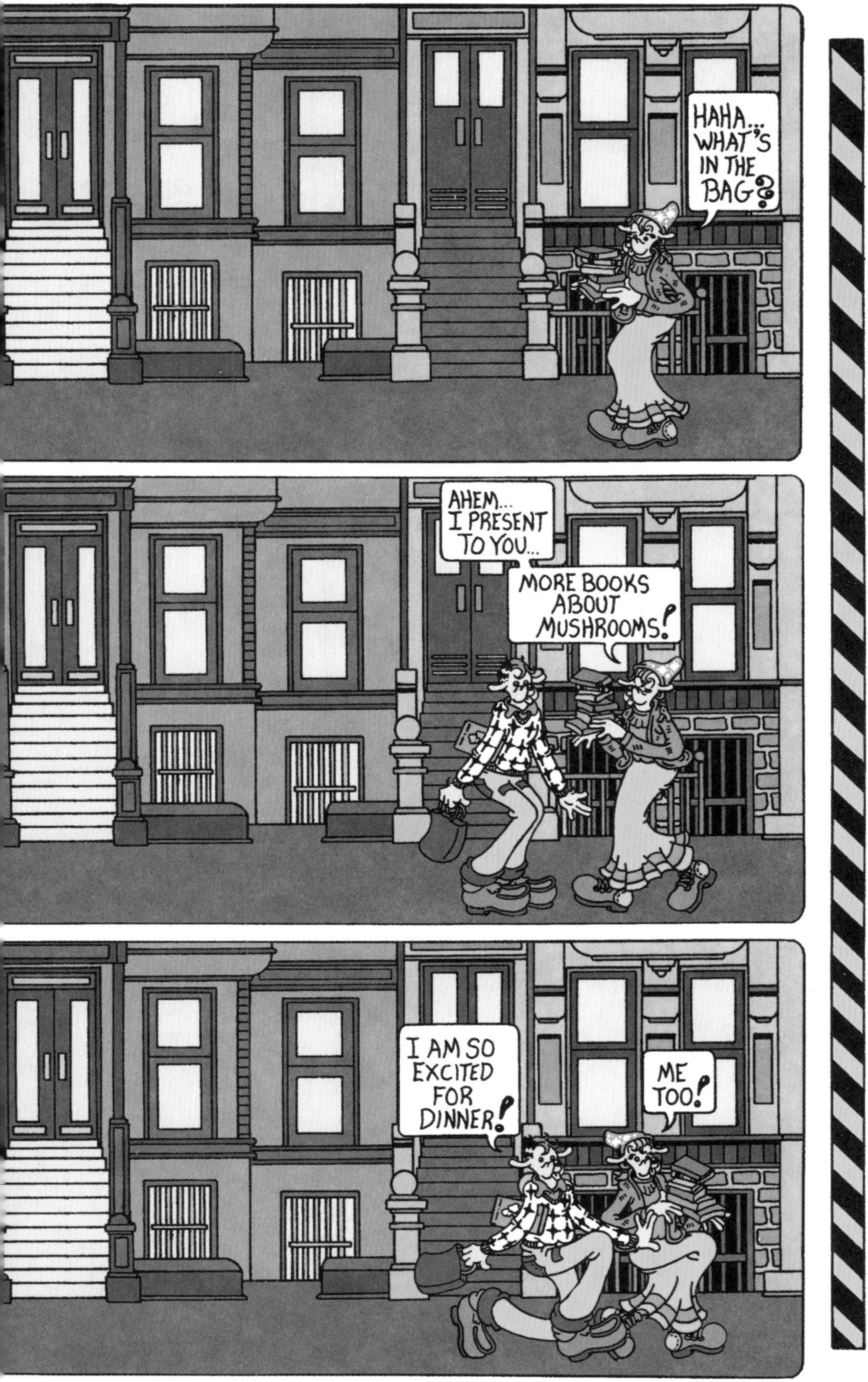
HAHA... WHAT'S IN THE BAG?
AHEM... I PRESENT TO YOU...
MORE BOOKS ABOUT MUSHROOMS!
I AM SO EXCITED FOR DINNER!
ME TOO!

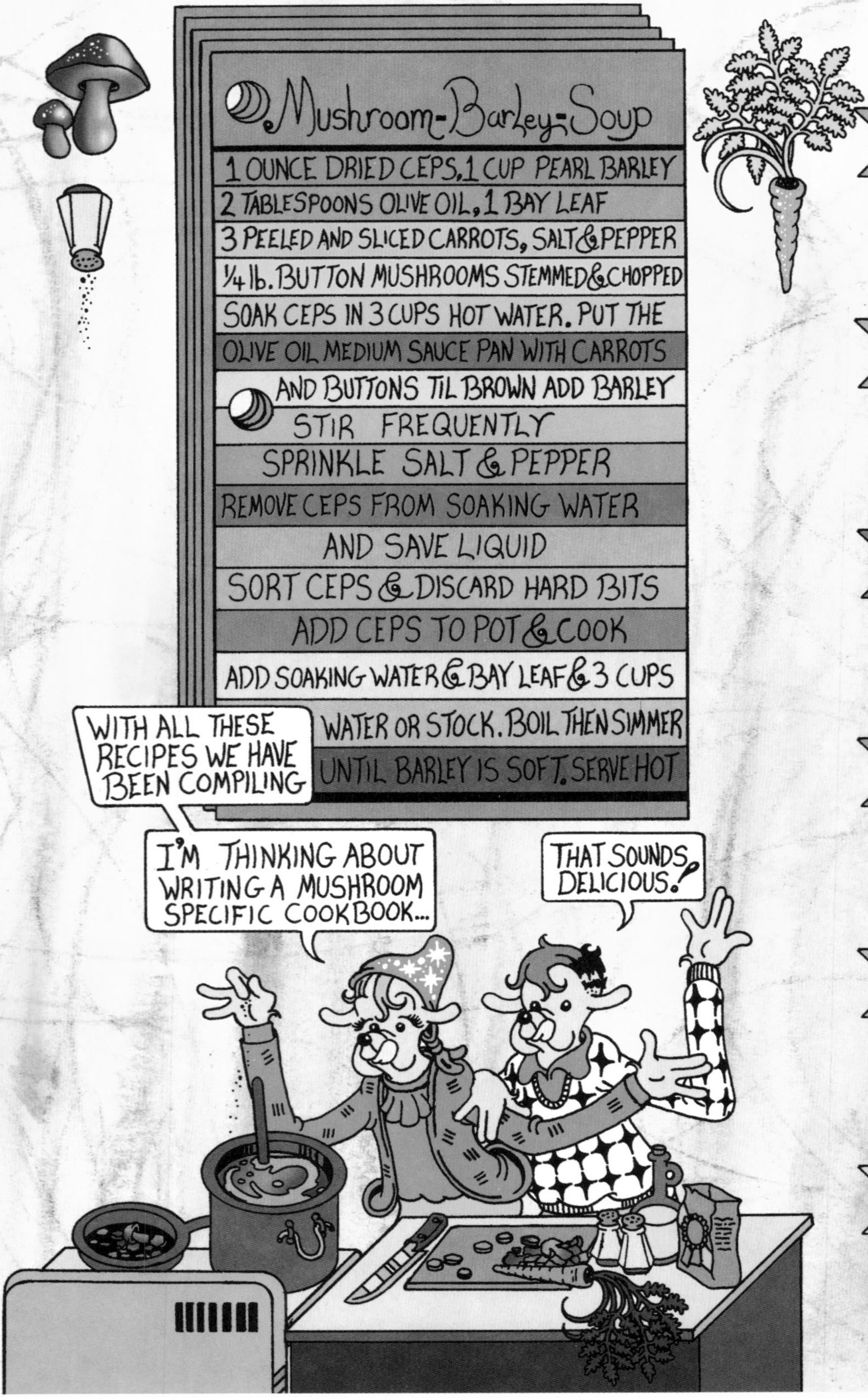
Mushroom-Barley-Soup
1 OUNCE DRIED CEPS, 1 CUP PEARL BARLEY
2 TABLESPOONS OLIVE OIL, 1 BAY LEAF
3 PEELED AND SLICED CARROTS, SALT & PEPPER
1/4 lb. BUTTON MUSHROOMS STEMMED & CHOPPED
SOAK CEPS IN 3 CUPS HOT WATER. PUT THE
OLIVE OIL MEDIUM SAUCE PAN WITH CARROTS
AND BUTTONS TIL BROWN ADD BARLEY
STIR FREQUENTLY
SPRINKLE SALT & PEPPER
REMOVE CEPS FROM SOAKING WATER
AND SAVE LIQUID
SORT CEPS & DISCARD HARD BITS
ADD CEPS TO POT & COOK
ADD SOAKING WATER & BAY LEAF & 3 CUPS
WATER OR STOCK. BOIL THEN SIMMER
UNTIL BARLEY IS SOFT. SERVE HOT
WITH ALL THESE RECIPES WE HAVE BEEN COMPILING
I'M THINKING ABOUT WRITING A MUSHROOM SPECIFIC COOKBOOK...
THAT SOUNDS DELICIOUS!

Mushroom-Julienne

24 OUNCE CREMINI MUSHROOMS
2 SHALLOTS, 2 TABLESPOONS CANOLA OIL
1/2 CUP SOUR CREAM, 1/2 CUP HEAVY CREAM,
SALT & PEPPER, 1 TABLESPOON GARLIC POWDER,
3/4 CUP SHREDDED MOZZARELLA CHEESE

SLICE MUSHROOMS & SHALLOTS THINLY
HEAT OIL IN COOKING PAN. SEASON
MUSHROOMS & ONIONS WITH SALT & PEPPER
SAUTE ON MEDIUM HEAT & DRAIN JUICES
MIX GARLIC POWDER, HEAVY CREAM, PEPPER,
SOUR CREAM IN A BOWL & MIX WELL
ADD CREAMY MIXTURE TO THE MUSHROOMS
STIR WELL
TRANSFER MIX TO BAKING DISH
SPREAD CHEESE ON TOP, BAKE AT 375°
FOR 10-15 MINUTES. SERVE WARM

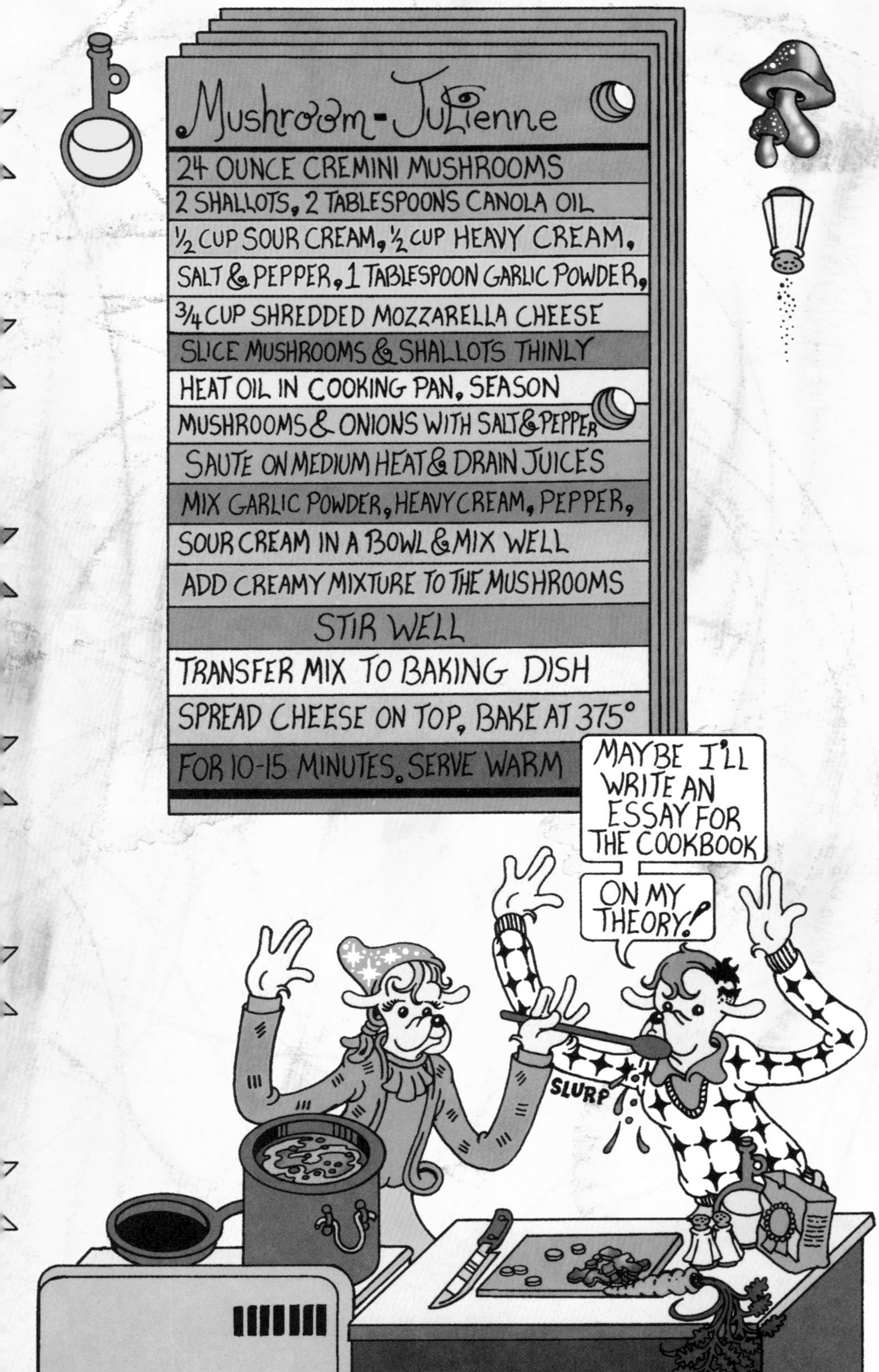
MAYBE I'LL WRITE AN ESSAY FOR THE COOKBOOK
ON MY THEORY!
SLURP

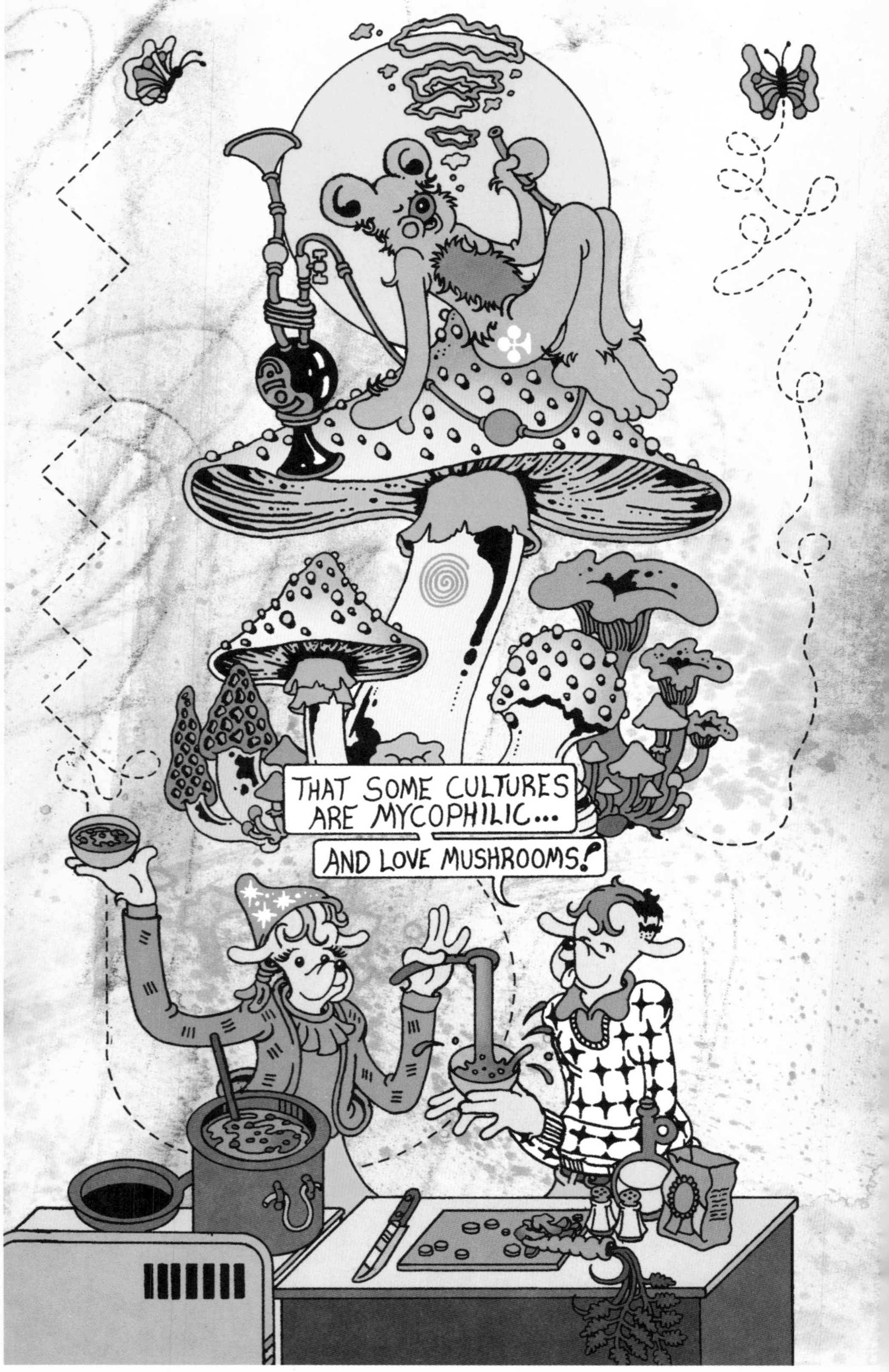
THAT SOME CULTURES
ARE MYCOPHILIC...
AND LOVE MUSHROOMS!

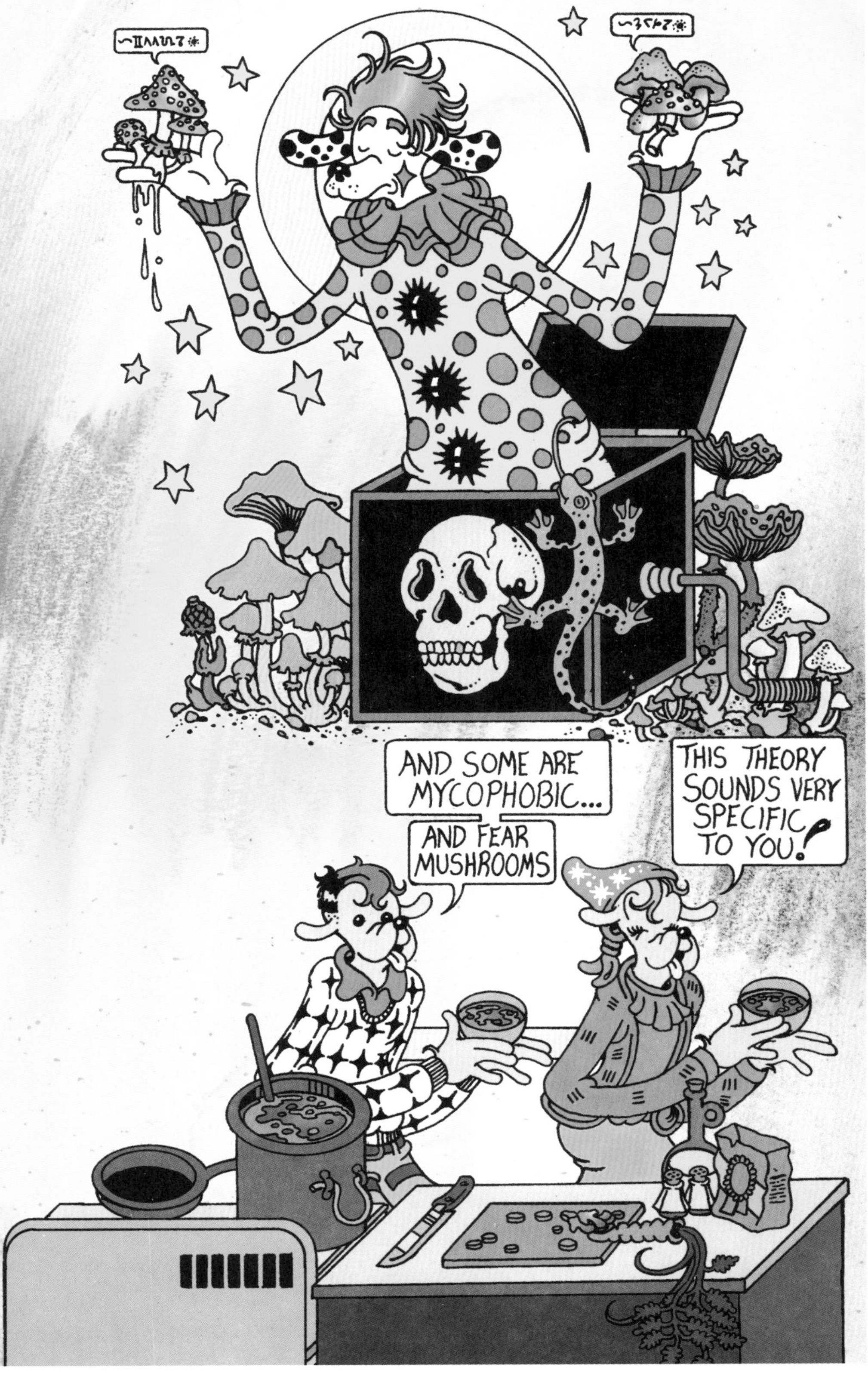
AND SOME ARE MYCOPHOBIC...
AND FEAR MUSHROOMS
THIS THEORY SOUNDS VERY SPECIFIC TO YOU!

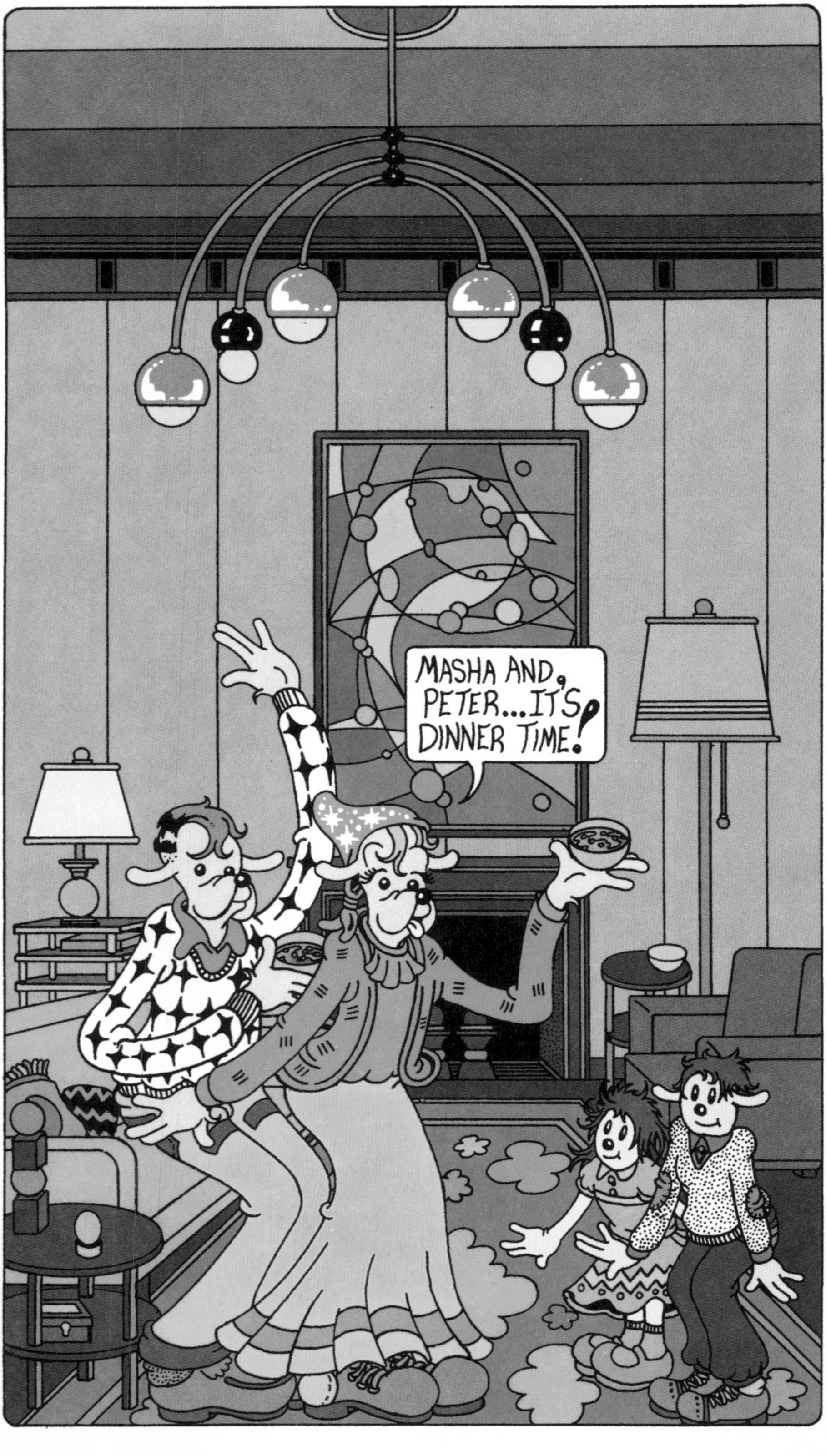
MASHA AND, PETER...IT'S DINNER TIME!

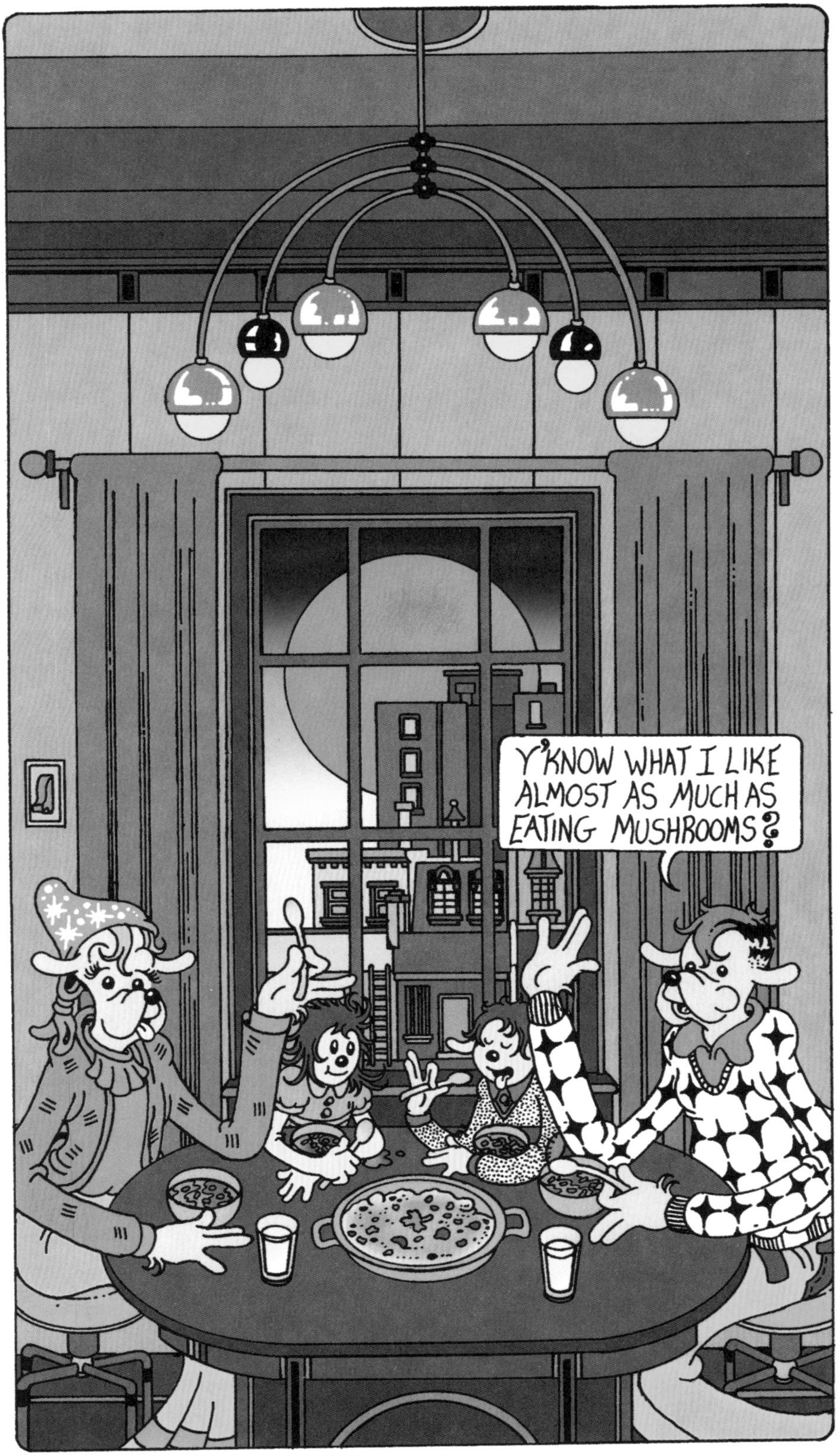
Y'KNOW WHAT I LIKE ALMOST AS MUCH AS EATING MUSHROOMS?

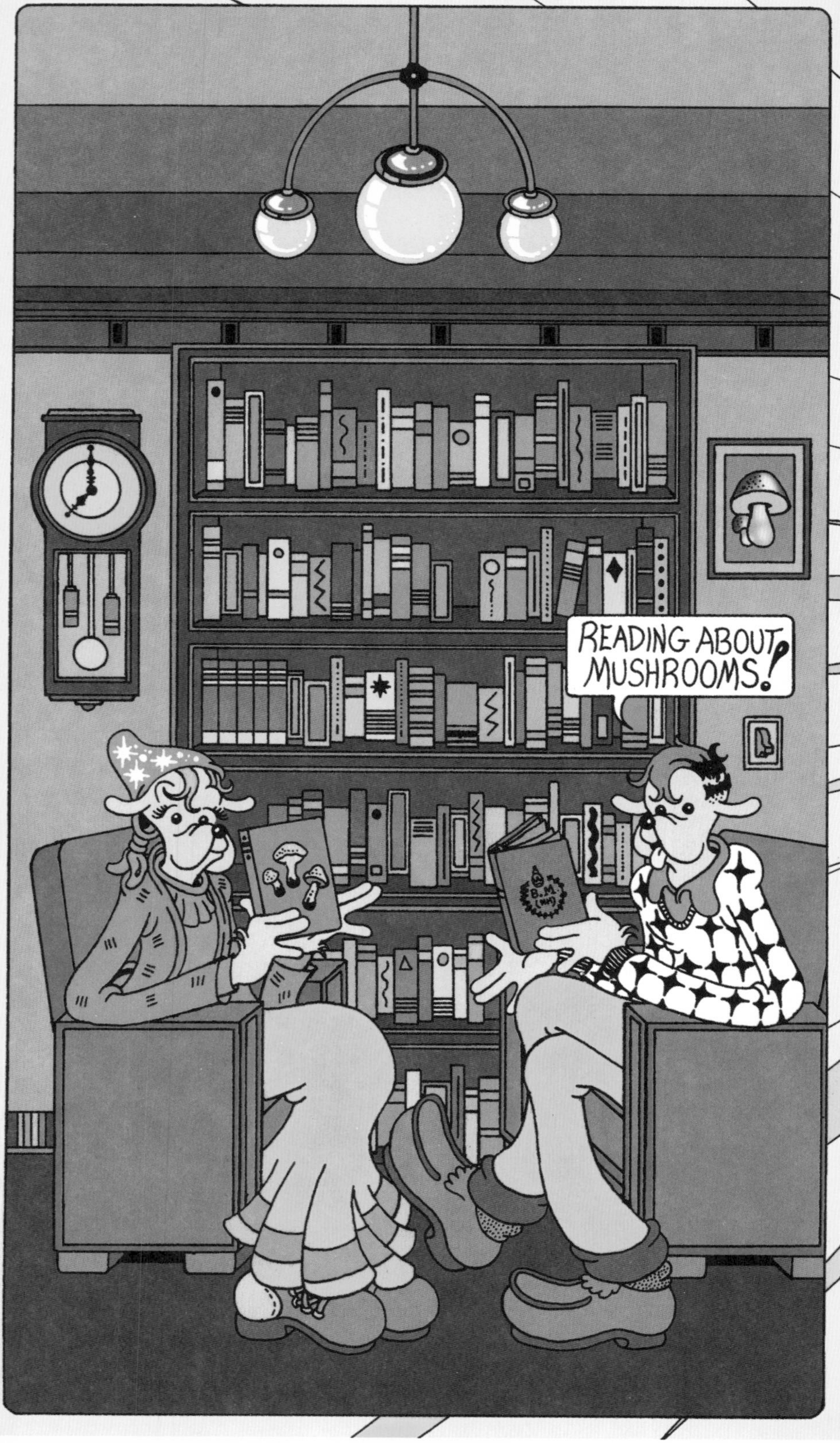
READING ABOUT MUSHROOMS!

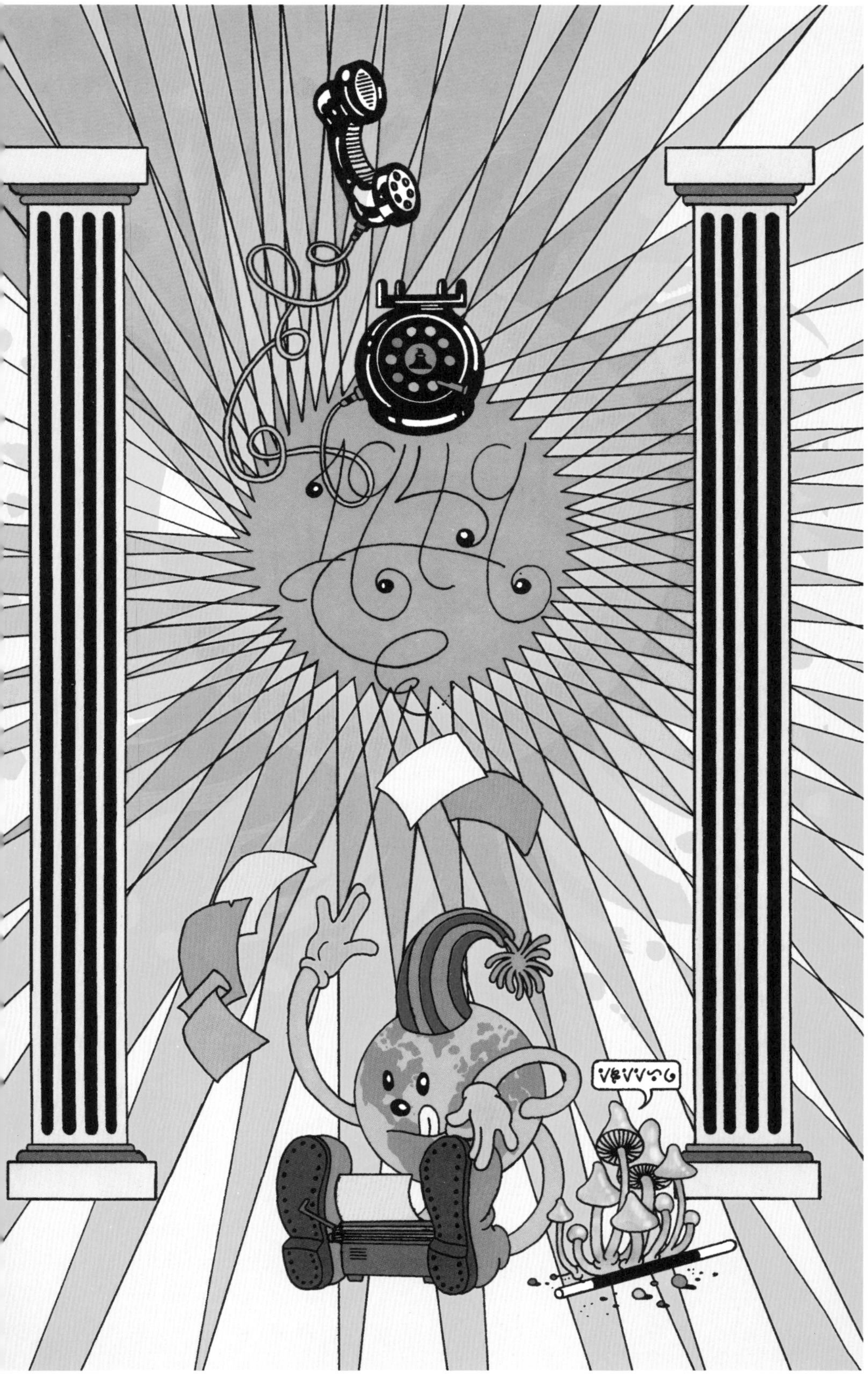

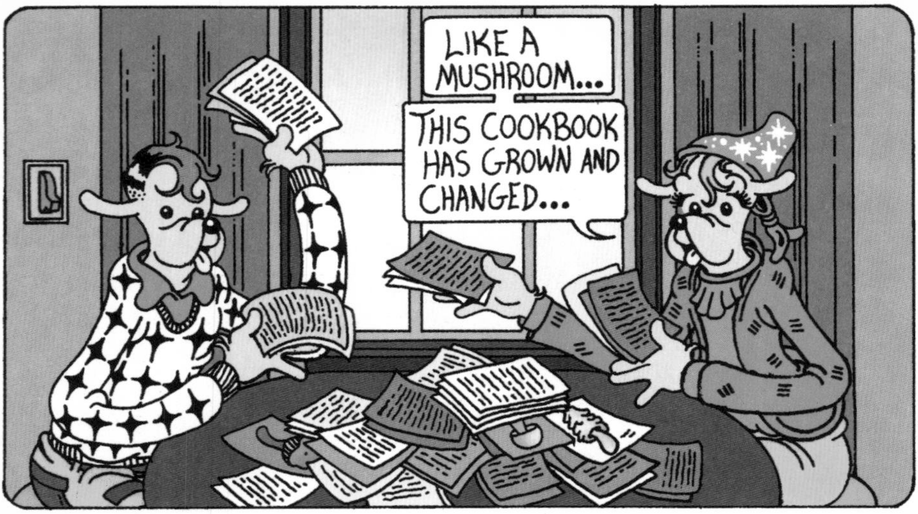
LIKE A MUSHROOM...
THIS COOKBOOK HAS GROWN AND CHANGED...

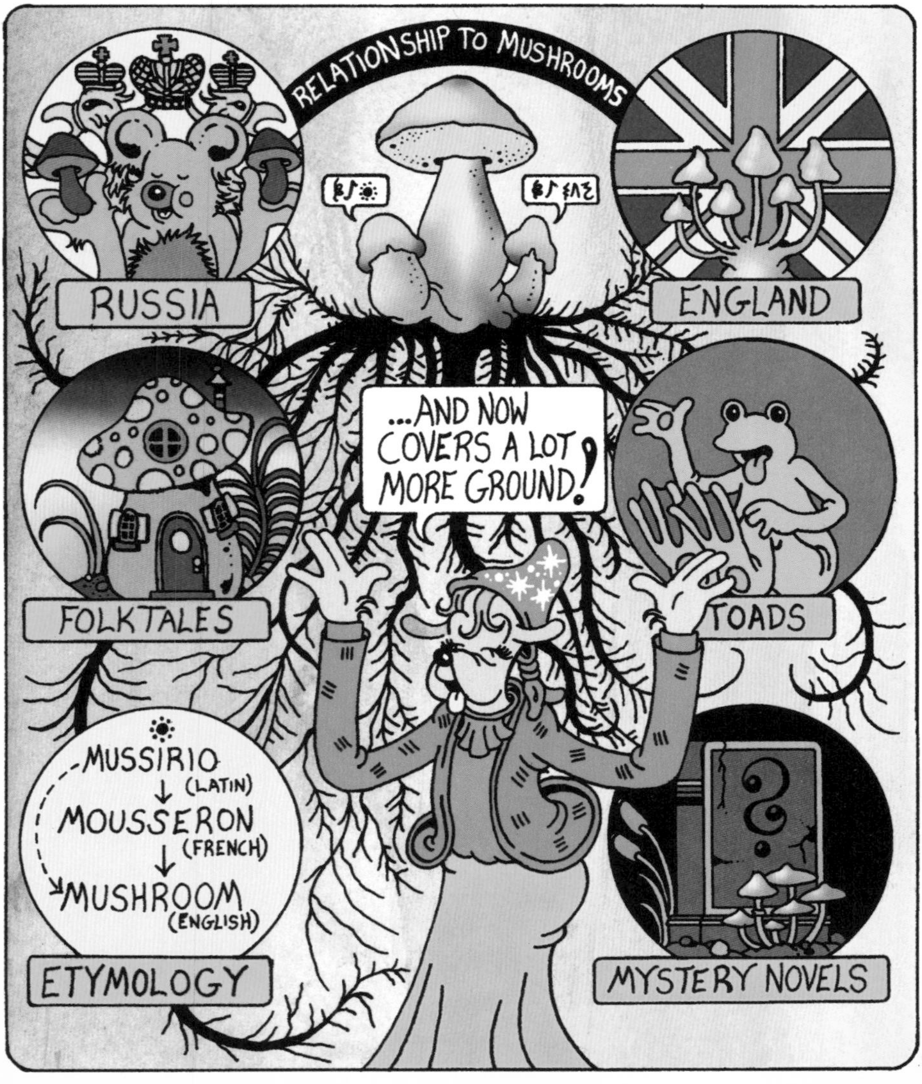
RELATIONSHIP TO MUSHROOMS
RUSSIA
ENGLAND
...AND NOW COVERS A LOT MORE GROUND!
FOLKTALES
TOADS
MUSSIRIO
(LATIN)
MOUSSERON
(FRENCH)
MUSHROOM
(ENGLISH)
ETYMOLOGY
MYSTERY NOVELS

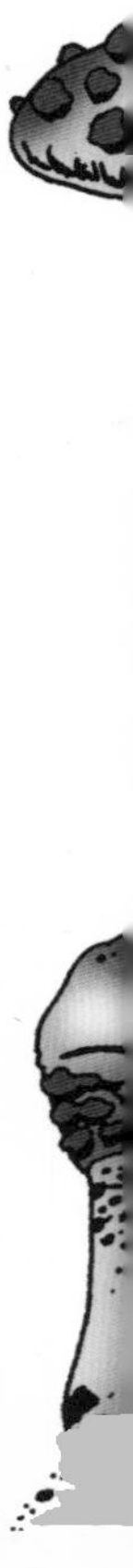

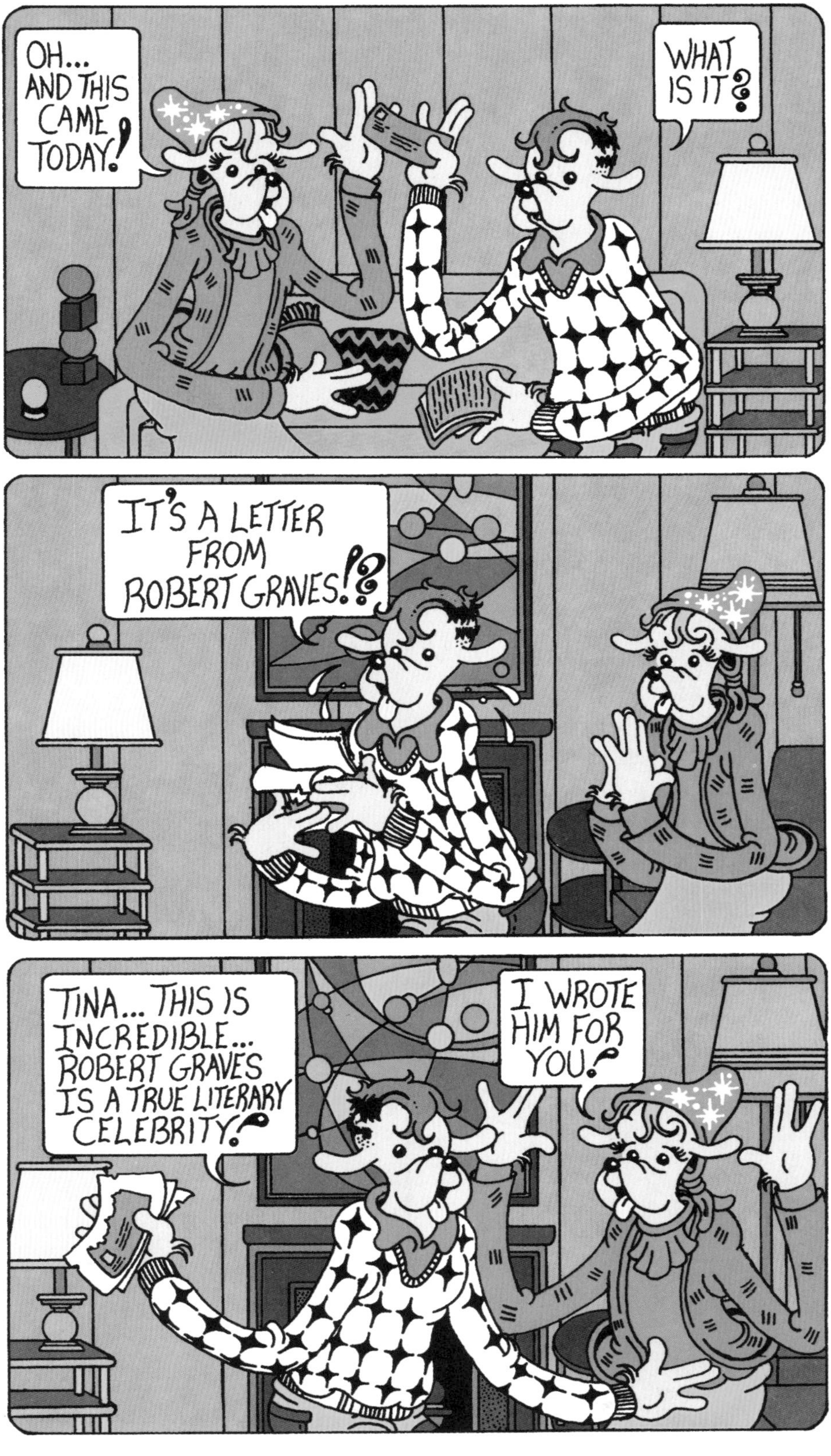
OH... AND THIS CAME TODAY!
WHAT IS IT?
IT'S A LETTER FROM ROBERT GRAVES!?
TINA... THIS IS INCREDIBLE... ROBERT GRAVES IS A TRUE LITERARY CELEBRITY!
I WROTE HIM FOR YOU!

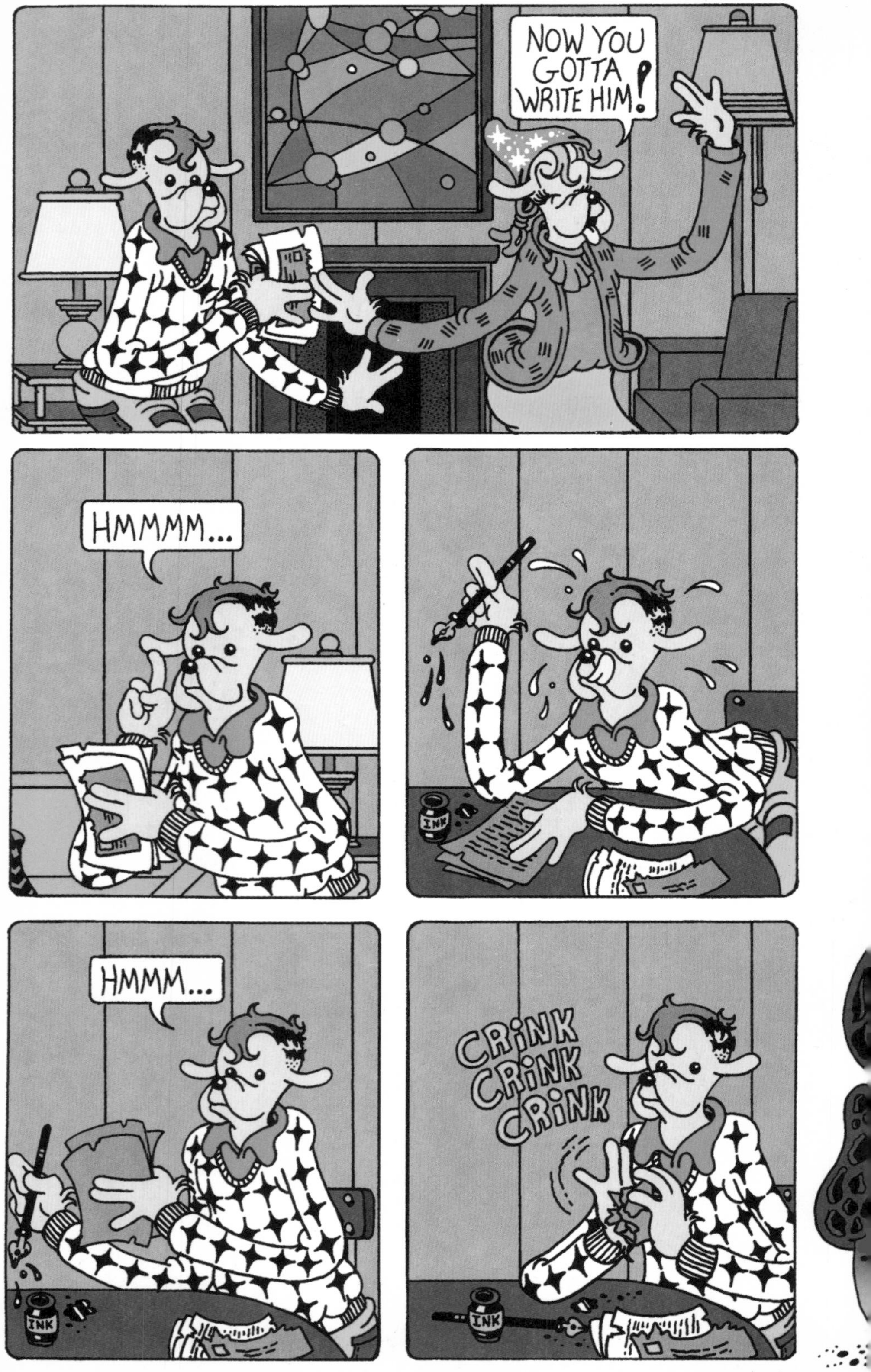
NOW YOU GOTTA WRITE HIM!
HMMMM...
INK
HMMM...
INK
CRiNK CRiNK CRiNK
INK

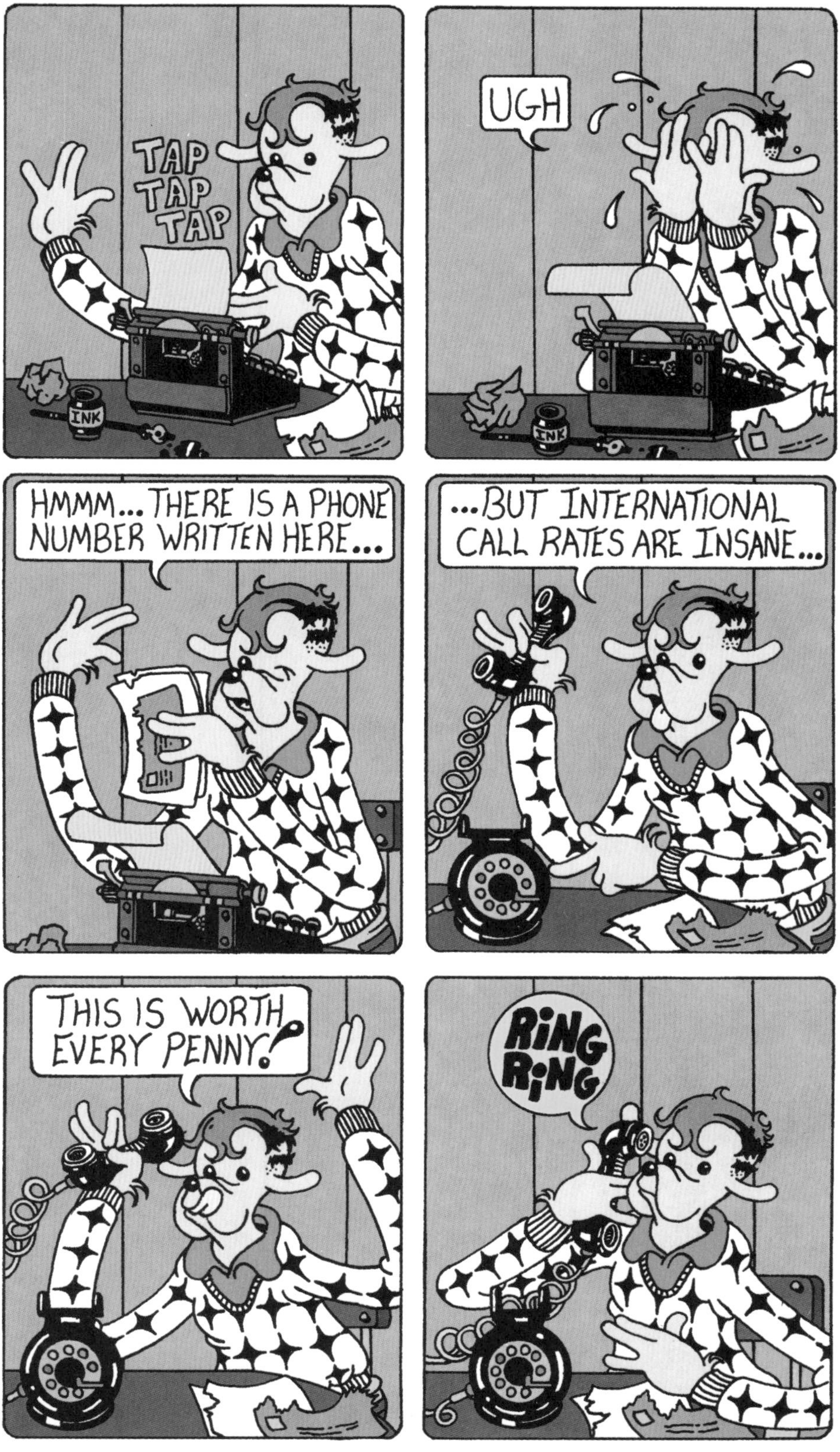
TAP TAP TAP
UGH
HMMM... THERE IS A PHONE NUMBER WRITTEN HERE...
...BUT INTERNATIONAL CALL RATES ARE INSANE...
THIS IS WORTH EVERY PENNY!
RING RING

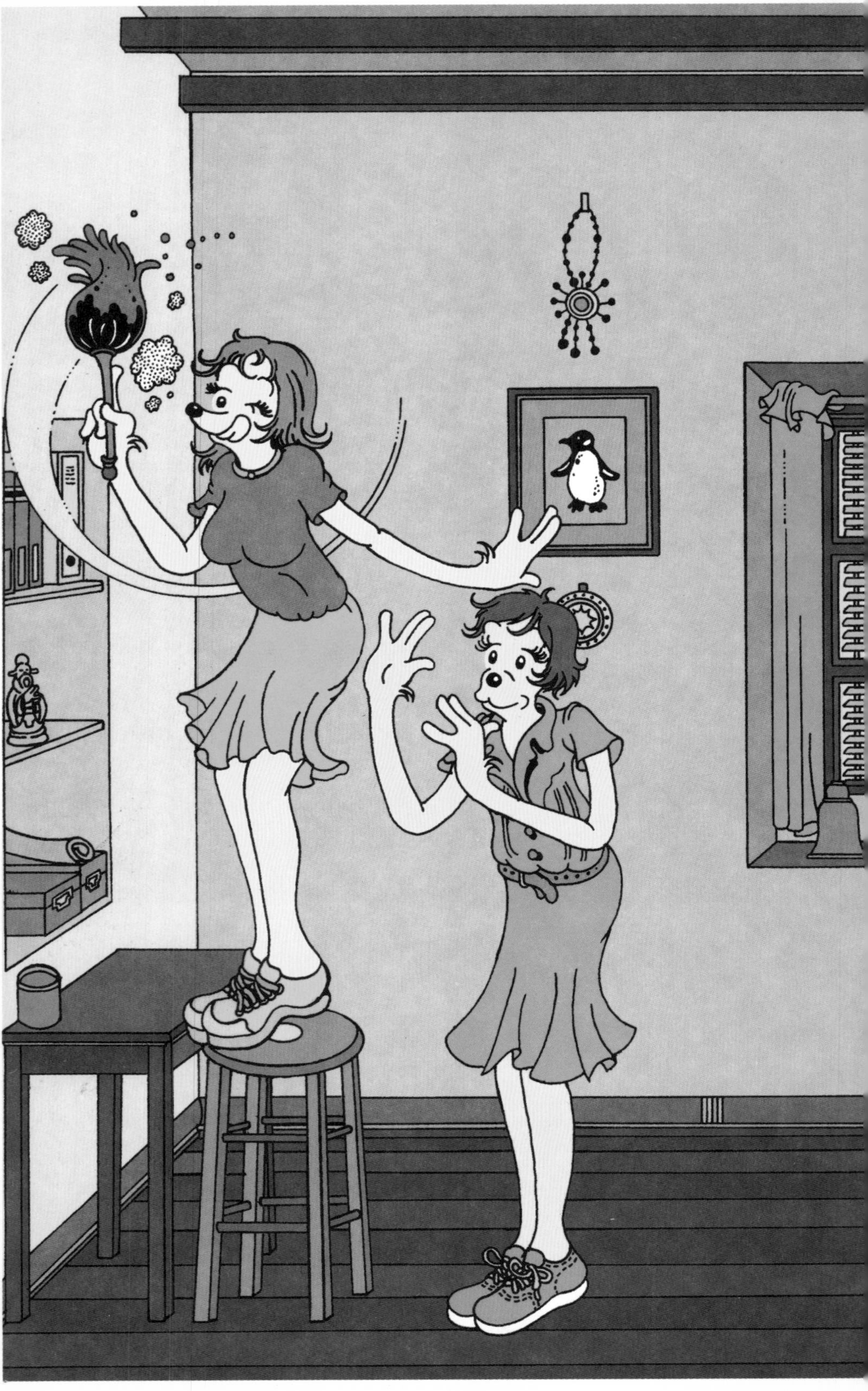

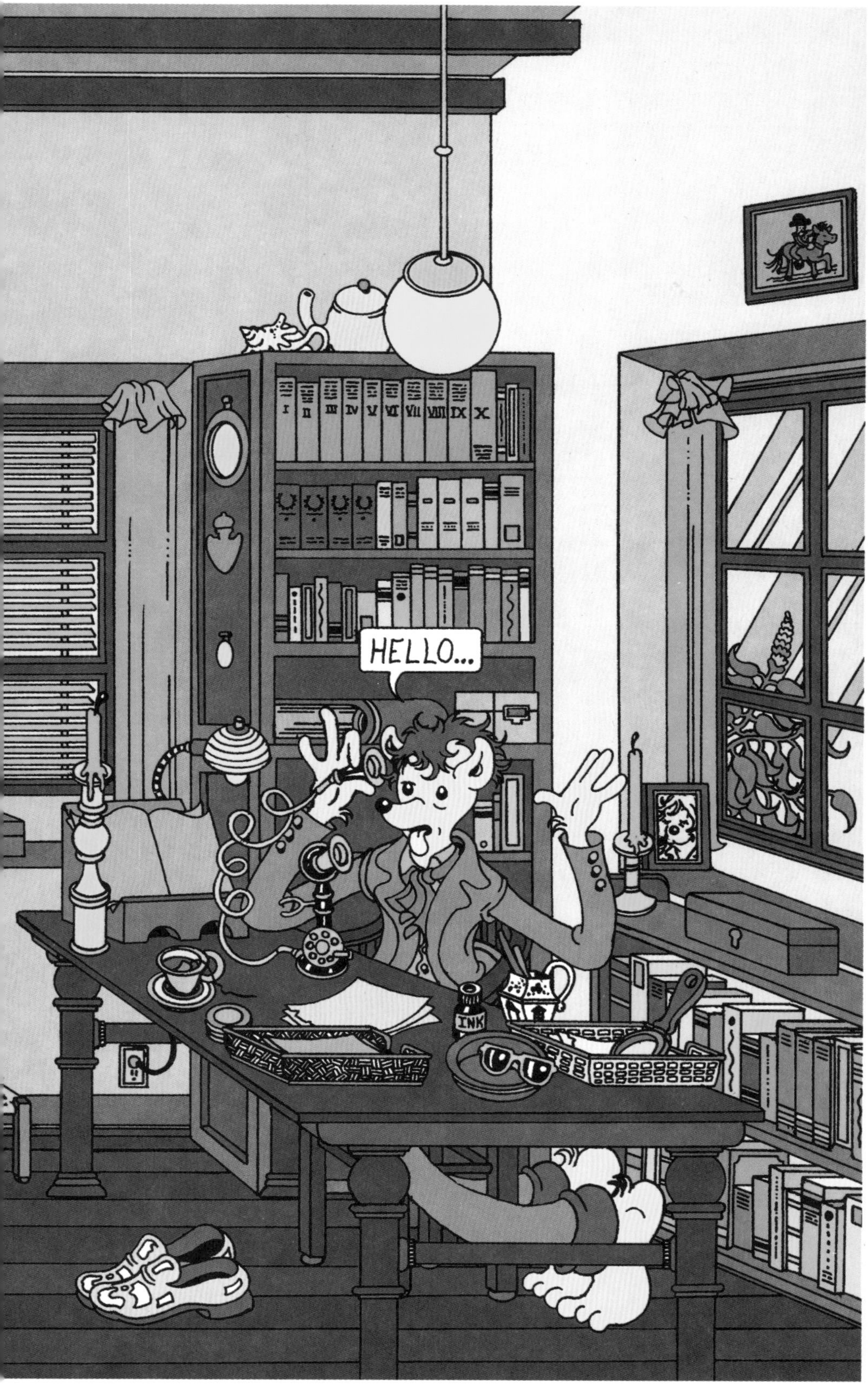
HELLO...

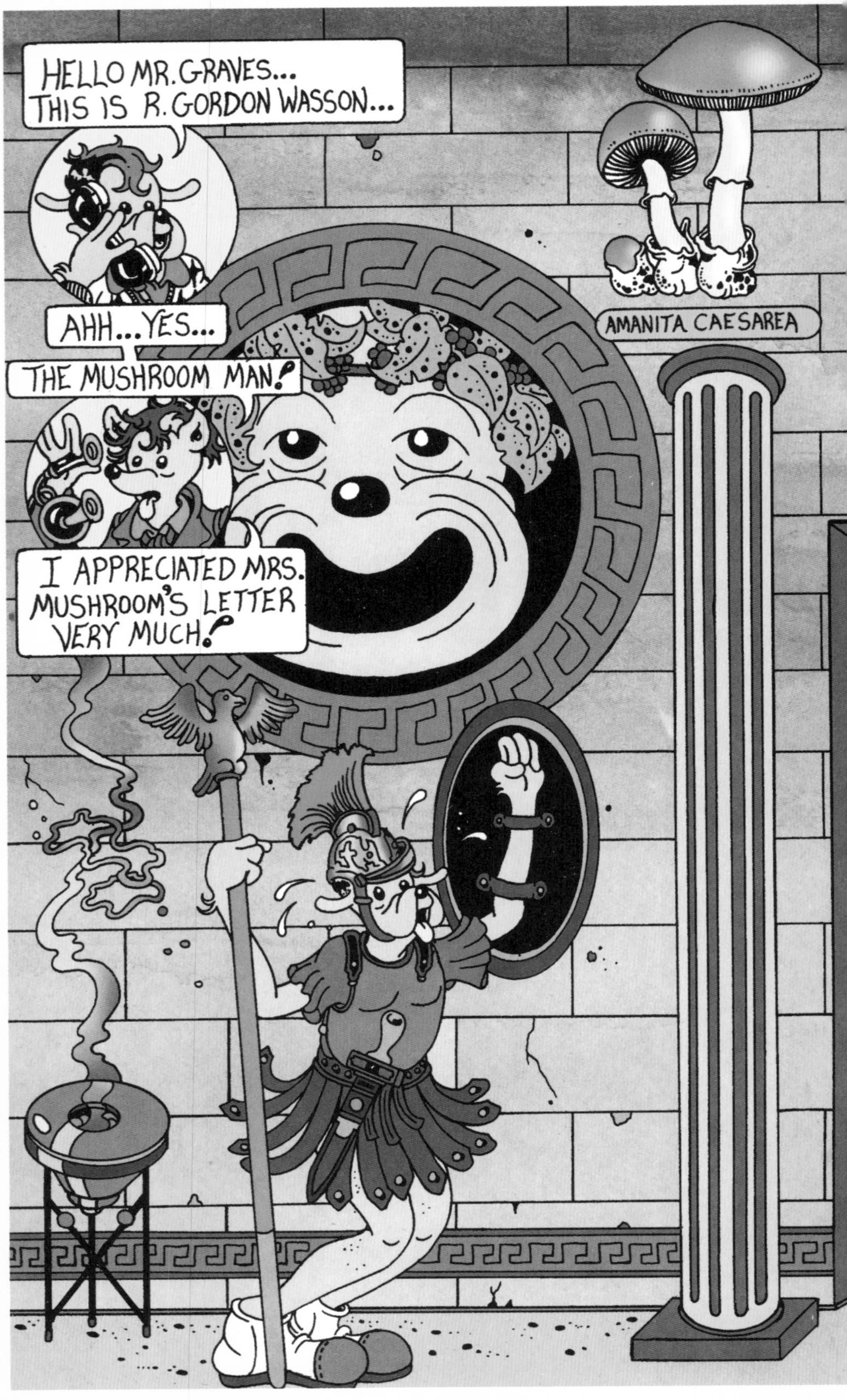
HELLO MR. GRAVES... THIS IS R. GORDON WASSON...
AMANITA CAESAREA
AHH...YES...
THE MUSHROOM MAN!
I APPRECIATED MRS. MUSHROOM'S LETTER VERY MUCH!

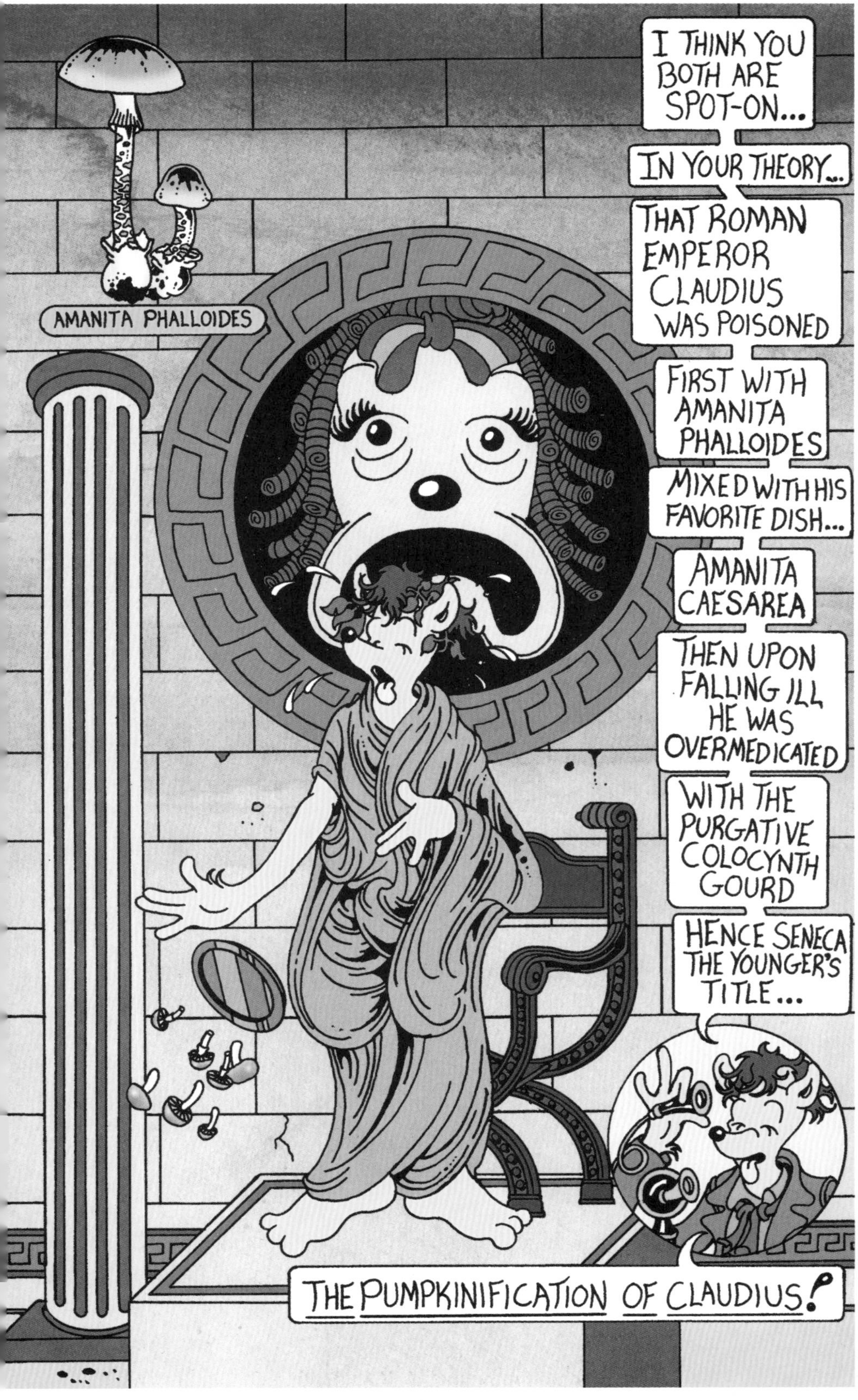
AMANITA PHALLOIDES
I THINK YOU BOTH ARE SPOT-ON...
IN YOUR THEORY...
THAT ROMAN EMPEROR CLAUDIUS WAS POISONED
FIRST WITH AMANITA PHALLOIDES
MIXED WITH HIS FAVORITE DISH...
AMANITA CAESAREA
THEN UPON FALLING ILL HE WAS OVERMEDICATED
WITH THE PURGATIVE COLOCYNTH GOURD
HENCE SENECA THE YOUNGER'S TITLE...
THE PUMPKINIFICATION OF CLAUDIUS!

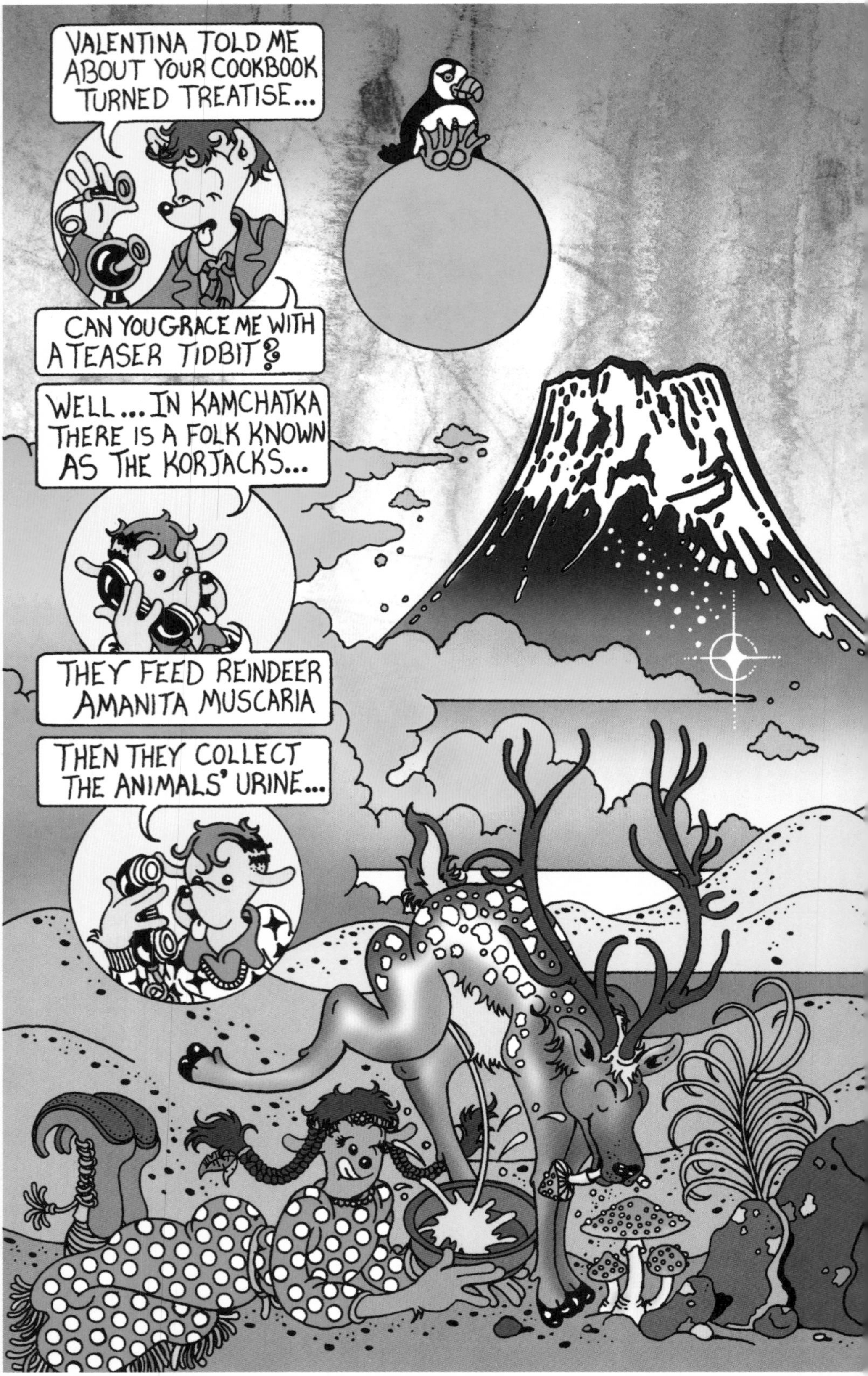

VALENTINA TOLD ME ABOUT YOUR COOKBOOK TURNED TREATISE...
CAN YOU GRACE ME WITH A TEASER TIDBIT?
WELL... IN KAMCHATKA THERE IS A FOLK KNOWN AS THE KORJACKS...
THEY FEED REINDEER AMANITA MUSCARIA
THEN THEY COLLECT THE ANIMALS' URINE...

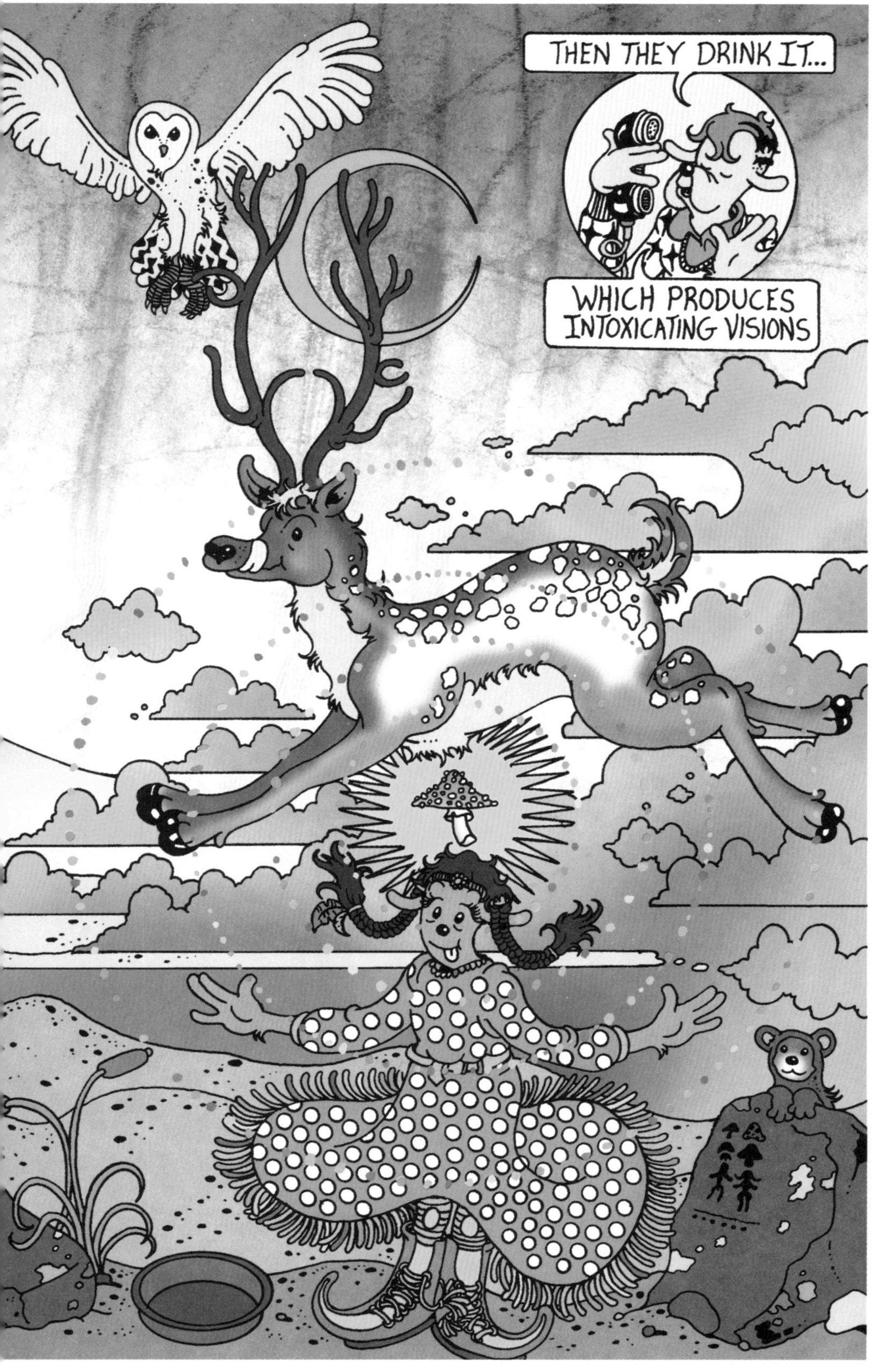
THEN THEY DRINK IT...
WHICH PRODUCES INTOXICATING VISIONS

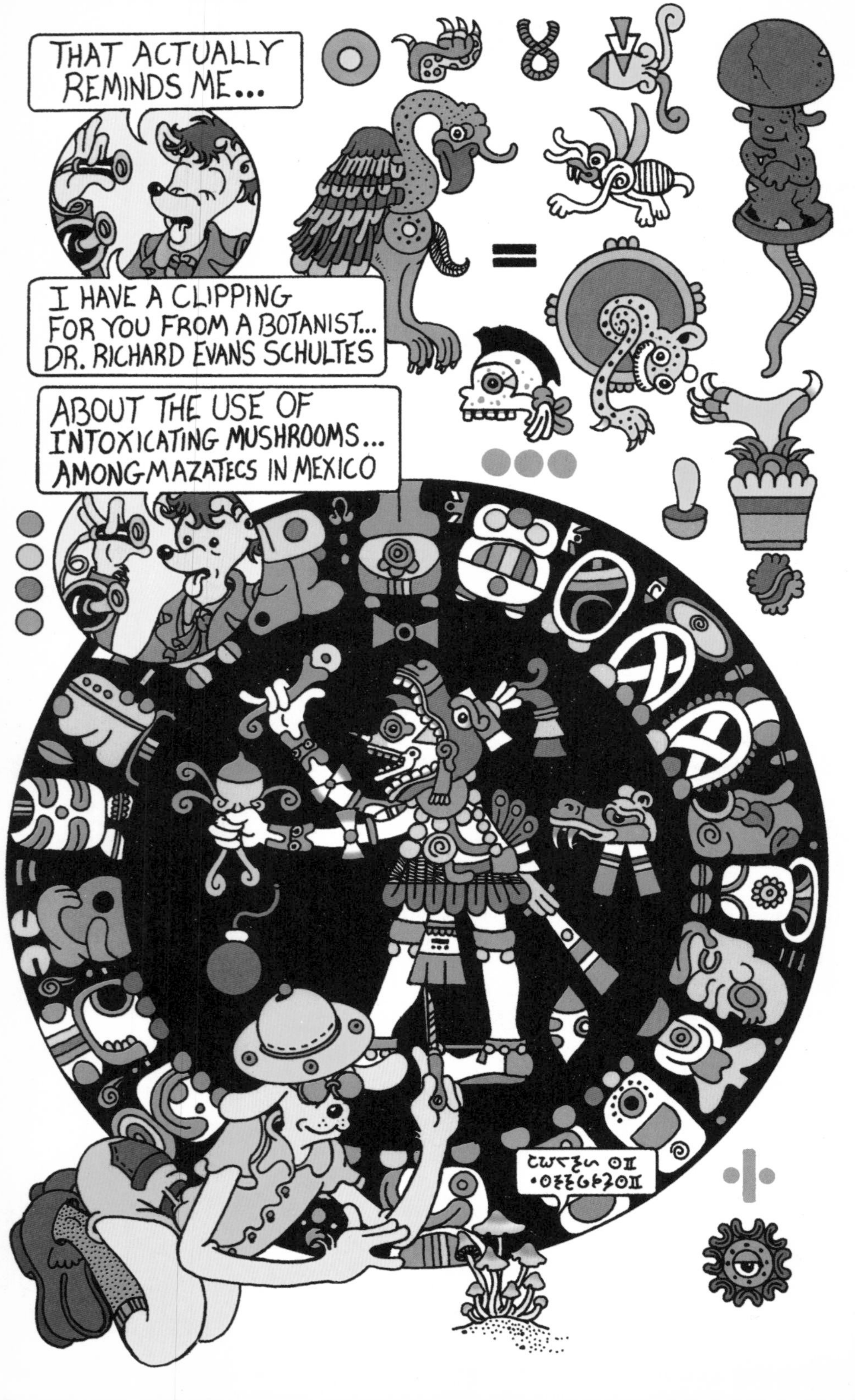

THAT ACTUALLY REMINDS ME...
I HAVE A CLIPPING FOR YOU FROM A BOTANIST... DR. RICHARD EVANS SCHULTES
ABOUT THE USE OF INTOXICATING MUSHROOMS... AMONG MAZATECS IN MEXICO

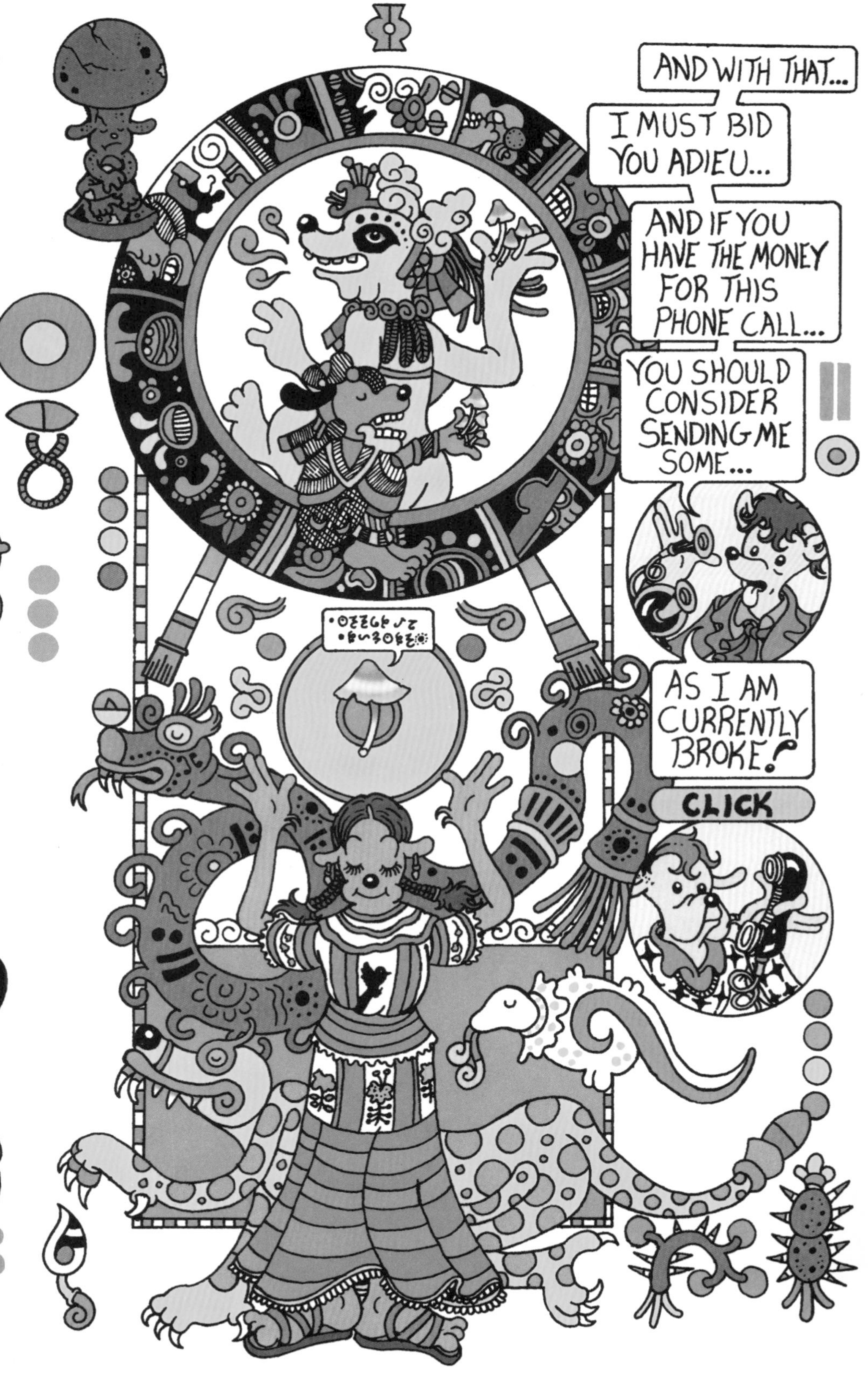

AND WITH THAT...
I MUST BID YOU ADIEU...
AND IF YOU HAVE THE MONEY FOR THIS PHONE CALL...
YOU SHOULD CONSIDER SENDING ME SOME...
AS I AM CURRENTLY BROKE!
CLICK

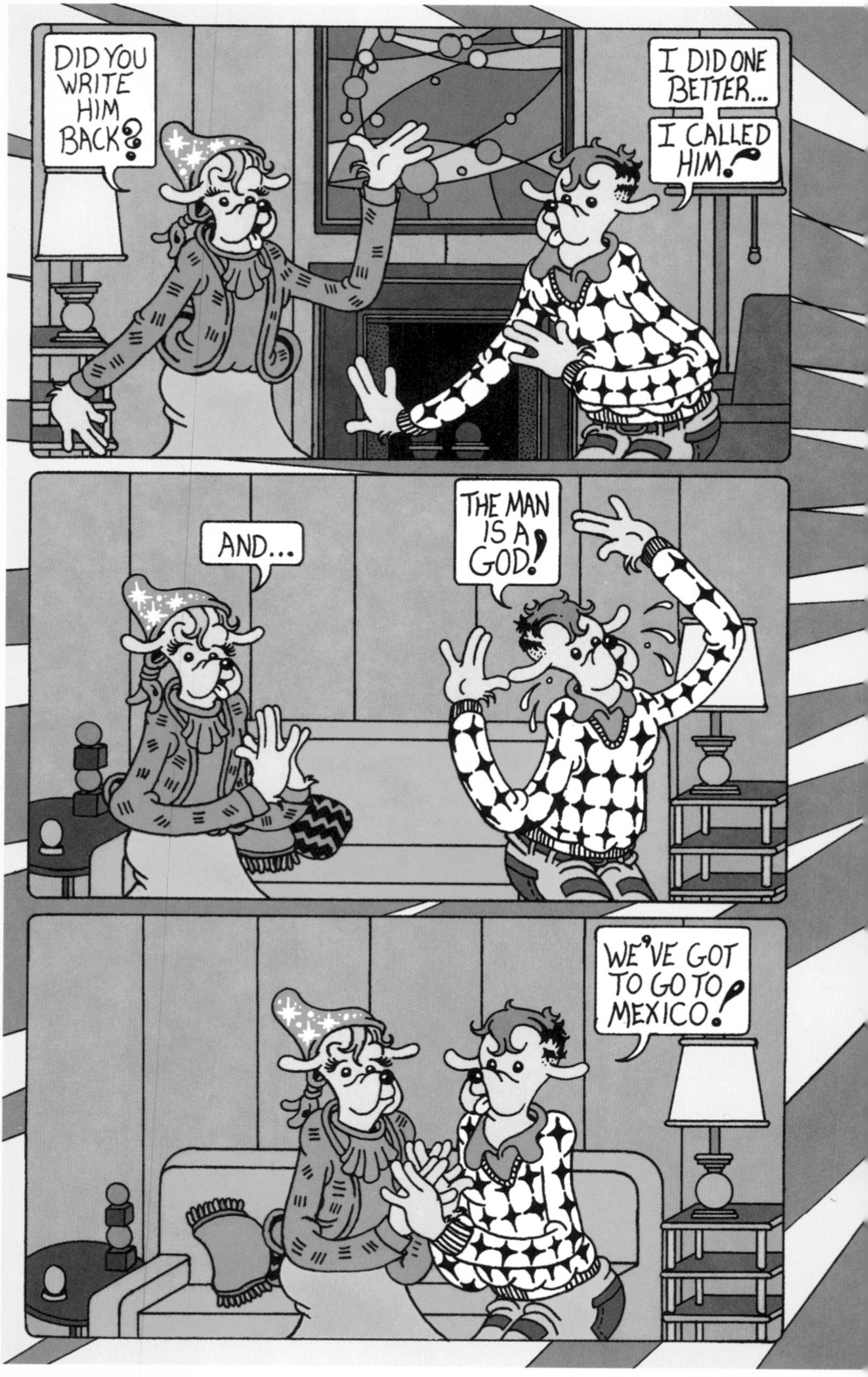
DID YOU WRITE HIM BACK?
I DID ONE BETTER...
I CALLED HIM!
AND...
THE MAN IS A GOD!
WE'VE GOT TO GO TO MEXICO!

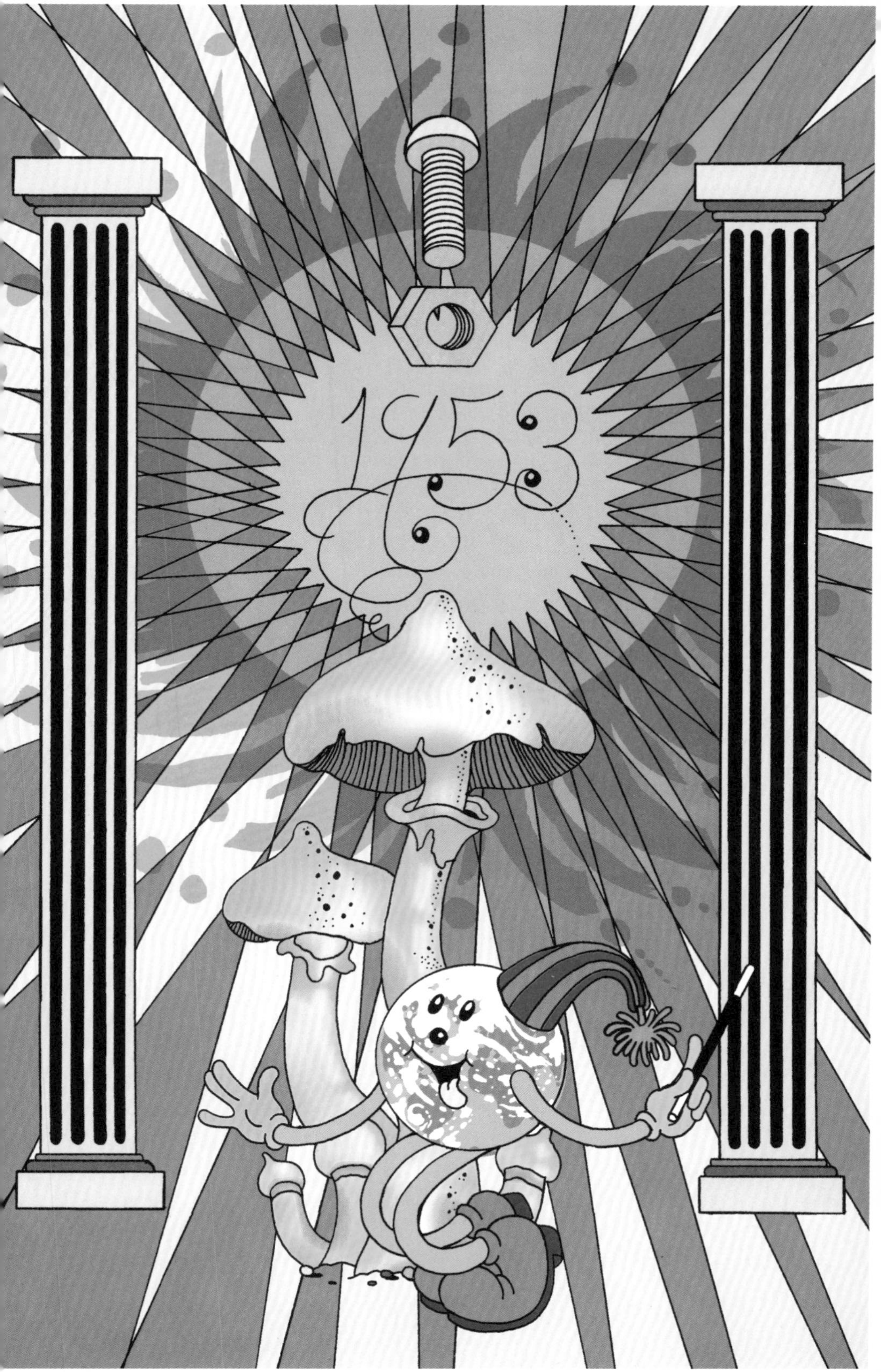

HUAUTLA DE JIMÉNEZ • OAXACA
MARCH 9, 1953

DEAR MR. WASSON,

I'M GLAD TO TELL YOU WHATEVER I CAN ABOUT THE MAZATEC MUSHROOM. MAZATECS SELDOM TALK ABOUT THE MUSHROOM TO OUTSIDERS BUT BELIEF IN IT IS WIDESPREAD. A BOY TOLD ME, "JESUS GAVE US THE MUSHROOM BECAUSE WE ARE POOR PEOPLE AND CAN'T AFFORD A DOCTOR AND EXPENSIVE MEDICINE."

THEY SAY THAT IT HELPS 'GOOD PEOPLE' BUT IF SOMEONE WHO IS BAD EATS IT, 'IT KILLS HIM OR MAKES HIM CRAZY.' WHEN THEY SPEAK OF 'BADNESS' THEY MEAN 'CEREMONIALLY UNCLEAN.' (A MURDERER IF HE IS CLEAN CAN EAT THE MUSHROOMS WITH NO ILL EFFECTS.) A PERSON IS SAFE IF HE OR SHE REFRAINS FROM INTERCOURSE FIVE DAYS BEFORE AND AFTER THEY EAT THE MUSHROOMS. A SHOEMAKER IN TOWN WENT CRAZY ABOUT FIVE YEARS AGO. THE NEIGHBORS SAY IT WAS BECAUSE HE ATE THE MUSHROOM AND THEN HAD INTERCOURSE WITH HIS WIFE. ~~~~~~~ ....

USUALLY IT IS NOT THE SICK PERSON NOR HIS FAMILY WHO EAT THE MUSHROOMS. THEY PAY A "WISEMAN" TO EAT IT AND TELL THEM WHAT THE MUSHROOM SAYS. THE WISEMAN ALWAYS EATS THE MUSHROOM AT NIGHT BECAUSE IT 'PREFERS TO WORK UNSEEN.' THE MAZATECS SPEAK OF THE MUSHROOM AS THOUGH IT HAD A PERSONALITY. THEY NEVER SAY, "THE WISEMAN SAID..." THEY QUOTE THE MUSHROOM DIRECT.

THE MUSHROOM TELLS THEM WHAT MADE THE PERSON SICK AND WHETHER THEY WILL LIVE OR DIE. EVERYONE WE HAVE ASKED INSISTS THEY ARE SEEING INTO HEAVEN. THEY ALSO SEE MOVING PICTURES OF THE U.S.A. AND THE OCEAN. THIS IS QUITE EXCITING FOR MOUNTAIN PEOPLE. THE MUSHROOM (called Si THO OR MORE AFFECTIONALLY CALLED 'NT: Si THO) IS BROWN AND GROWS BIGGEST IN JUNE AND JULY AFTER THE RAIN. THE MUSHROOM GROWS IN THE GRASS AND IS OFTEN FOUND ON COW MANURE. IF THEY CANNOT FIND ONE GROWING, THEY GO WITHOUT.

I REGRET THE SURVIVAL OF THE USE OF THE MUSHROOM. I WISH THEY WOULD CONSULT THE BIBLE FOR CHRIST'S WISHES AND NOT BE DECEIVED BY THE MUSHROOM. I WILL BE ABSENT DURING YOUR VISIT BUT RECOMMEND VICTOR HERNANDEZ AS A GUIDE.

SINCERELY,

Eunice V. Pike

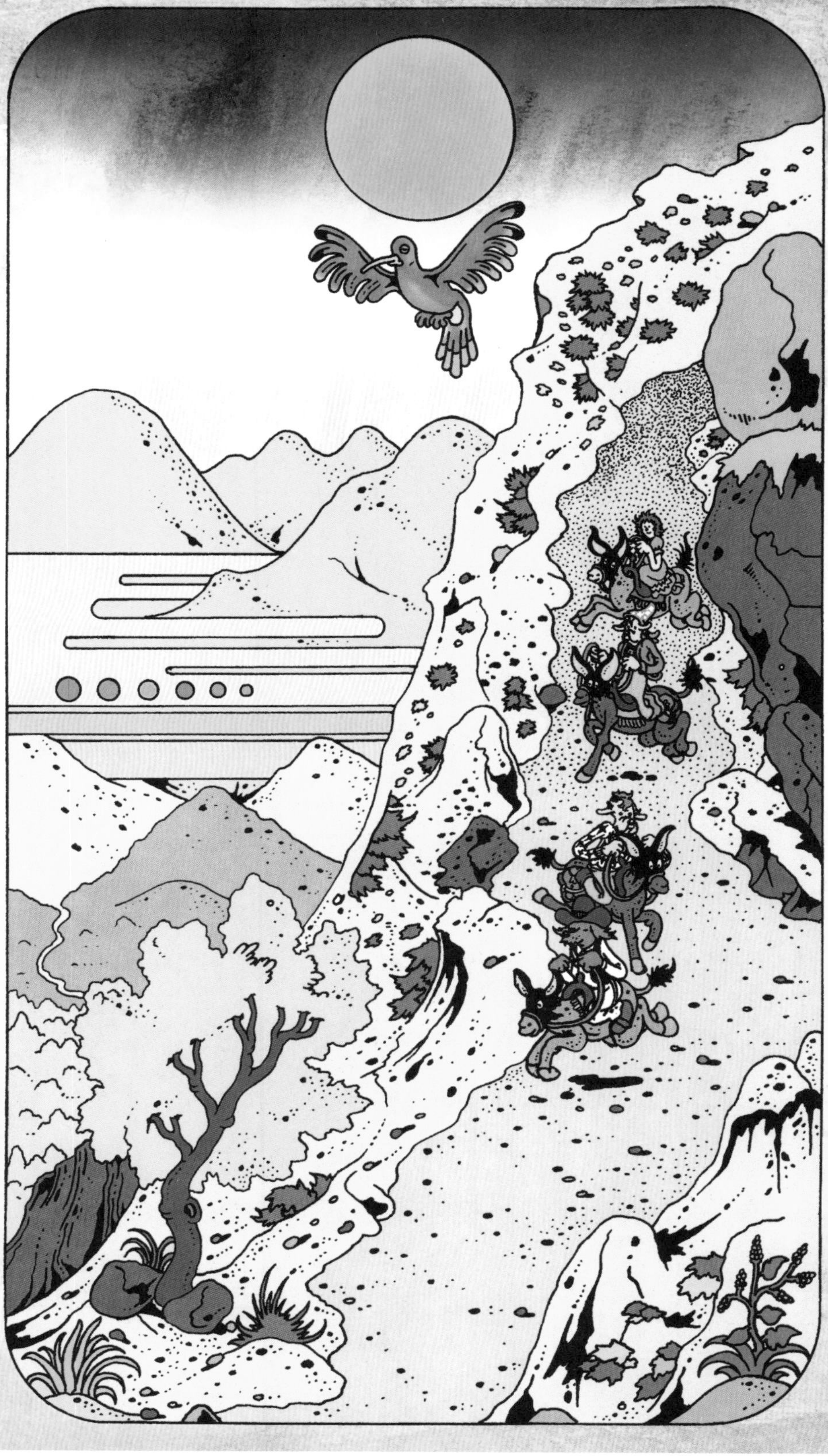

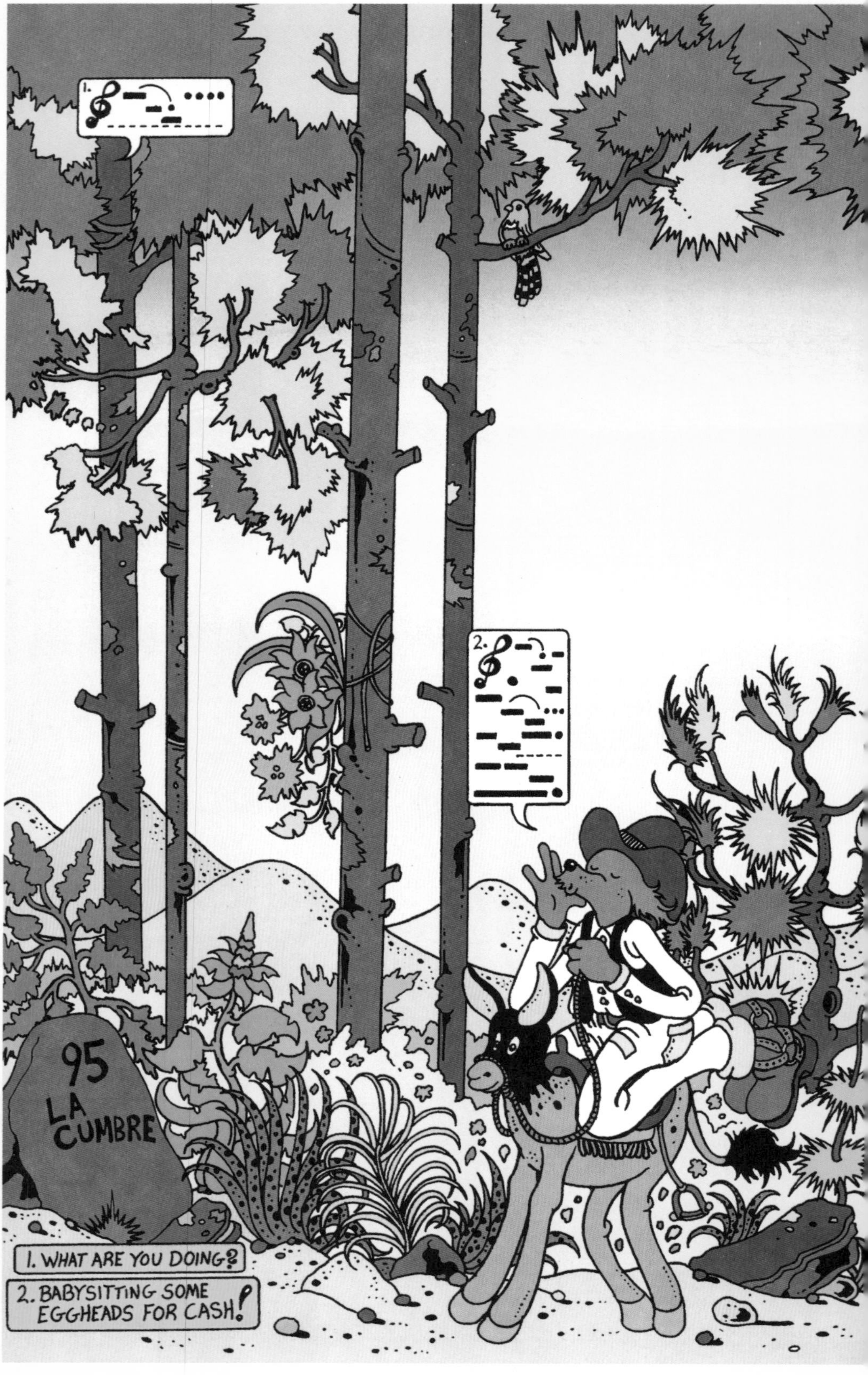
1.
2.
95
LA CUMBRE
1. WHAT ARE YOU DOING?
2. BABYSITTING SOME EGGHEADS FOR CASH!

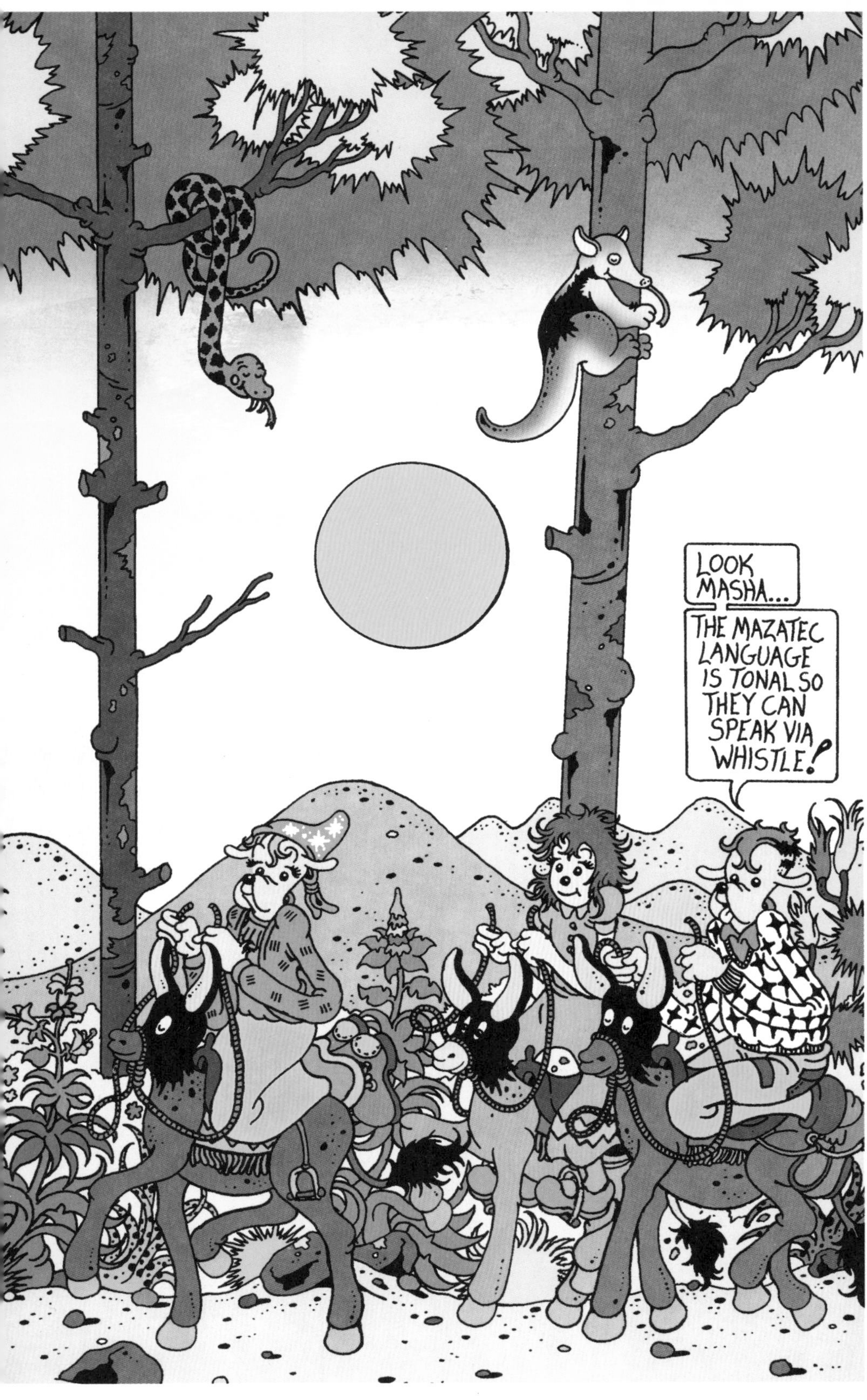
LOOK MASHA...
THE MAZATEC LANGUAGE IS TONAL SO THEY CAN SPEAK VIA WHISTLE!

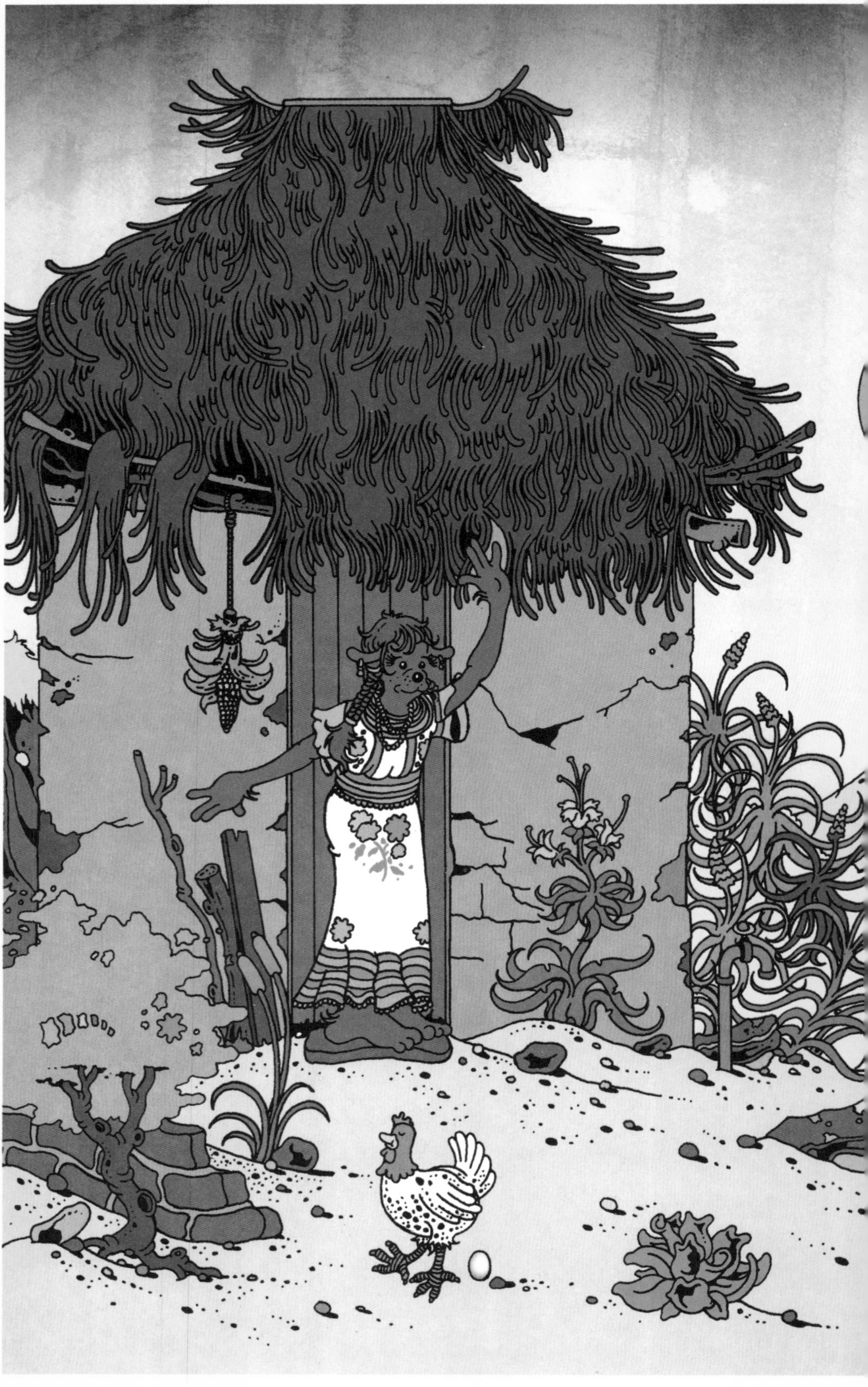

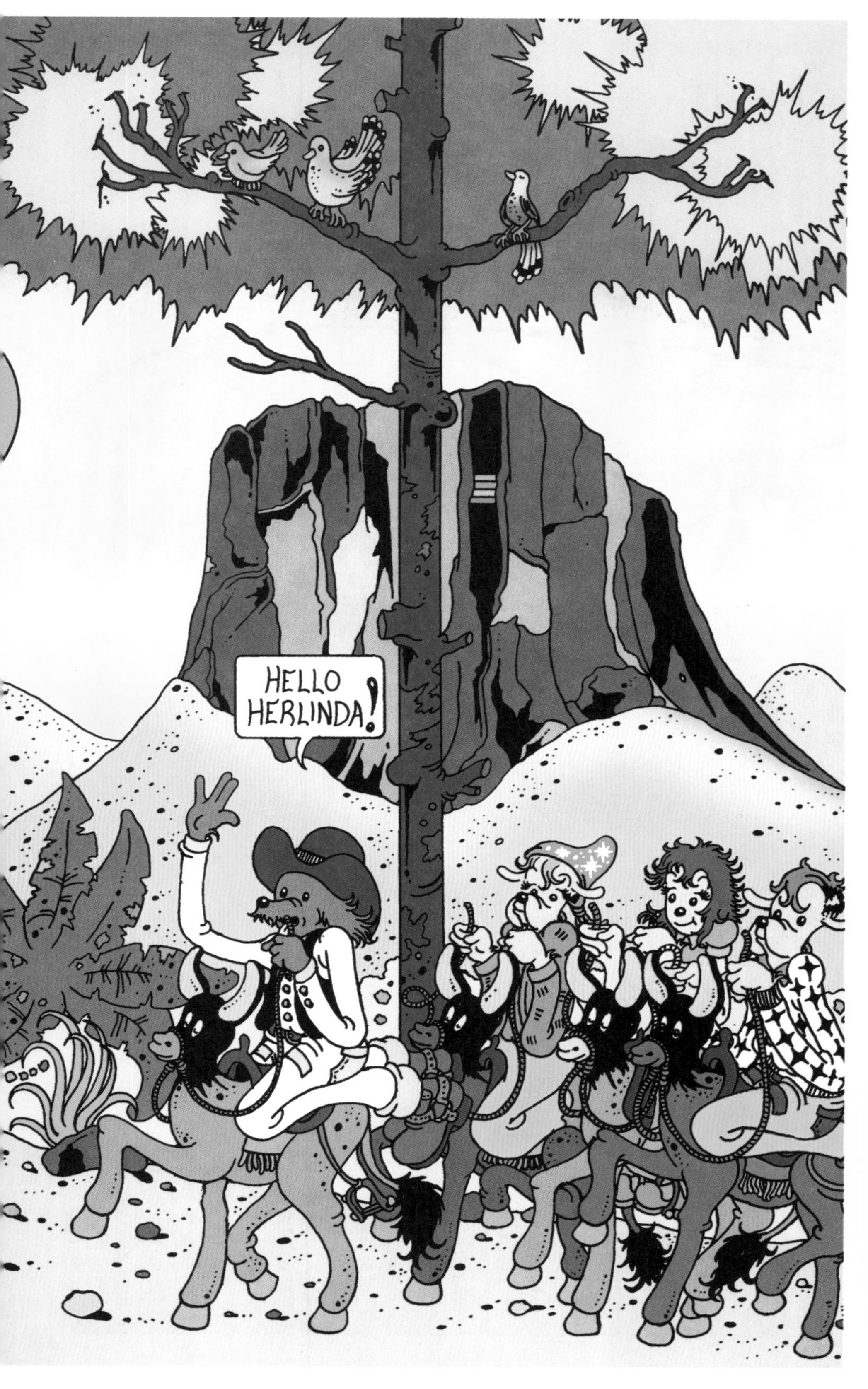
HELLO HERLINDA!

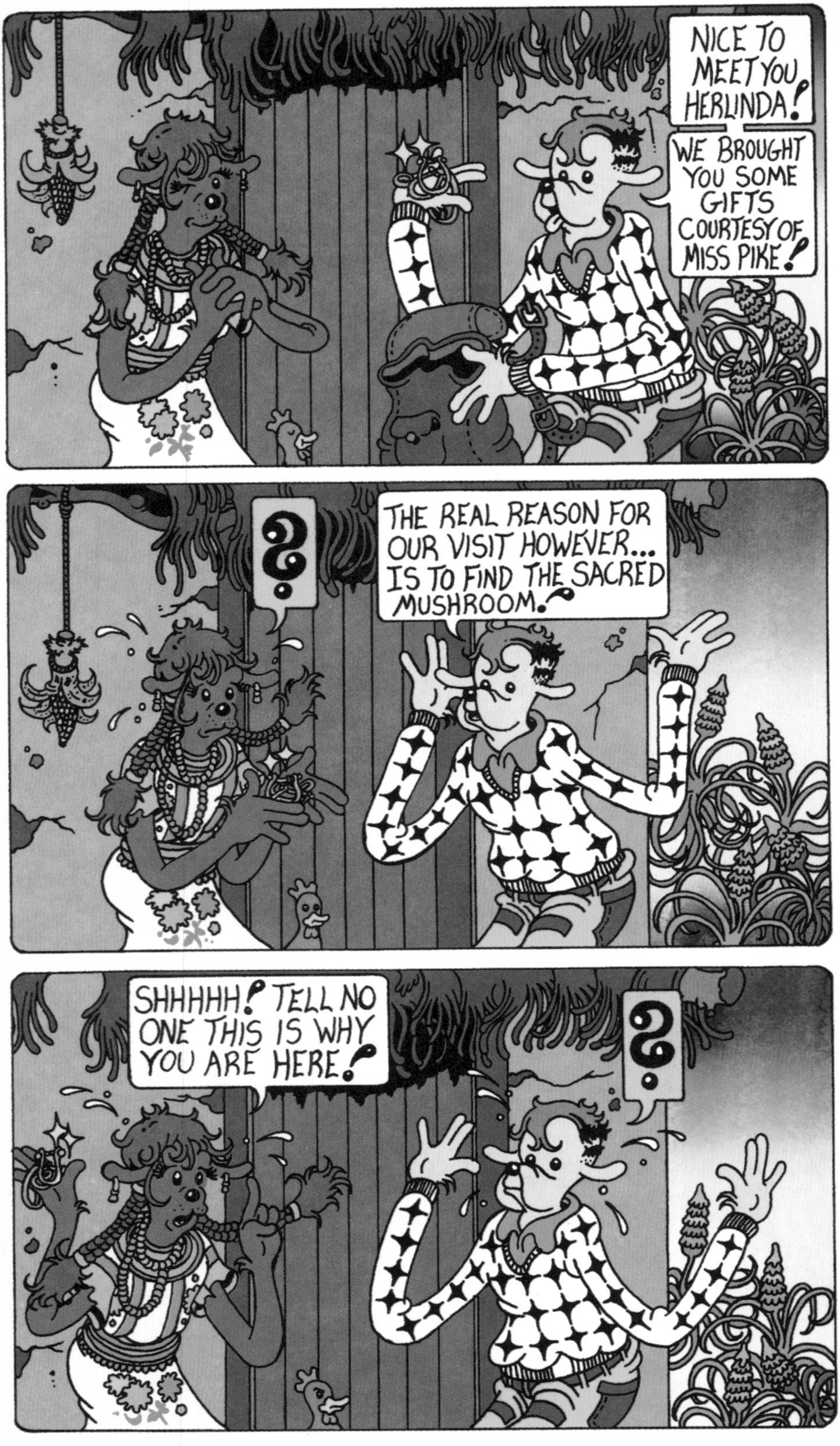
NICE TO MEET YOU HERLINDA!
WE BROUGHT YOU SOME GIFTS COURTESY OF MISS PIKE!
?
THE REAL REASON FOR OUR VISIT HOWEVER... IS TO FIND THE SACRED MUSHROOM.
SHHHHH! TELL NO ONE THIS IS WHY YOU ARE HERE!
?

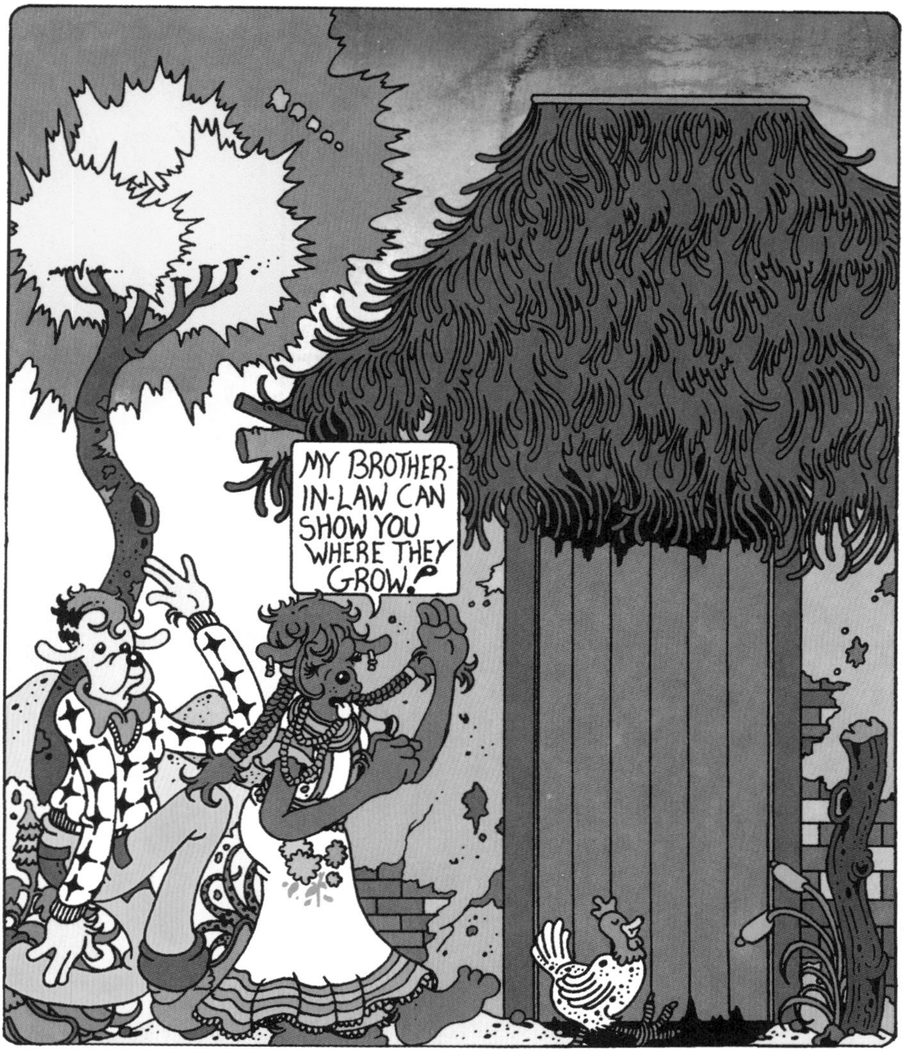
MY BROTHER-IN-LAW CAN SHOW YOU WHERE THEY GROW!

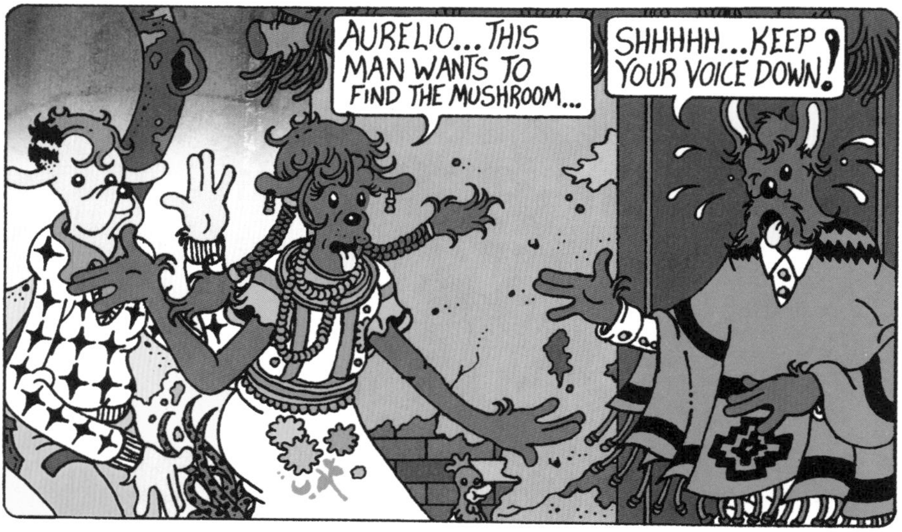
AURELIO... THIS MAN WANTS TO FIND THE MUSHROOM...
SHHHHH...KEEP YOUR VOICE DOWN!

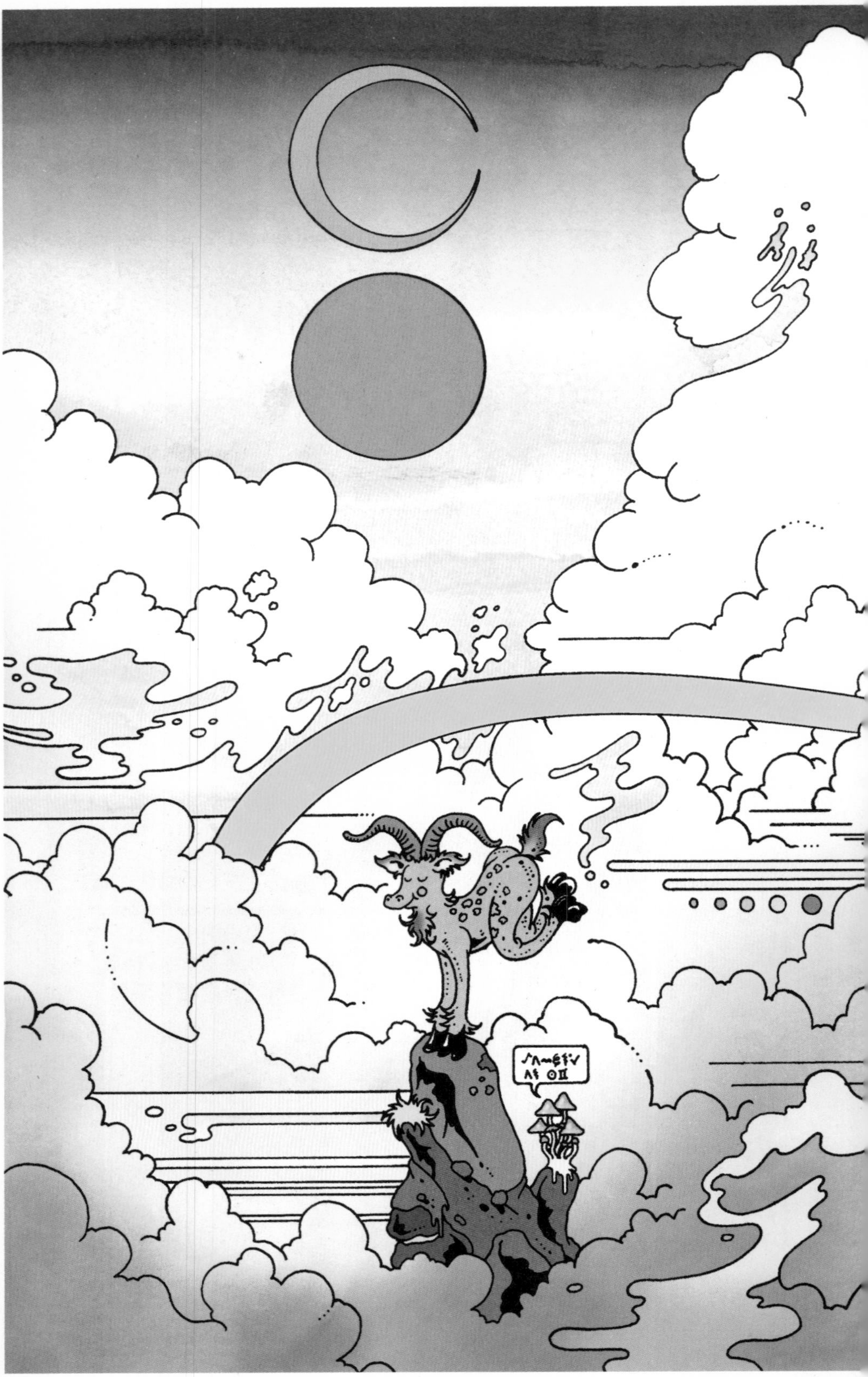

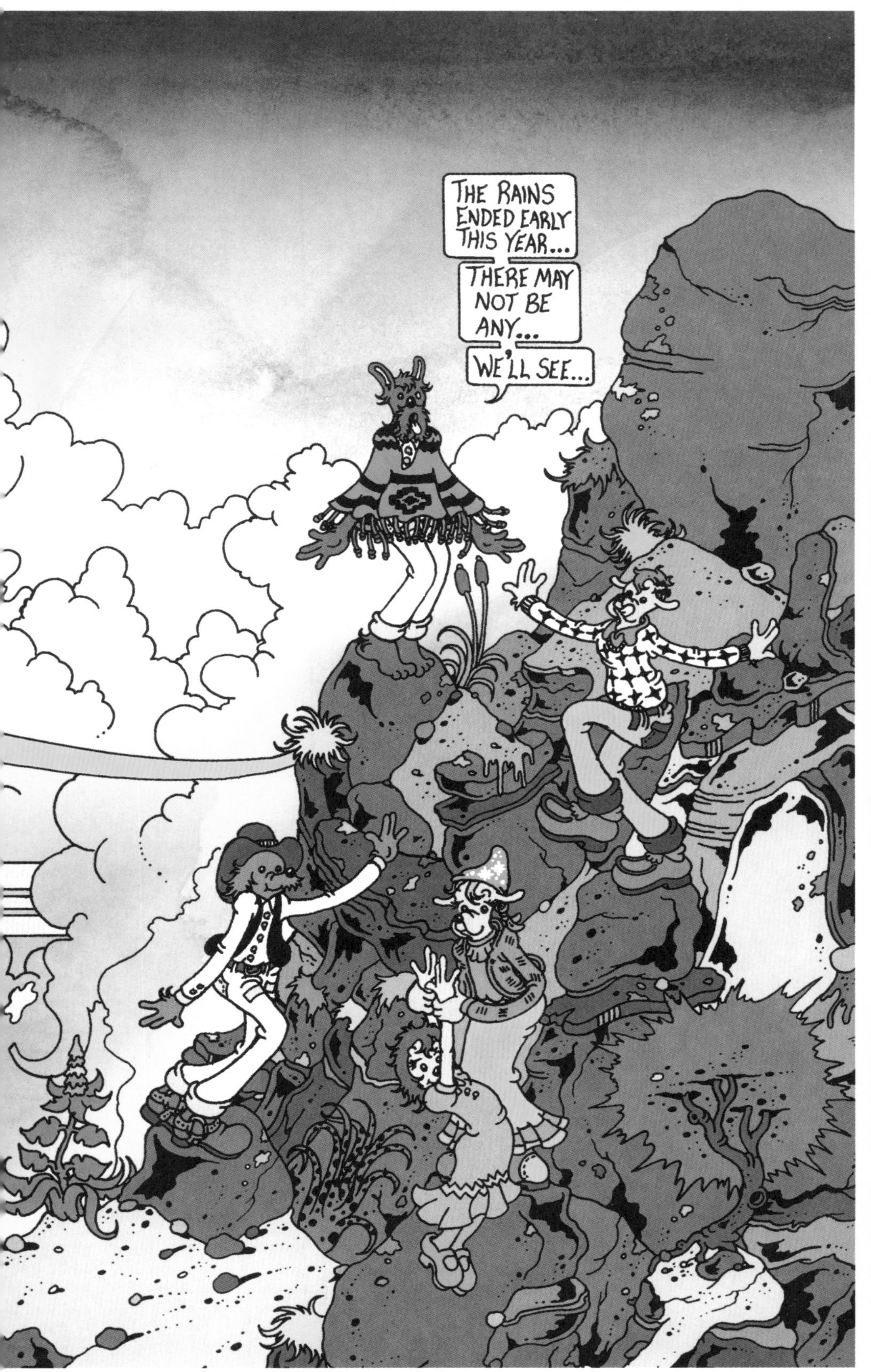
THE RAINS ENDED EARLY THIS YEAR...
THERE MAY NOT BE ANY...
WE'LL SEE...

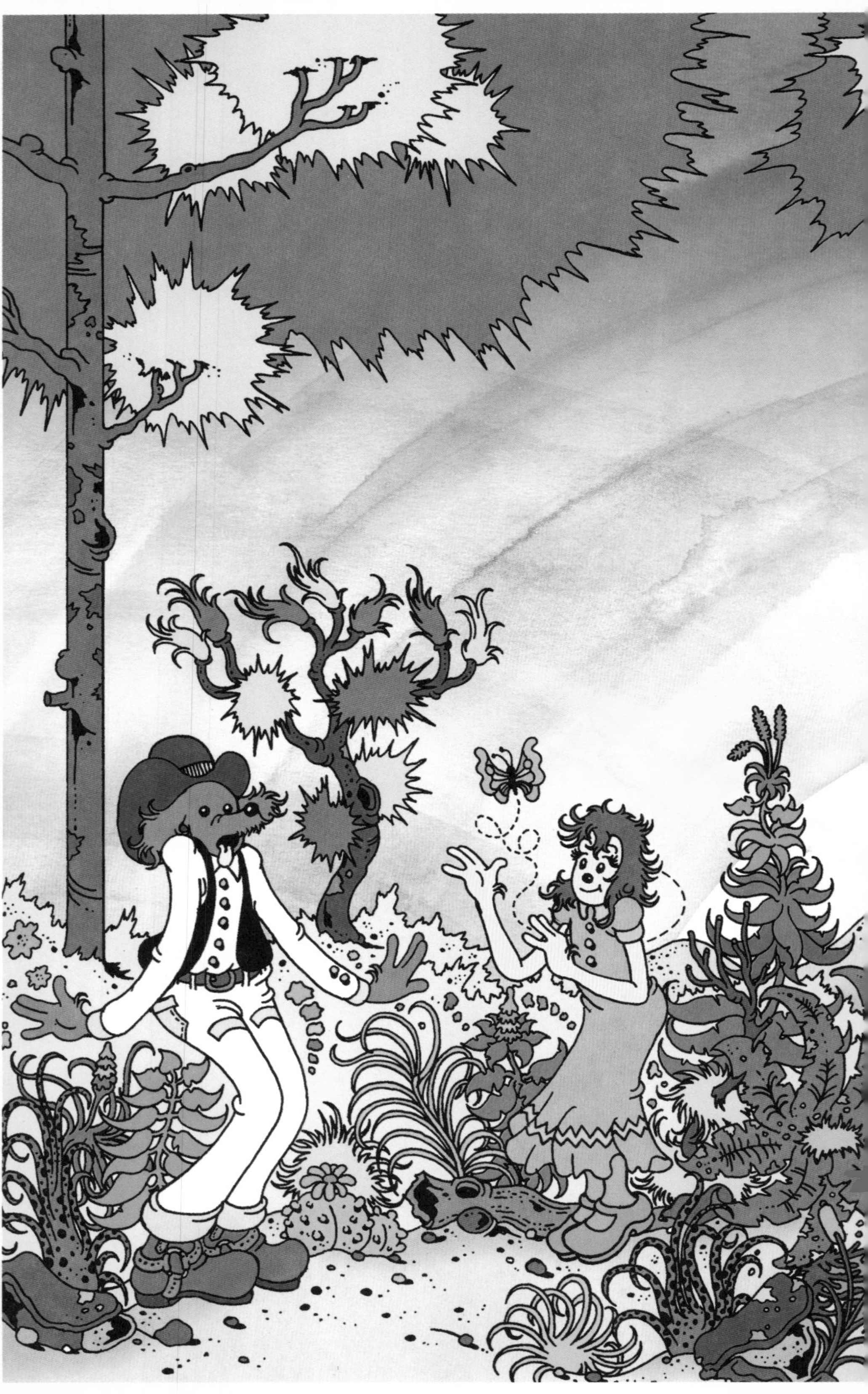

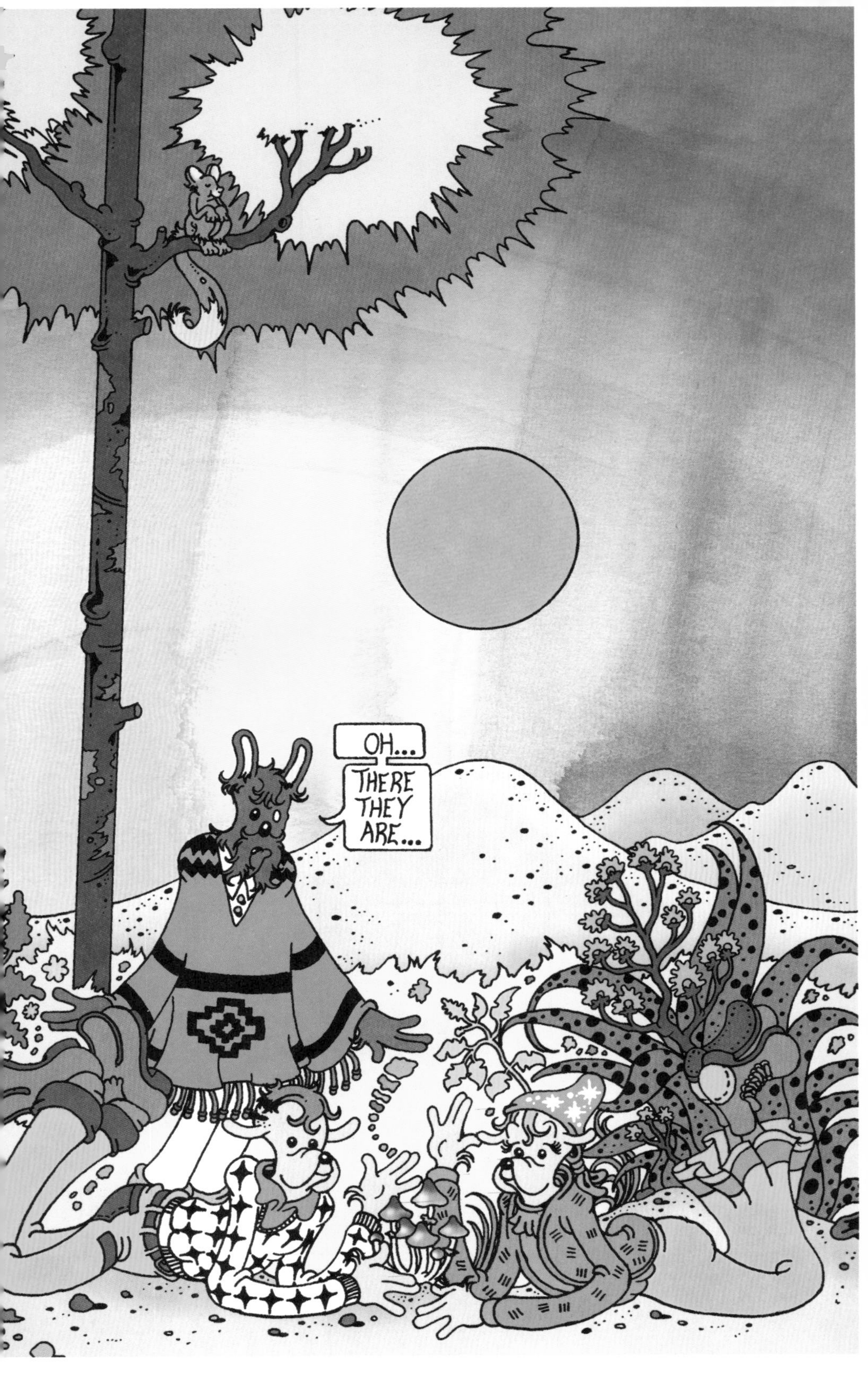
OH...
THERE THEY ARE...

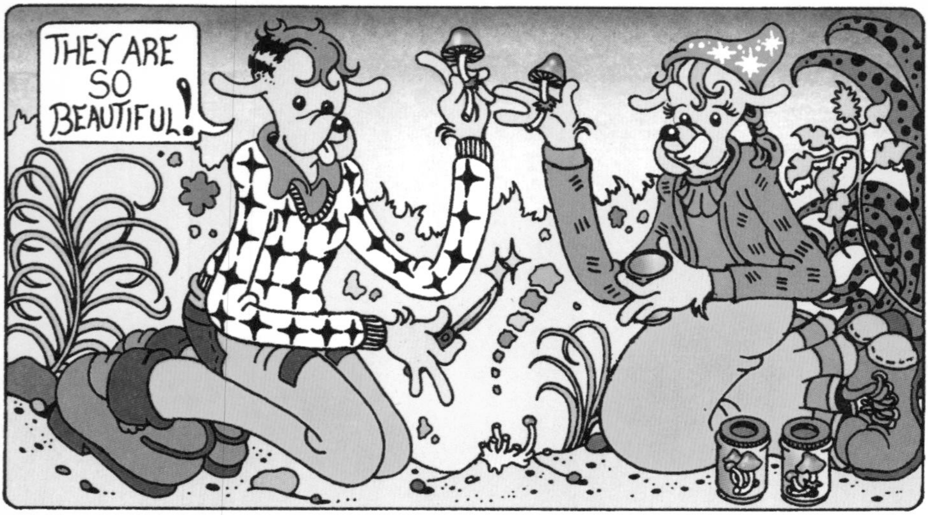
THEY ARE SO BEAUTIFUL!

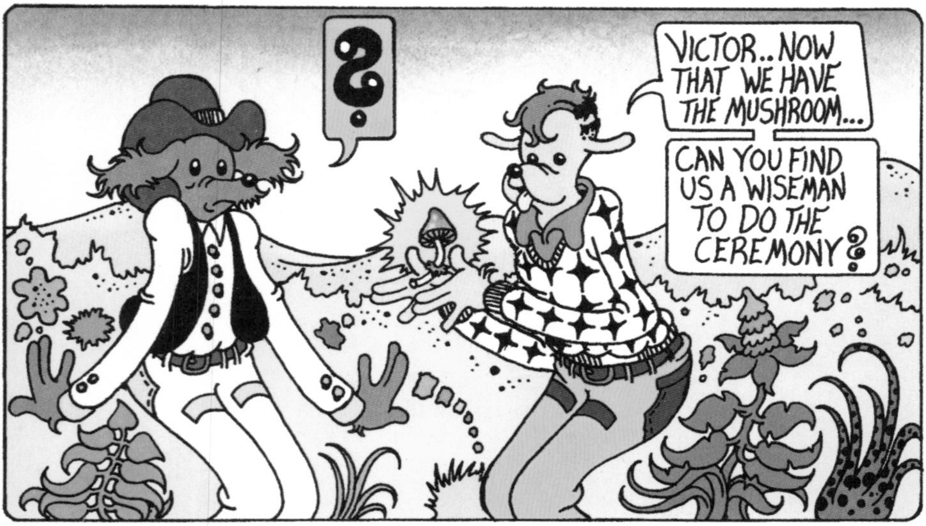
?
VICTOR.. NOW THAT WE HAVE THE MUSHROOM...
CAN YOU FIND US A WISEMAN TO DO THE CEREMONY?

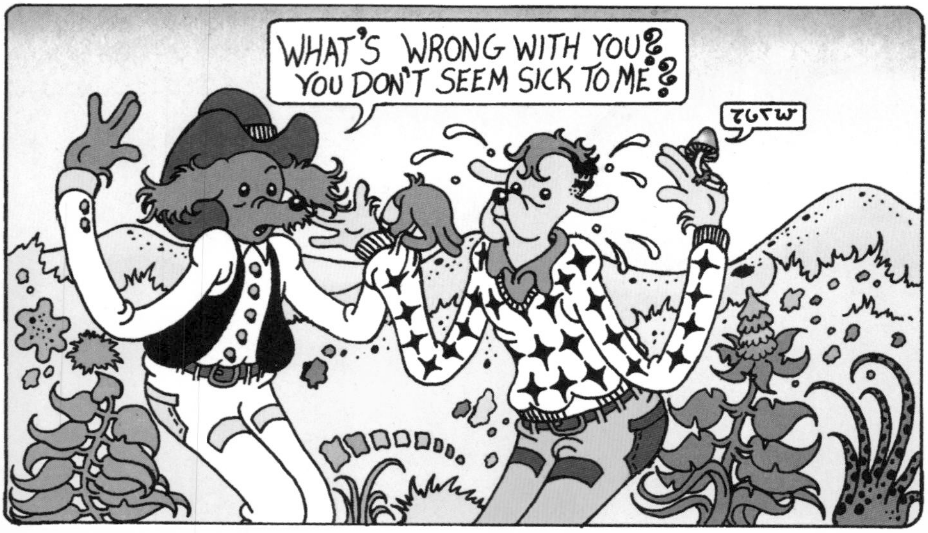
WHAT'S WRONG WITH YOU? YOU DON'T SEEM SICK TO ME?

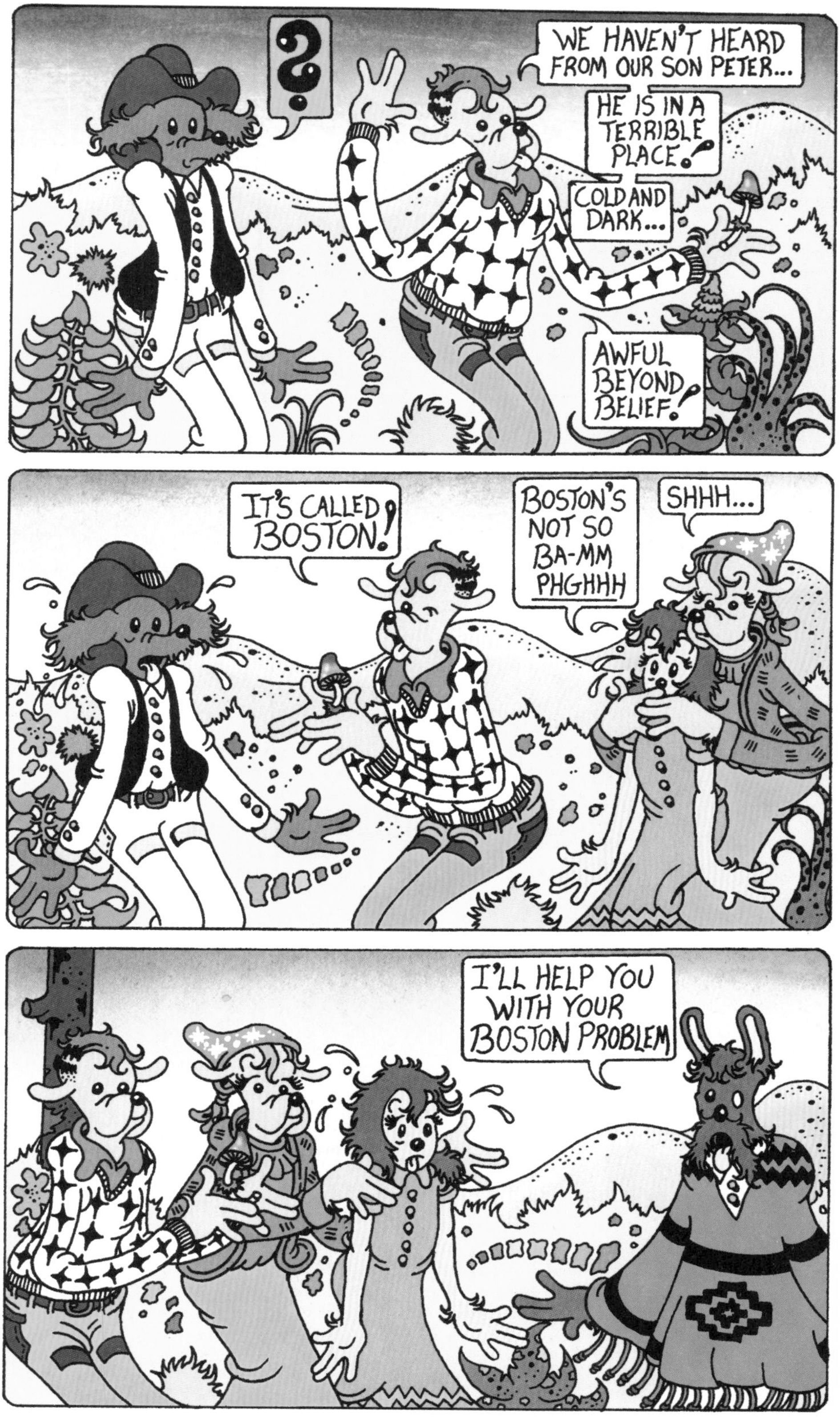
?
WE HAVEN'T HEARD FROM OUR SON PETER...
HE IS IN A TERRIBLE PLACE!
COLD AND DARK...
AWFUL BEYOND BELIEF!
IT'S CALLED BOSTON!
BOSTON'S NOT SO BA-MM PHGHHH
SHHH...
I'LL HELP YOU WITH YOUR BOSTON PROBLEM

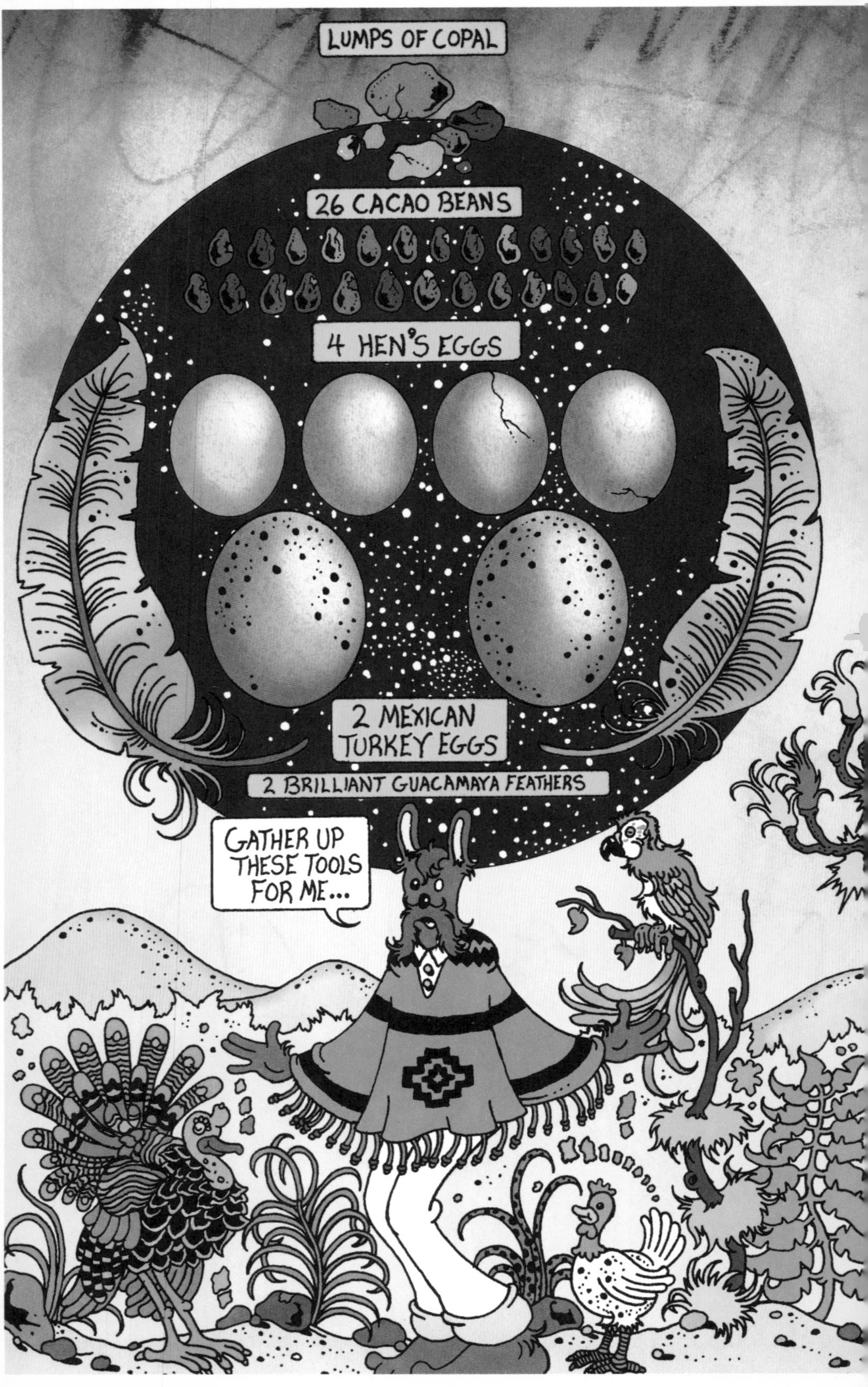
LUMPS OF COPAL
26 CACAO BEANS
4 HEN'S EGGS
2 MEXICAN TURKEY EGGS
2 BRILLIANT GUACAMAYA FEATHERS
GATHER UP THESE TOOLS FOR ME...

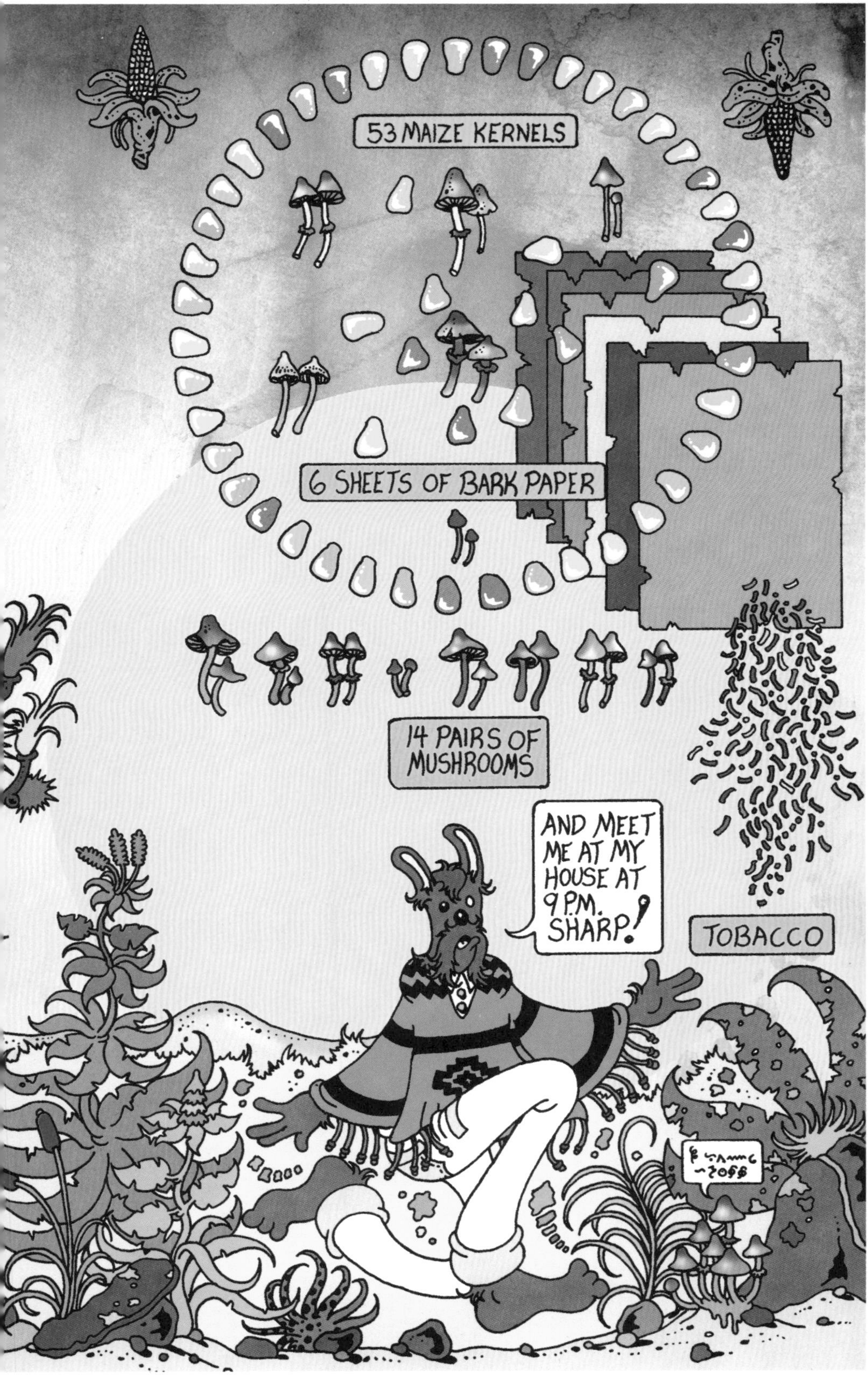

53 MAIZE KERNELS
6 SHEETS OF BARK PAPER
14 PAIRS OF MUSHROOMS
TOBACCO
AND MEET ME AT MY HOUSE AT 9 P.M. SHARP!

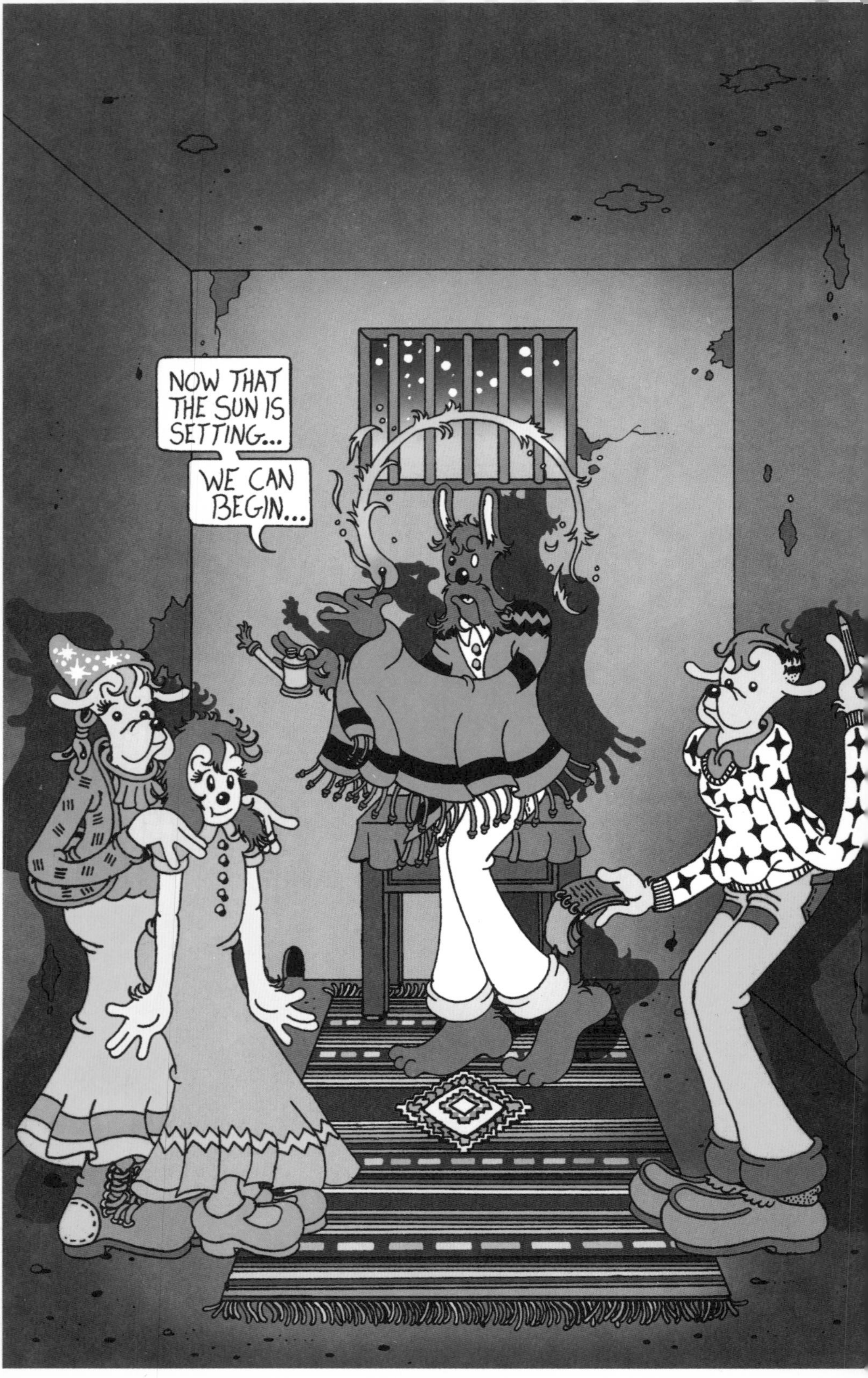
NOW THAT THE SUN IS SETTING...
WE CAN BEGIN...

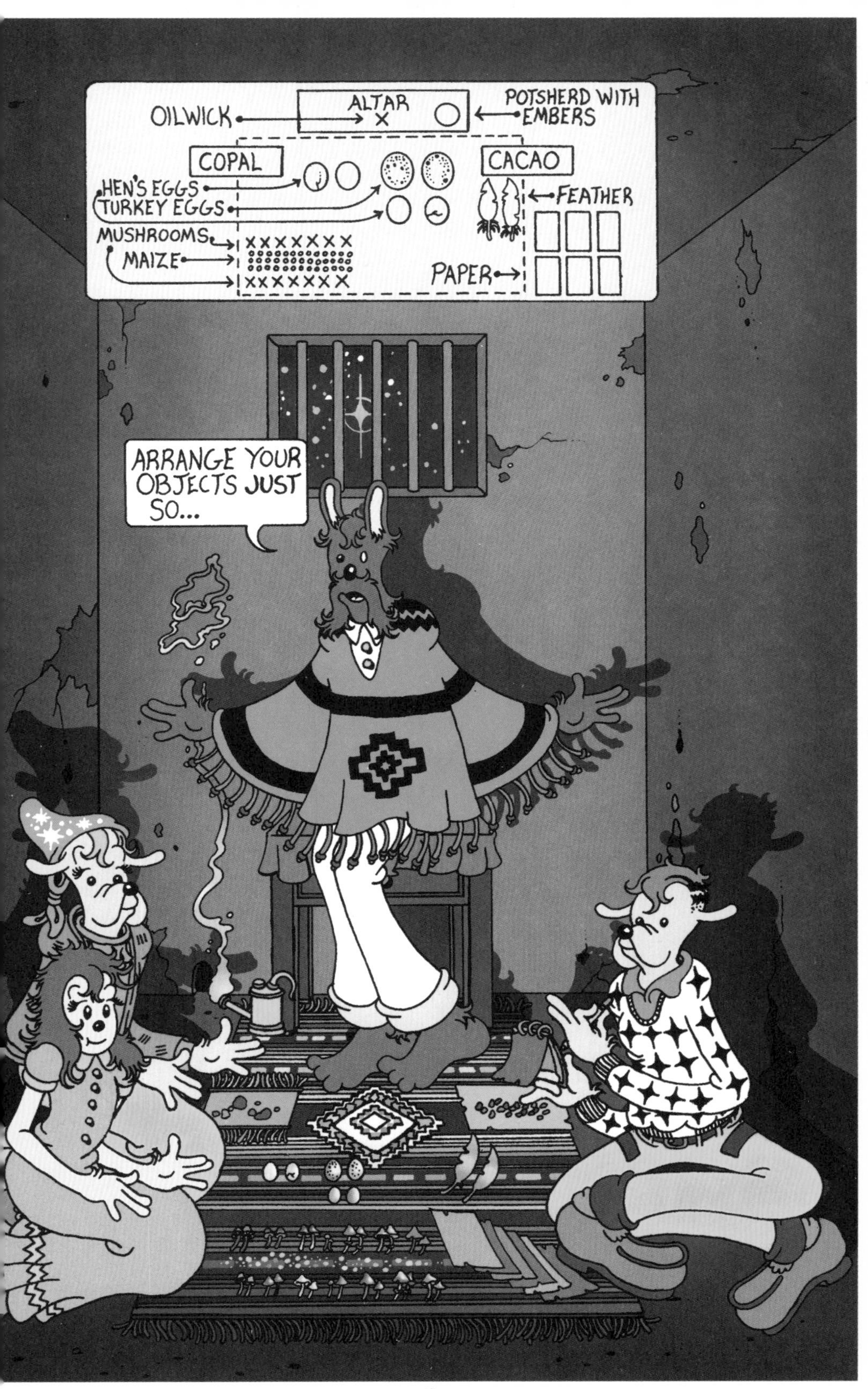
ALTAR
OILWICK
POTSHERD WITH EMBERS
COPAL
CACAO
HEN'S EGGS
TURKEY EGGS
FEATHER
MUSHROOMS
MAIZE
PAPER
ARRANGE YOUR OBJECTS JUST SO...

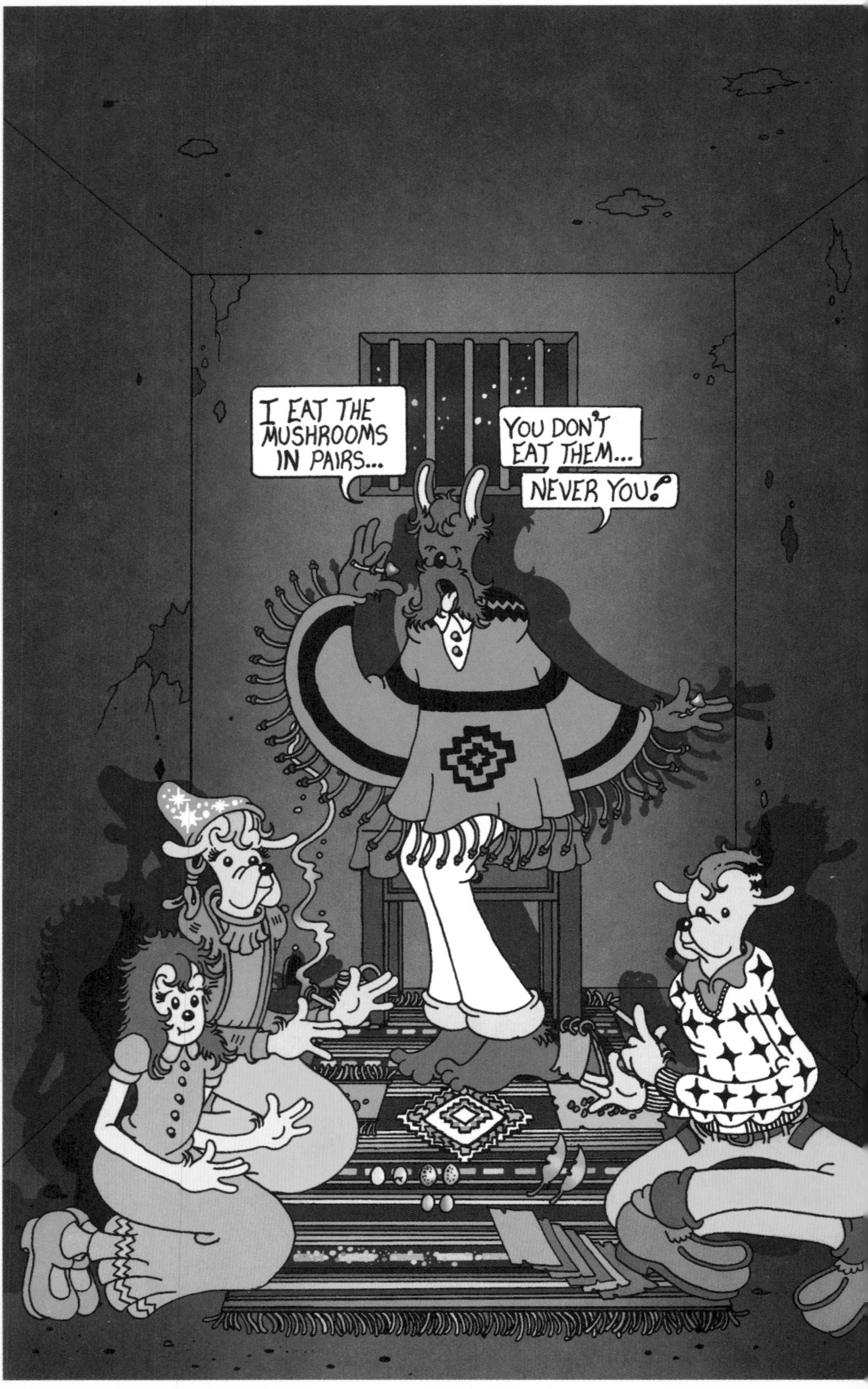
I EAT THE MUSHROOMS IN PAIRS...
YOU DON'T EAT THEM... NEVER YOU!

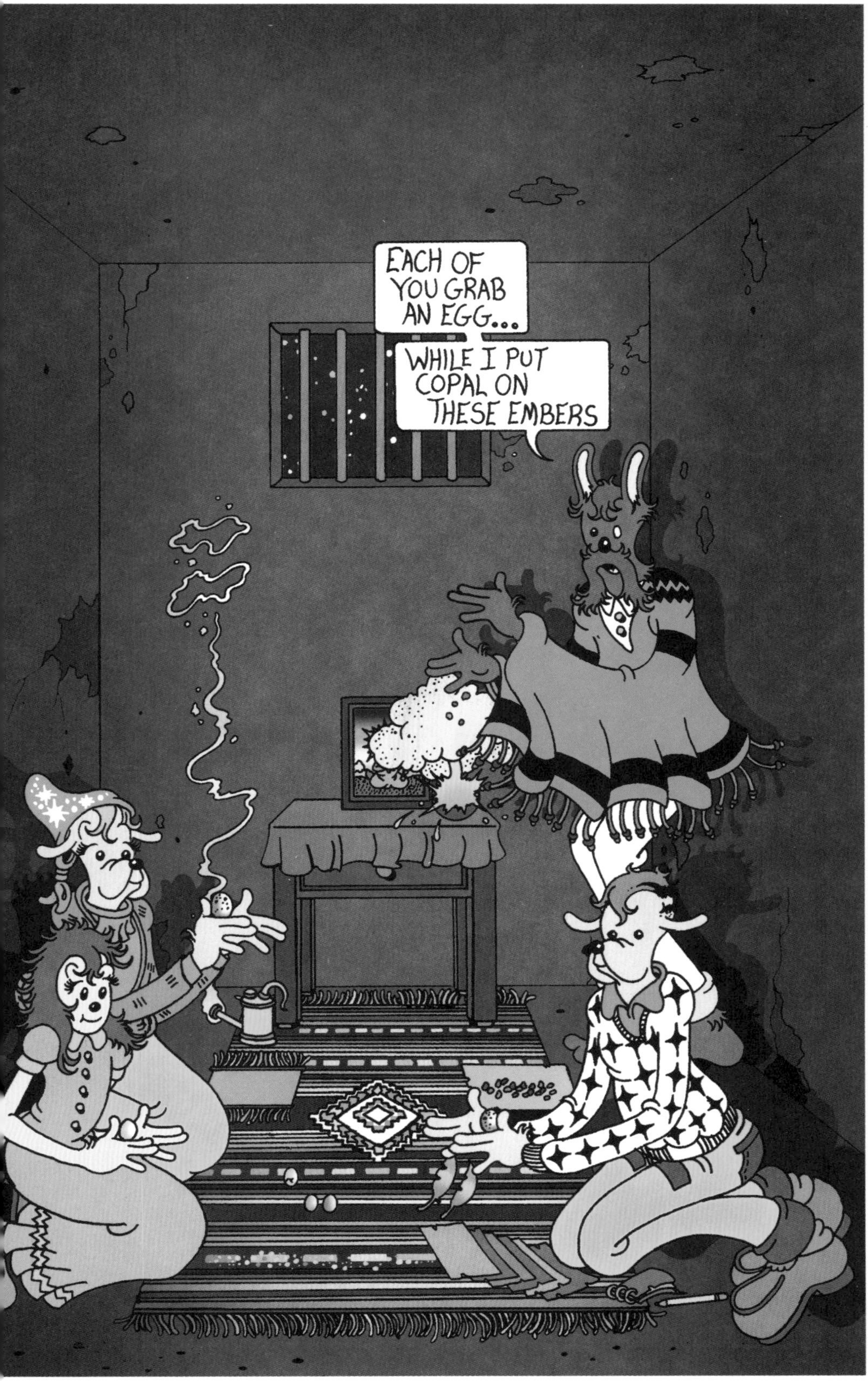
EACH OF YOU GRAB AN EGG...
WHILE I PUT COPAL ON THESE EMBERS

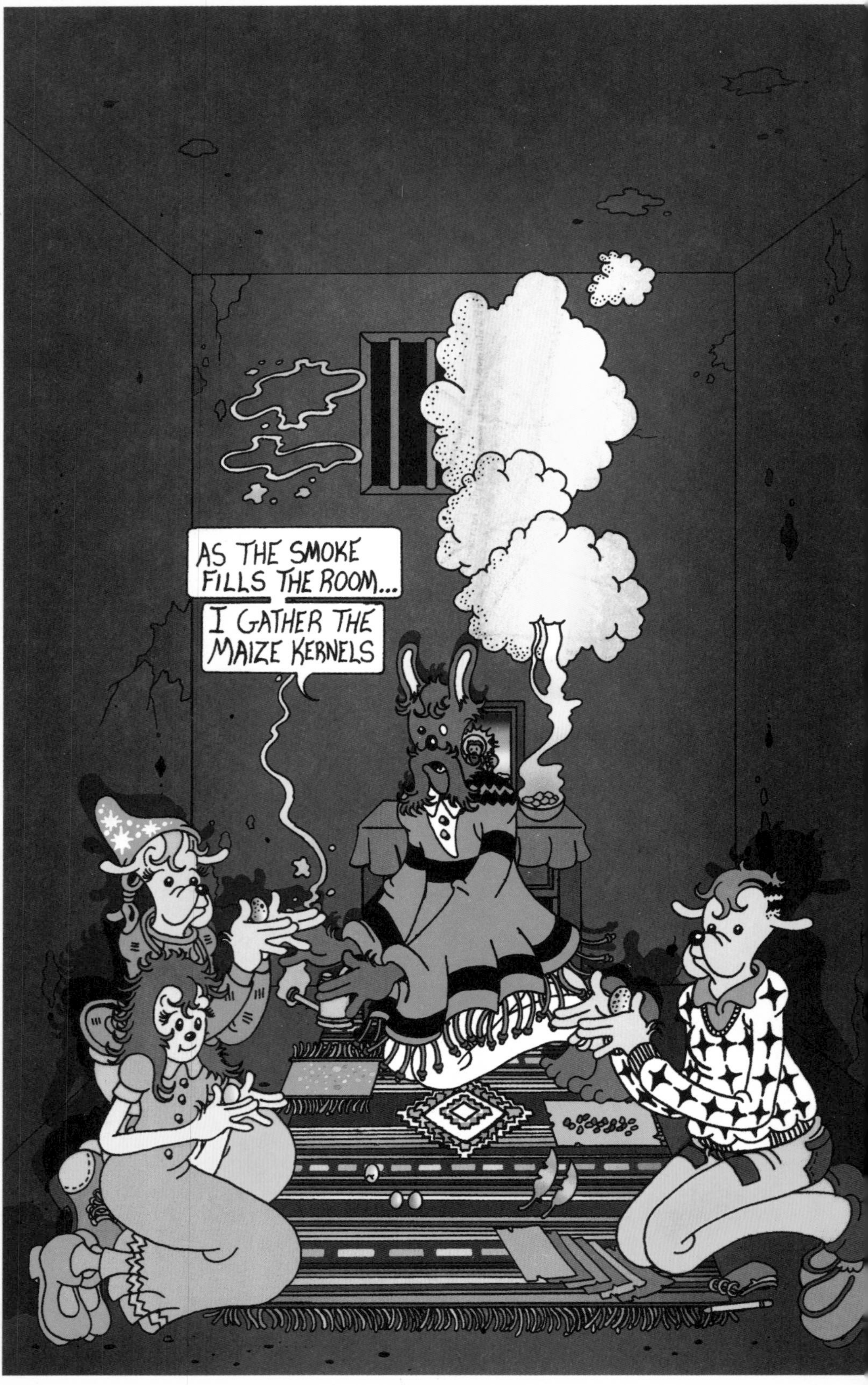
AS THE SMOKE FILLS THE ROOM...
I GATHER THE MAIZE KERNELS

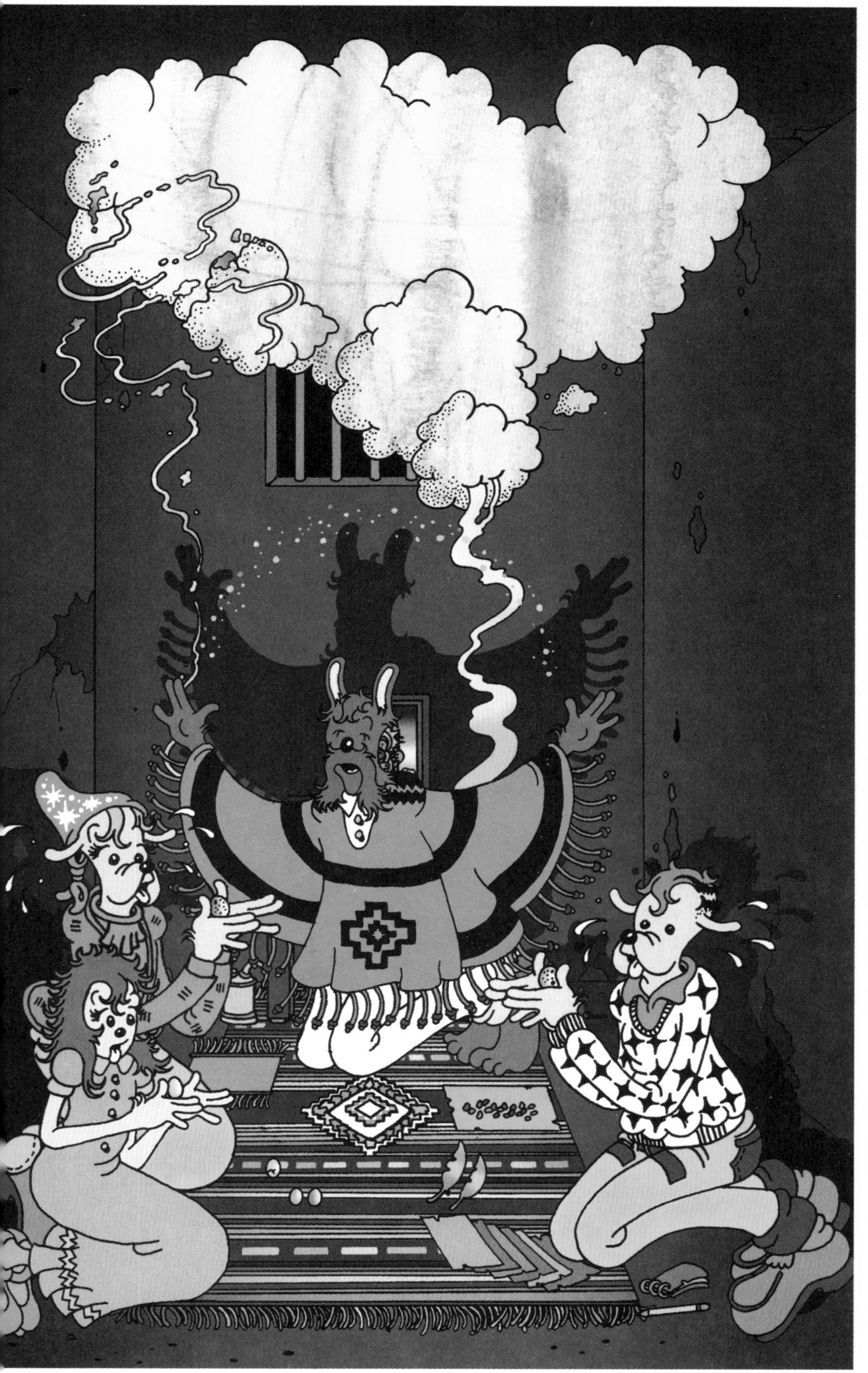

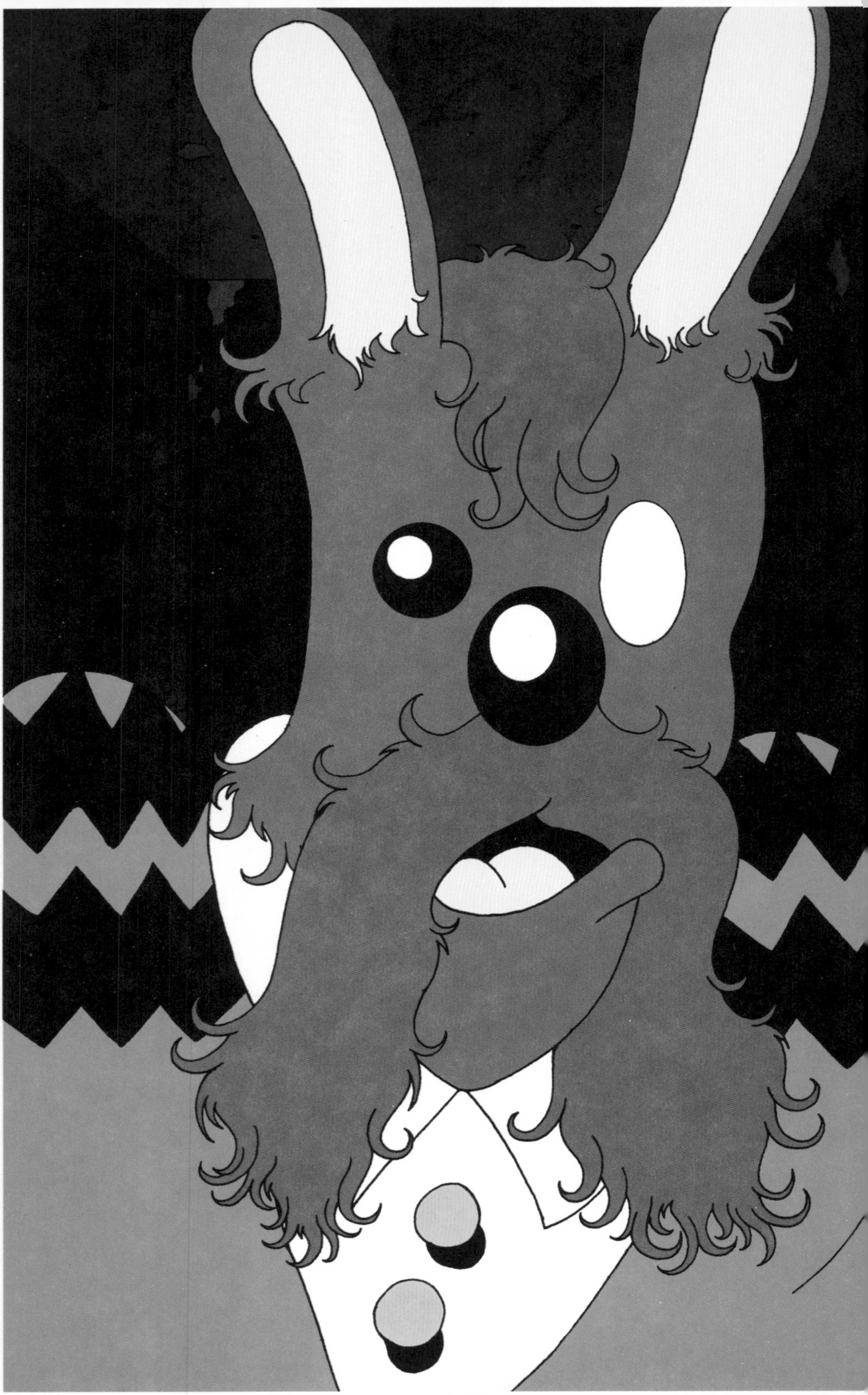

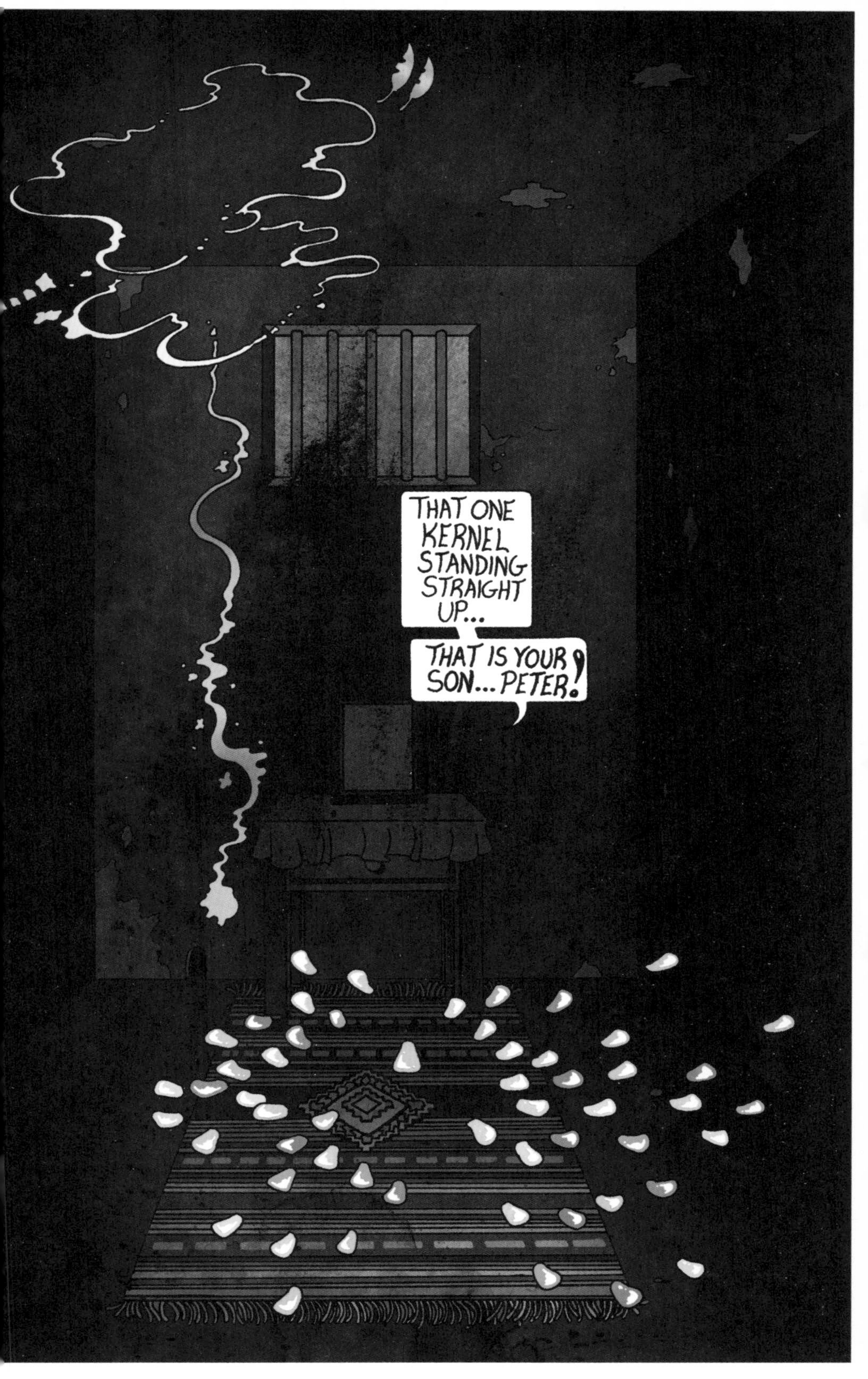
THAT ONE KERNEL STANDING STRAIGHT UP...
THAT IS YOUR SON... PETER!

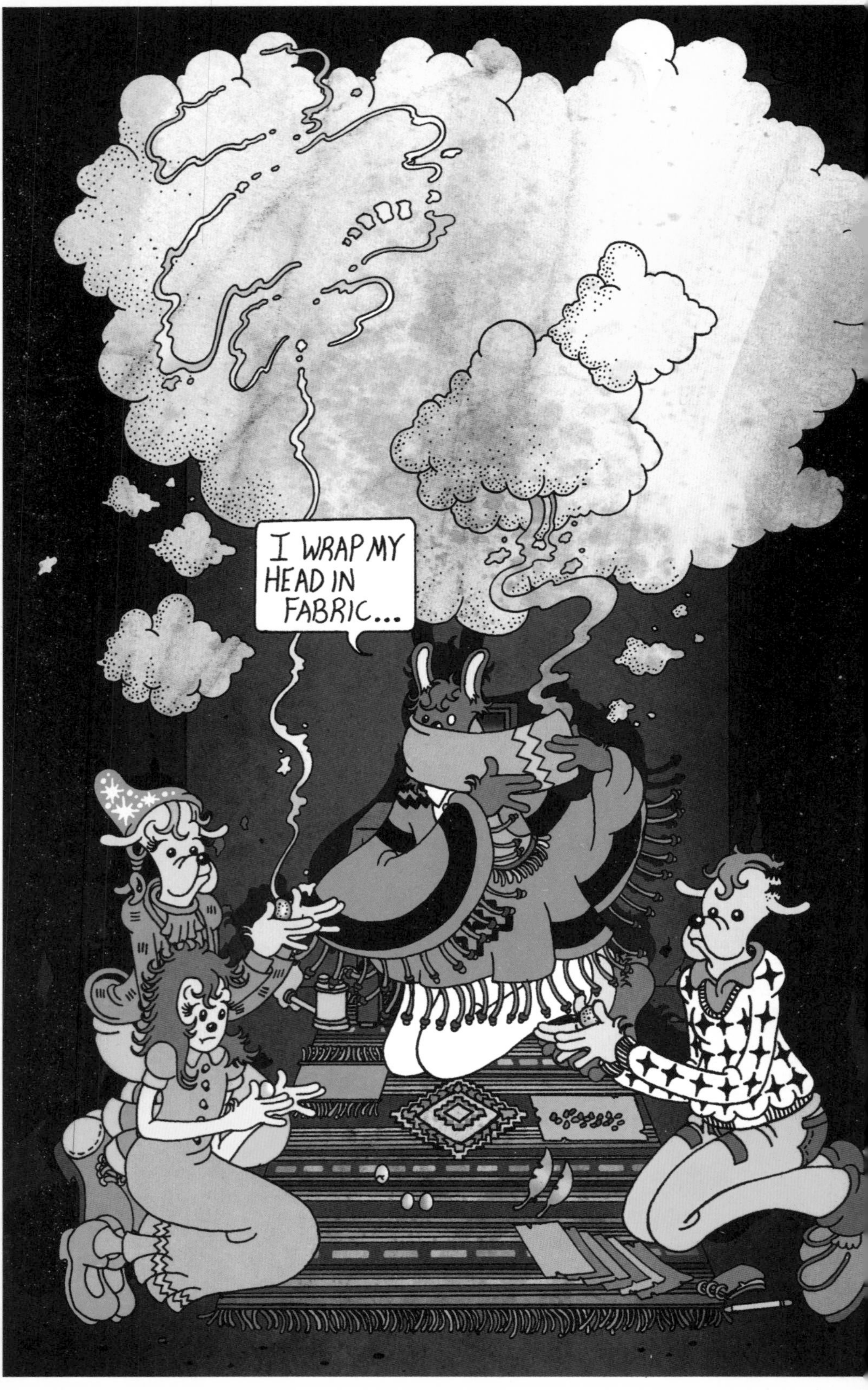
I WRAP MY HEAD IN FABRIC...

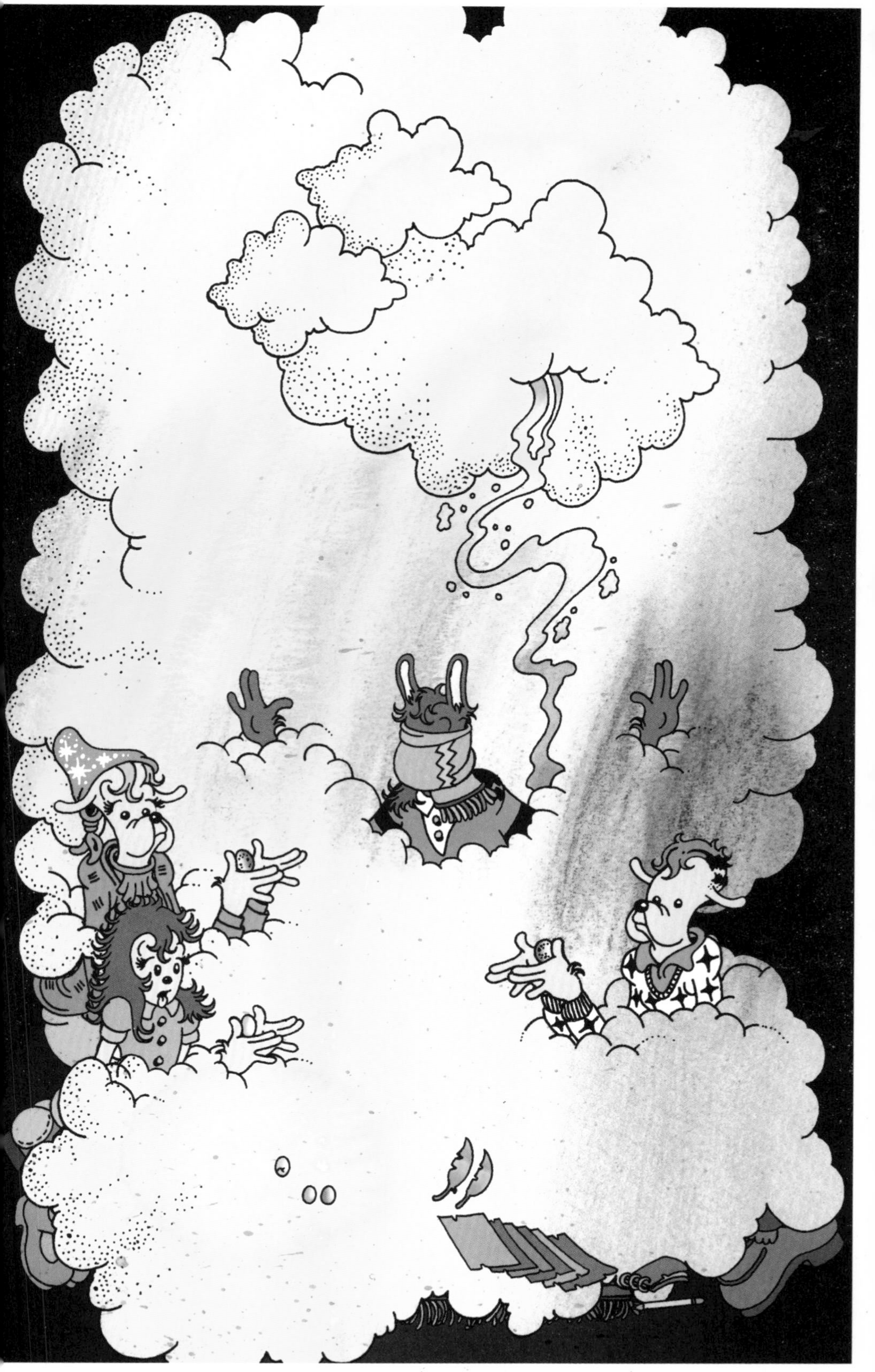

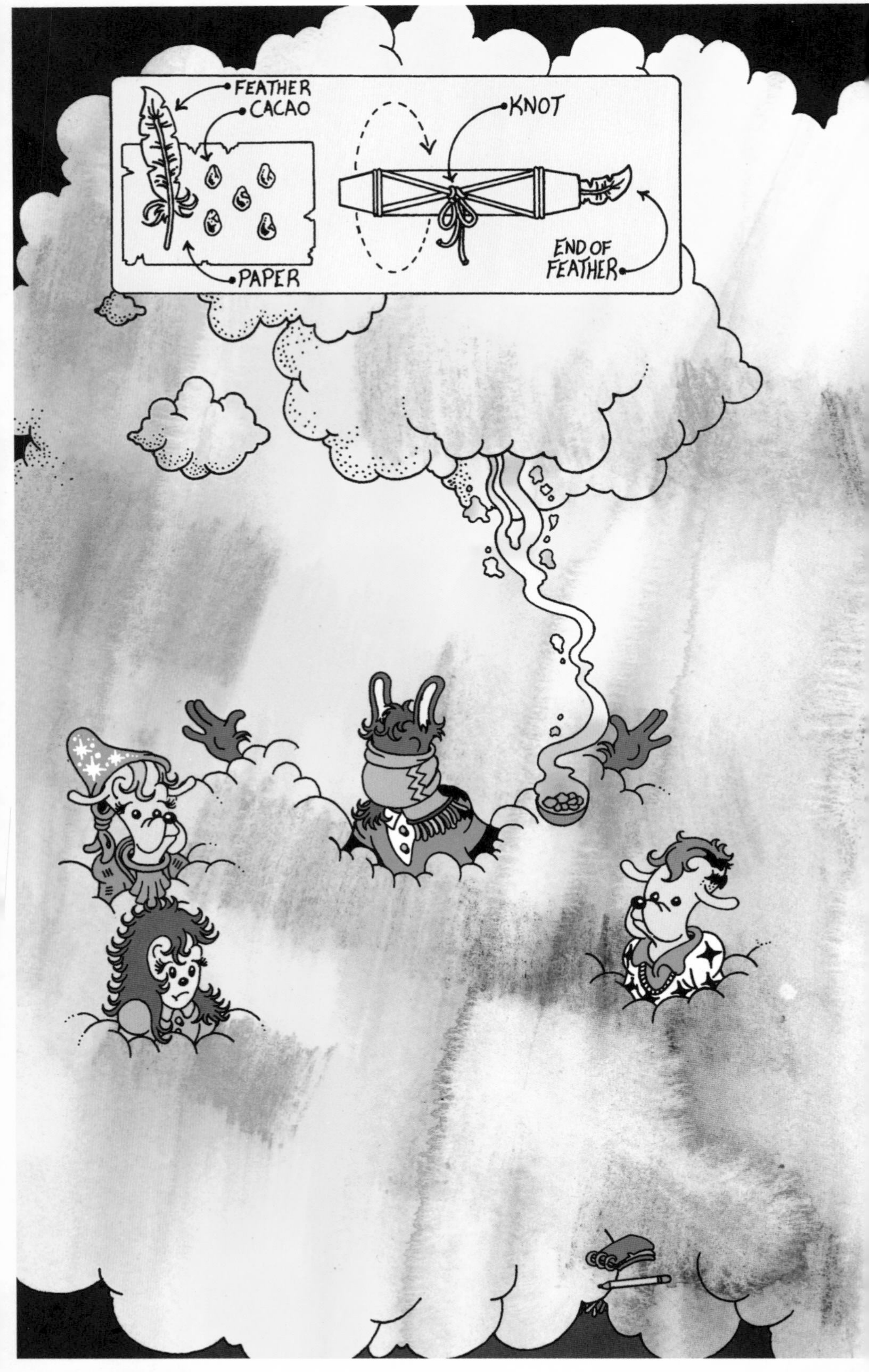
FEATHER
CACAO
PAPER
KNOT
END OF FEATHER

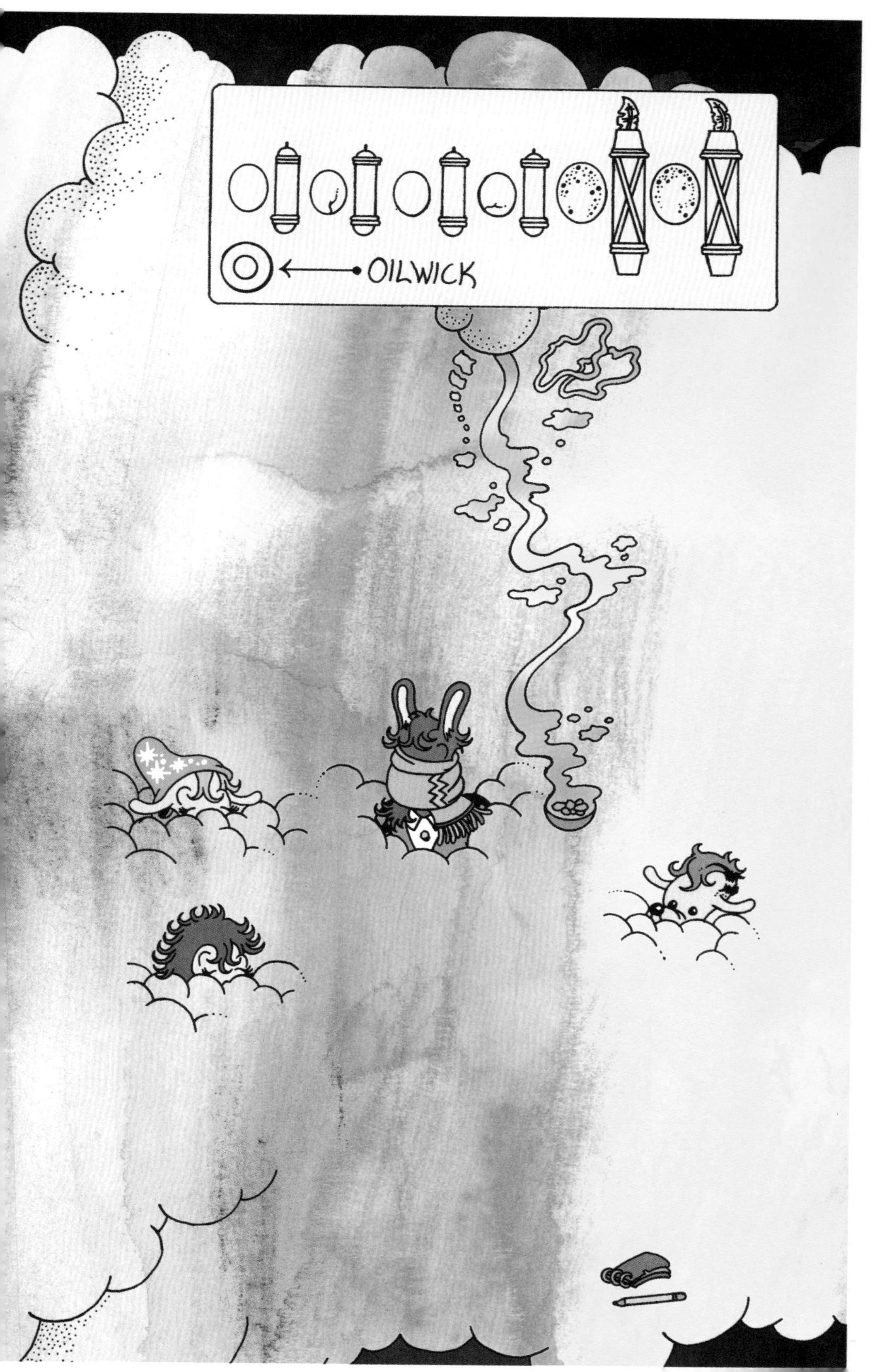
OILWICK

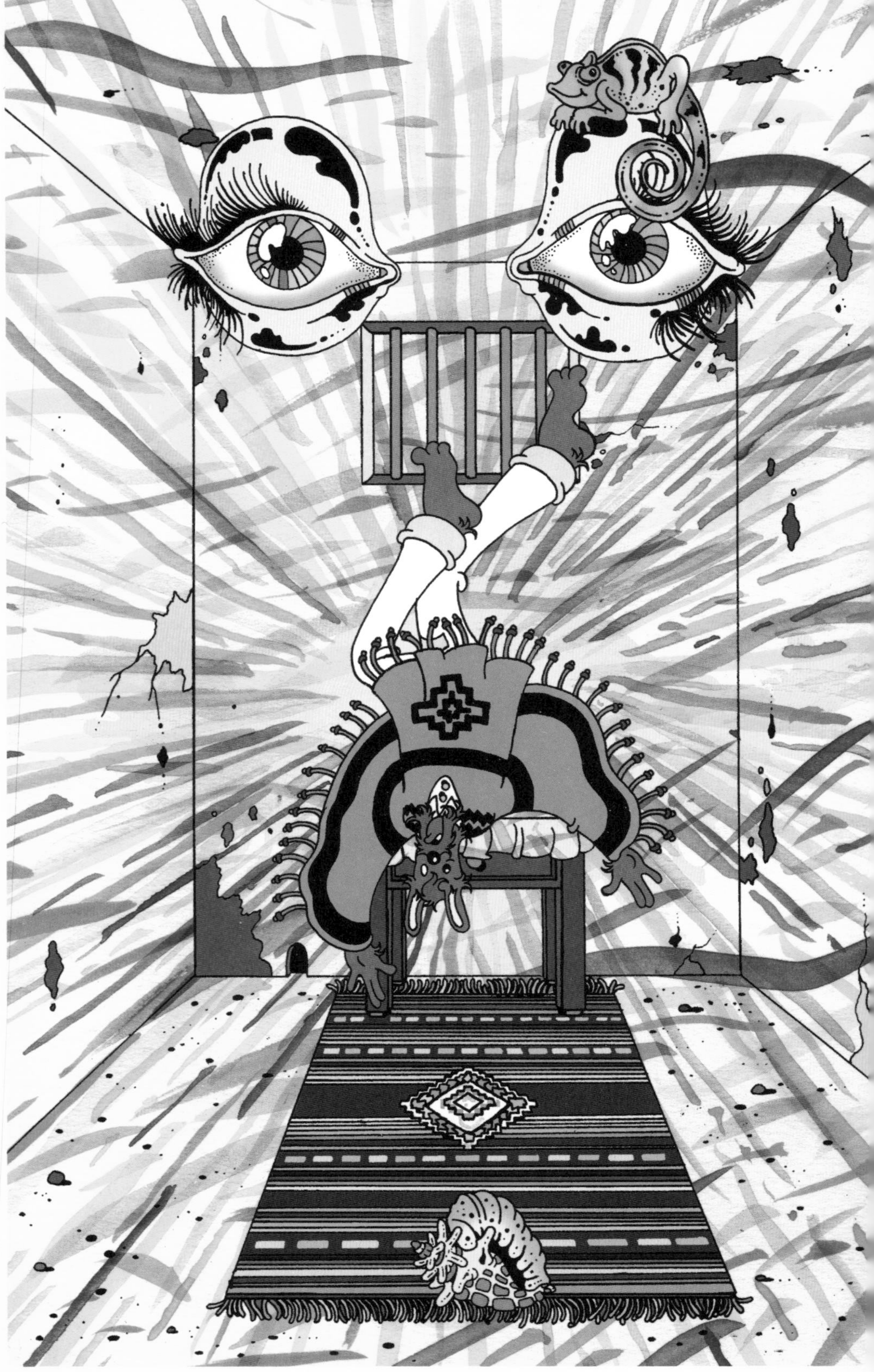

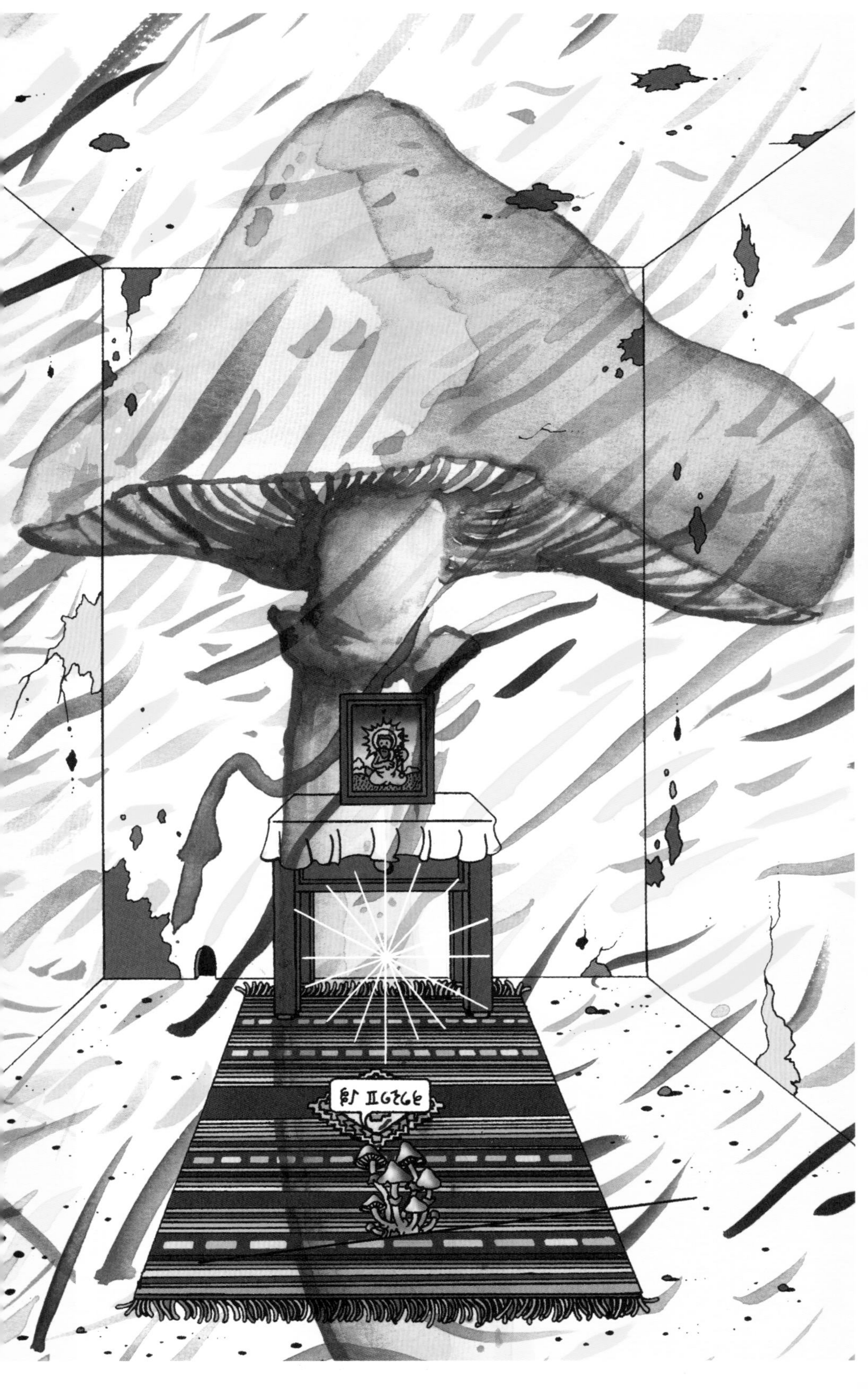

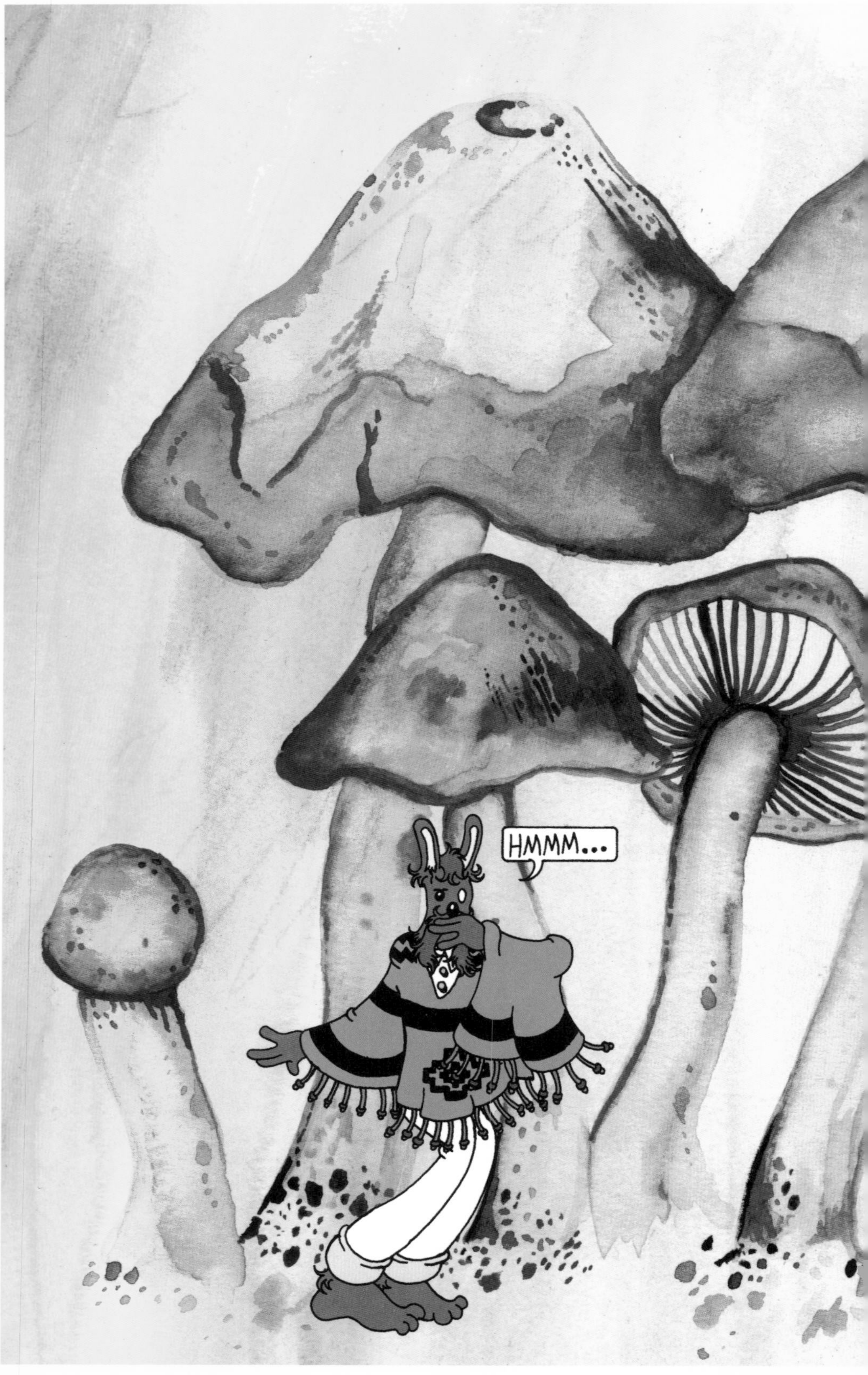
HMMM...

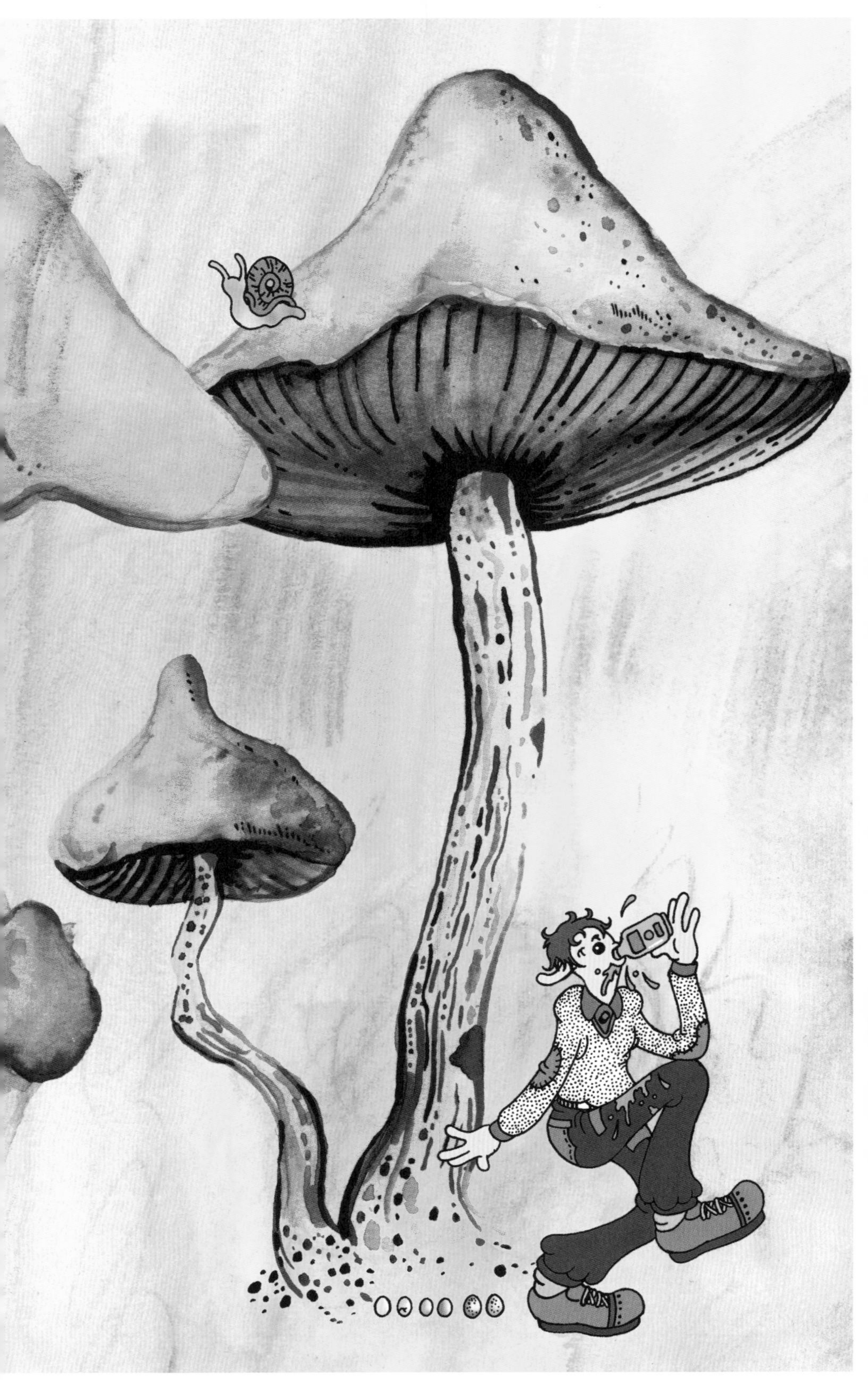

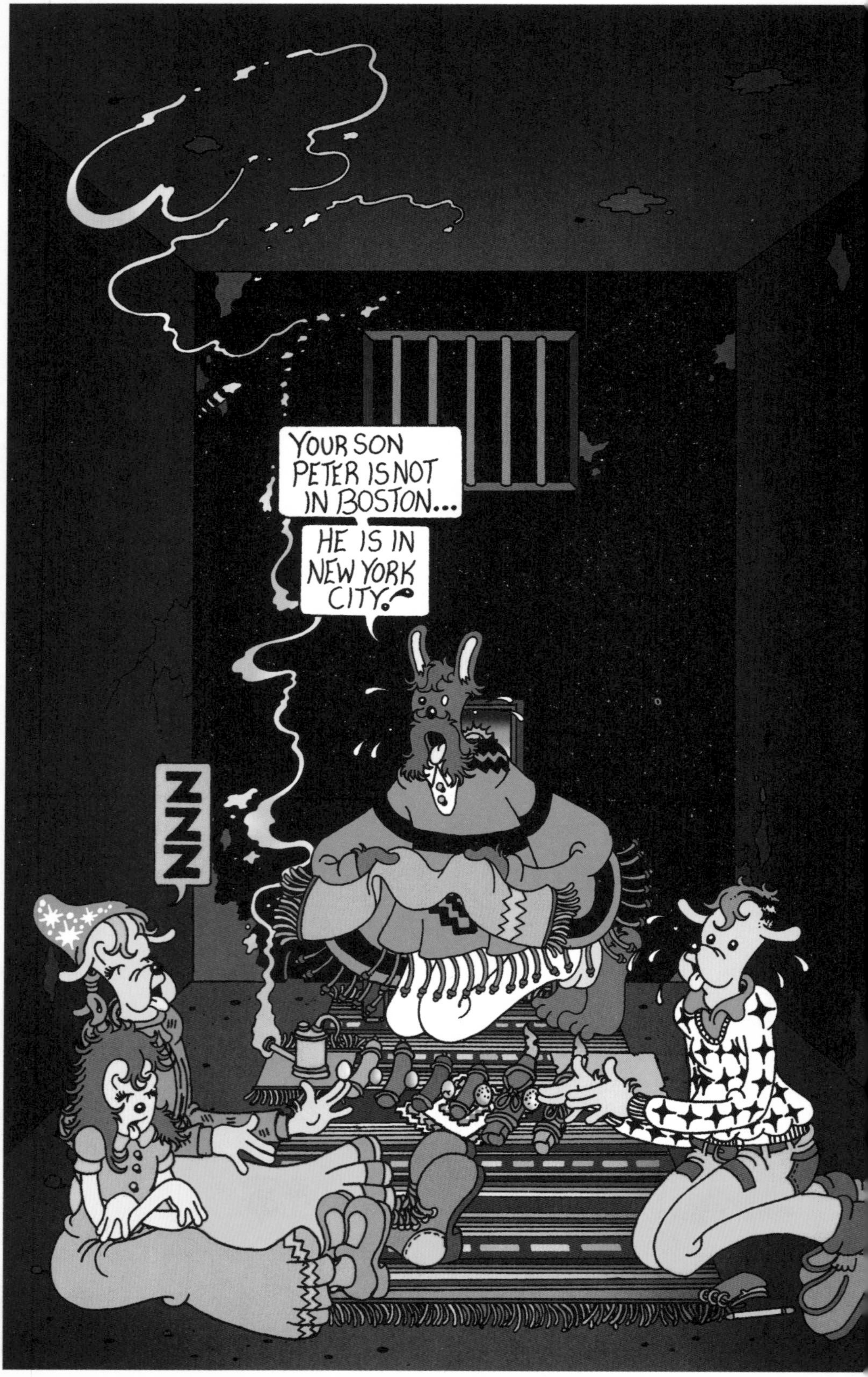
YOUR SON PETER IS NOT IN BOSTON...
HE IS IN NEW YORK CITY!
ZZZ

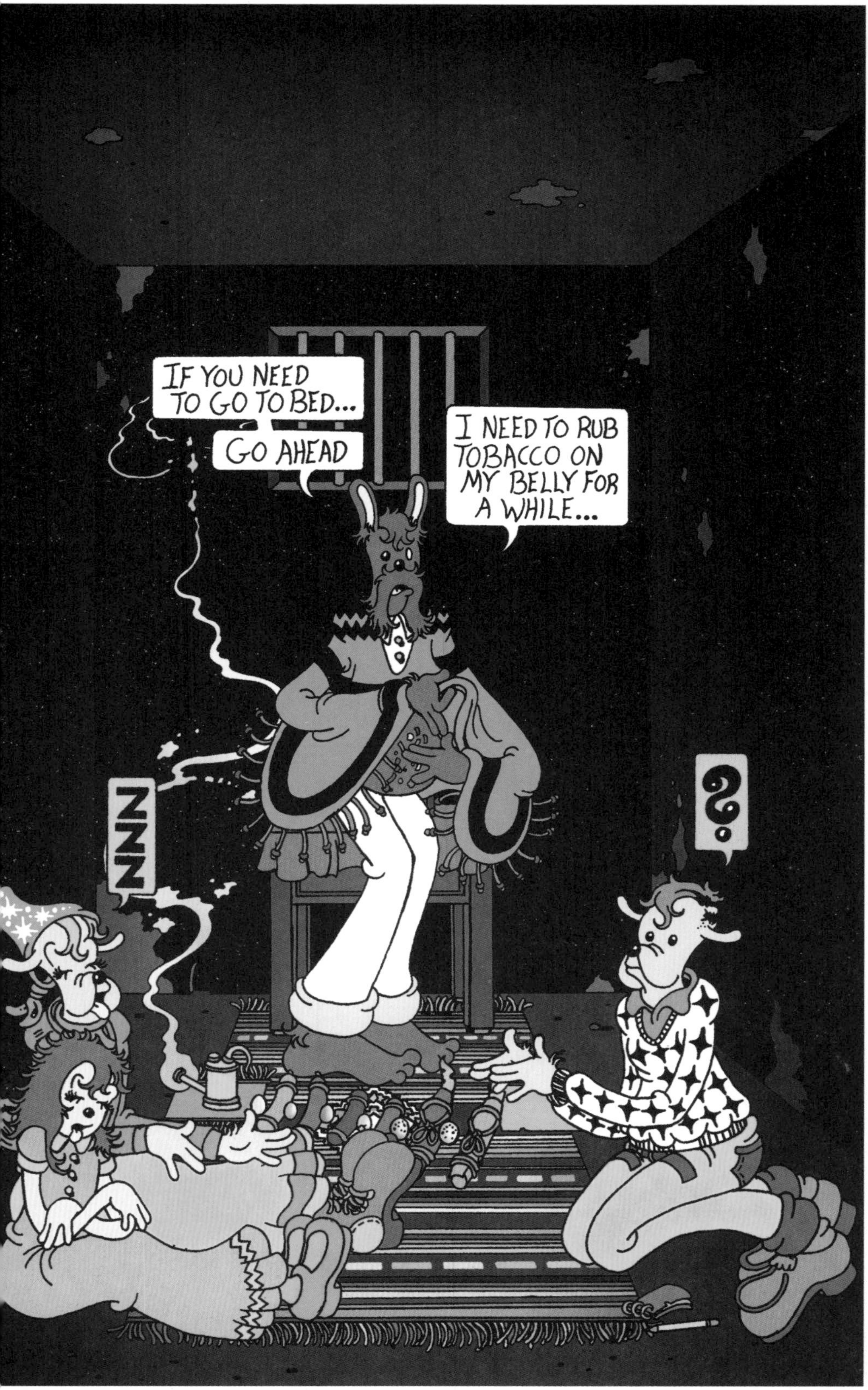
IF YOU NEED TO GO TO BED...
GO AHEAD
I NEED TO RUB TOBACCO ON MY BELLY FOR A WHILE...
ZZZ
?

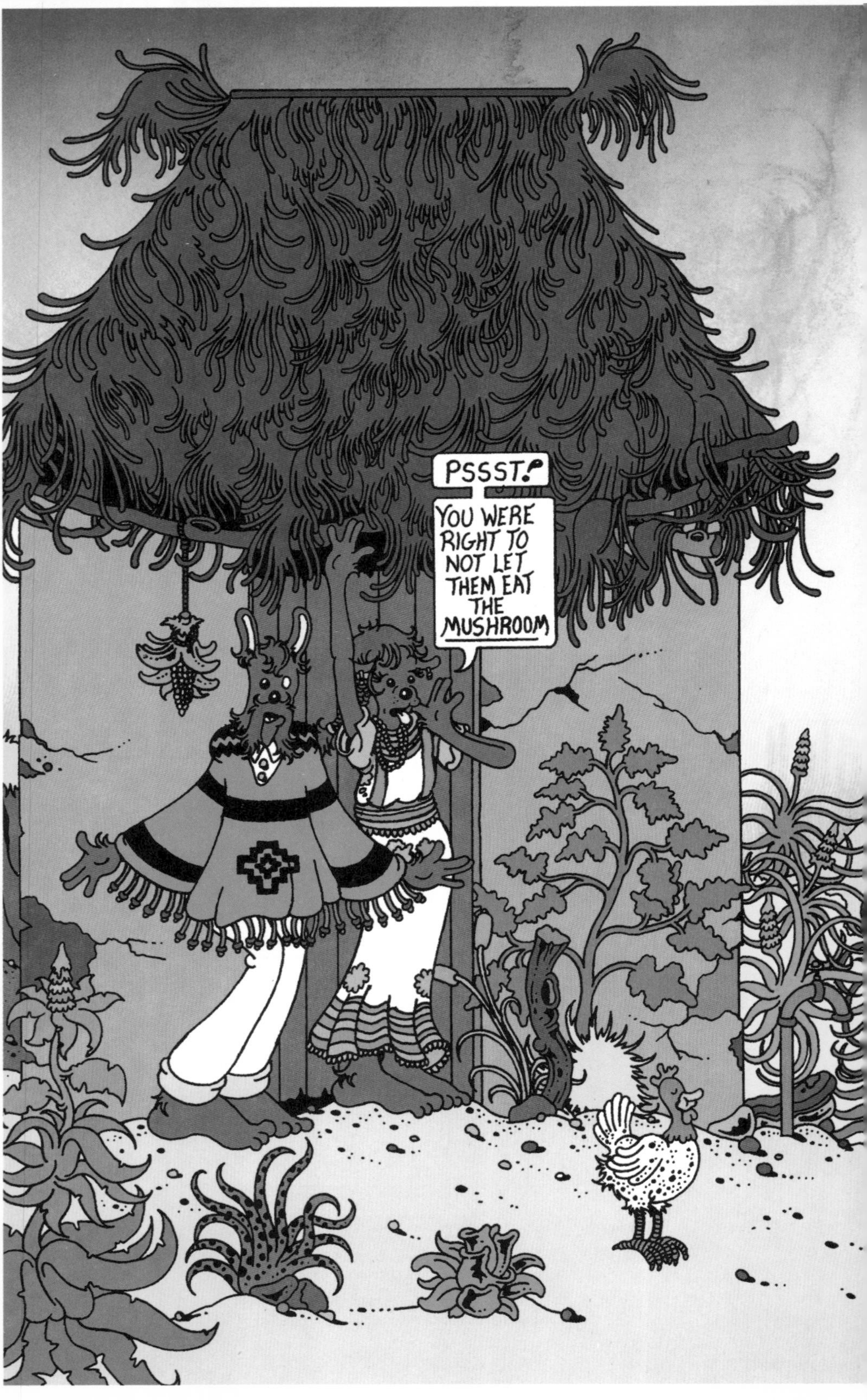
PSSST!
YOU WERE RIGHT TO NOT LET THEM EAT THE MUSHROOM

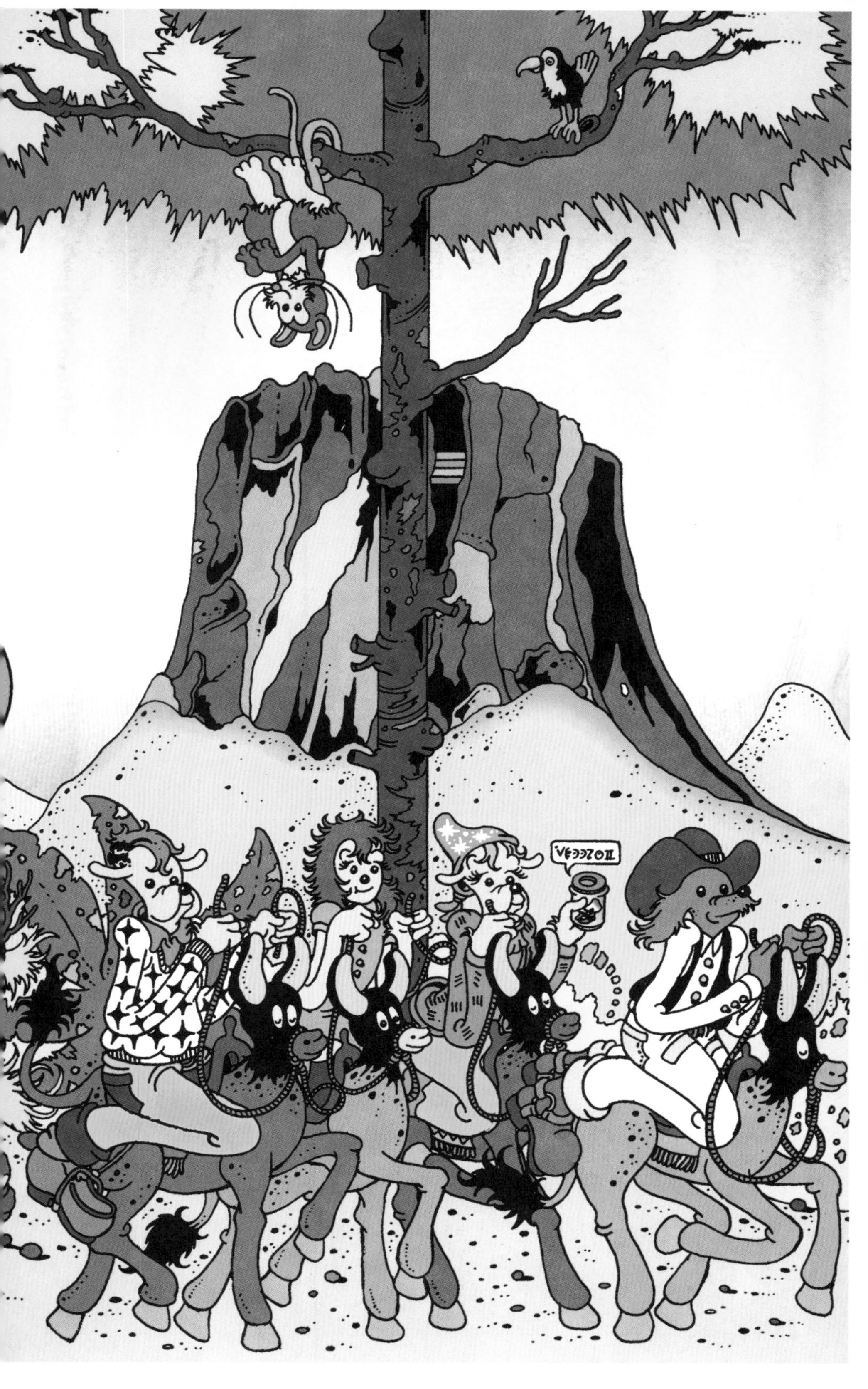

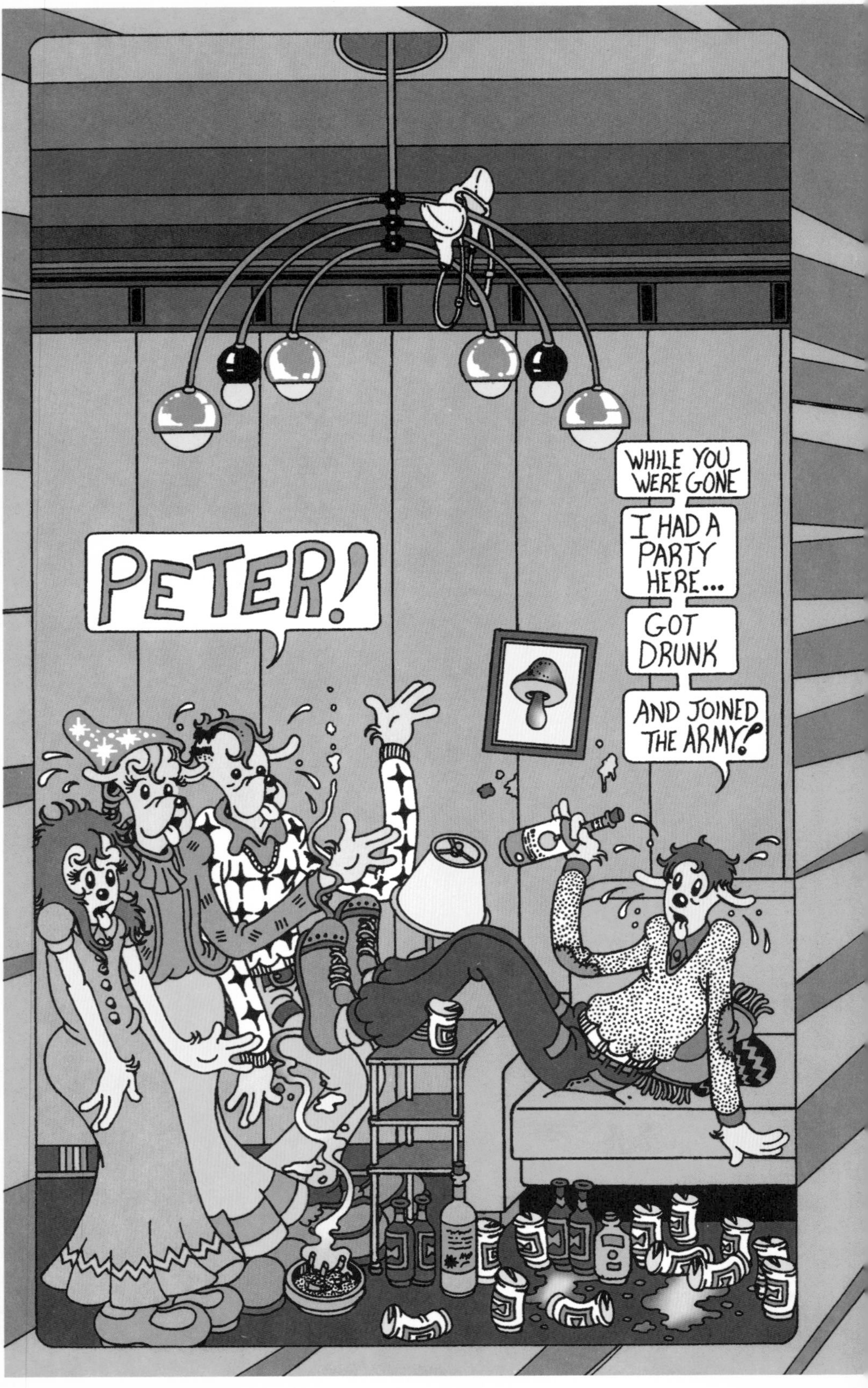
PETER!
WHILE YOU WERE GONE
I HAD A PARTY HERE...
GOT DRUNK
AND JOINED THE ARMY!

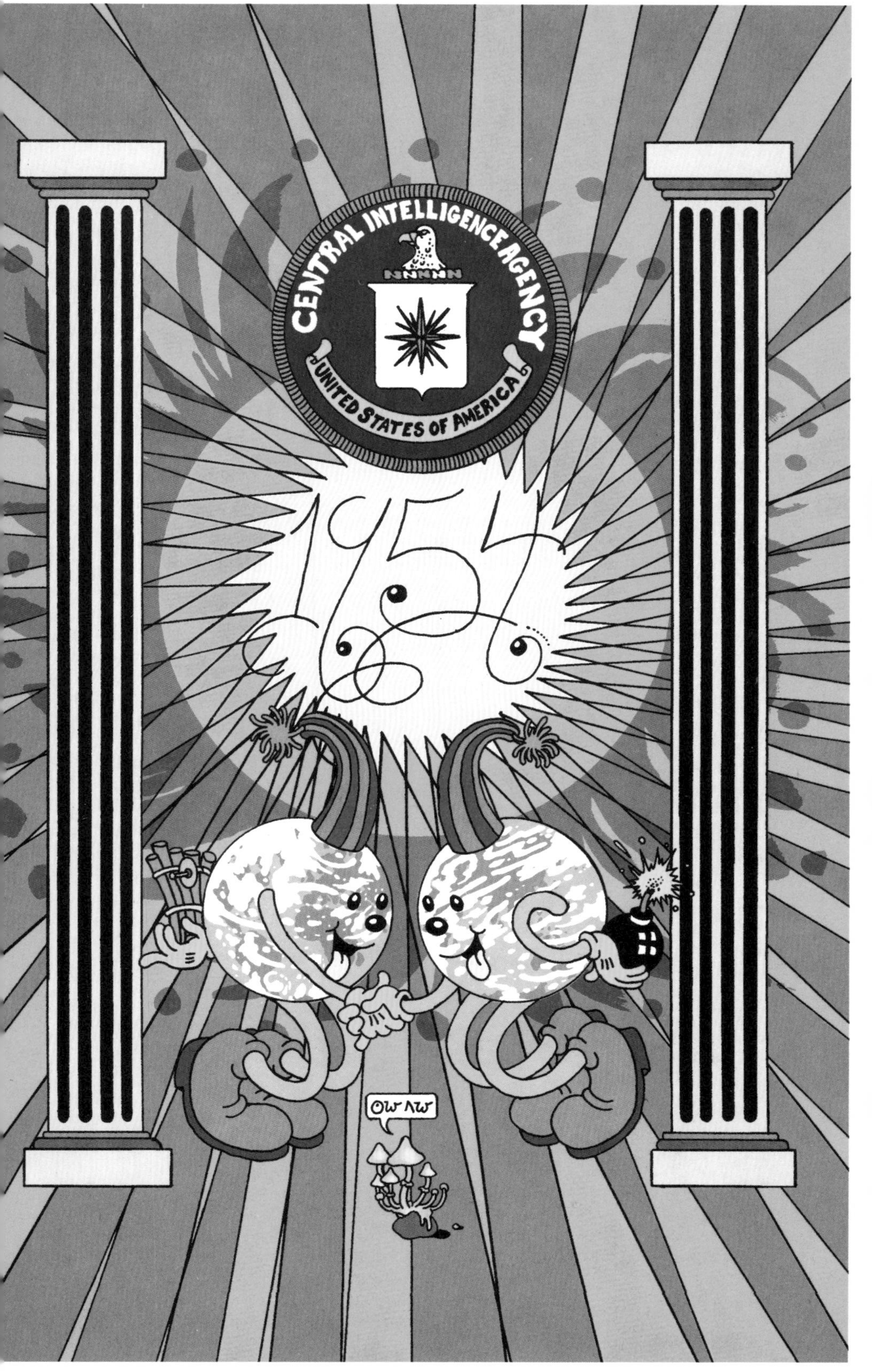
CENTRAL INTELLIGENCE AGENCY
UNITED STATES OF AMERICA

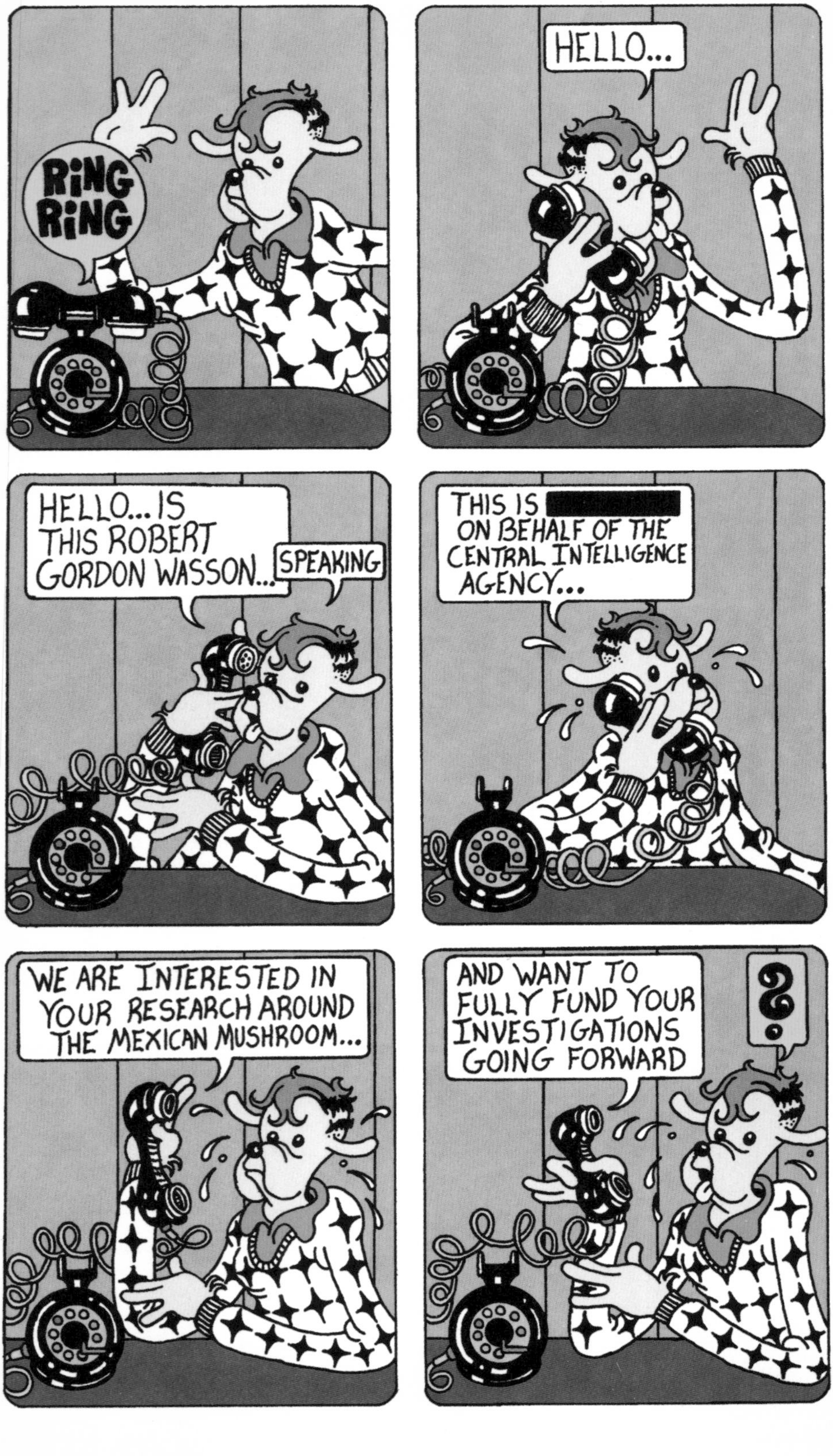
RING RING
HELLO...
HELLO... IS THIS ROBERT GORDON WASSON...
SPEAKING
THIS IS [redacted] ON BEHALF OF THE CENTRAL INTELLIGENCE AGENCY...
WE ARE INTERESTED IN YOUR RESEARCH AROUND THE MEXICAN MUSHROOM...
AND WANT TO FULLY FUND YOUR INVESTIGATIONS GOING FORWARD
?

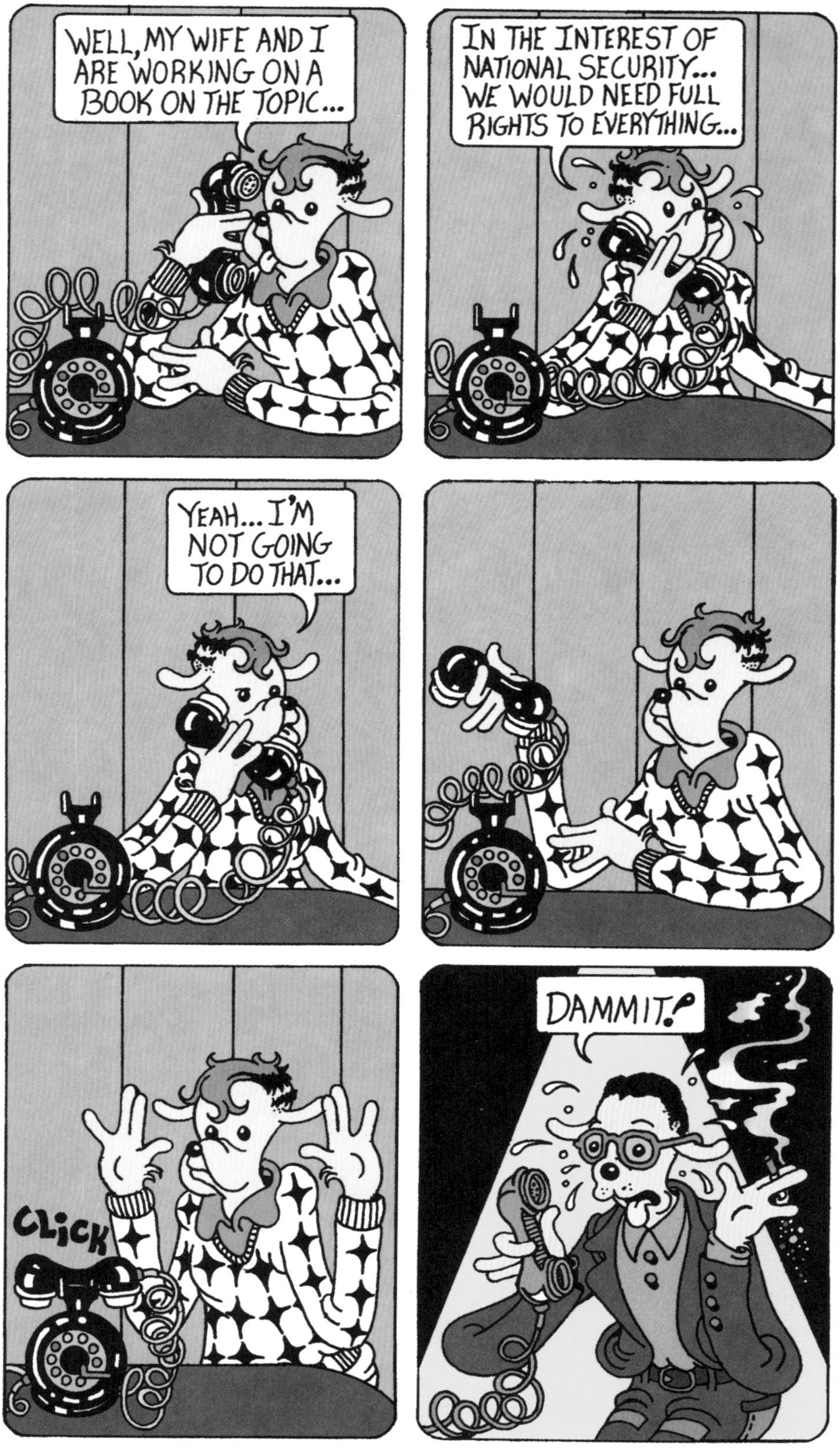
WELL, MY WIFE AND I ARE WORKING ON A BOOK ON THE TOPIC...
IN THE INTEREST OF NATIONAL SECURITY... WE WOULD NEED FULL RIGHTS TO EVERYTHING...
YEAH... I'M NOT GOING TO DO THAT...
CLICK
DAMMIT!

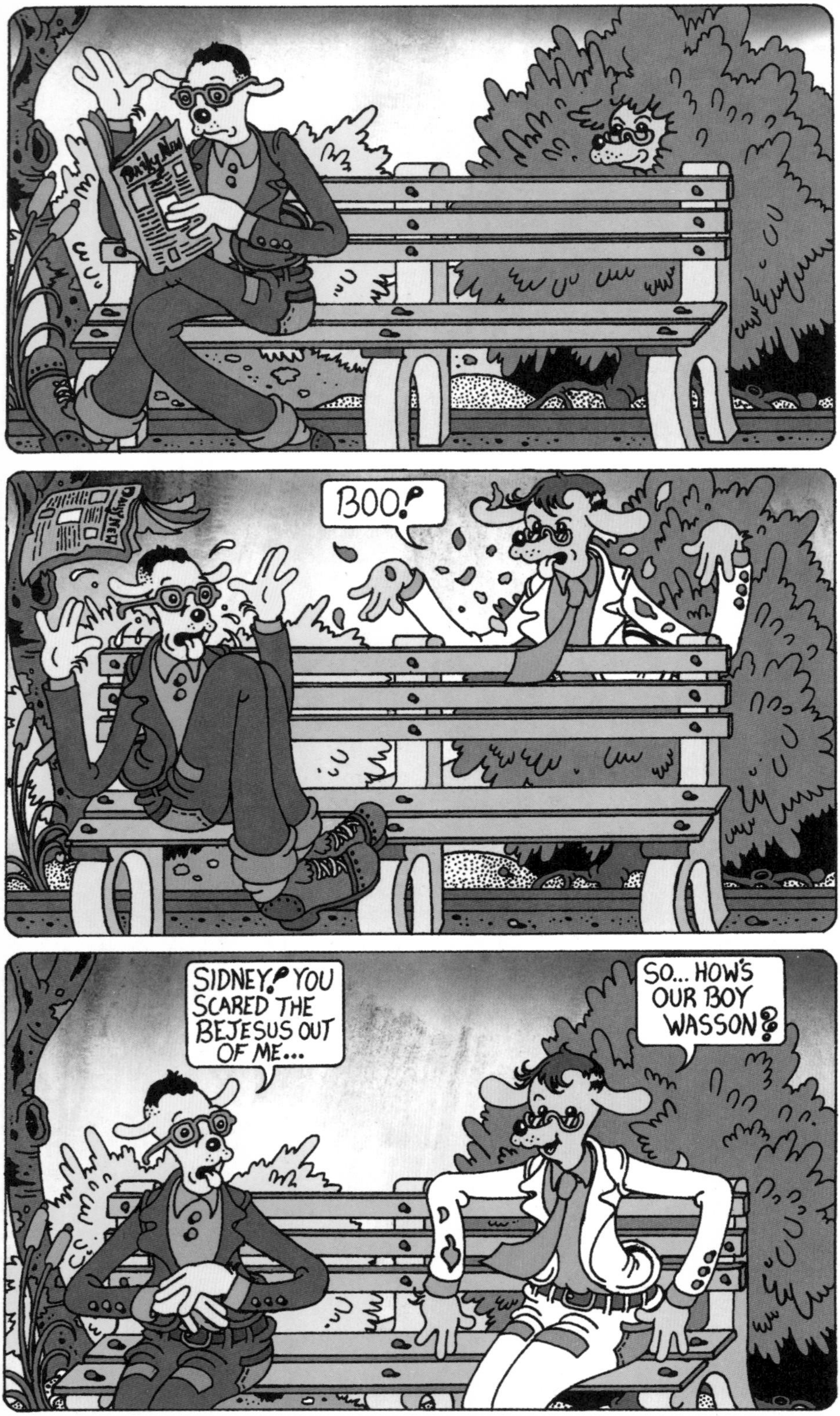
BOO!
SIDNEY! YOU SCARED THE BEJESUS OUT OF ME...
SO... HOW'S OUR BOY WASSON?

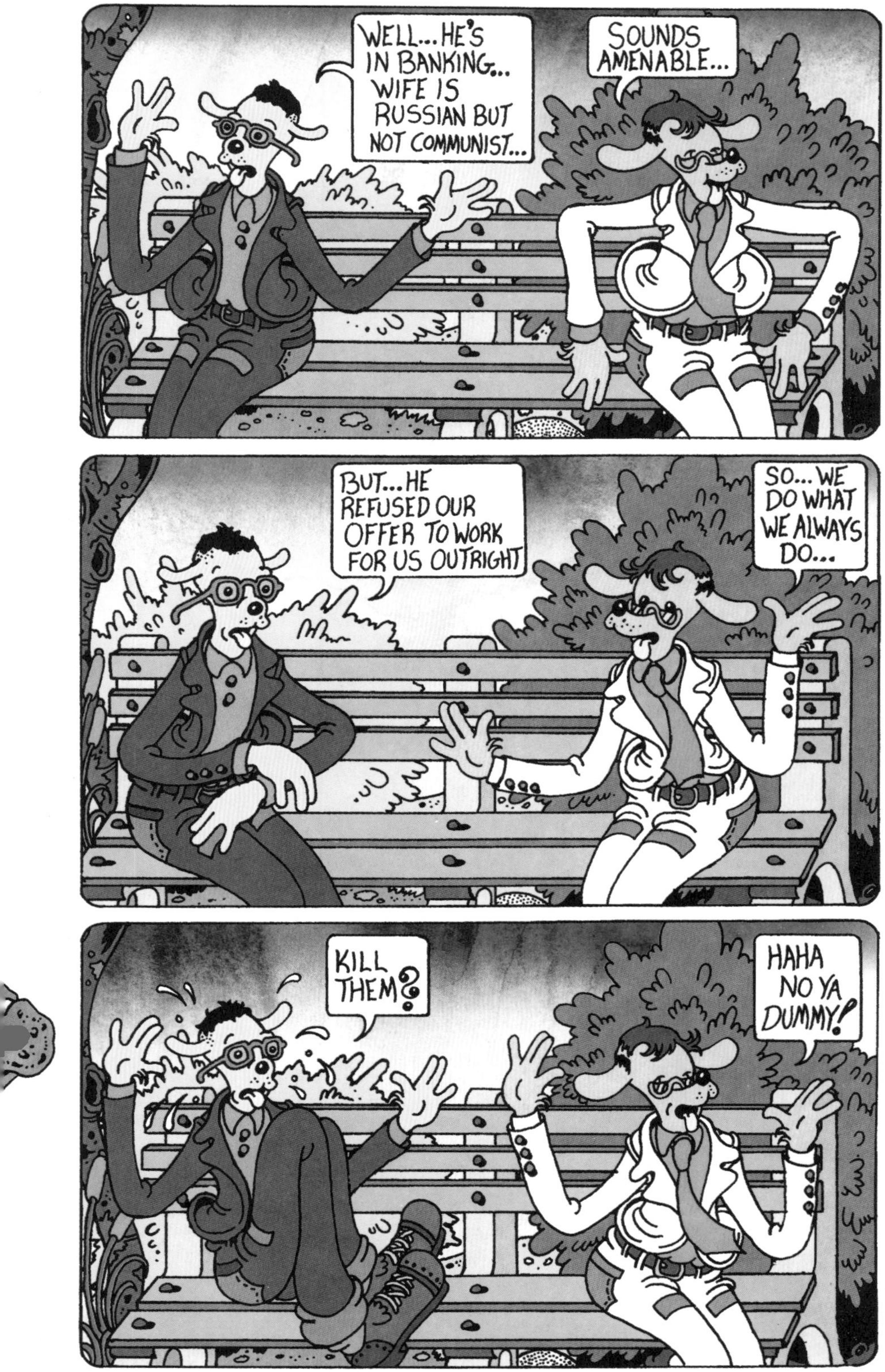
WELL...HE'S IN BANKING... WIFE IS RUSSIAN BUT NOT COMMUNIST...
SOUNDS AMENABLE...
BUT...HE REFUSED OUR OFFER TO WORK FOR US OUTRIGHT
SO... WE DO WHAT WE ALWAYS DO...
KILL THEM?
HAHA NO YA DUMMY!

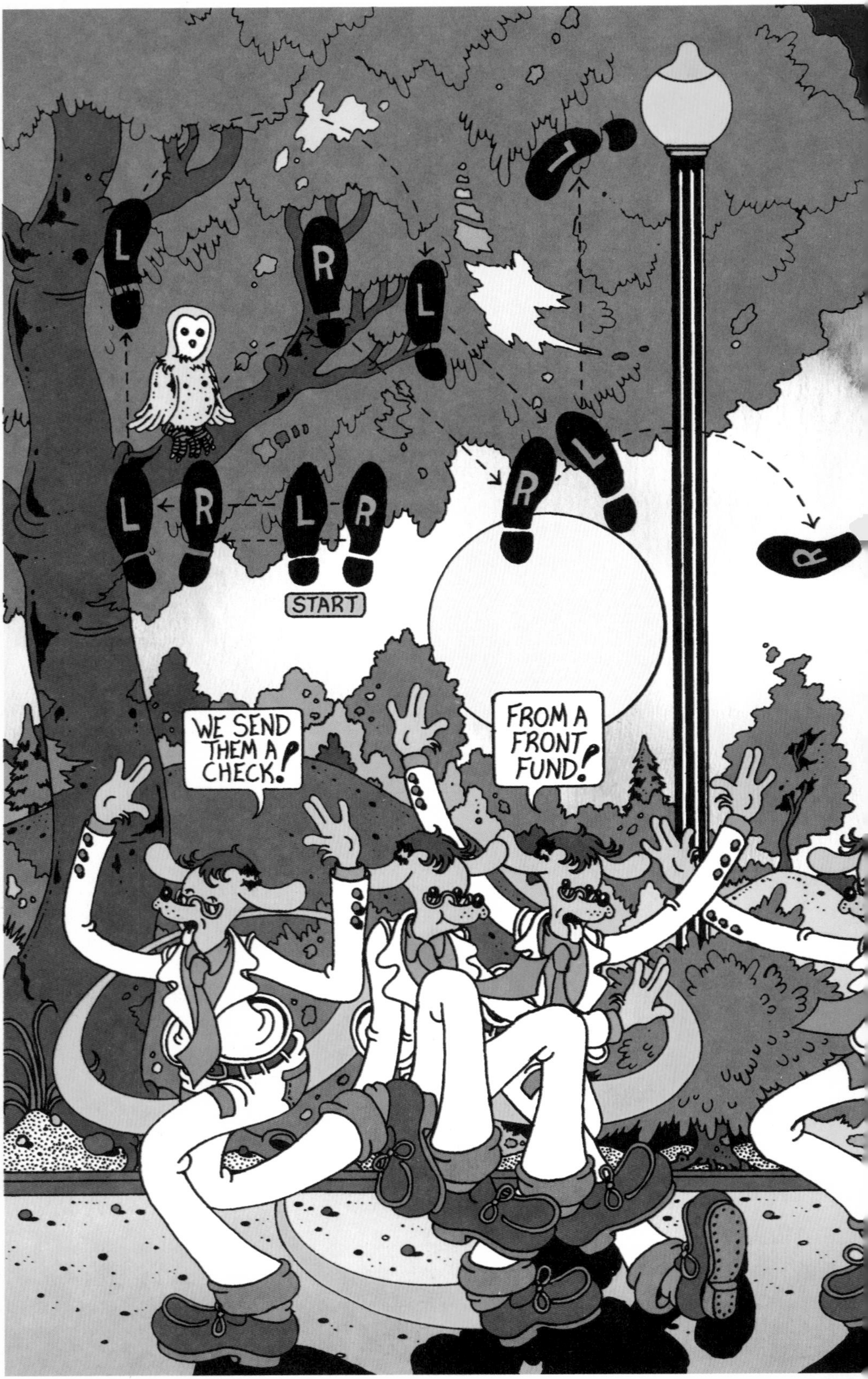
START
WE SEND THEM A CHECK!
FROM A FRONT FUND!

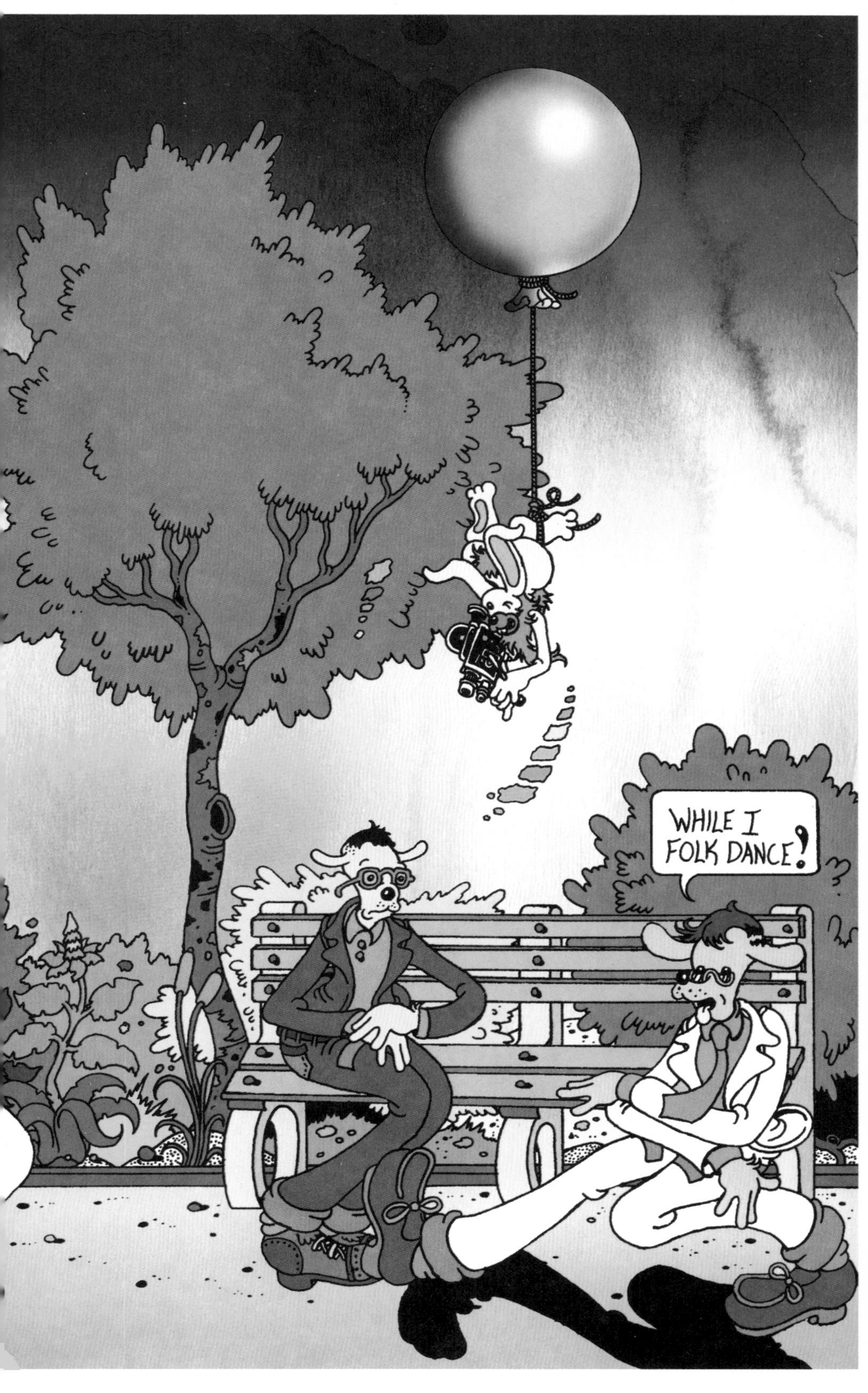
WHILE I FOLK DANCE?

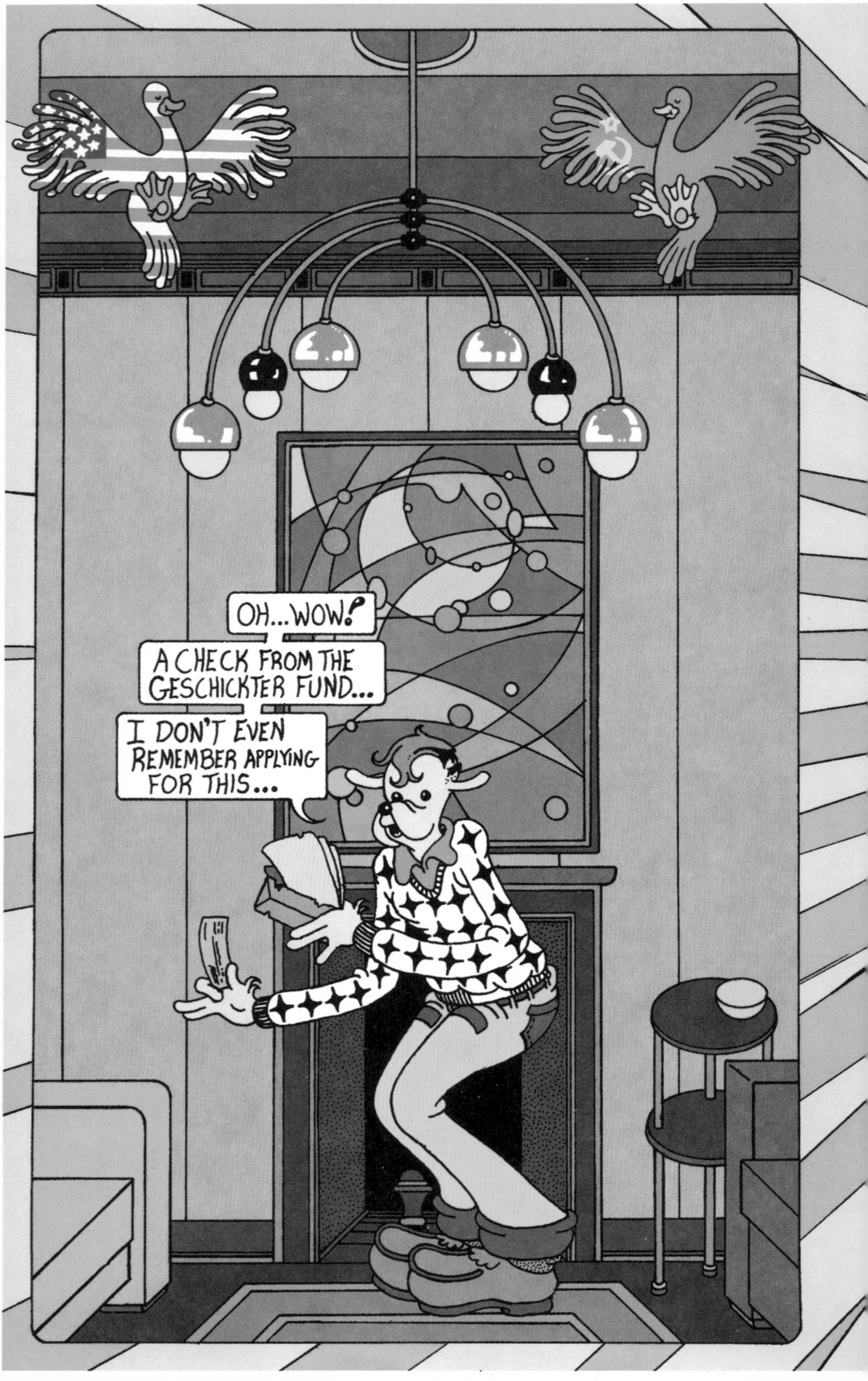
OH...WOW!
A CHECK FROM THE GESCHICKTER FUND...
I DON'T EVEN REMEMBER APPLYING FOR THIS...

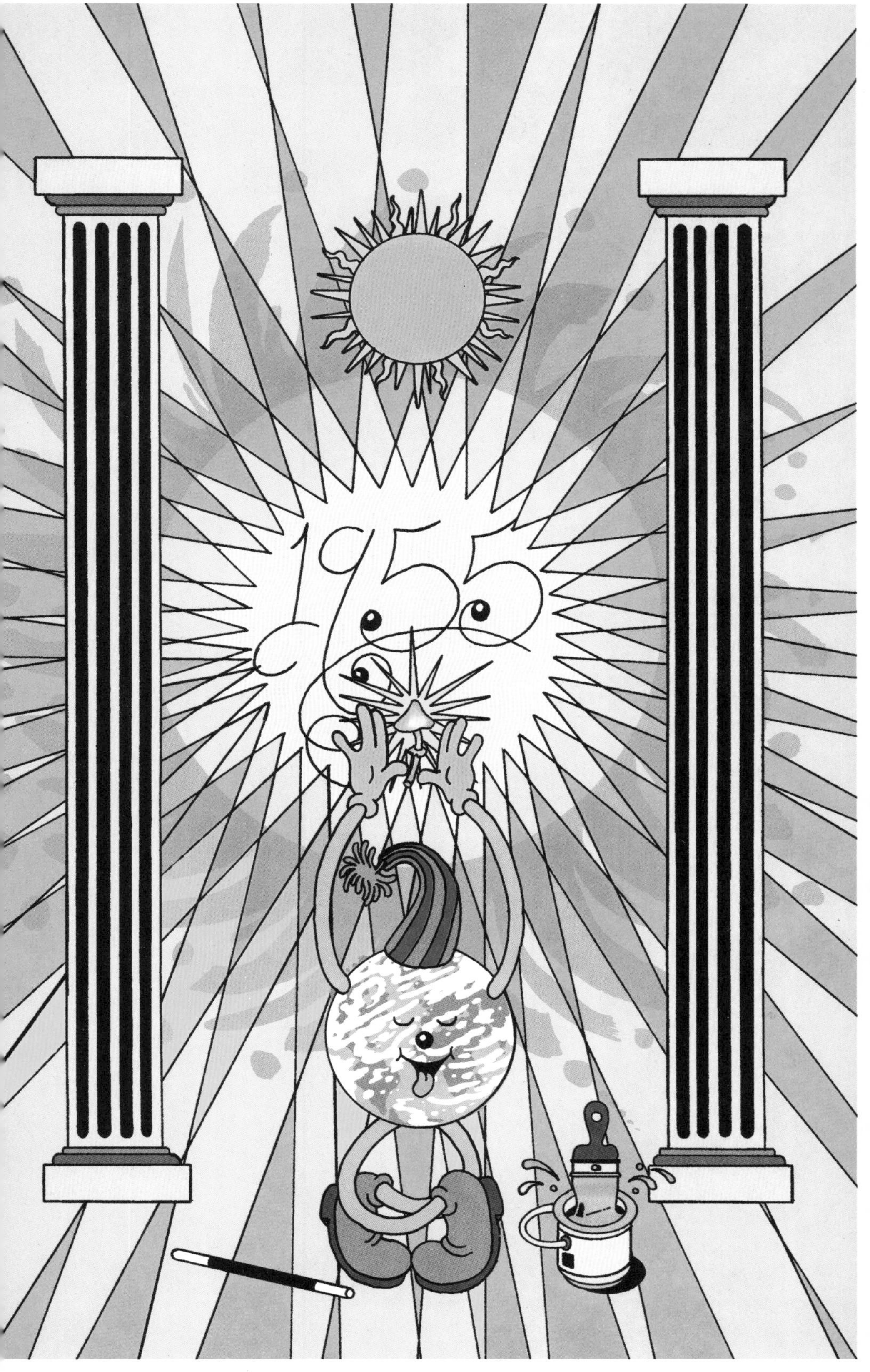
1955

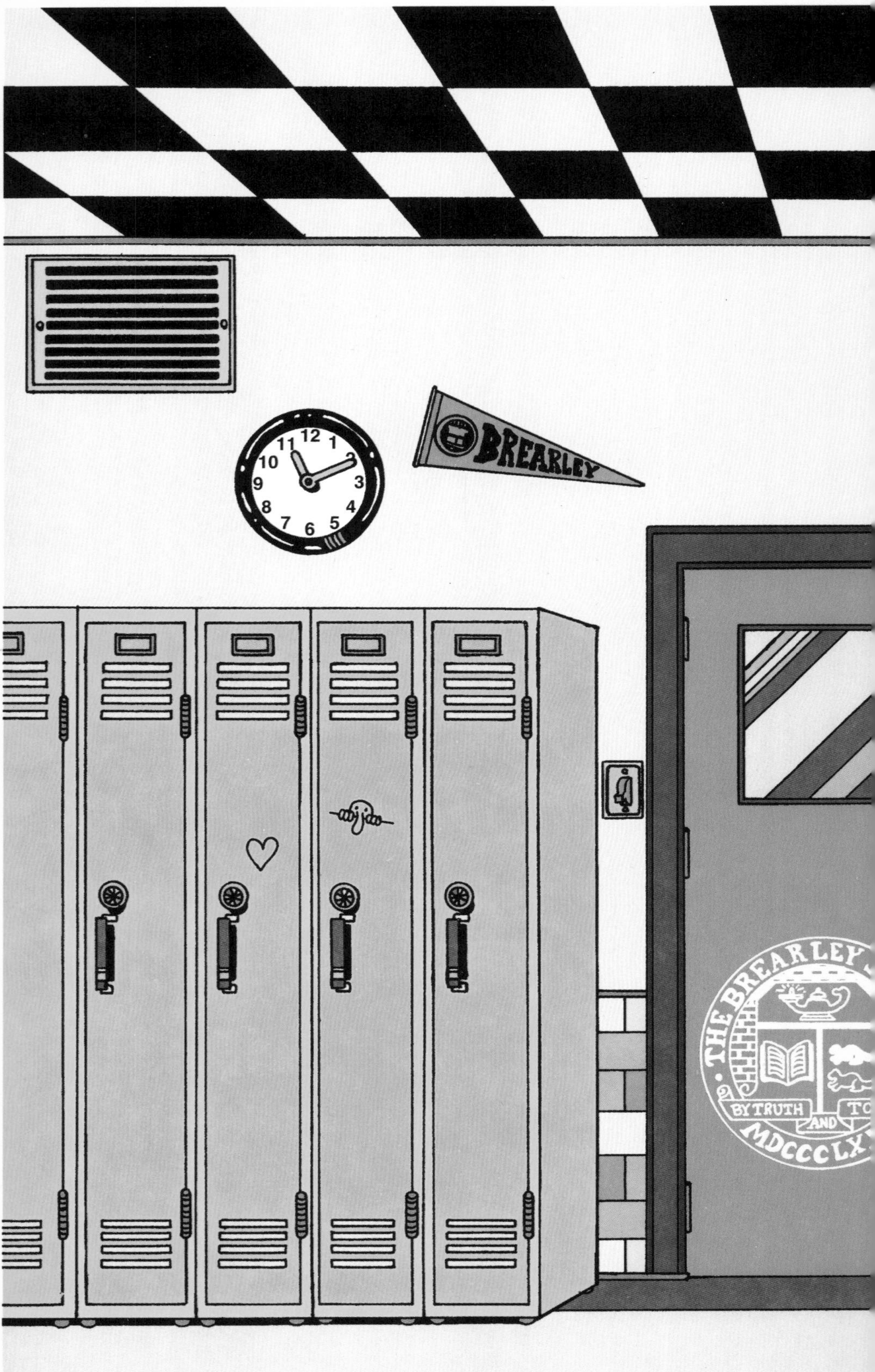
BREARLEY
THE BREARLEY
BY TRUTH
AND
MDCCCLX

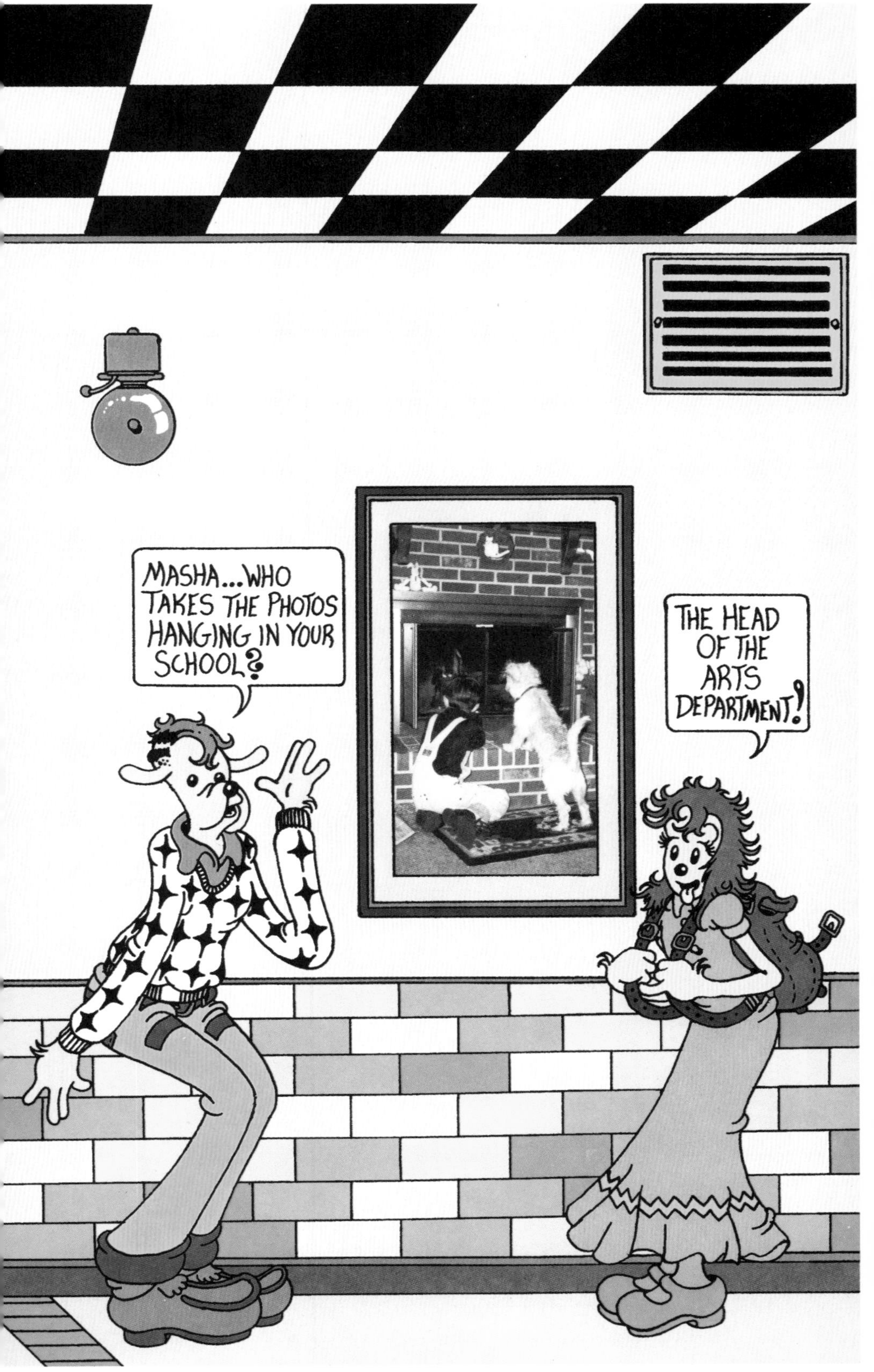
MASHA...WHO TAKES THE PHOTOS HANGING IN YOUR SCHOOL?
THE HEAD OF THE ARTS DEPARTMENT!

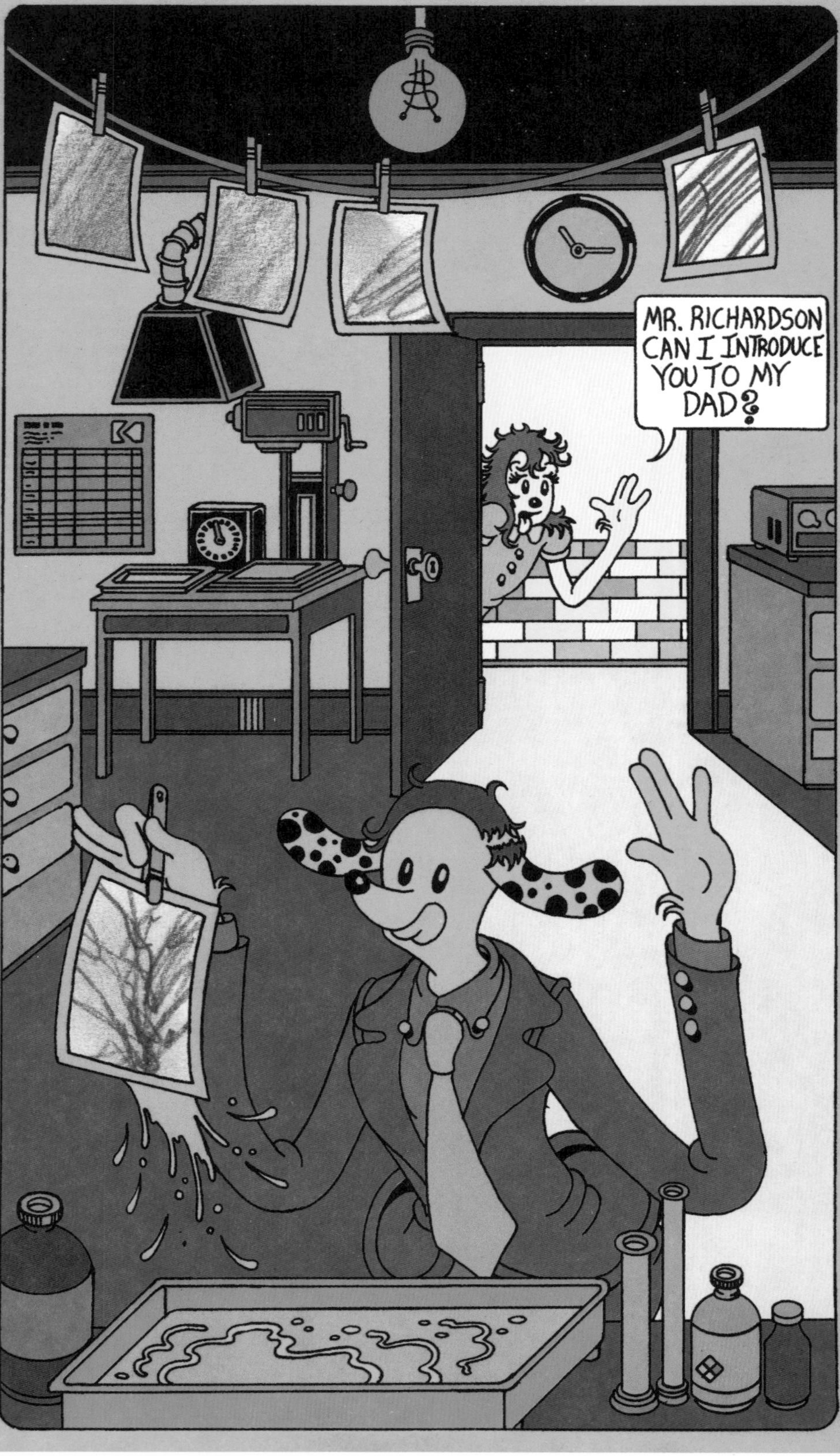
MR. RICHARDSON CAN I INTRODUCE YOU TO MY DAD?

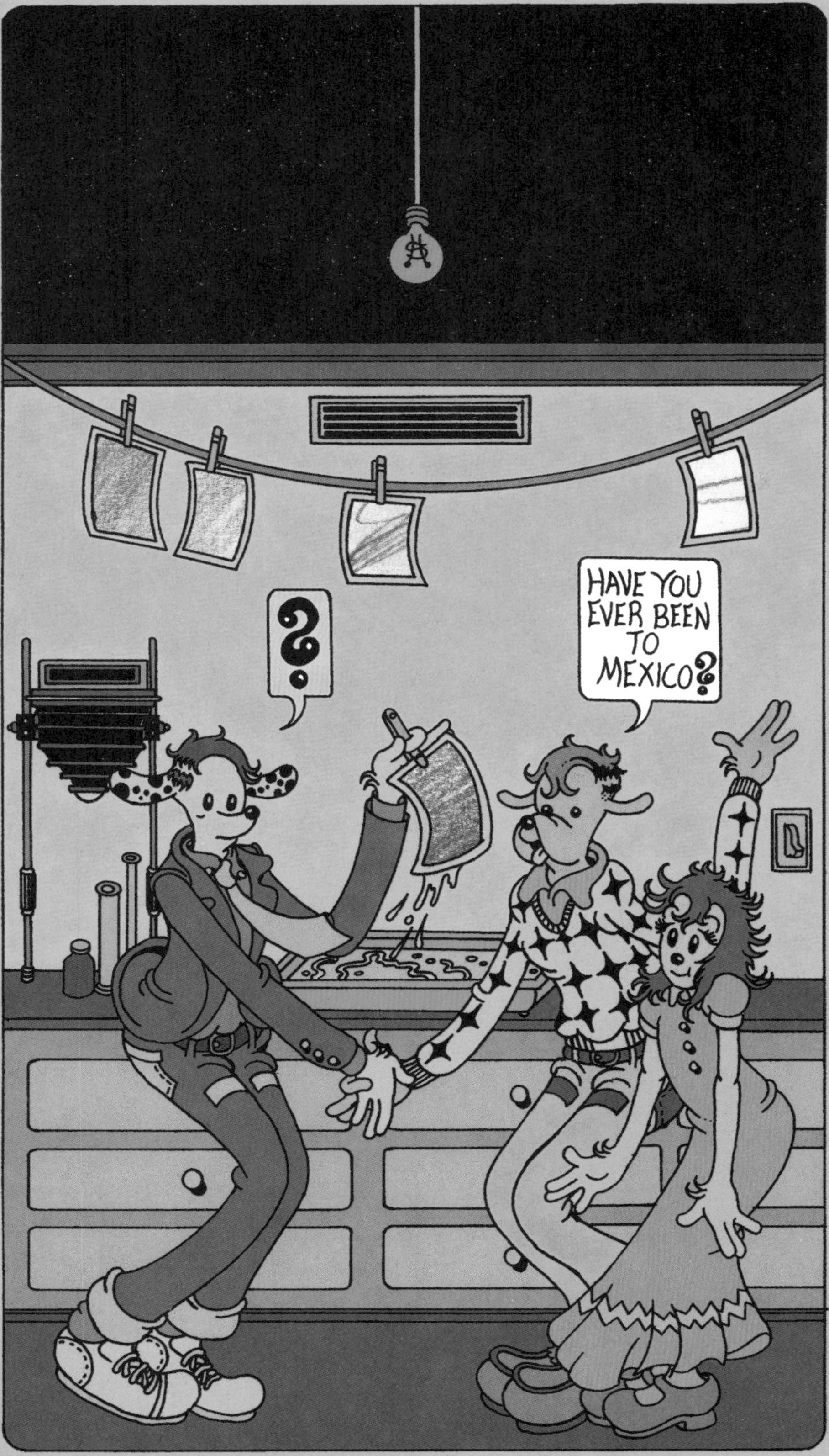
?
HAVE YOU EVER BEEN TO MEXICO?

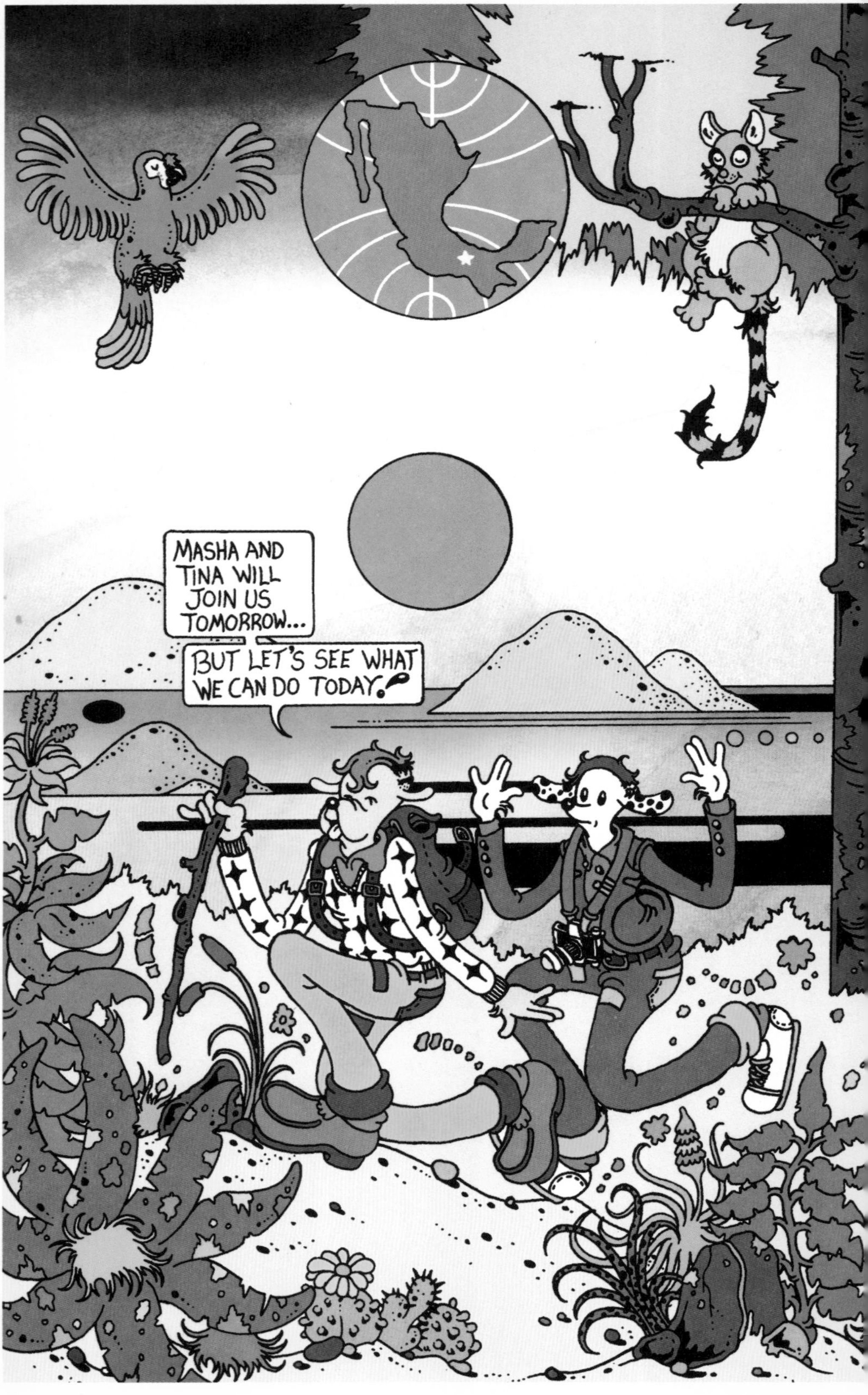
MASHA AND TINA WILL JOIN US TOMORROW...
BUT LET'S SEE WHAT WE CAN DO TODAY!

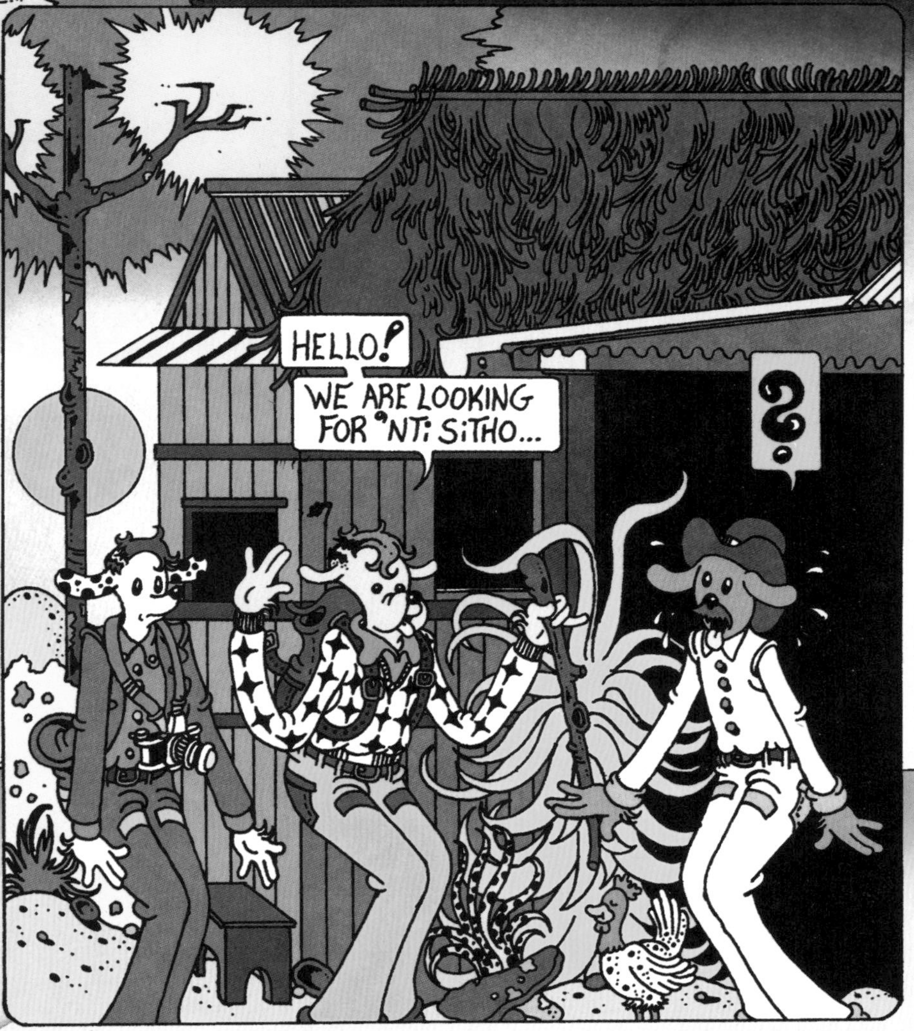
HELLO!
WE ARE LOOKING FOR 'NTi SiTHO...
?

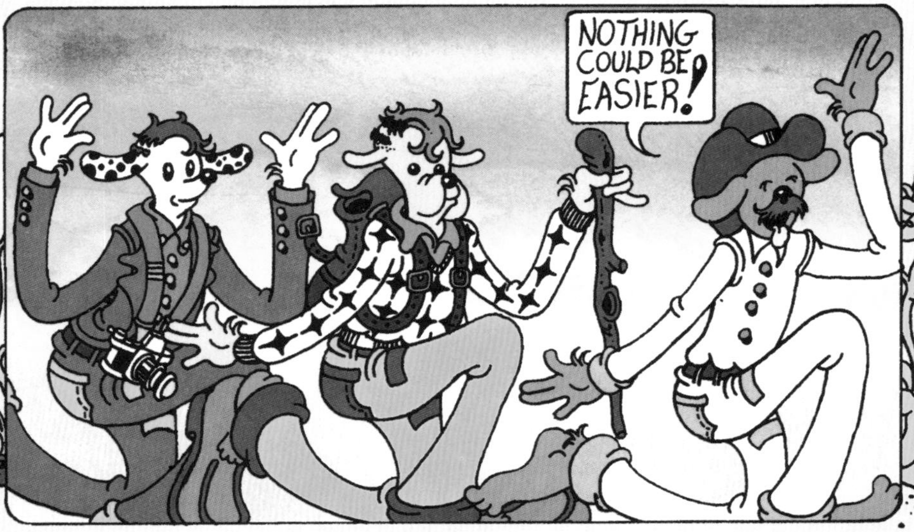
NOTHING COULD BE EASIER!

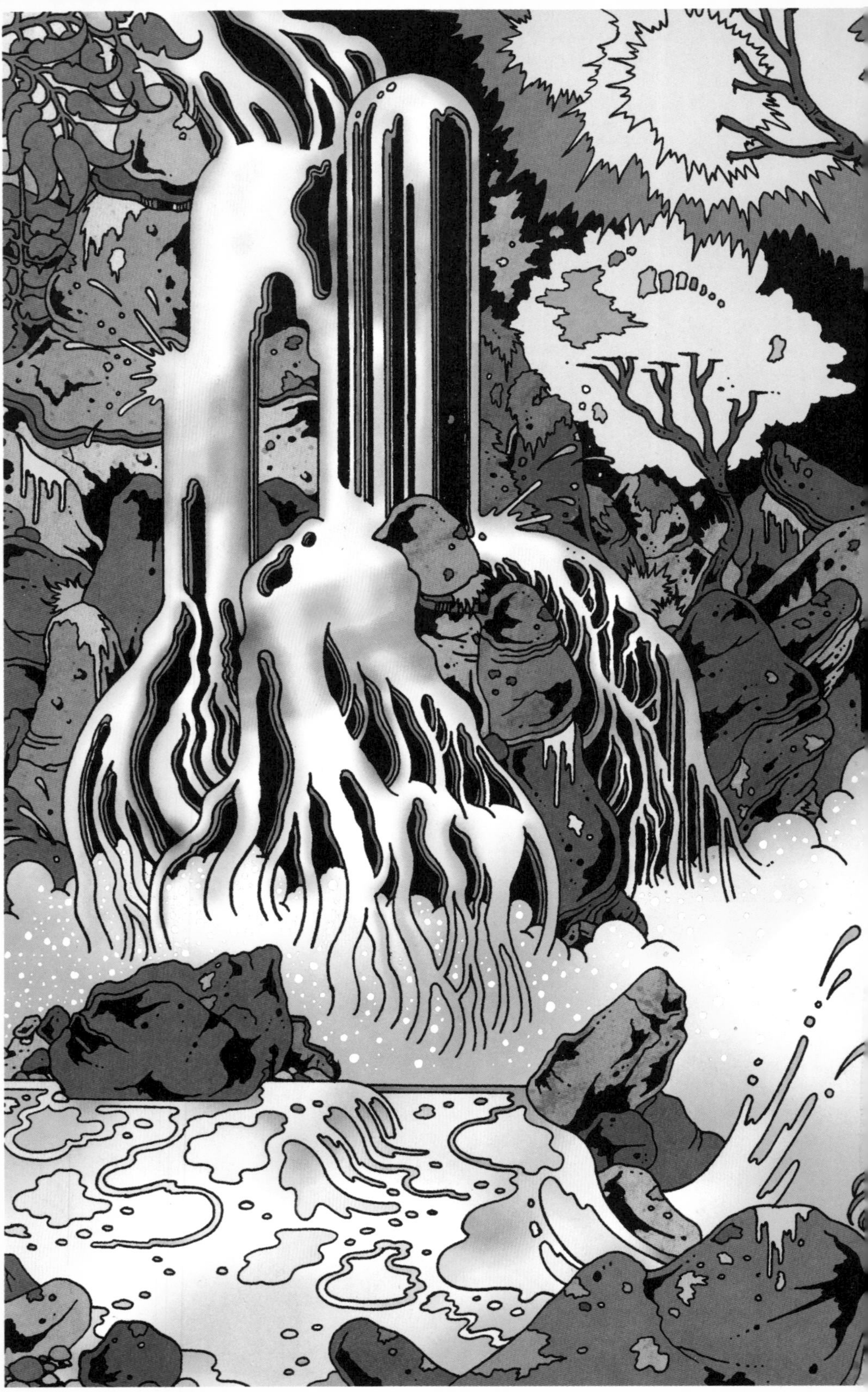

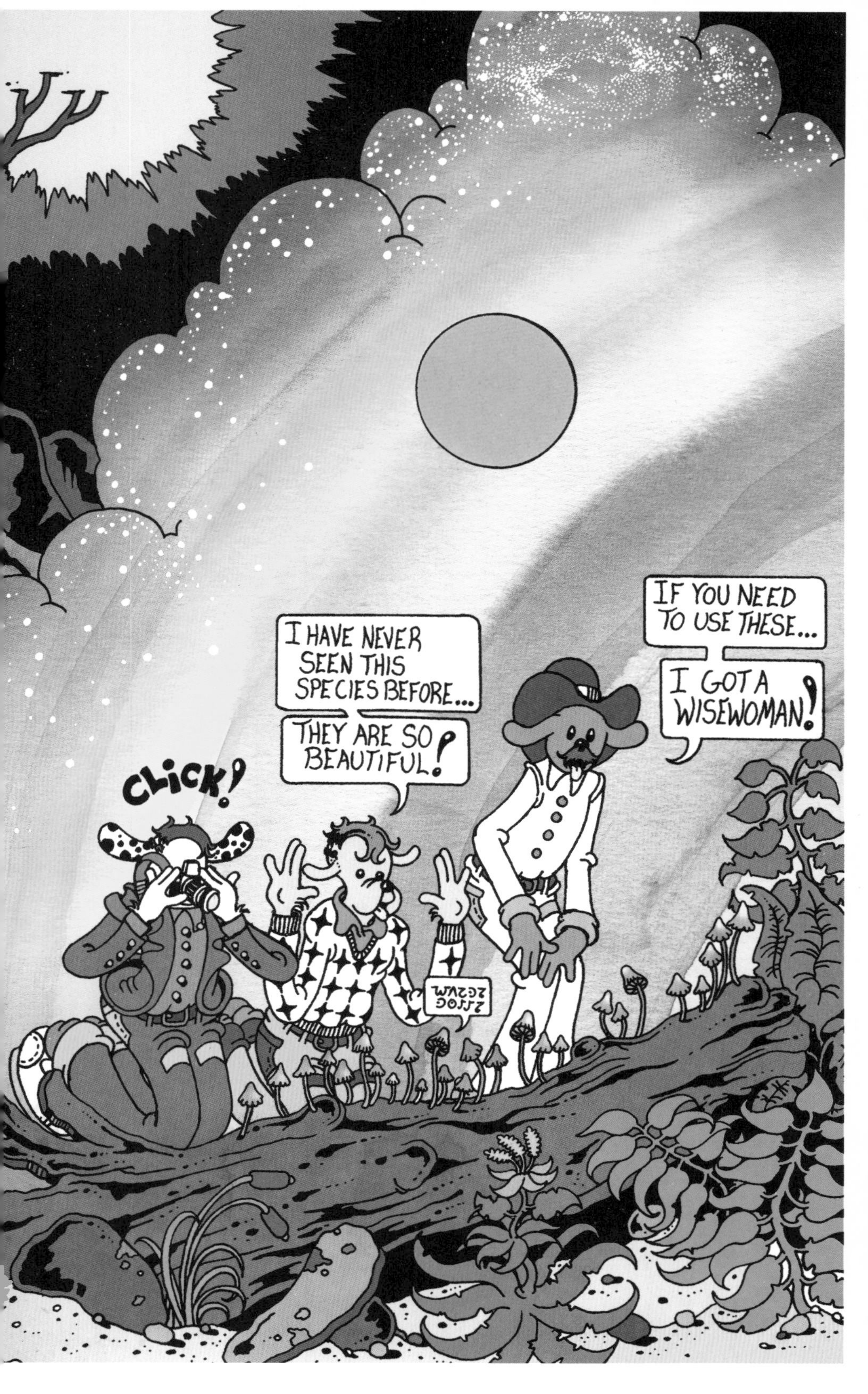
CLICK!
I HAVE NEVER SEEN THIS SPECIES BEFORE...
THEY ARE SO BEAUTIFUL!
IF YOU NEED TO USE THESE...
I GOT A WISEWOMAN!

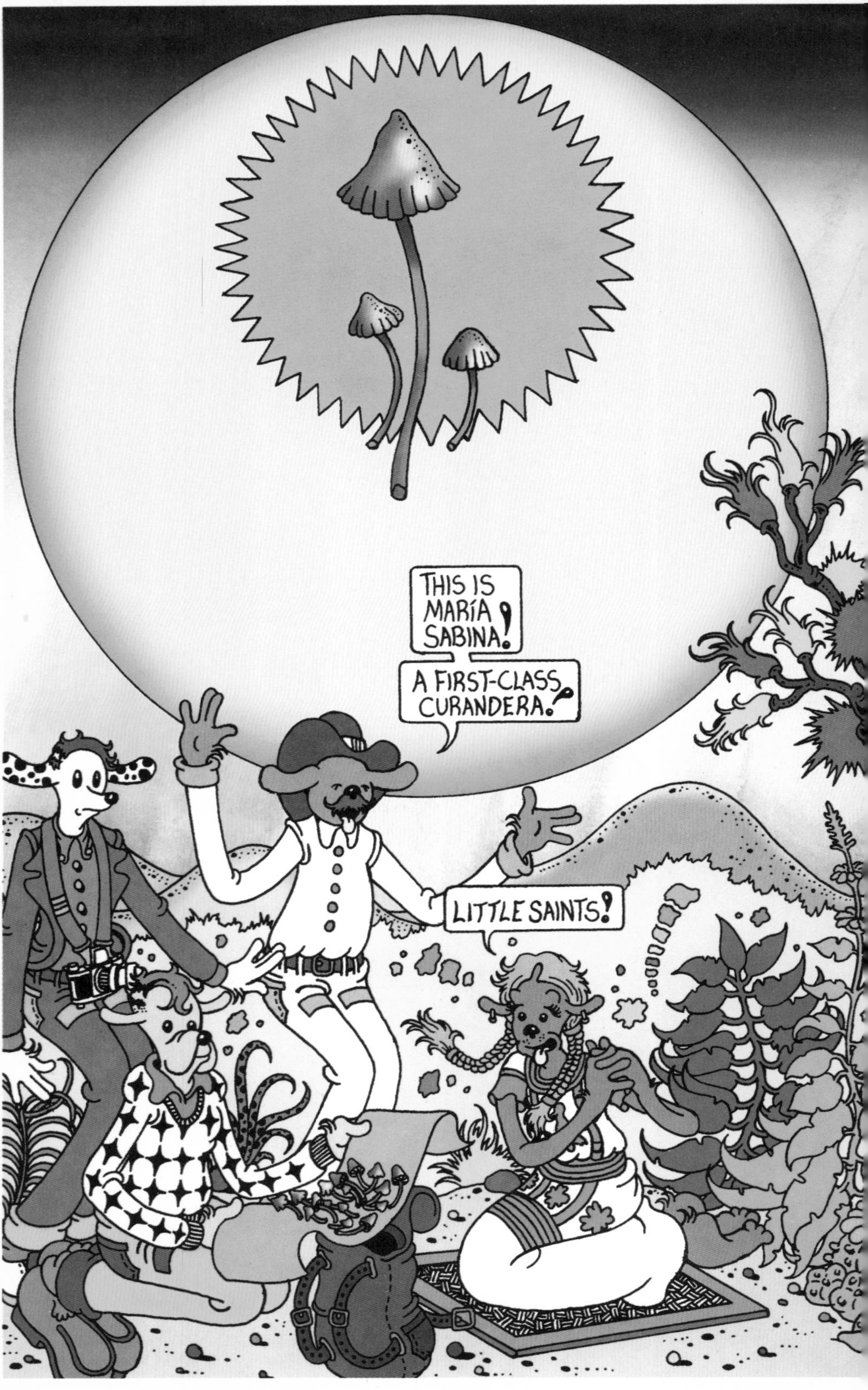
THIS IS MARÍA SABINA!
A FIRST-CLASS CURANDERA!
LITTLE SAINTS!

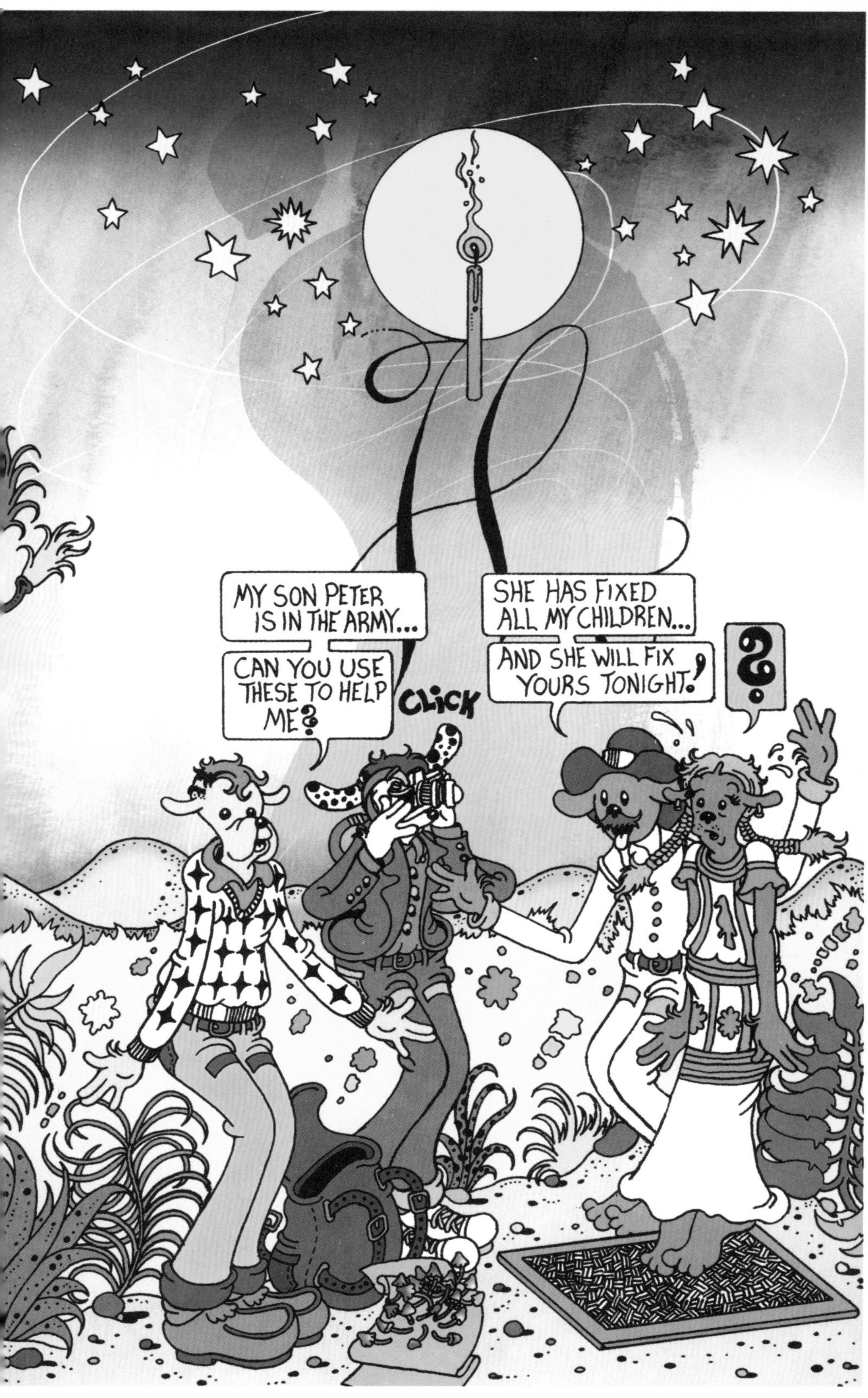
MY SON PETER IS IN THE ARMY...
CAN YOU USE THESE TO HELP ME?
CLICK
SHE HAS FIXED ALL MY CHILDREN...
AND SHE WILL FIX YOURS TONIGHT!
?

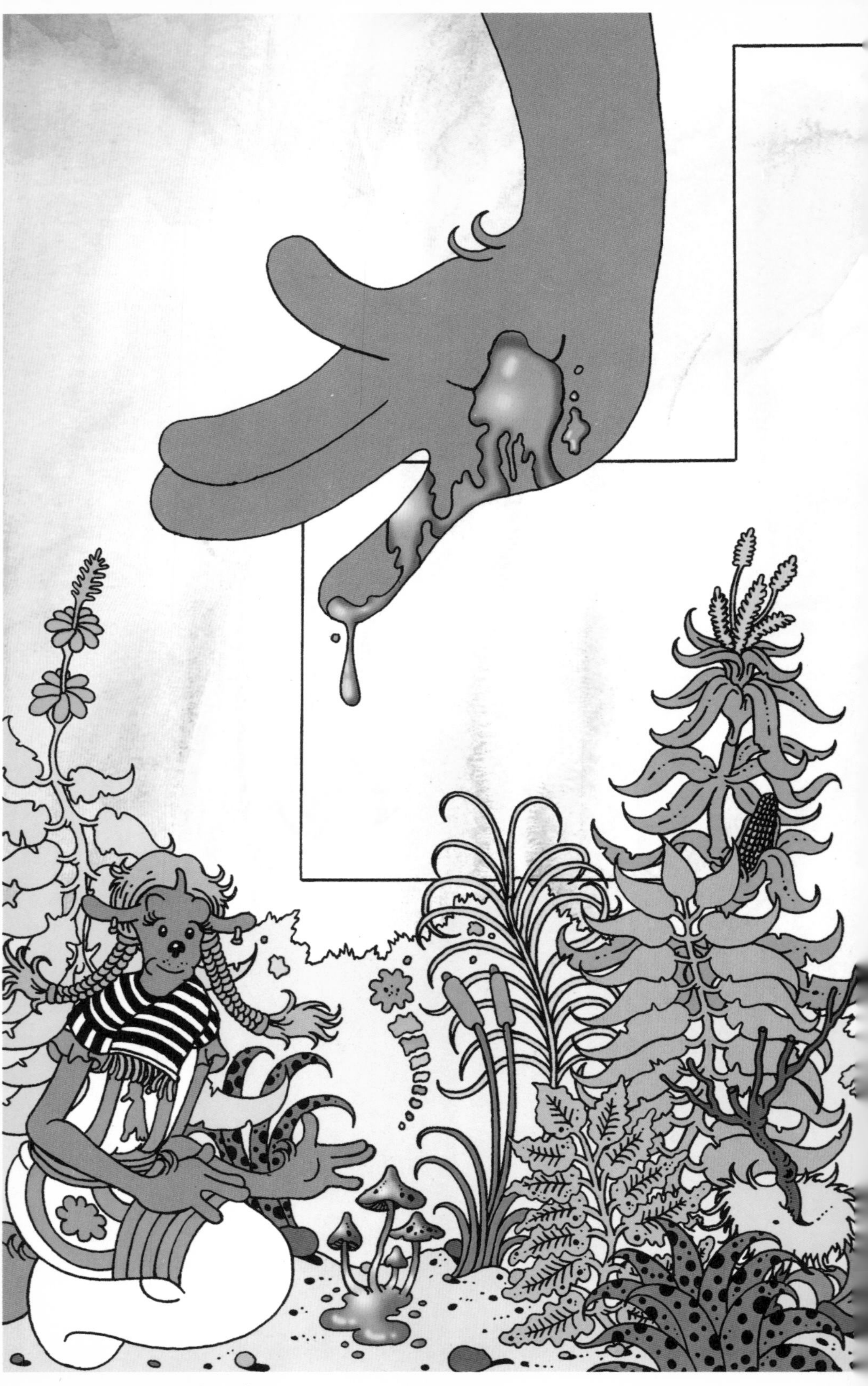

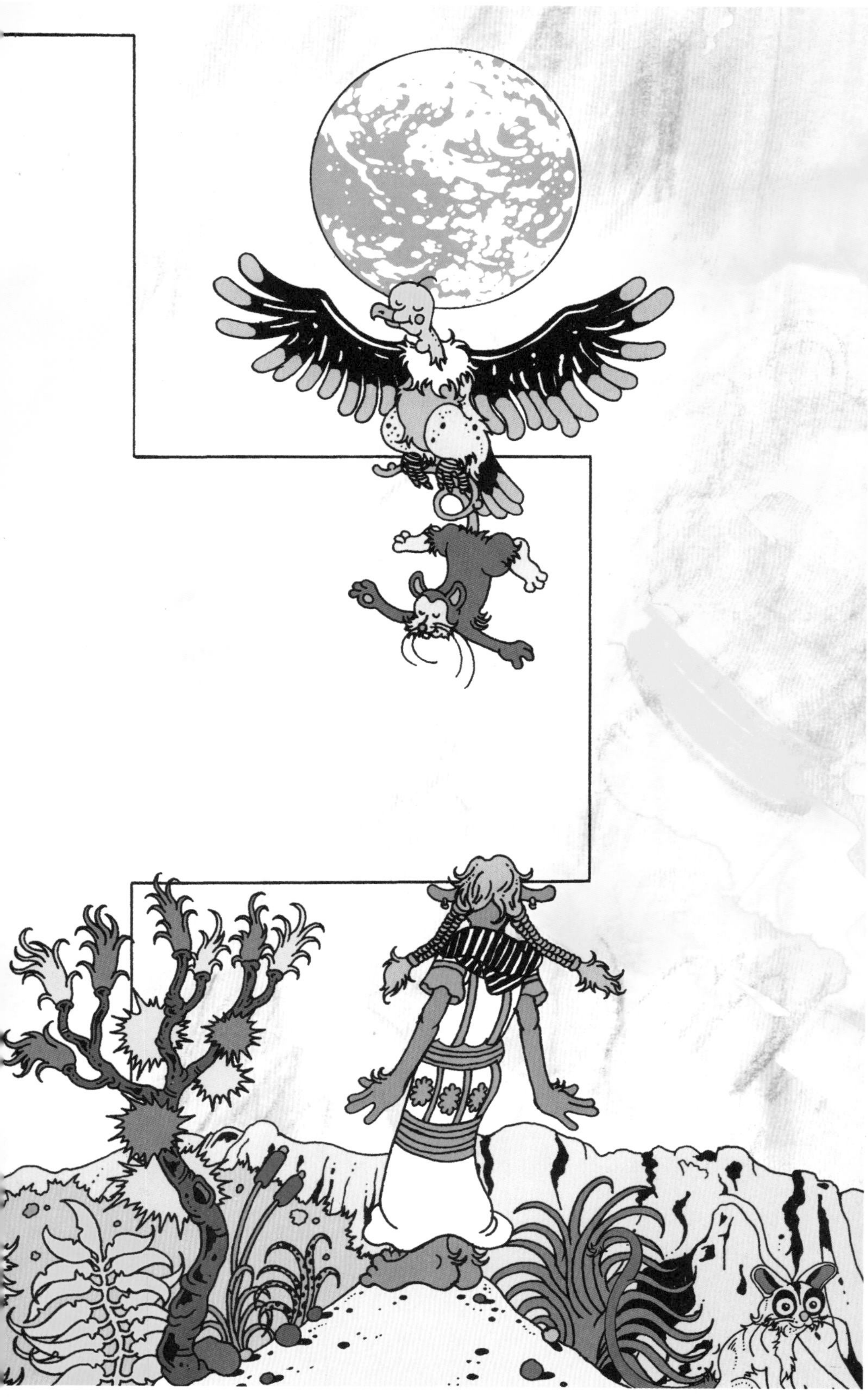

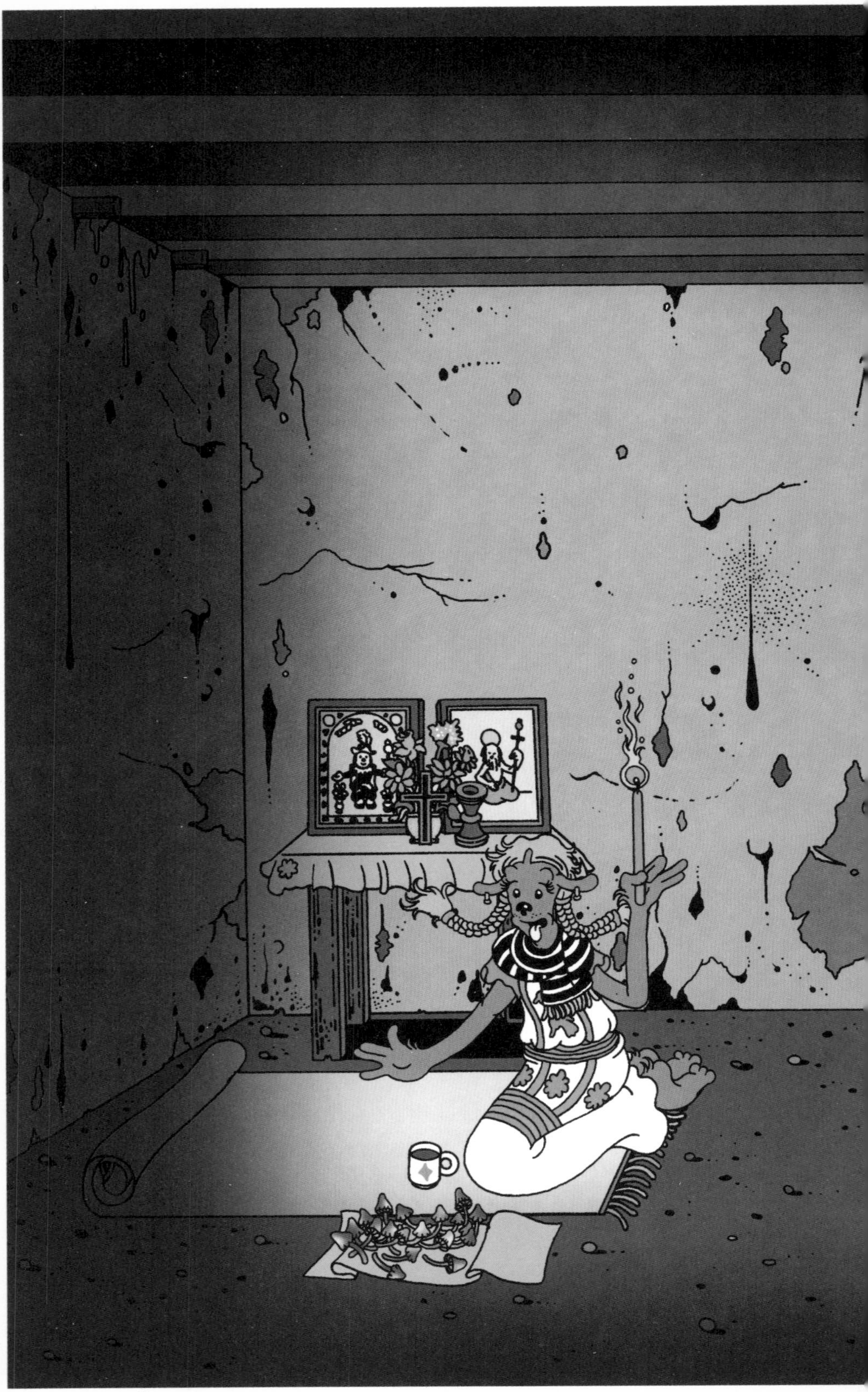

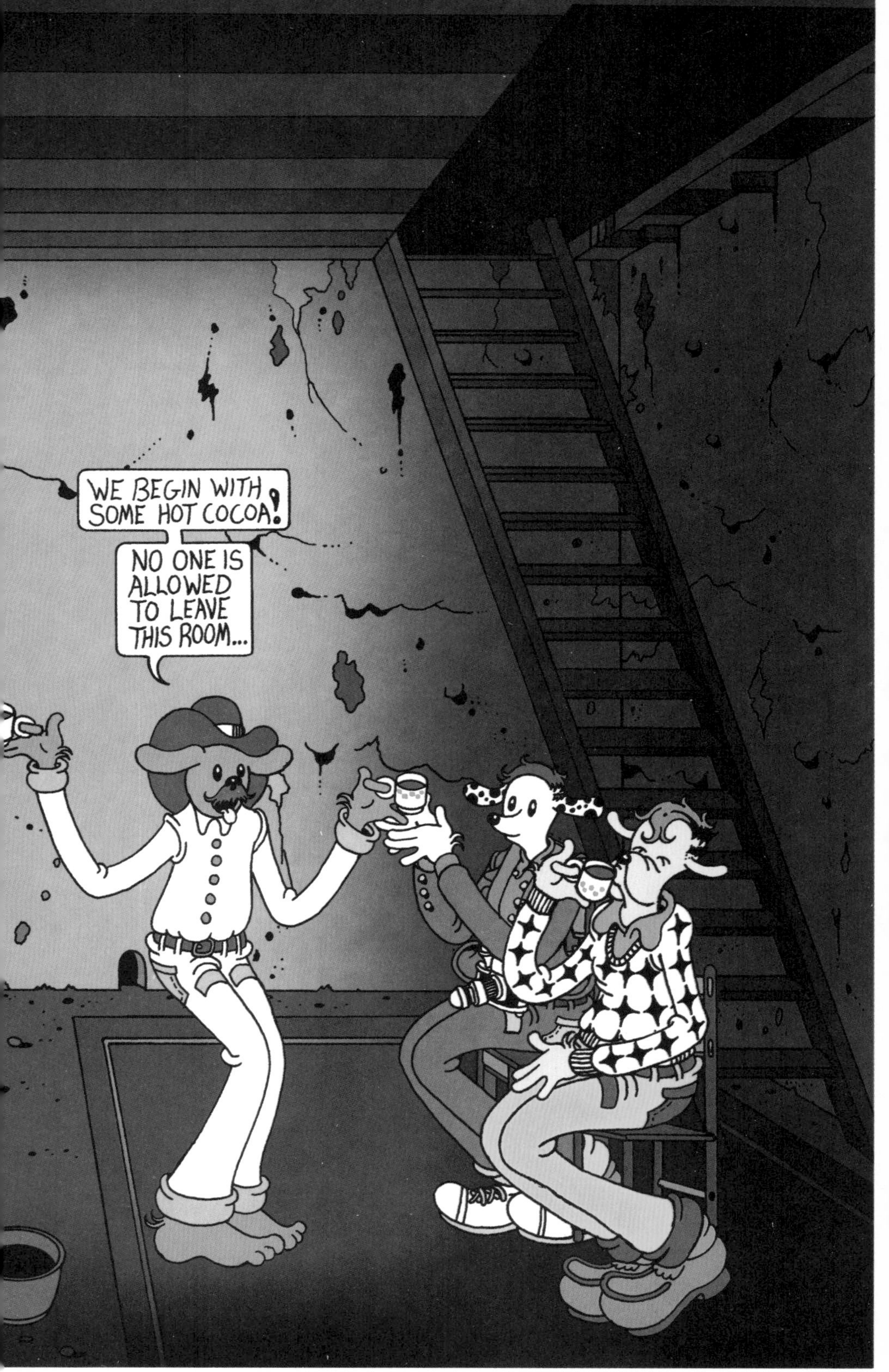
WE BEGIN WITH SOME HOT COCOA!
NO ONE IS ALLOWED TO LEAVE THIS ROOM...

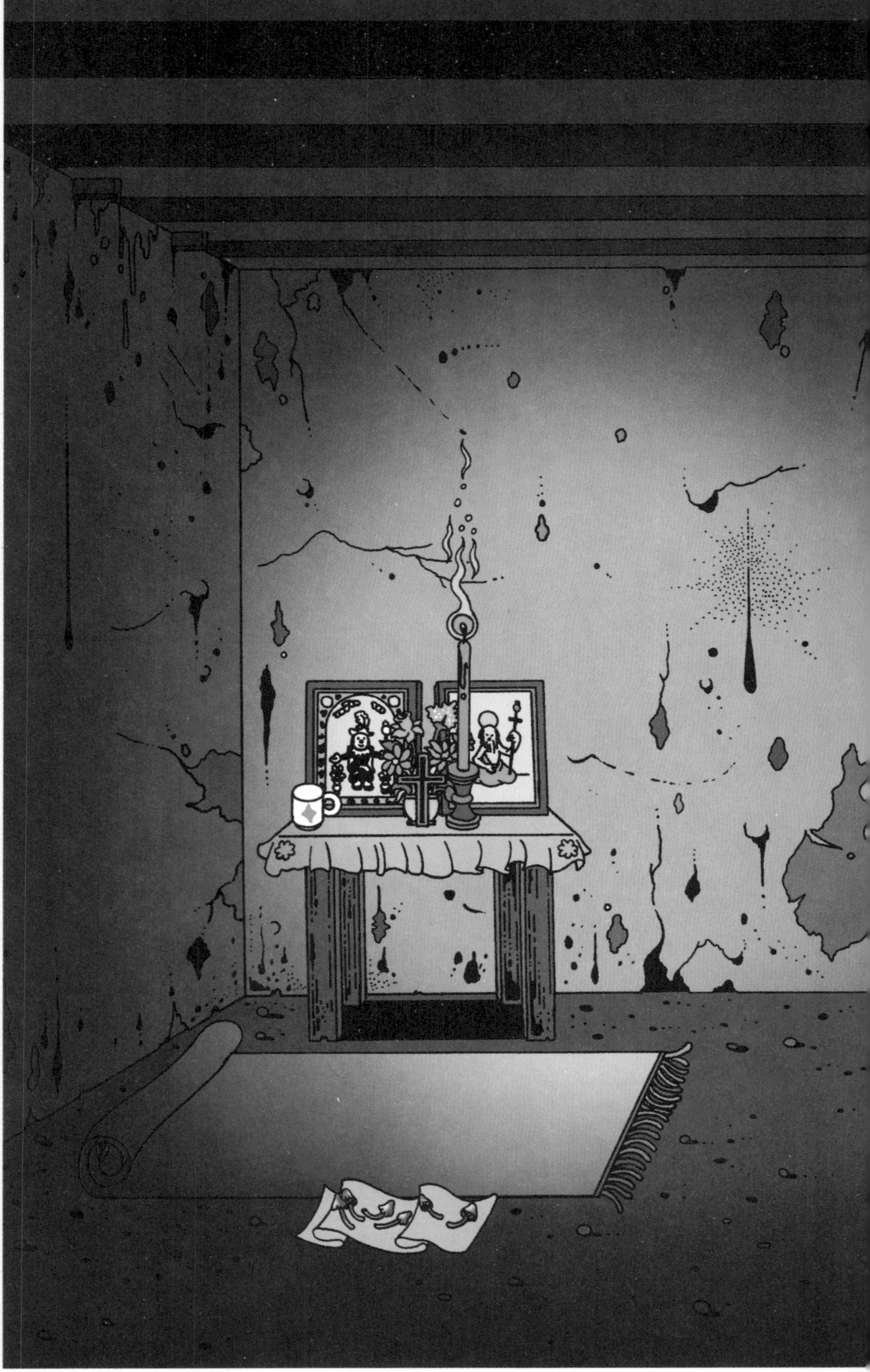

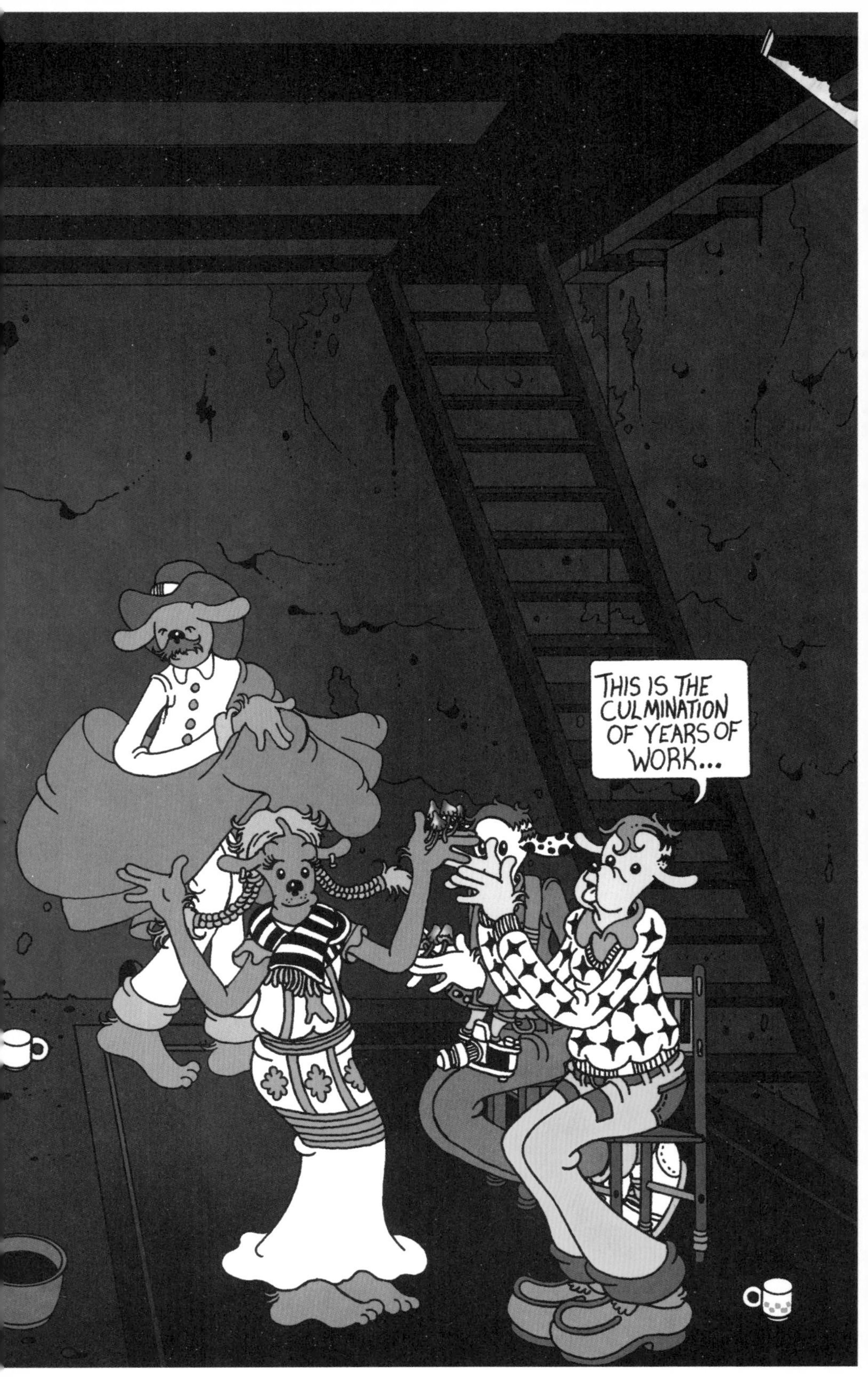
THIS IS THE CULMINATION OF YEARS OF WORK...

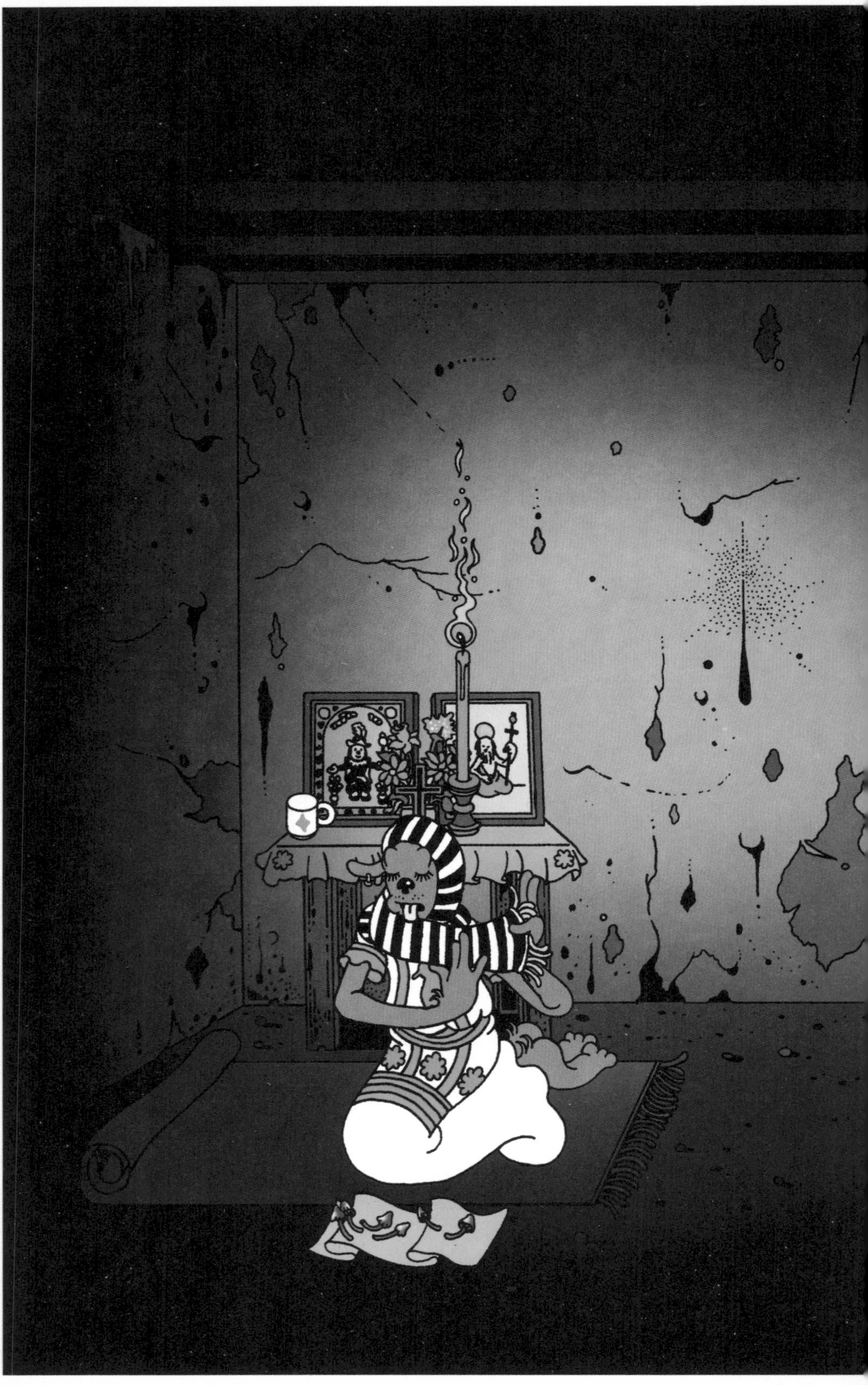

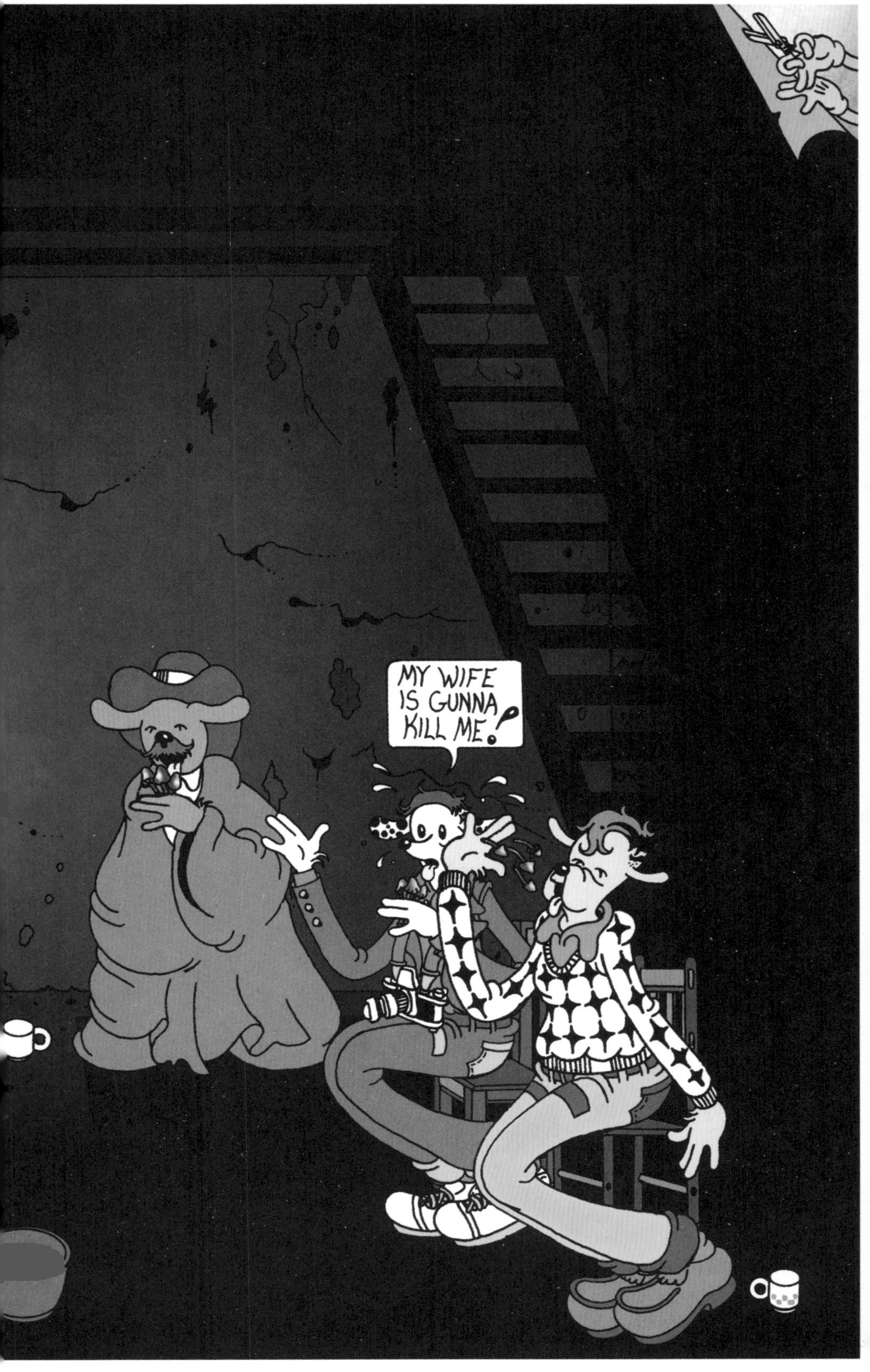
MY WIFE IS GUNNA KILL ME!

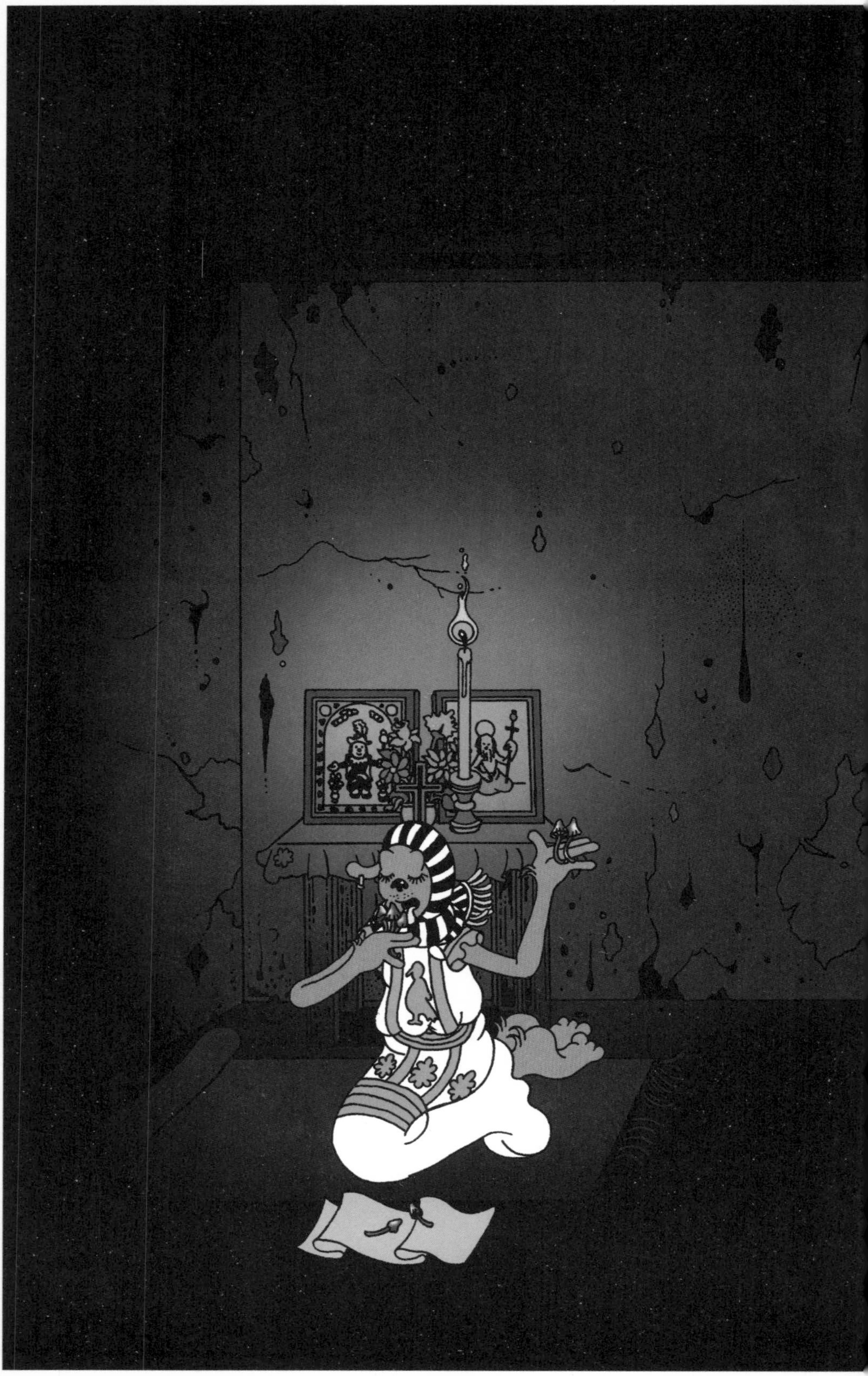

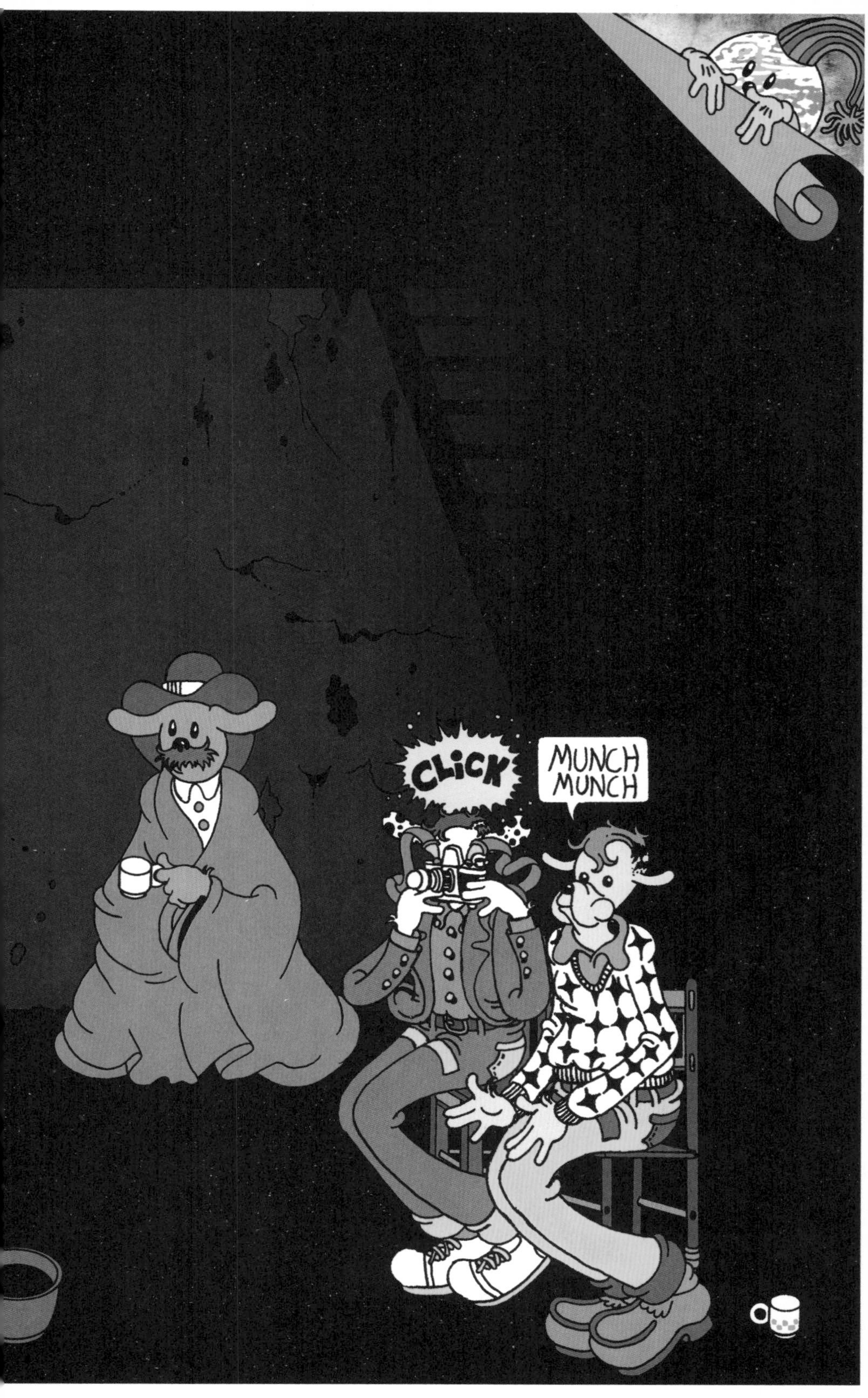
CLICK
MUNCH MUNCH

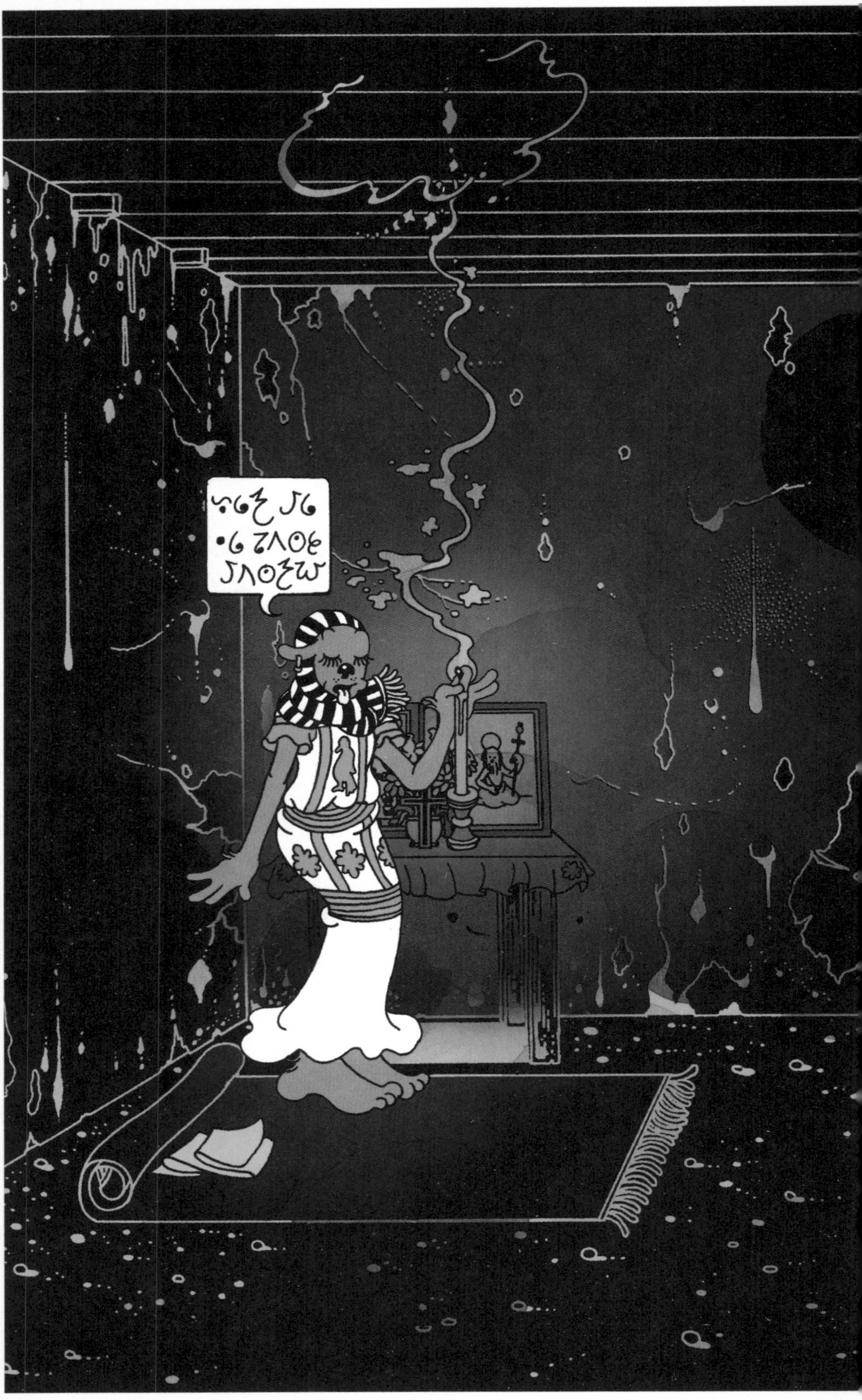

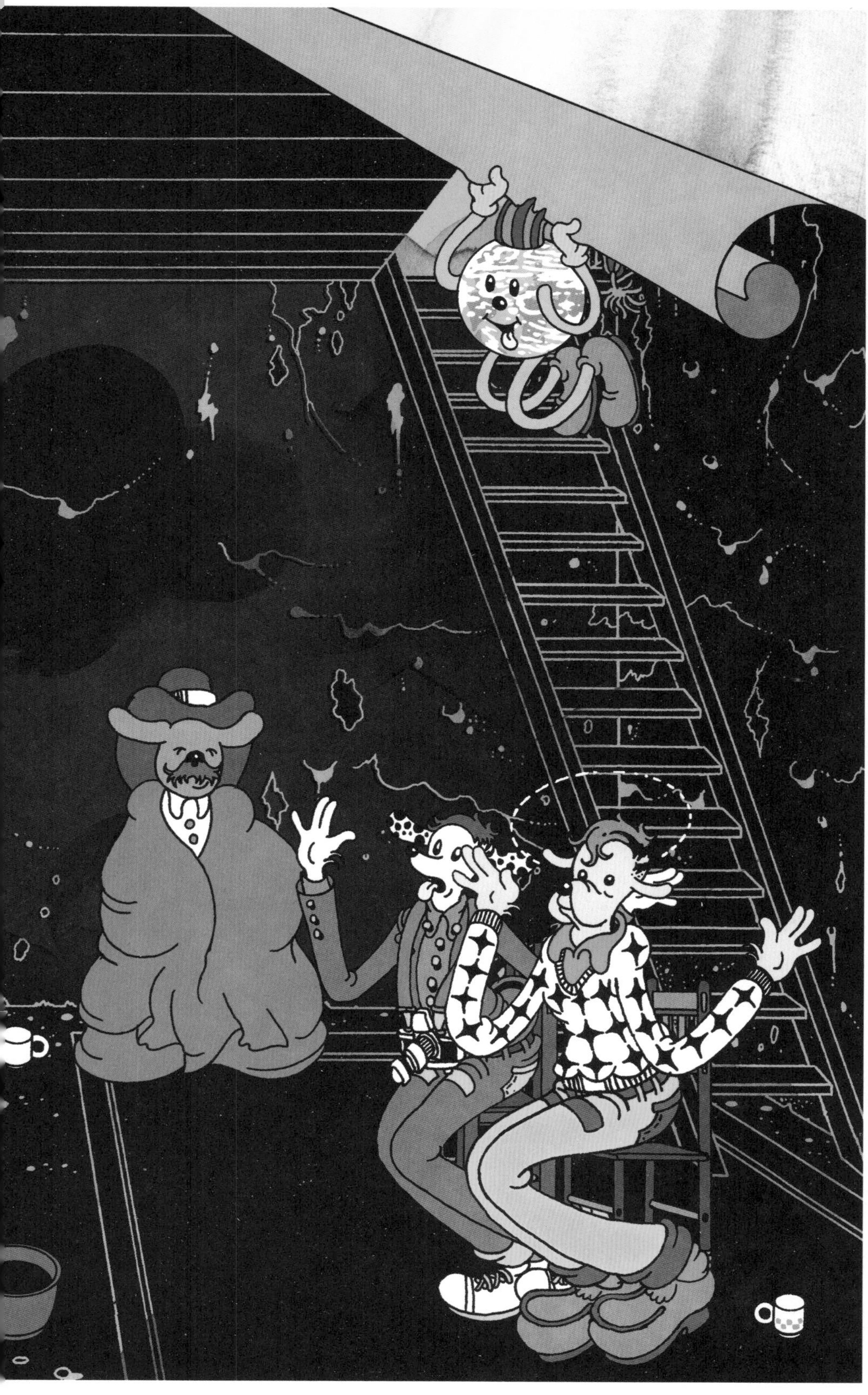

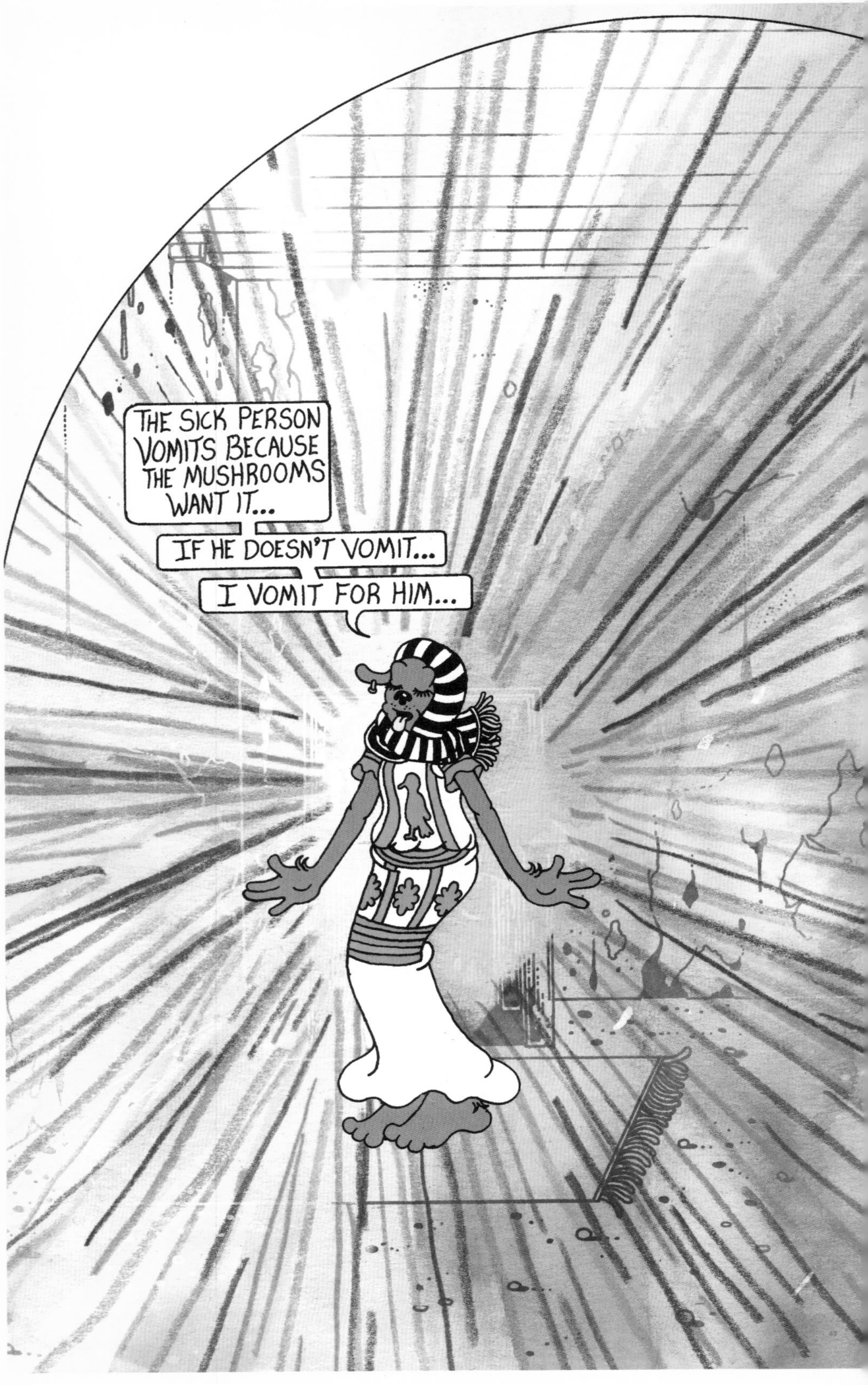
THE SICK PERSON VOMITS BECAUSE THE MUSHROOMS WANT IT...
IF HE DOESN'T VOMIT...
I VOMIT FOR HIM...

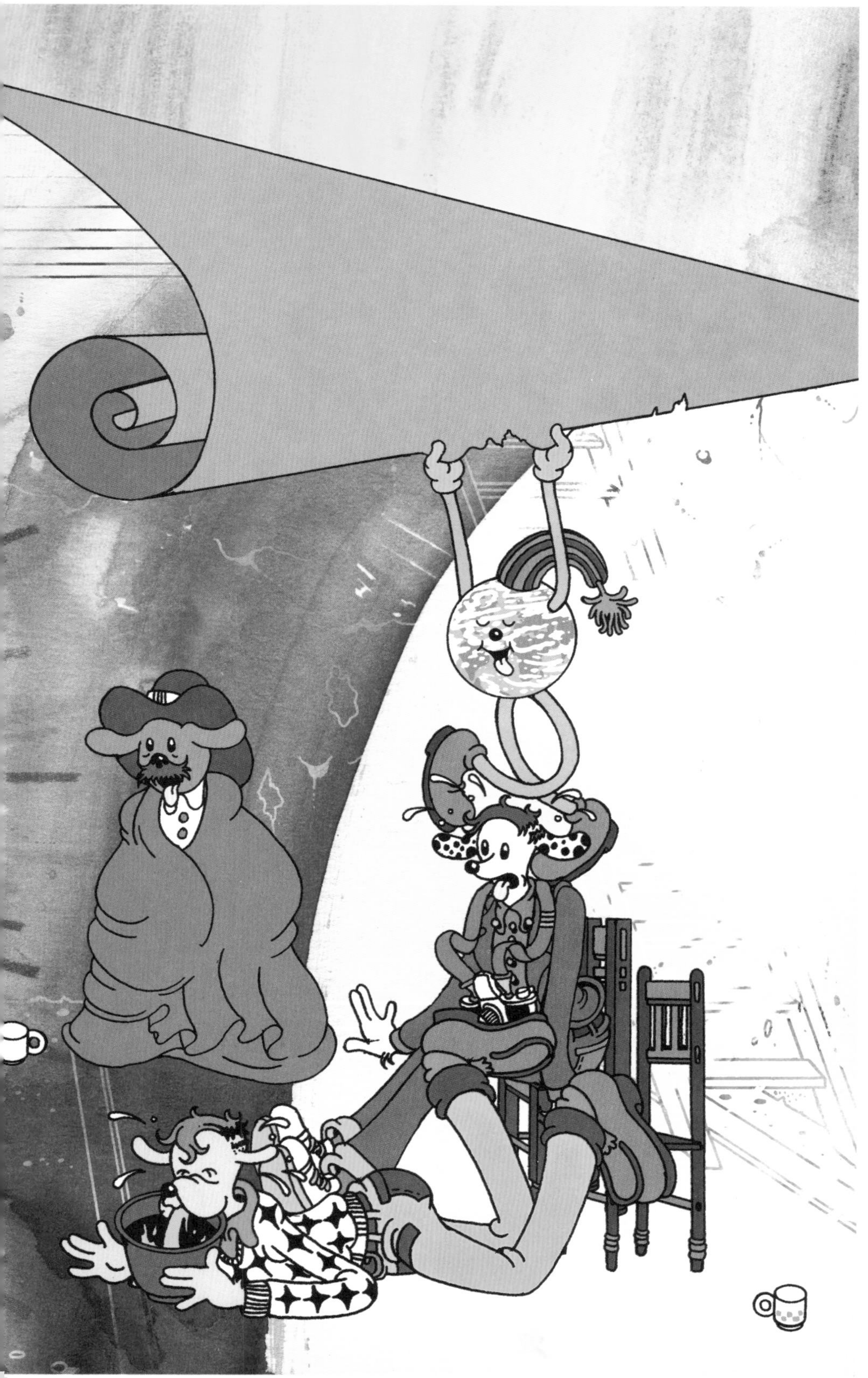

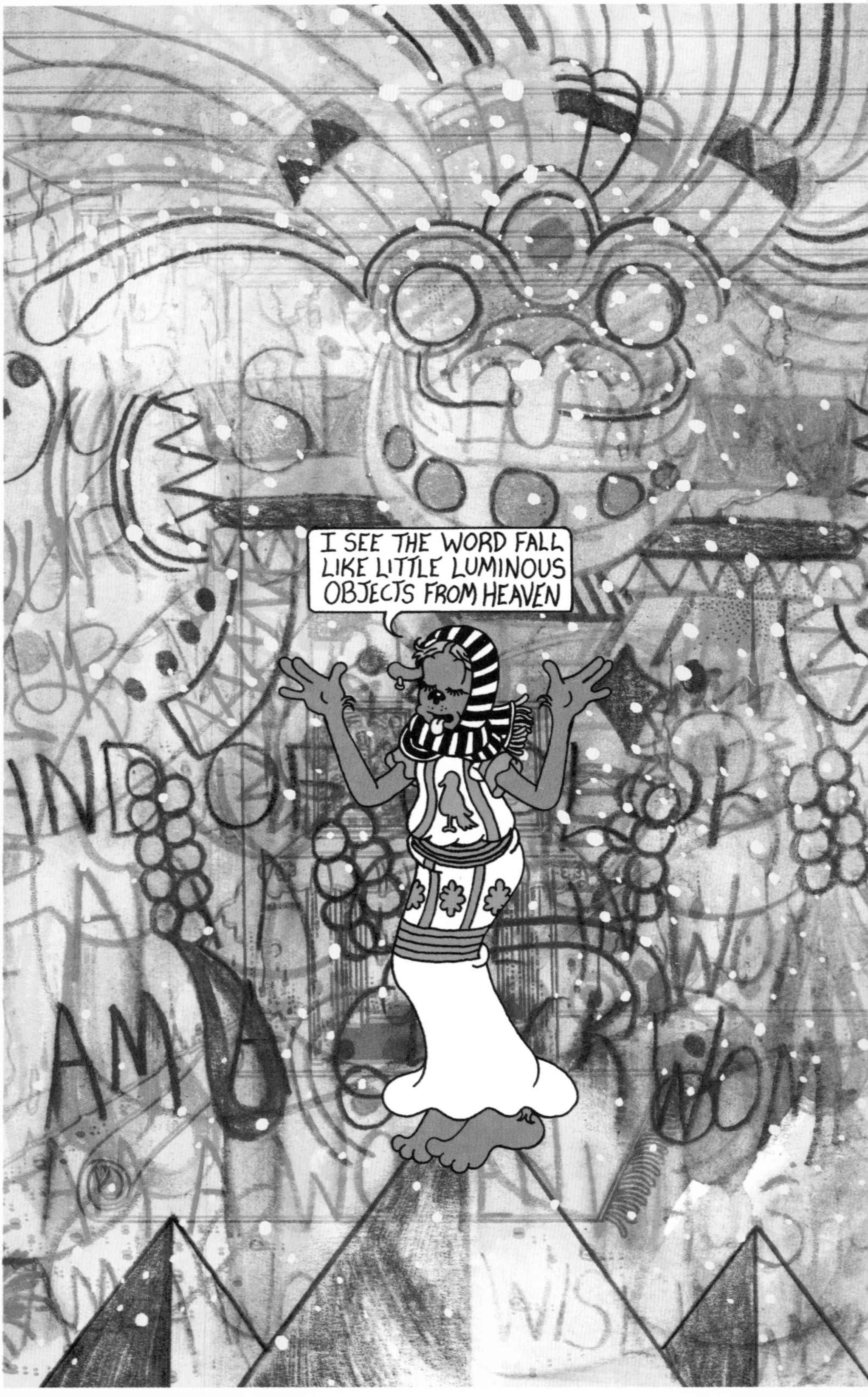
I SEE THE WORD FALL LIKE LITTLE LUMINOUS OBJECTS FROM HEAVEN

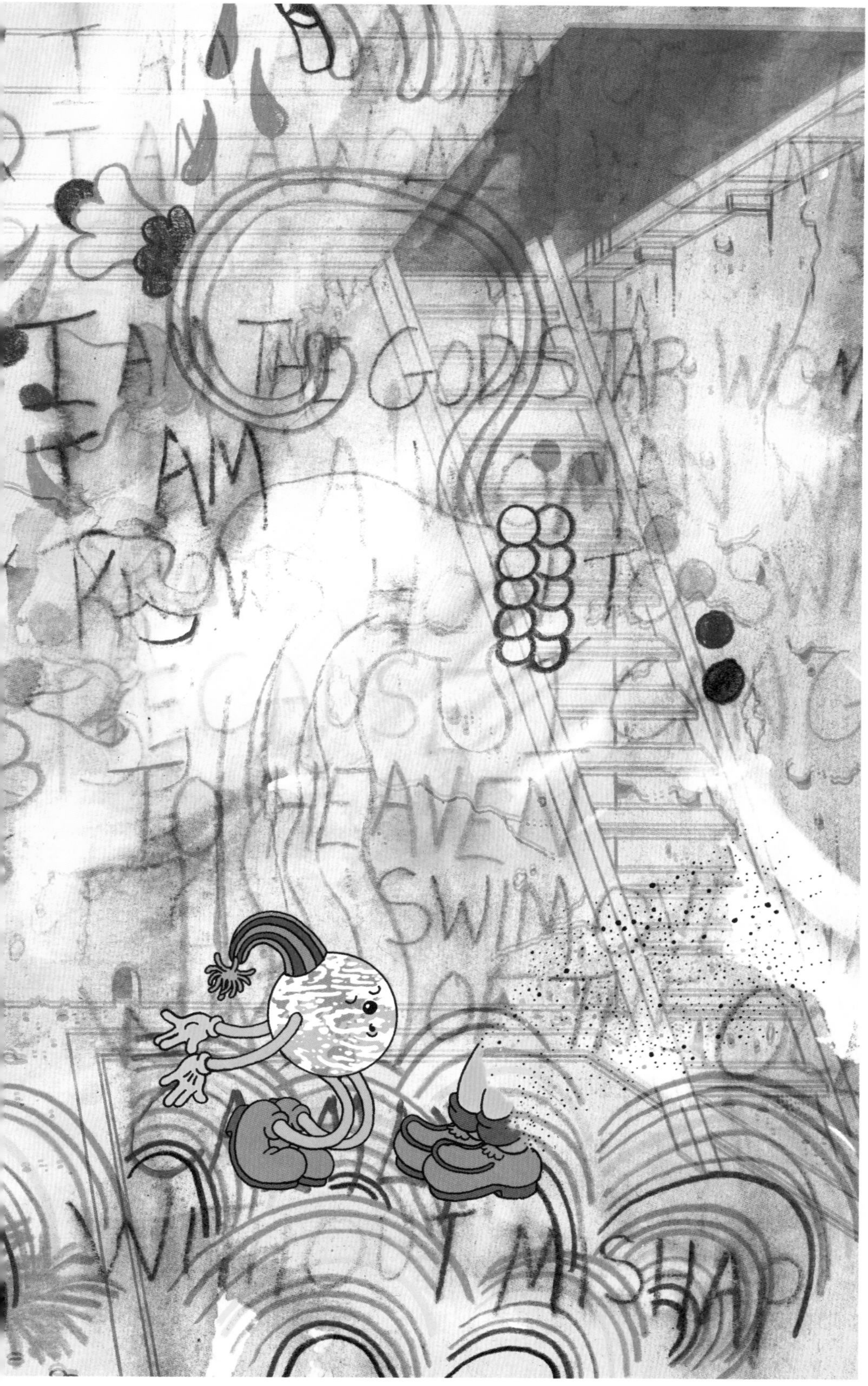
I AM THE GODSTAR
I AM
TO HEAVEN
SWIM
MISHAP

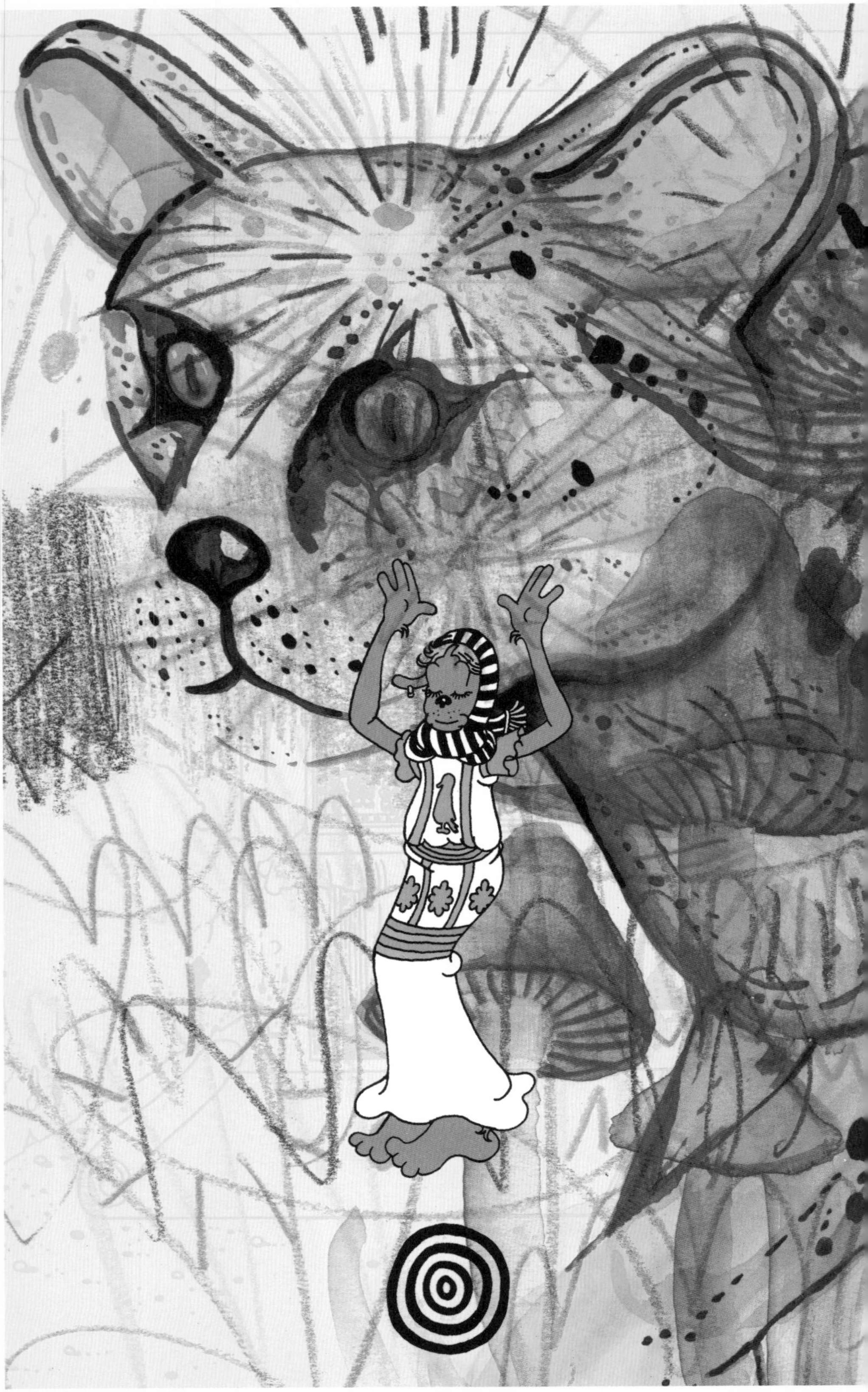

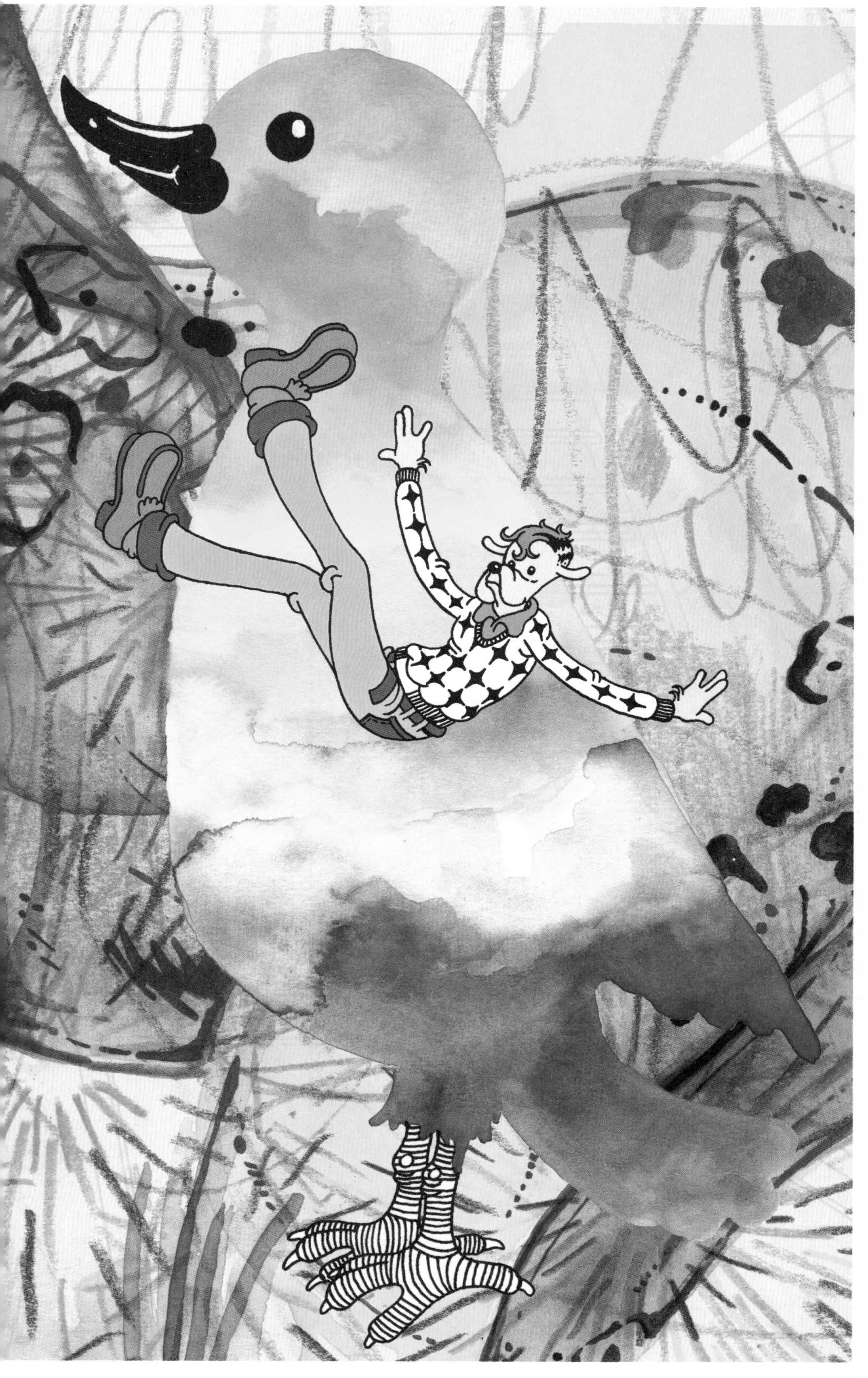

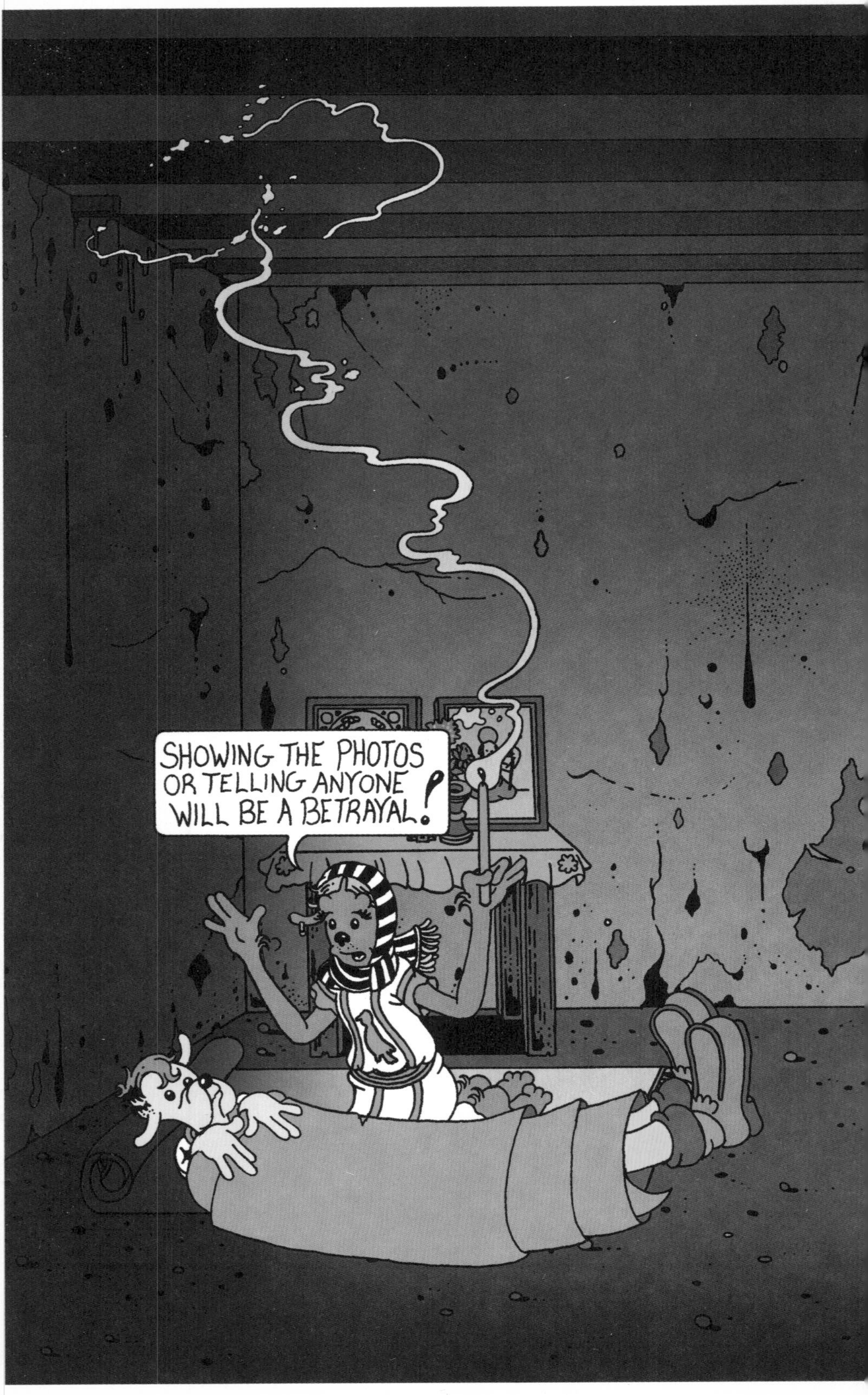
SHOWING THE PHOTOS OR TELLING ANYONE WILL BE A BETRAYAL!

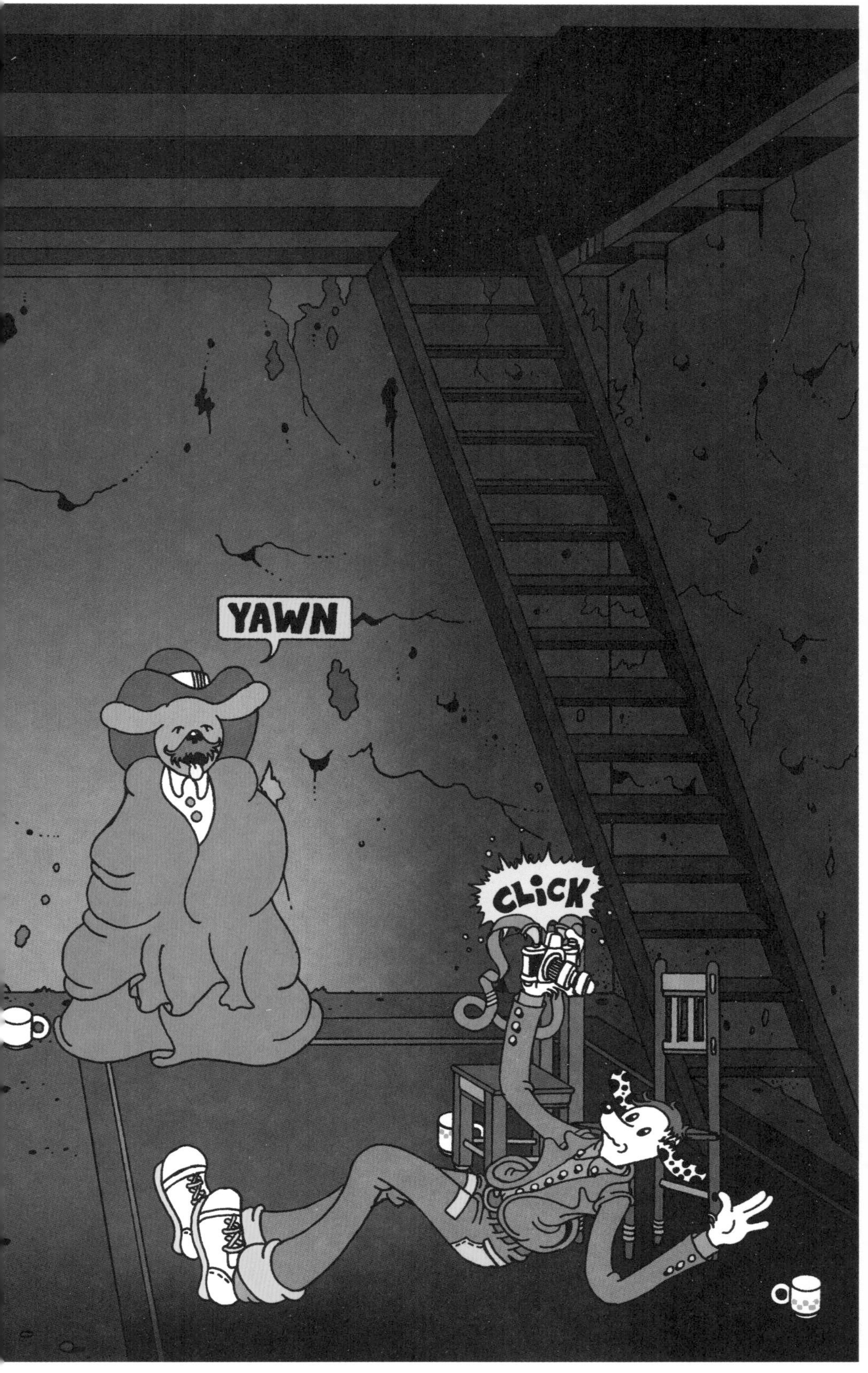
YAWN
CLICK

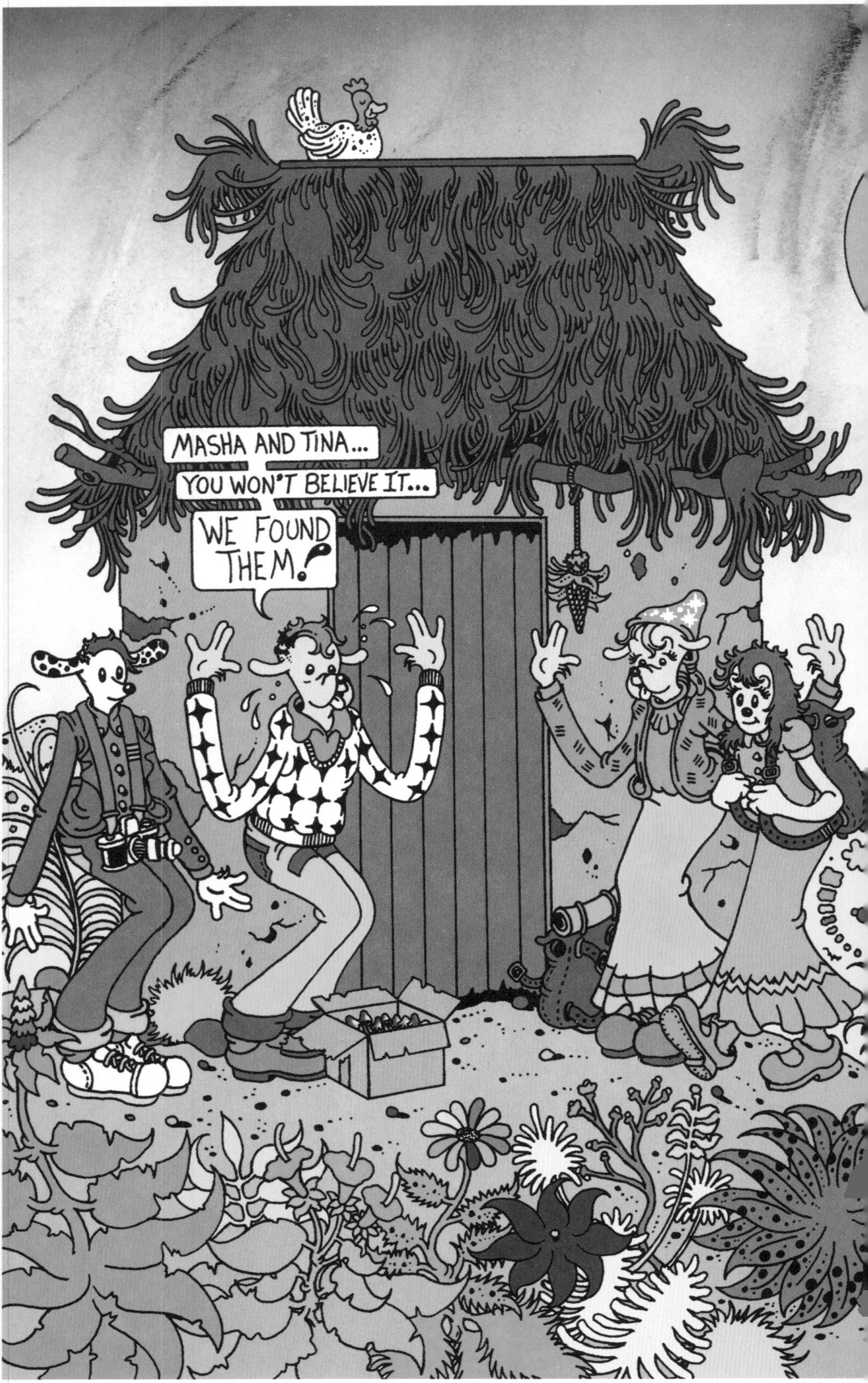
MASHA AND TINA...
YOU WON'T BELIEVE IT...
WE FOUND THEM!

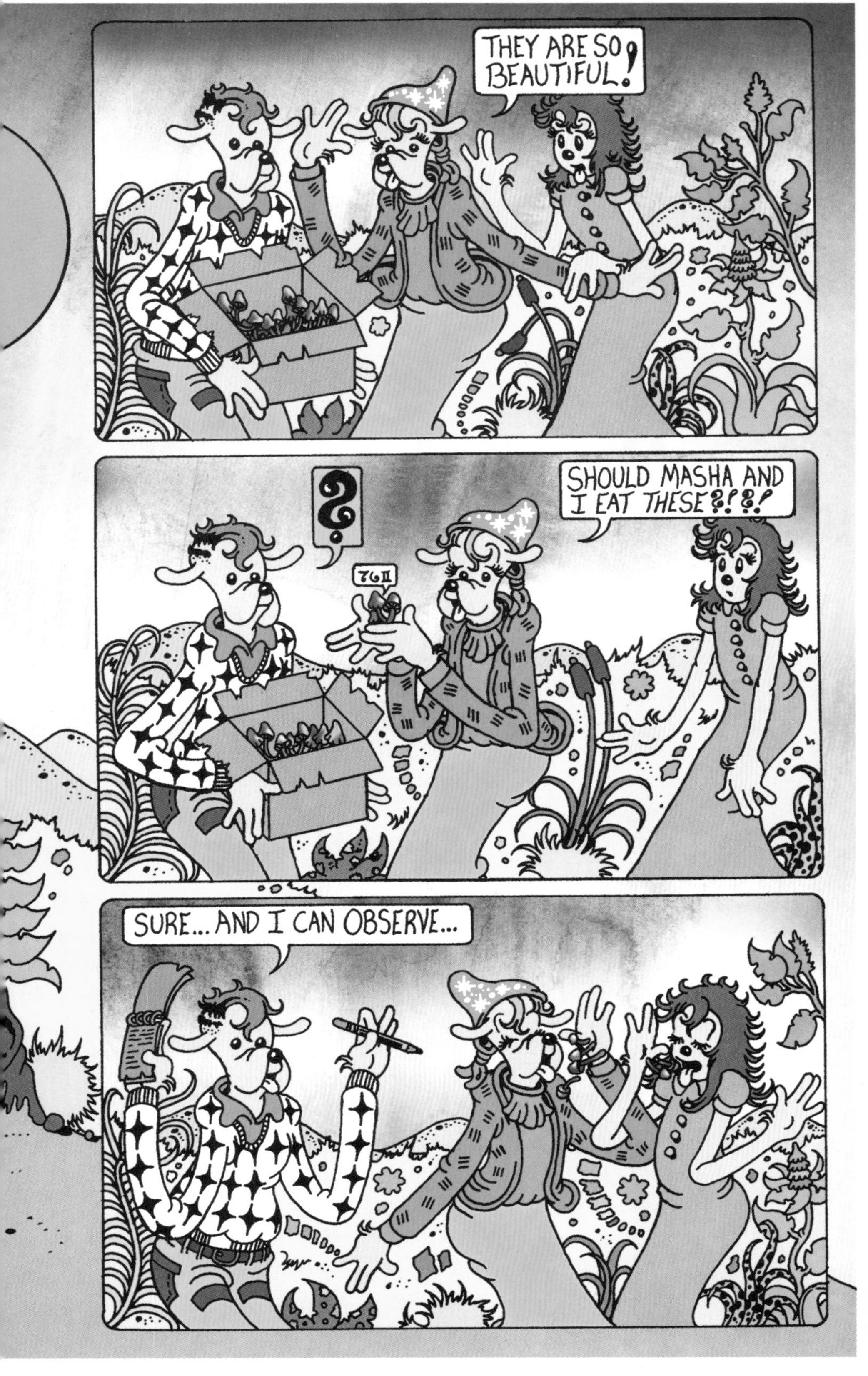
THEY ARE SO BEAUTIFUL!
SHOULD MASHA AND I EAT THESE?!?!
SURE... AND I CAN OBSERVE...

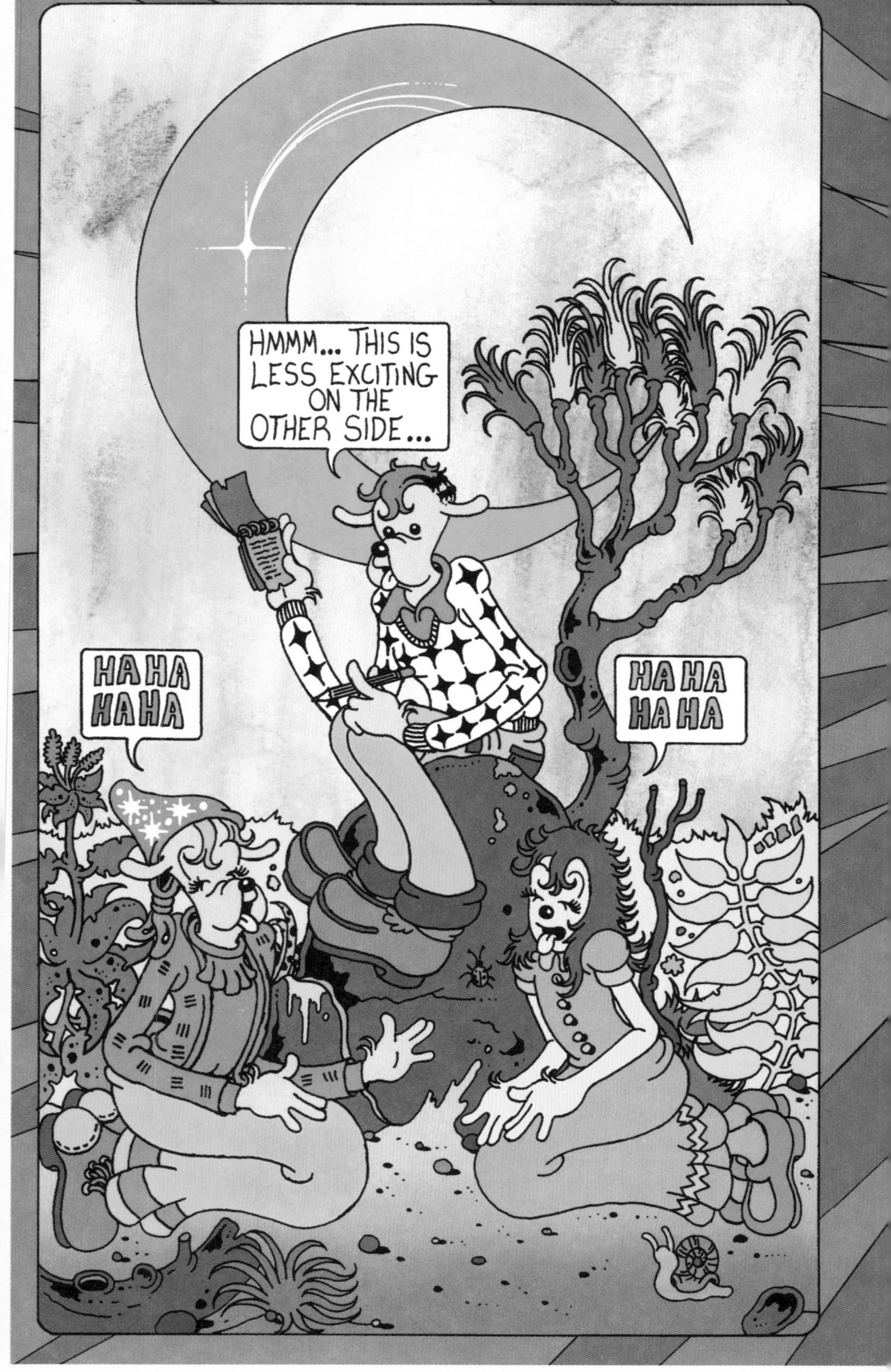
HMMM... THIS IS LESS EXCITING ON THE OTHER SIDE...
HA HA HA HA
HA HA HA HA

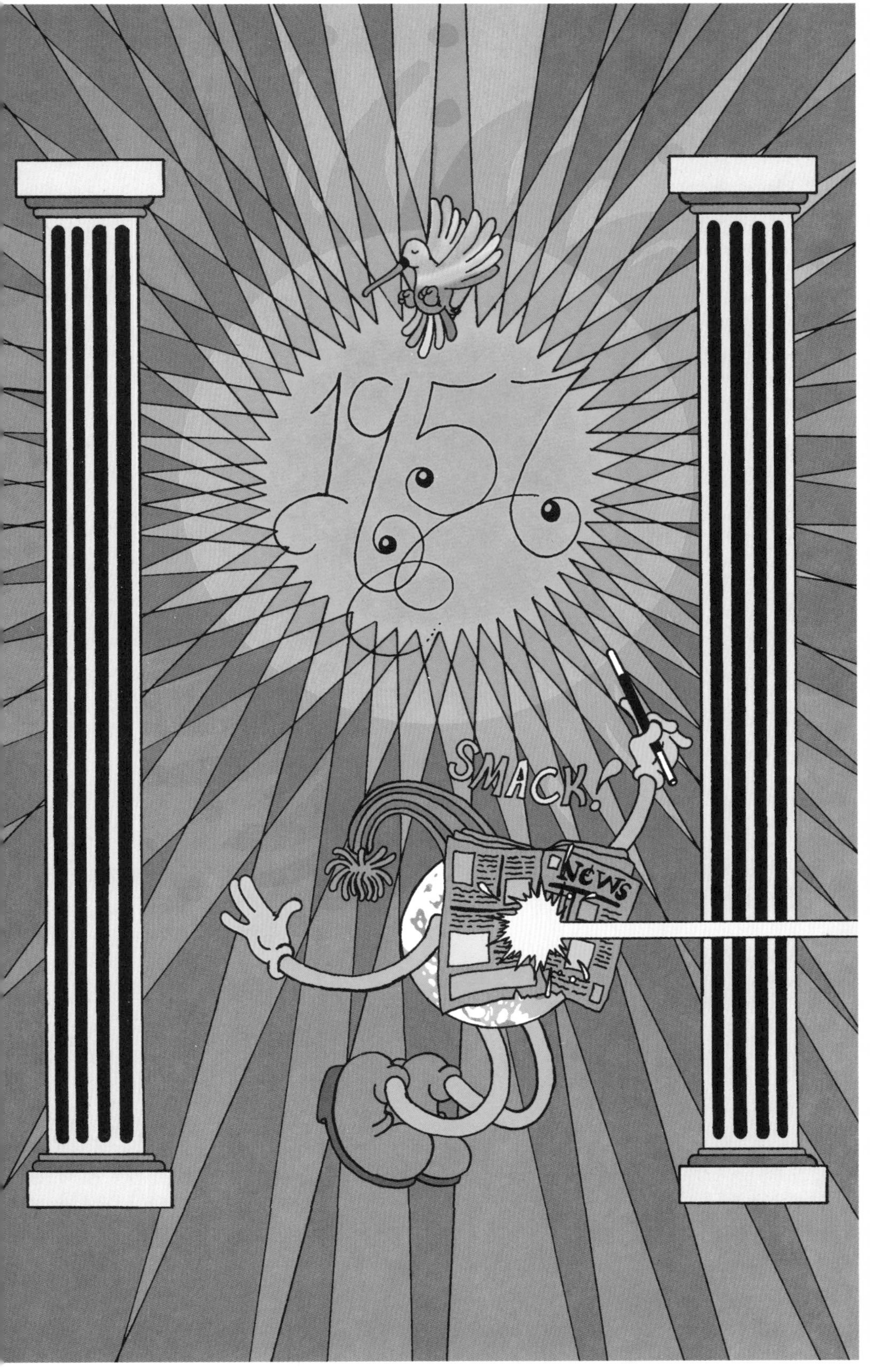
1957
SMACK!
News

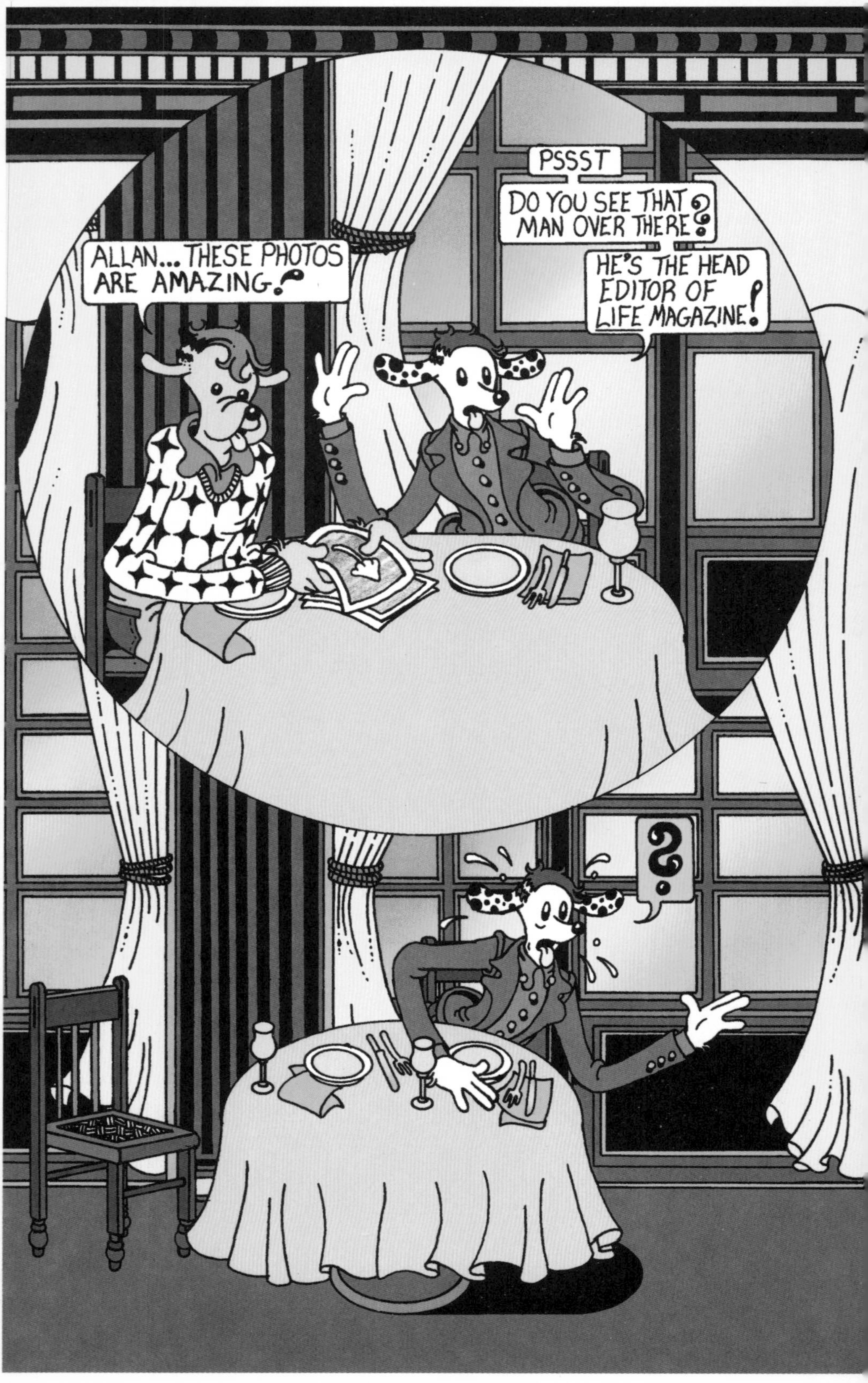
ALLAN... THESE PHOTOS ARE AMAZING!
PSSST
DO YOU SEE THAT MAN OVER THERE?
HE'S THE HEAD EDITOR OF LIFE MAGAZINE!
?

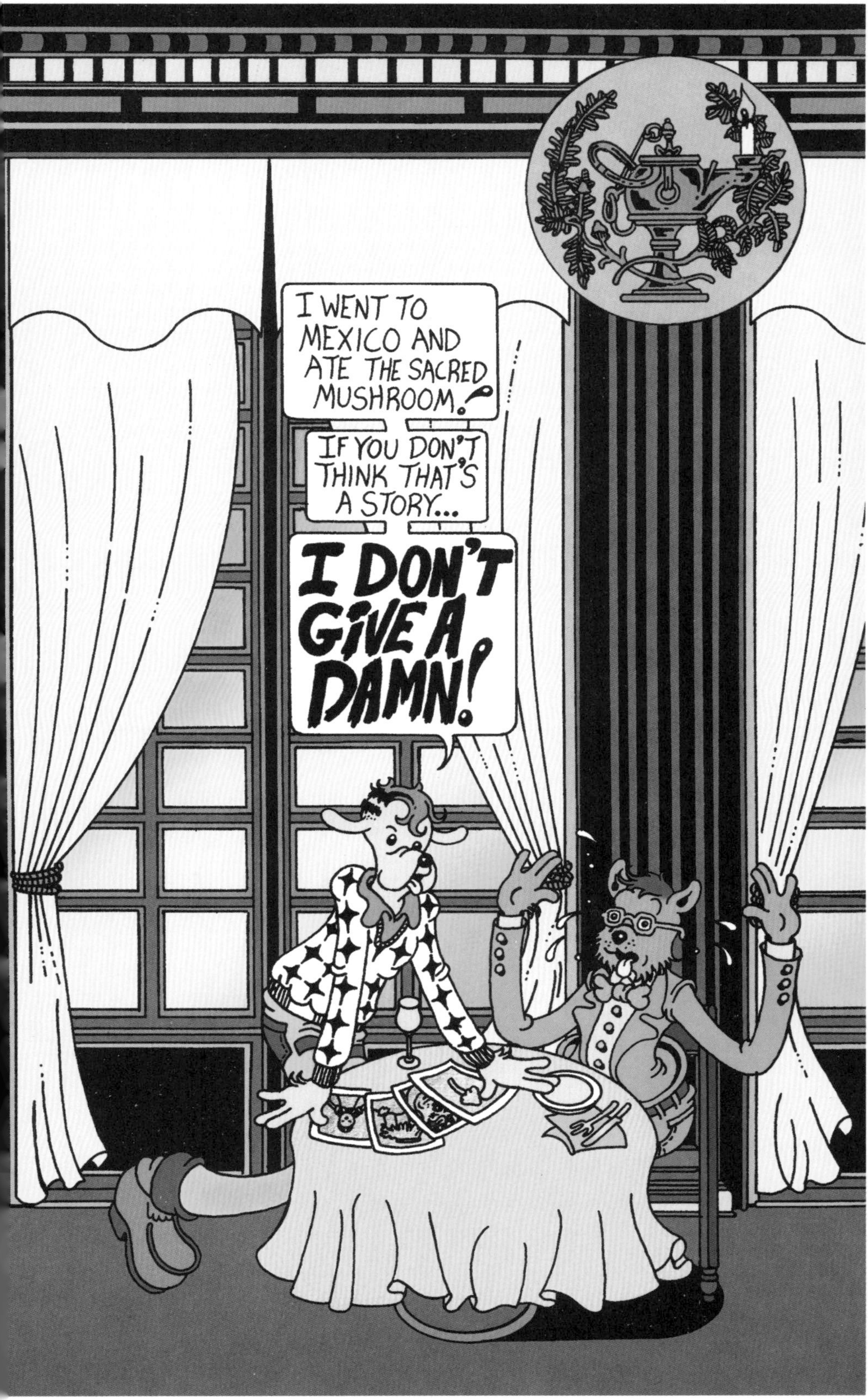

I WENT TO MEXICO AND ATE THE SACRED MUSHROOM!
IF YOU DON'T THINK THAT'S A STORY...
I DON'T GIVE A DAMN!

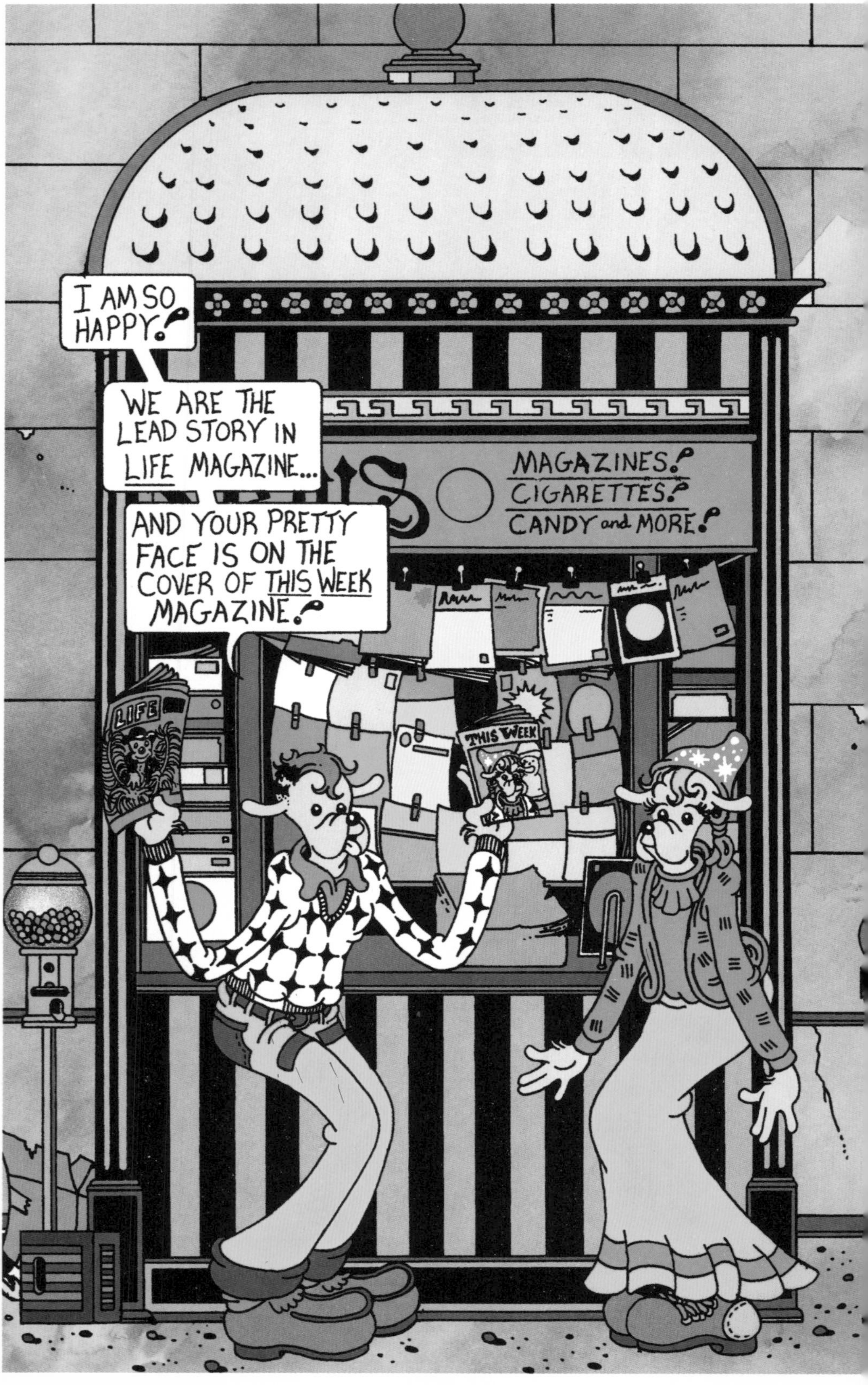
I AM SO HAPPY!
WE ARE THE LEAD STORY IN LIFE MAGAZINE...
AND YOUR PRETTY FACE IS ON THE COVER OF THIS WEEK MAGAZINE!
MAGAZINES!
CIGARETTES!
CANDY and MORE!
LIFE
THIS WEEK

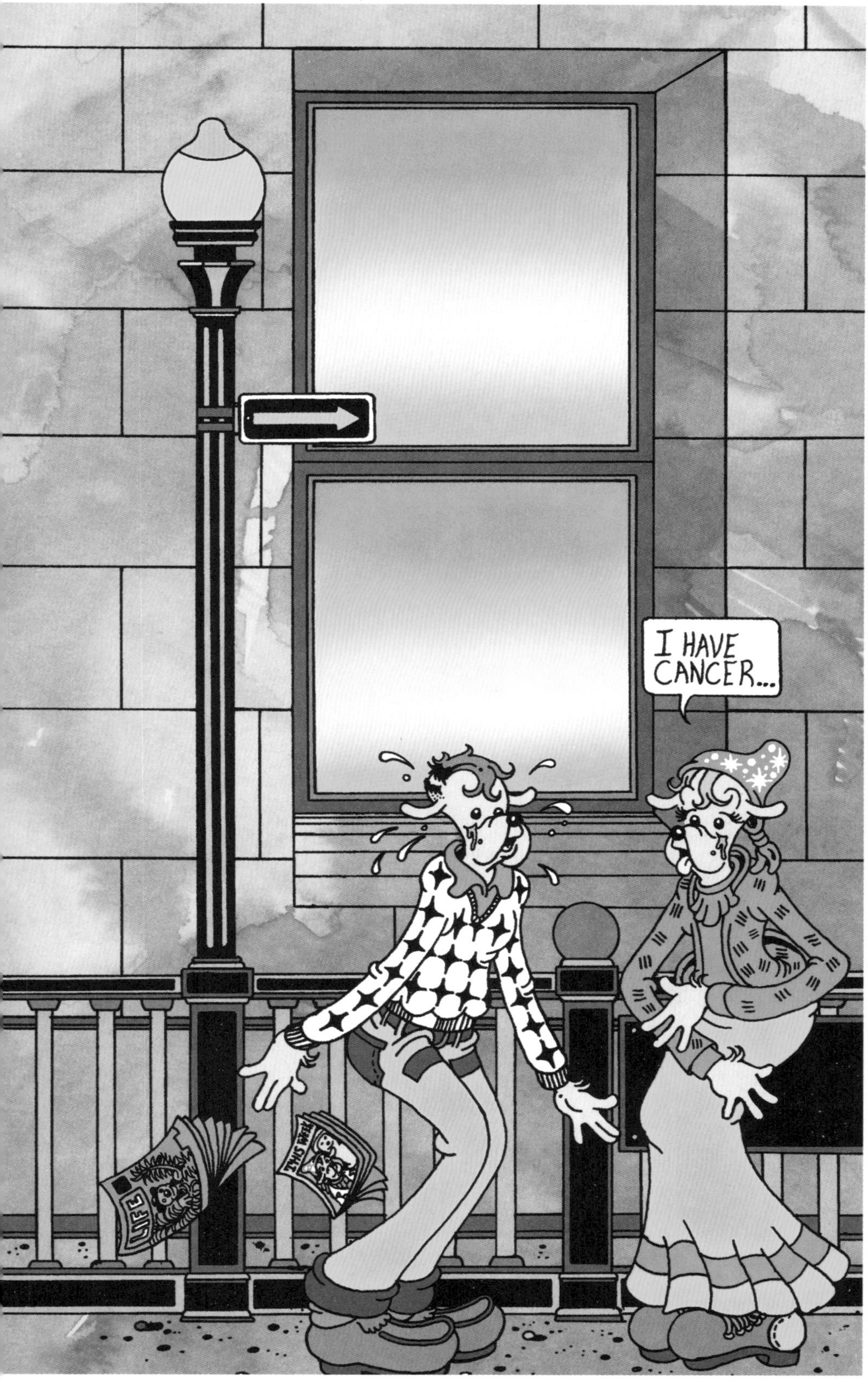
I HAVE CANCER...
LIFE
THIS WEEK

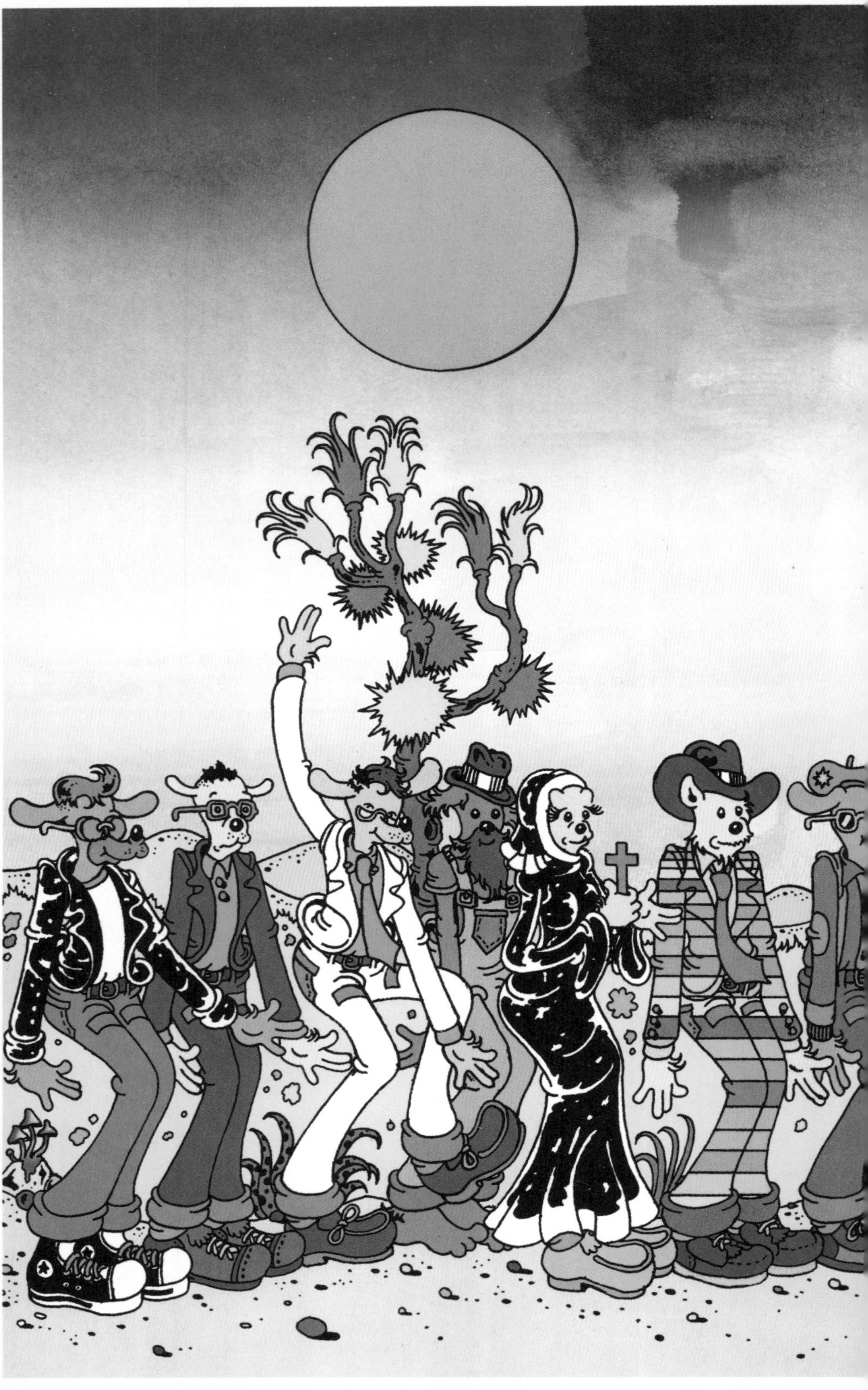

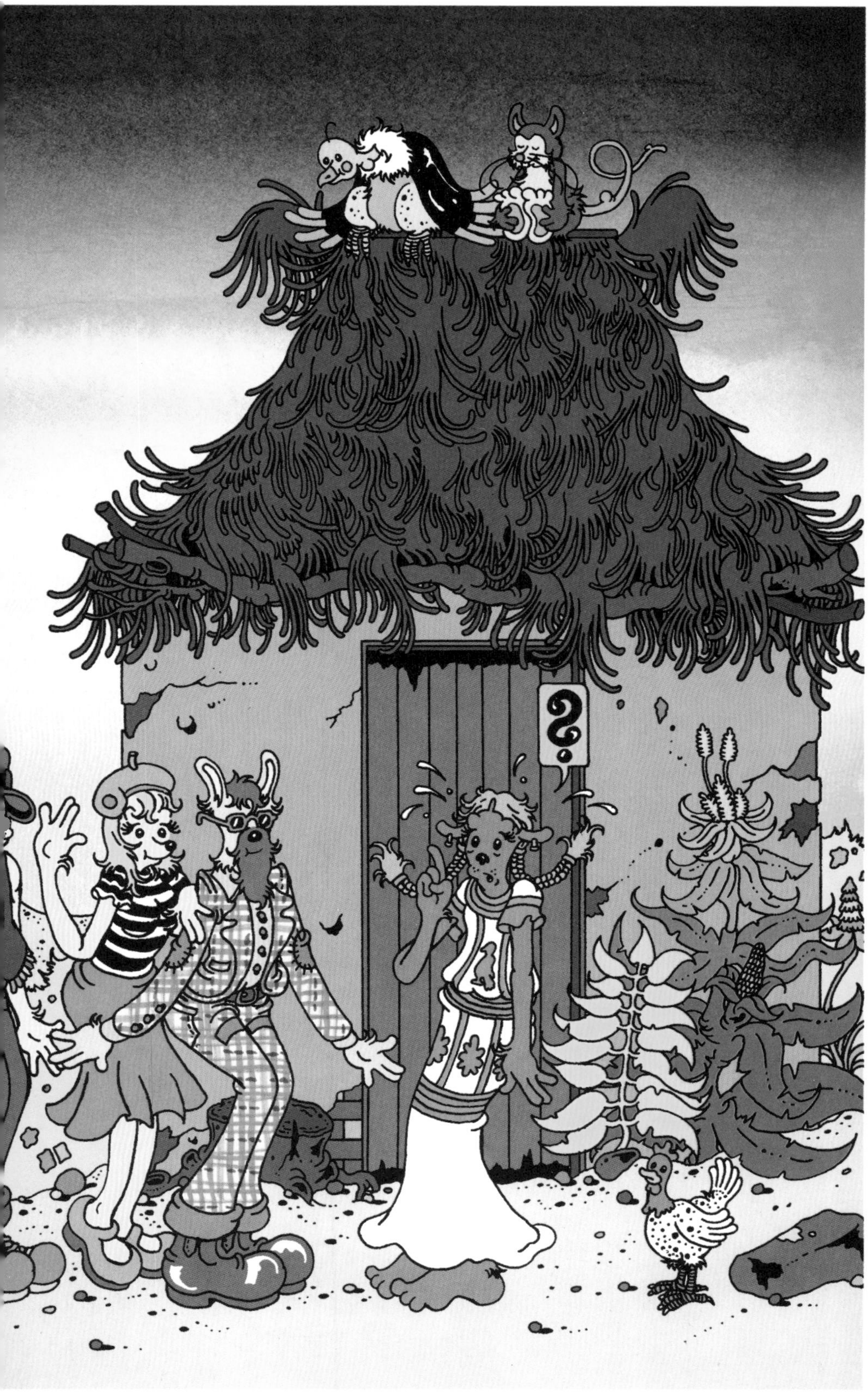

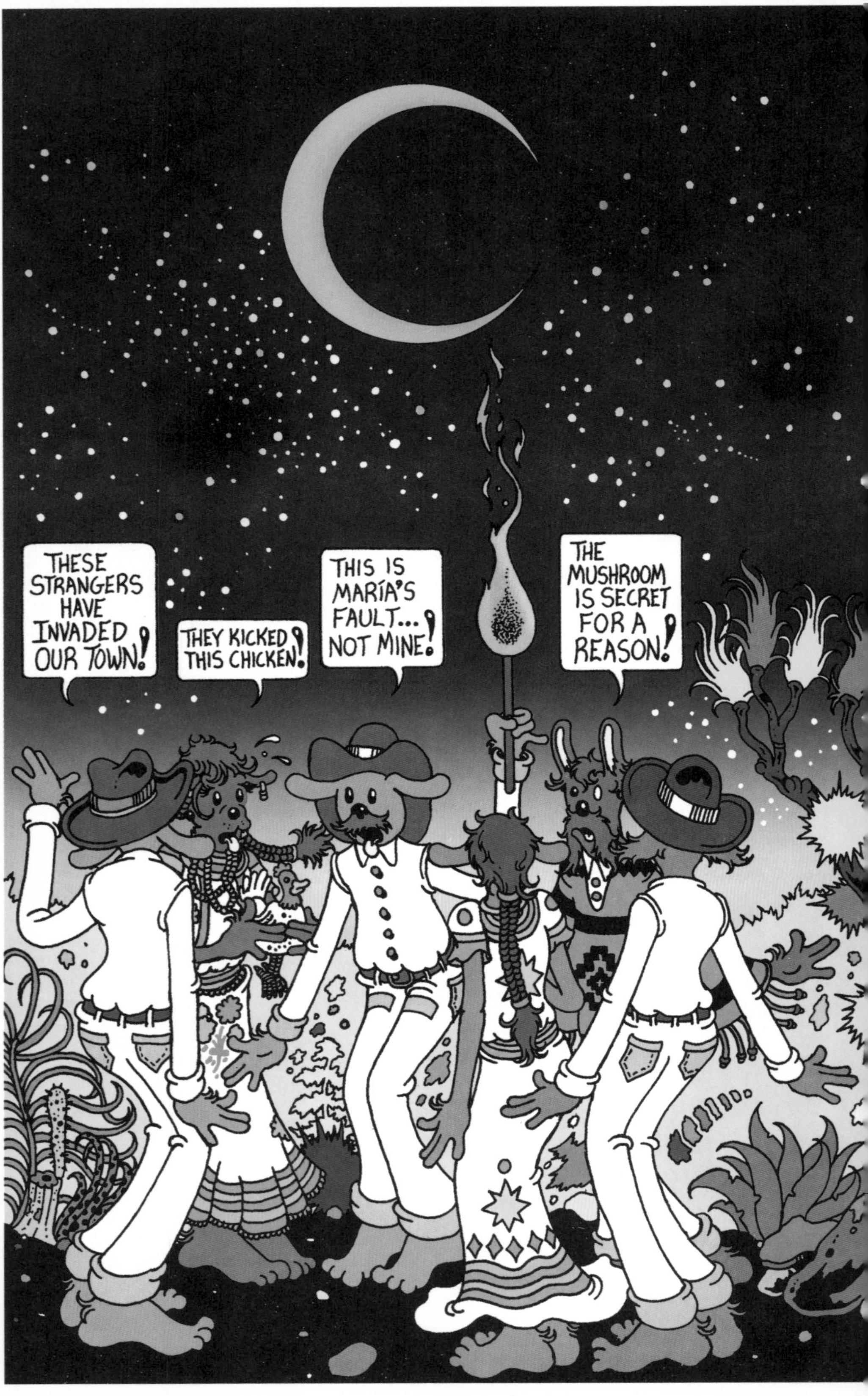
THESE STRANGERS HAVE INVADED OUR TOWN!
THEY KICKED THIS CHICKEN!
THIS IS MARÍA'S FAULT... NOT MINE!
THE MUSHROOM IS SECRET FOR A REASON!

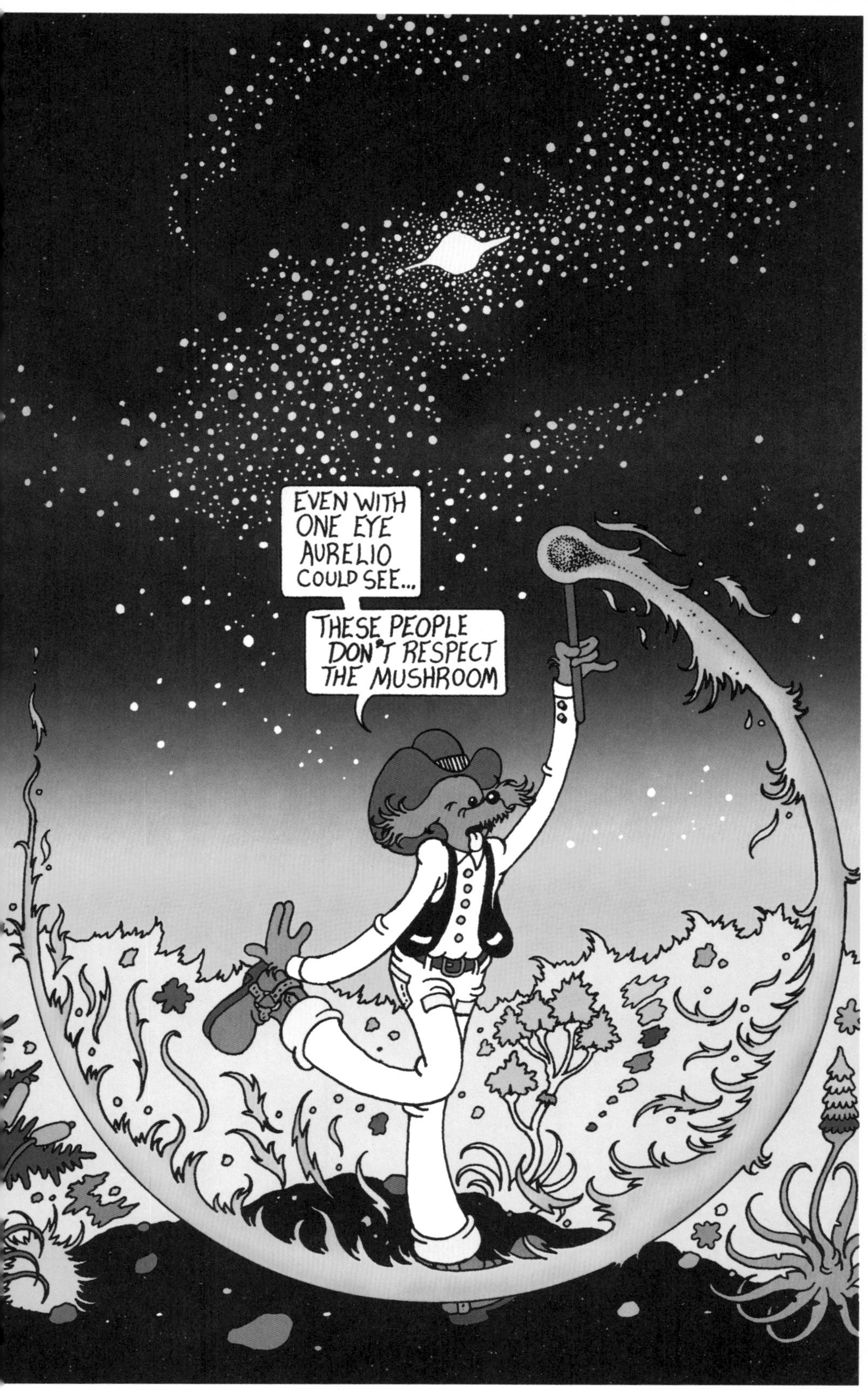
EVEN WITH ONE EYE AURELIO COULD SEE...
THESE PEOPLE DON'T RESPECT THE MUSHROOM

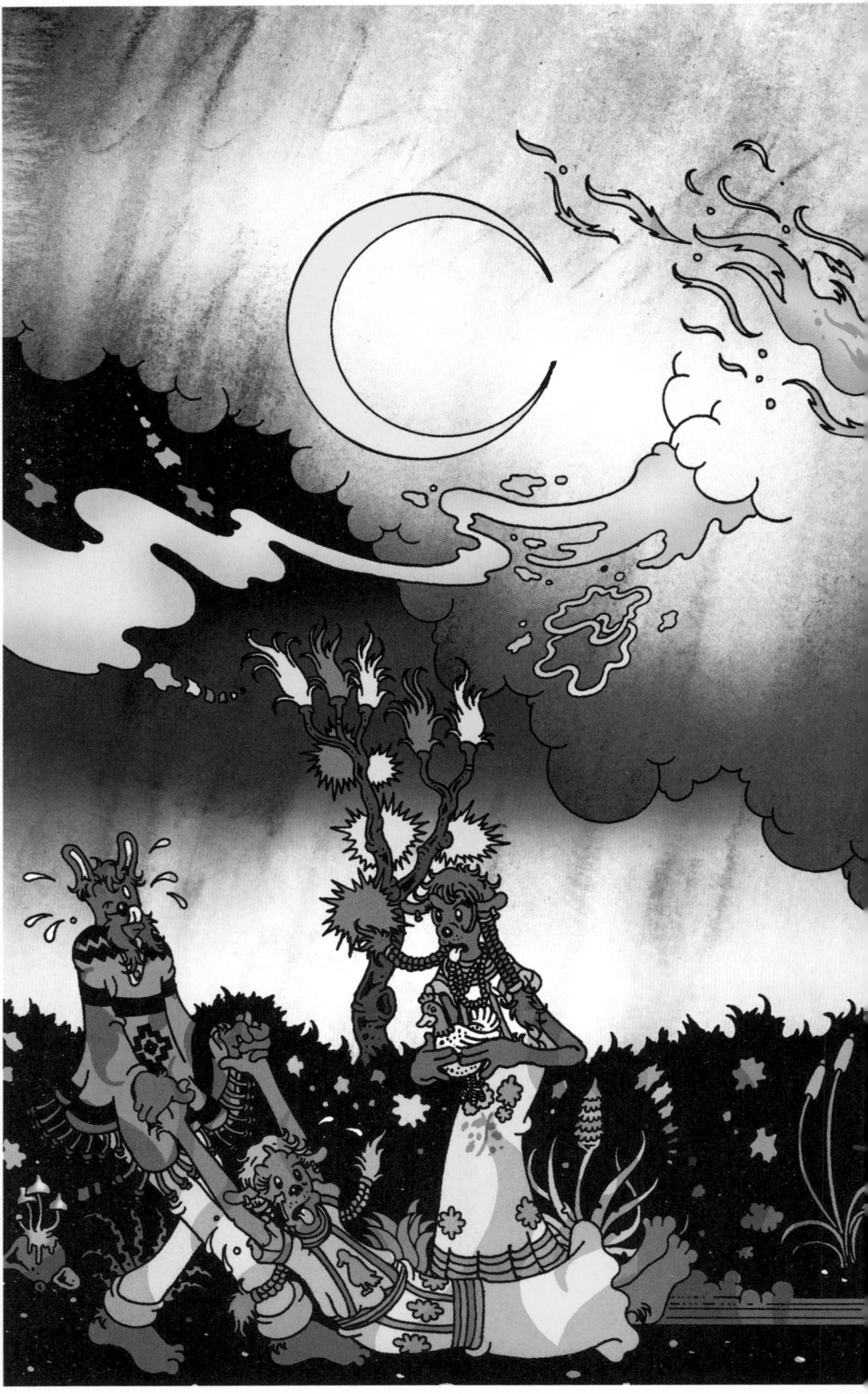

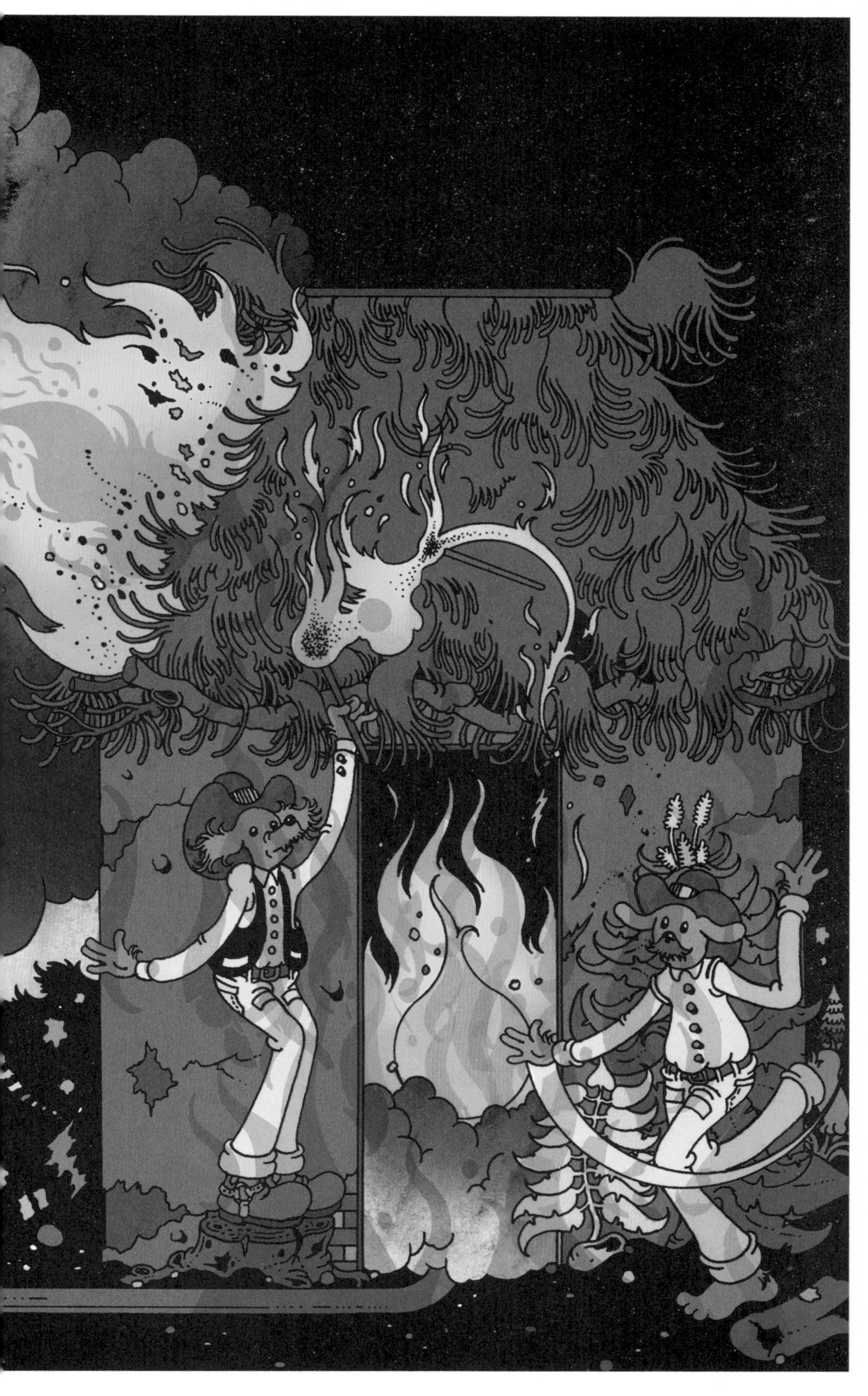

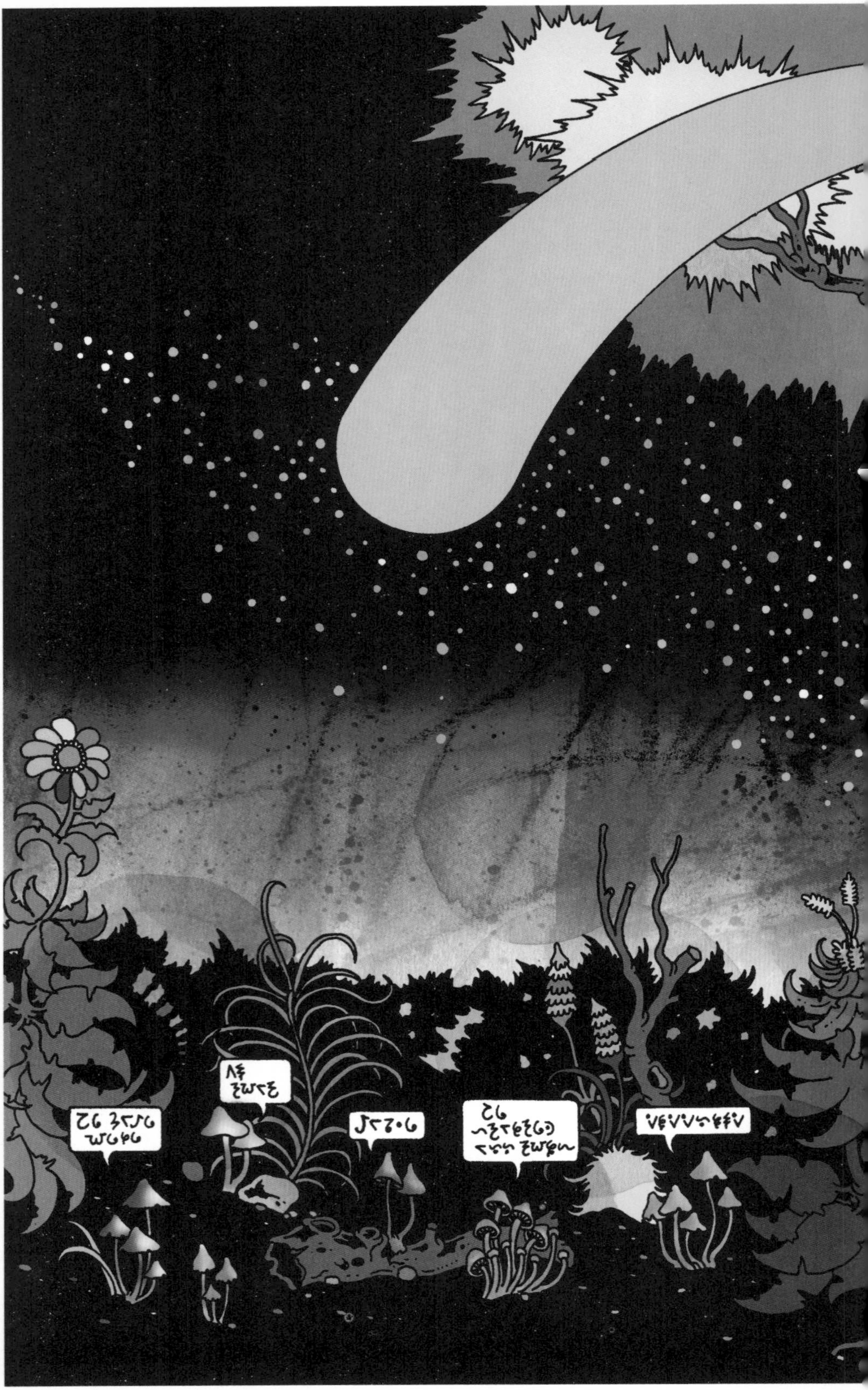

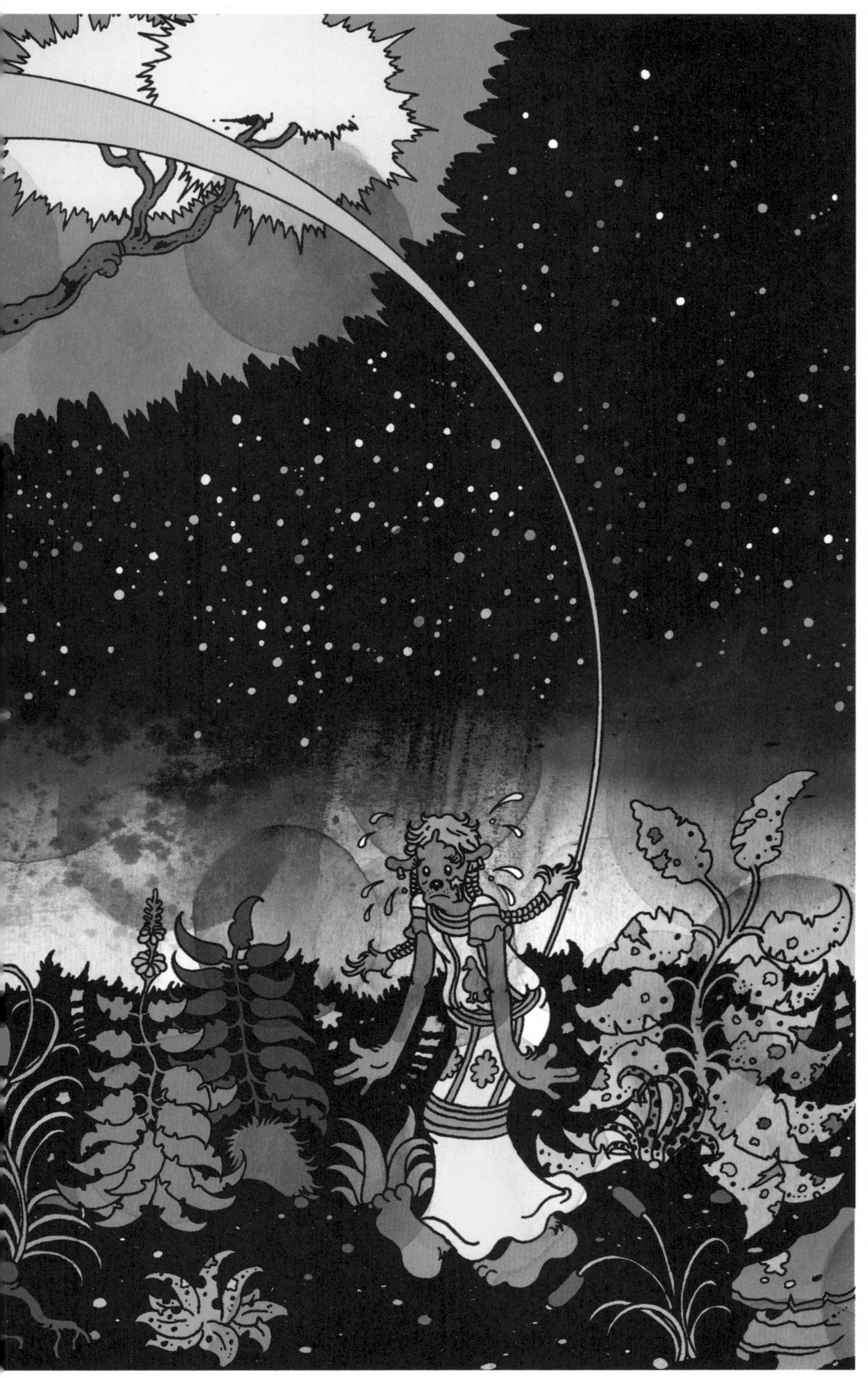

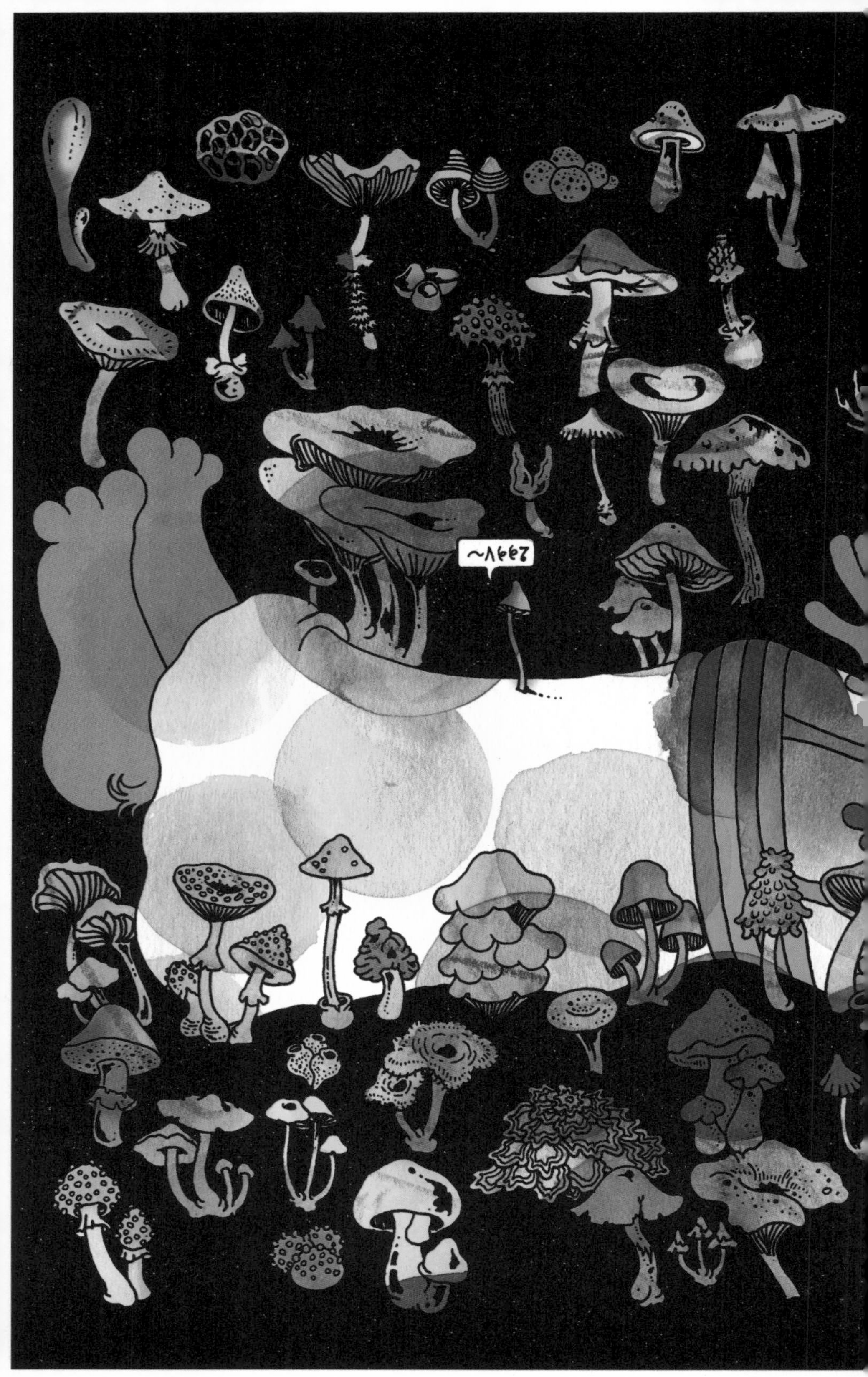

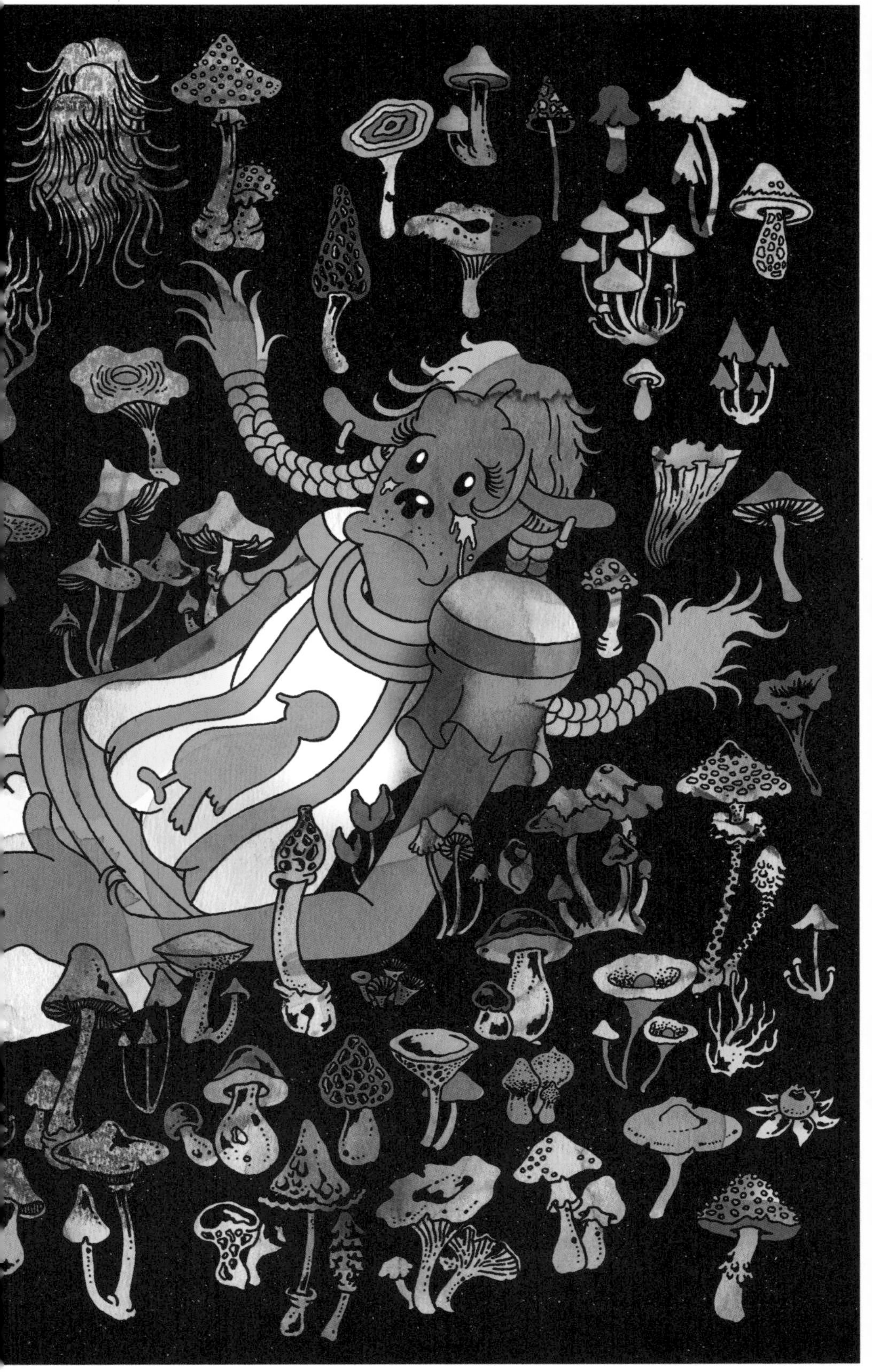

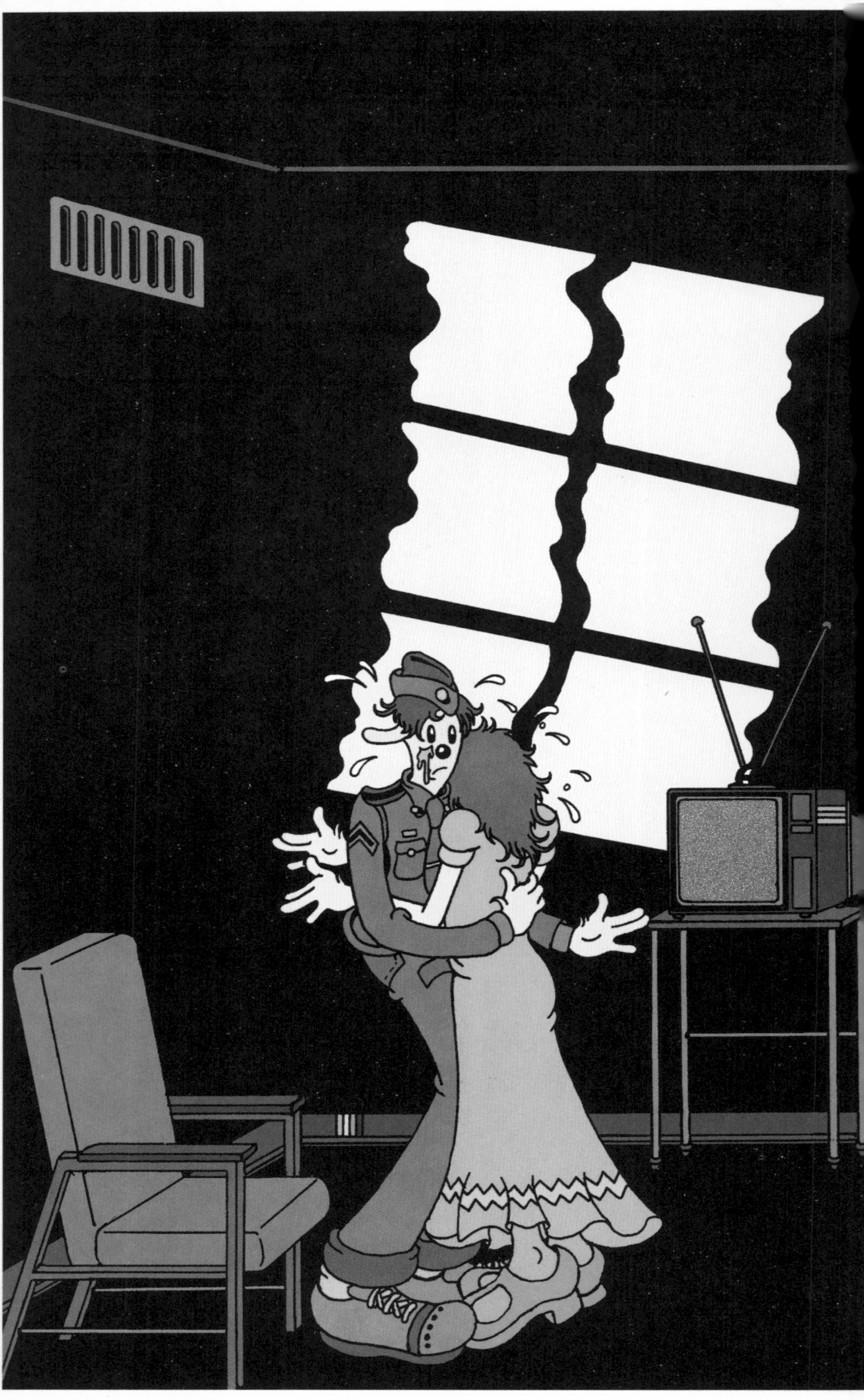

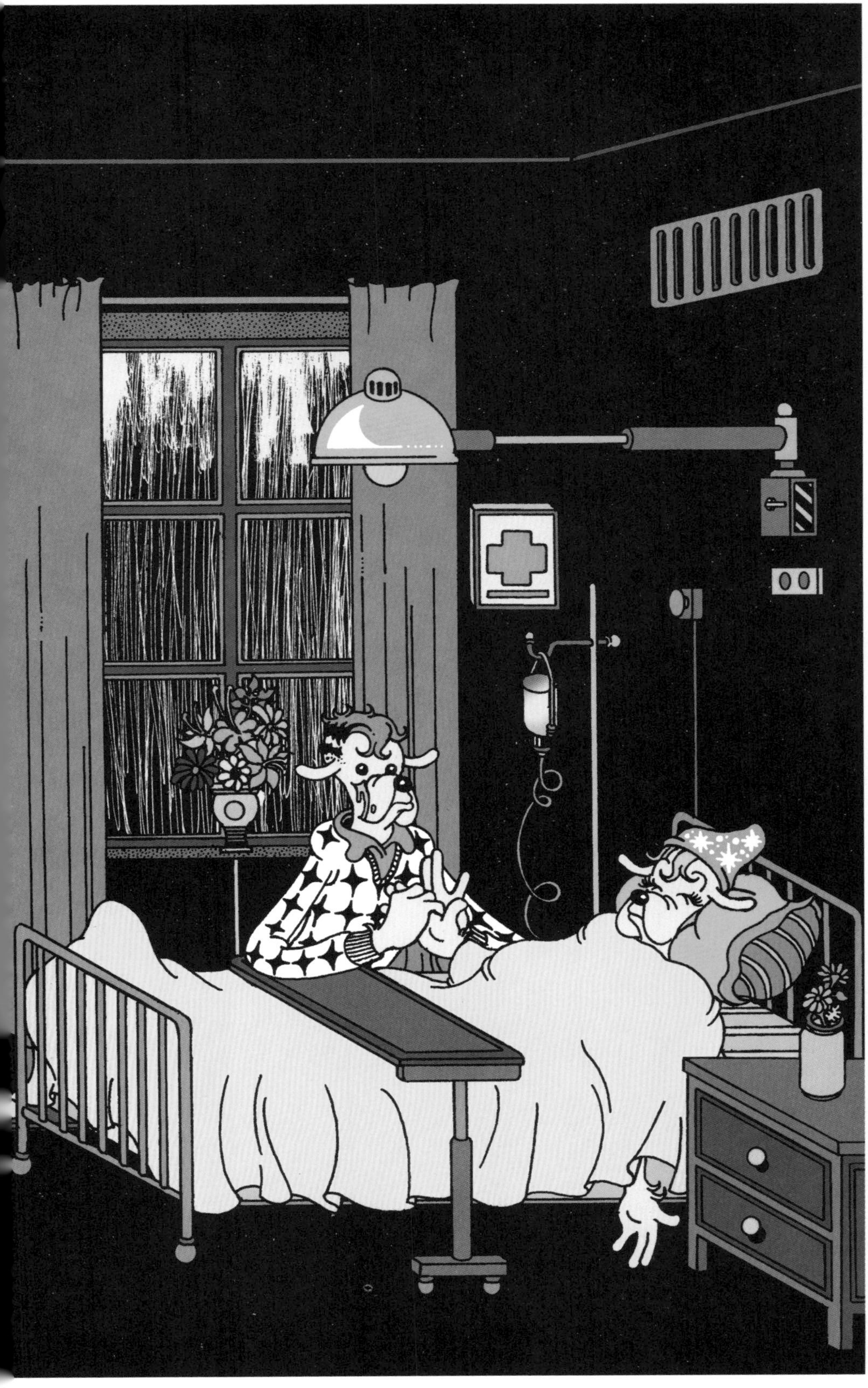

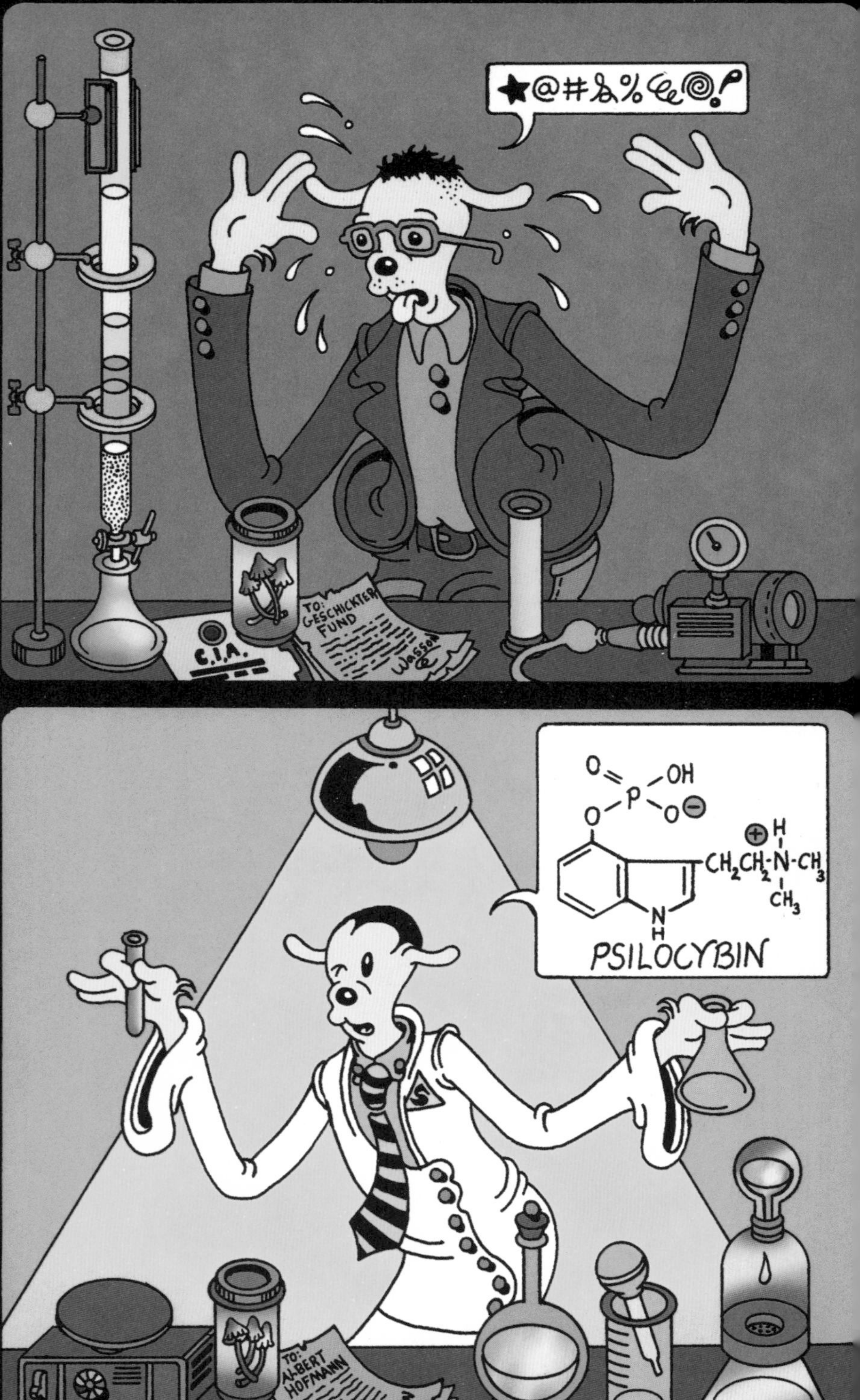
C.I.A.
TO: GESCHICKTER FUND
WASSON
PSILOCYBIN
TO: ALBERT HOFMANN
WASSON

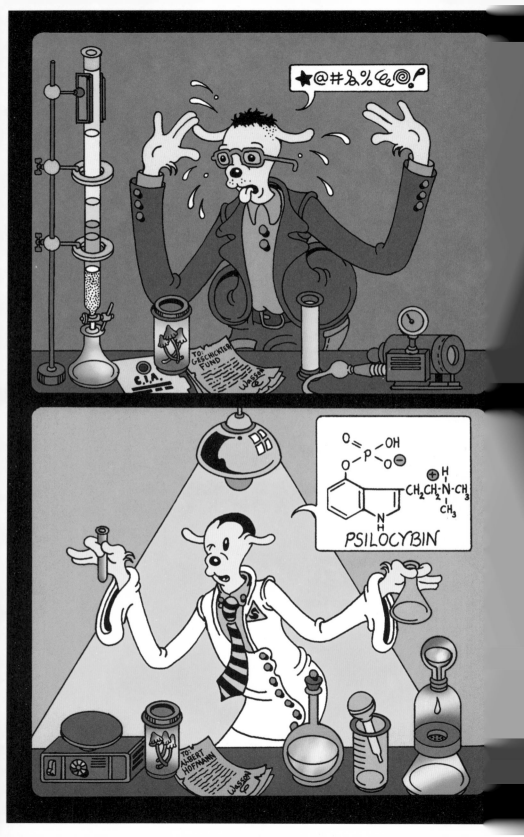

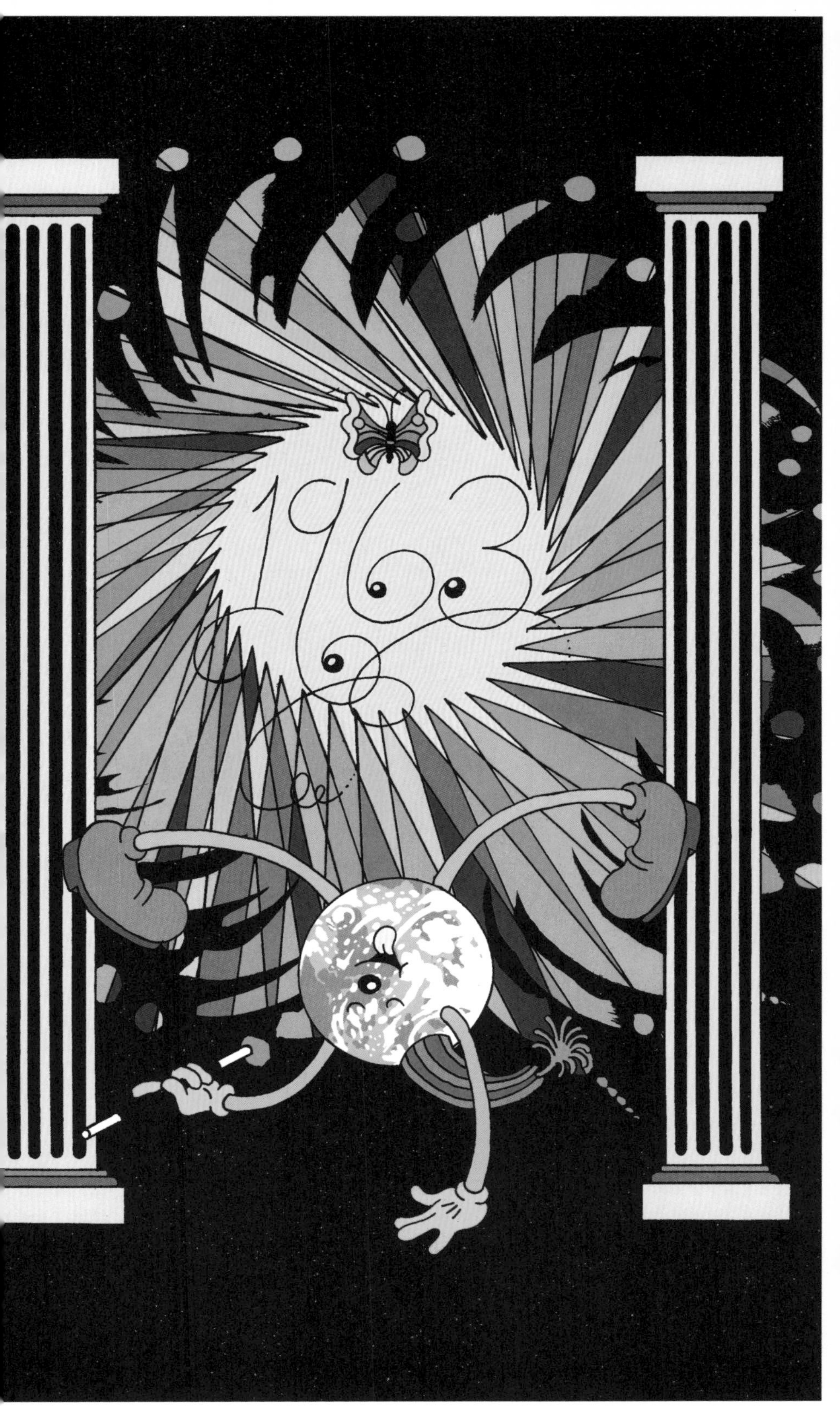
1963

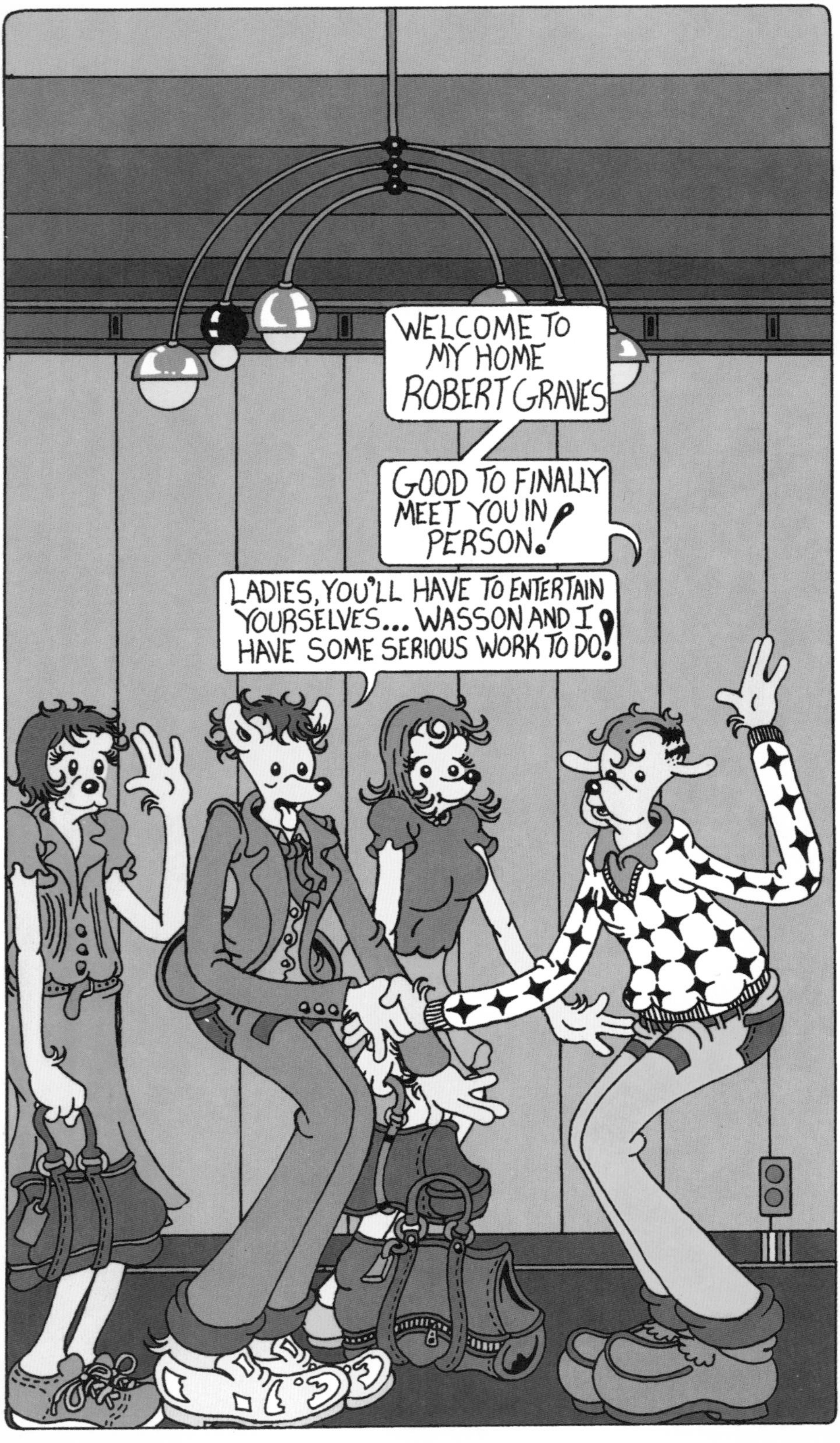
WELCOME TO MY HOME ROBERT GRAVES
GOOD TO FINALLY MEET YOU IN PERSON!
LADIES, YOU'LL HAVE TO ENTERTAIN YOURSELVES... WASSON AND I HAVE SOME SERIOUS WORK TO DO!

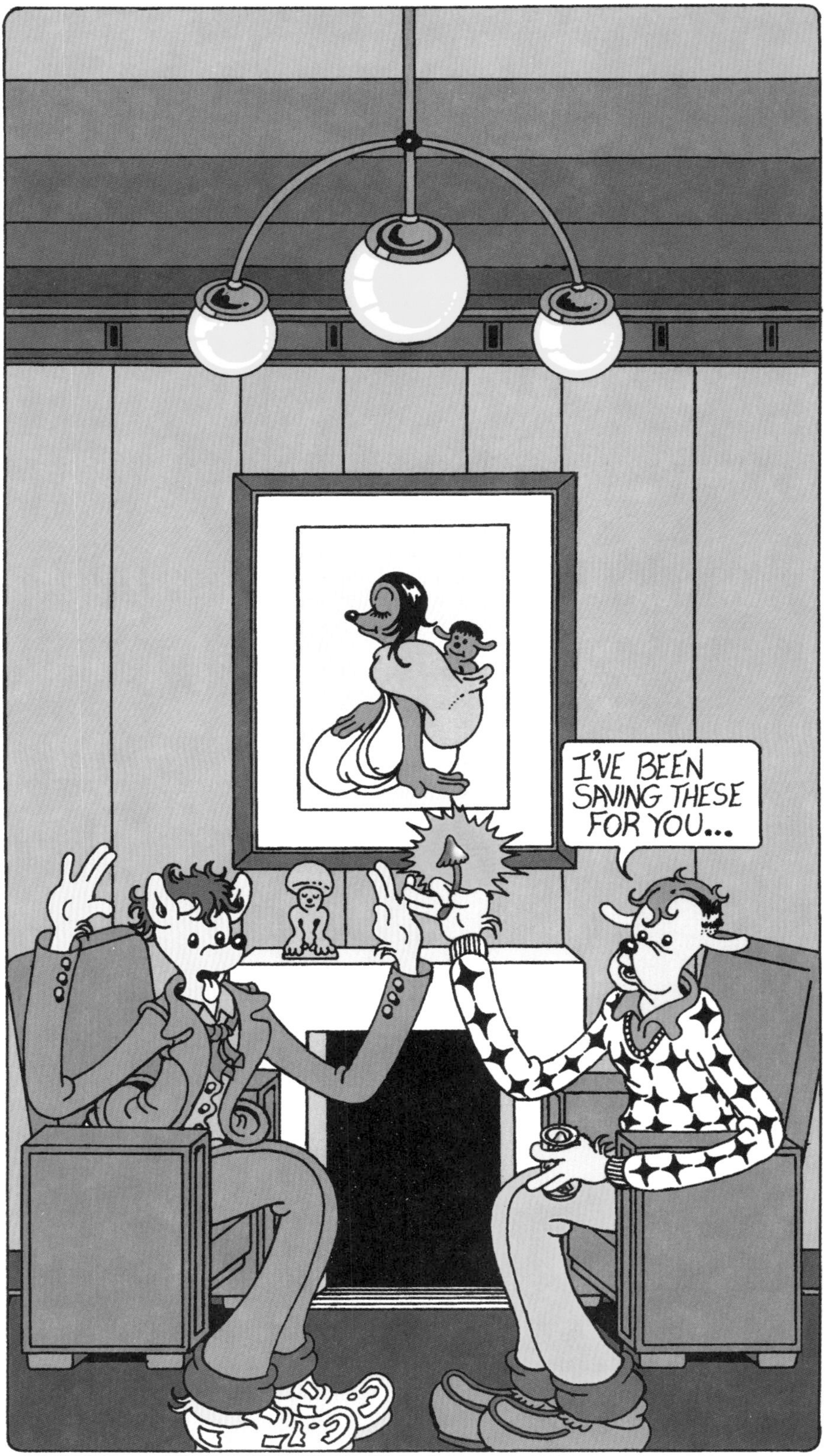
I'VE BEEN SAVING THESE FOR YOU...

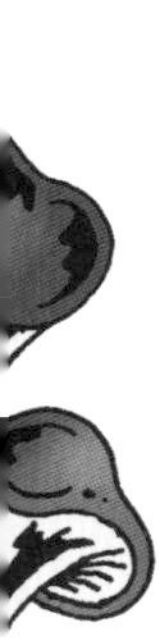

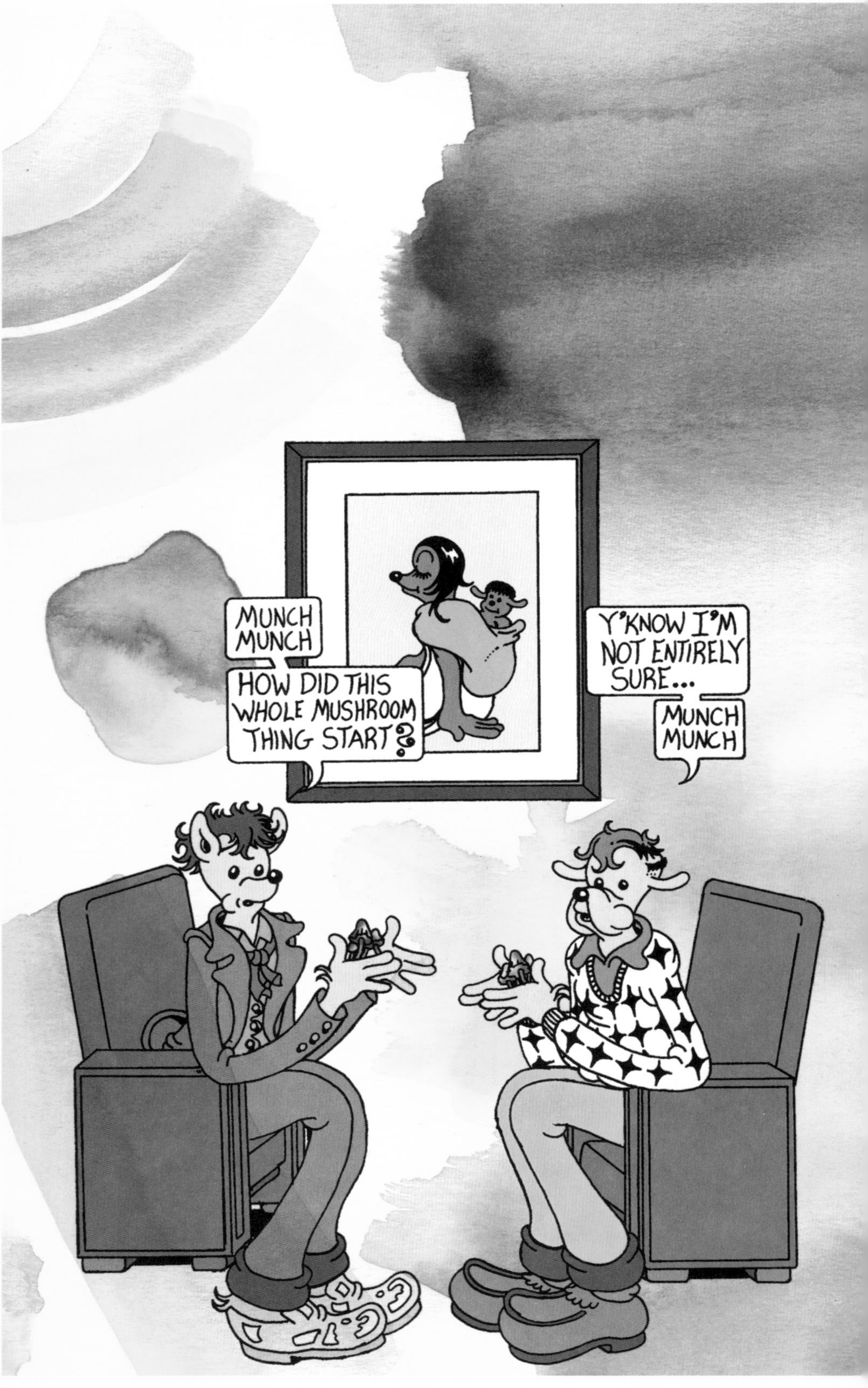
MUNCH MUNCH
HOW DID THIS WHOLE MUSHROOM THING START?
Y'KNOW I'M NOT ENTIRELY SURE...
MUNCH MUNCH

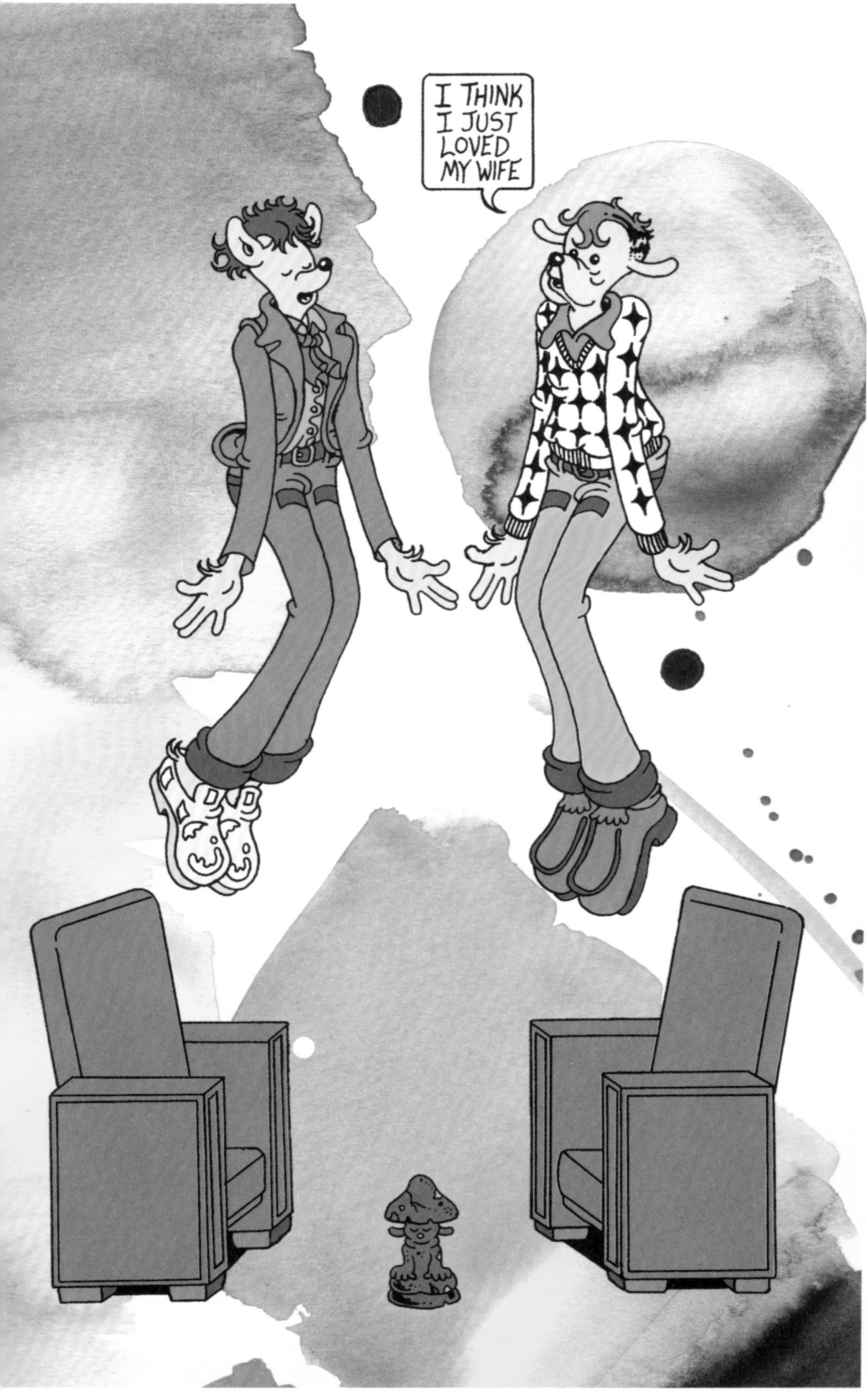
I THINK I JUST LOVED MY WIFE

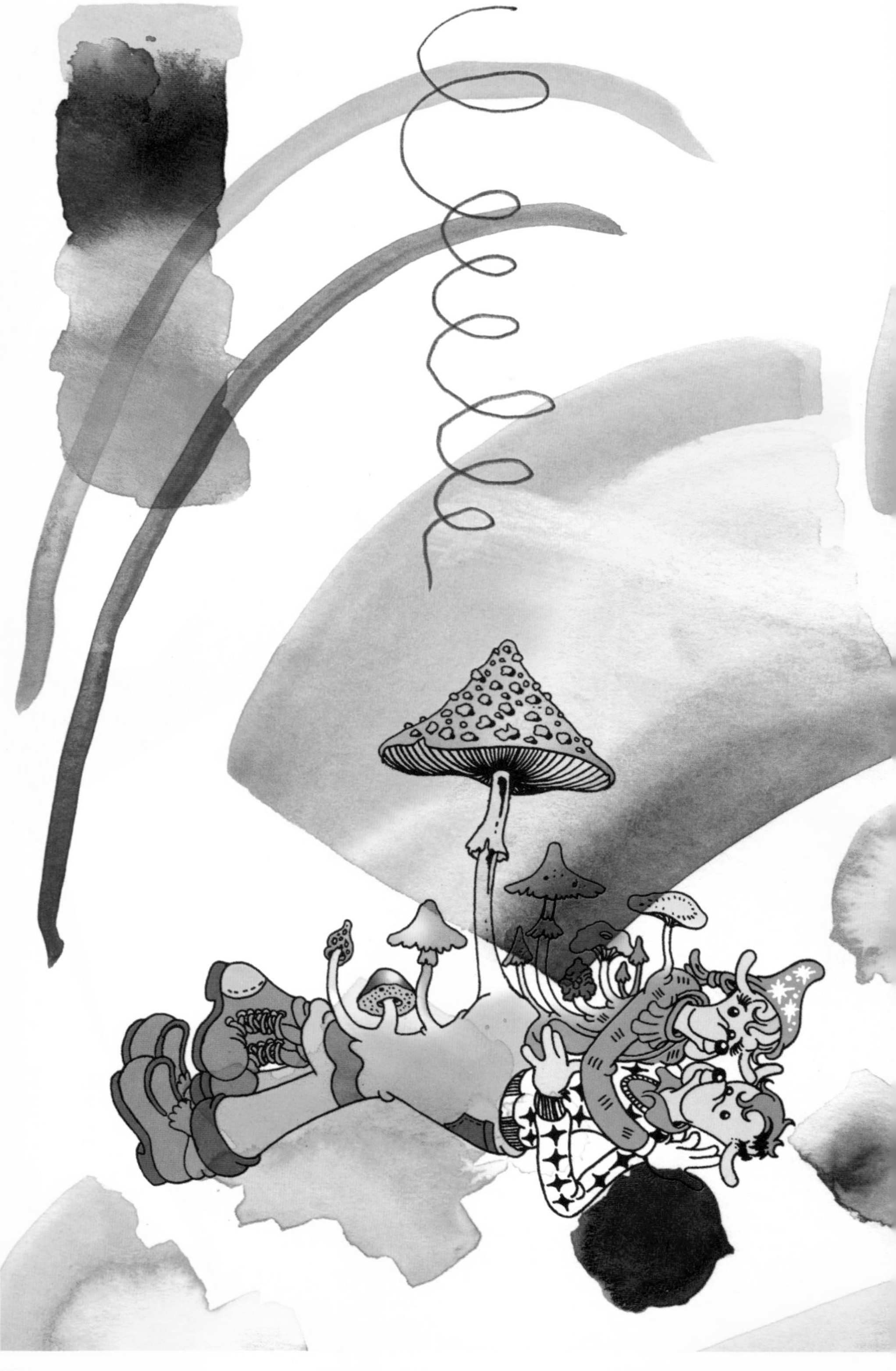

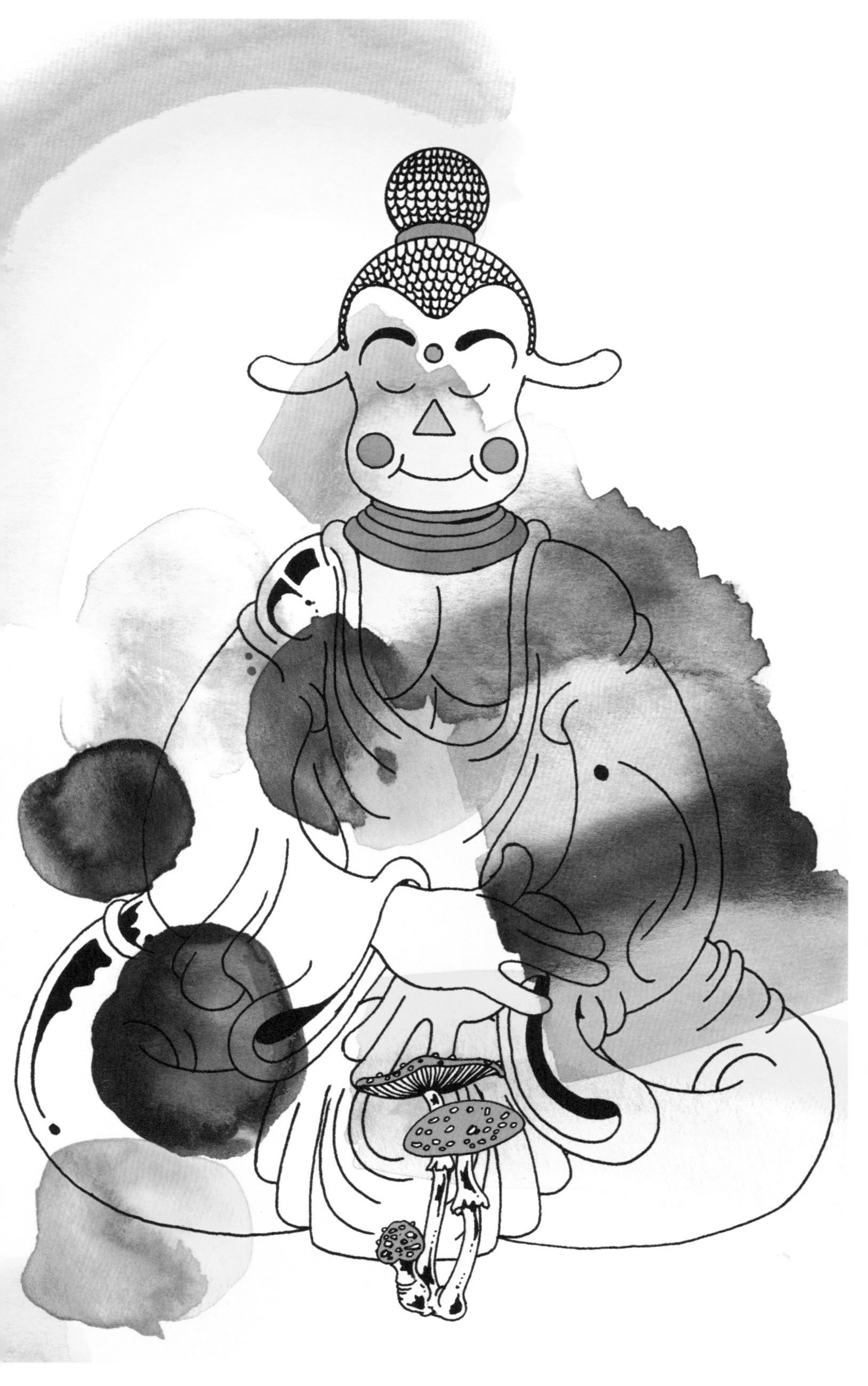

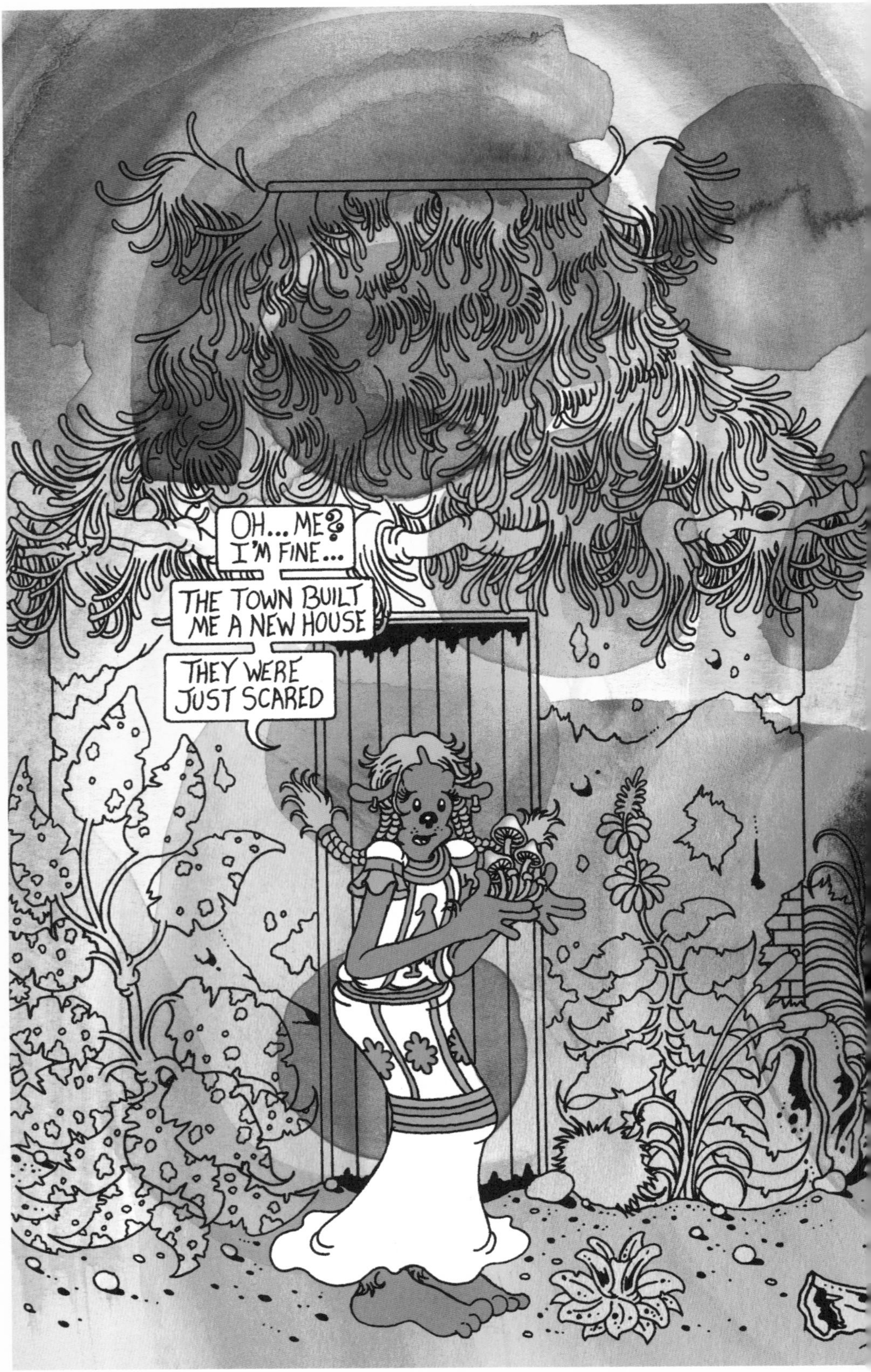
OH... ME? I'M FINE...
THE TOWN BUILT ME A NEW HOUSE
THEY WERE JUST SCARED

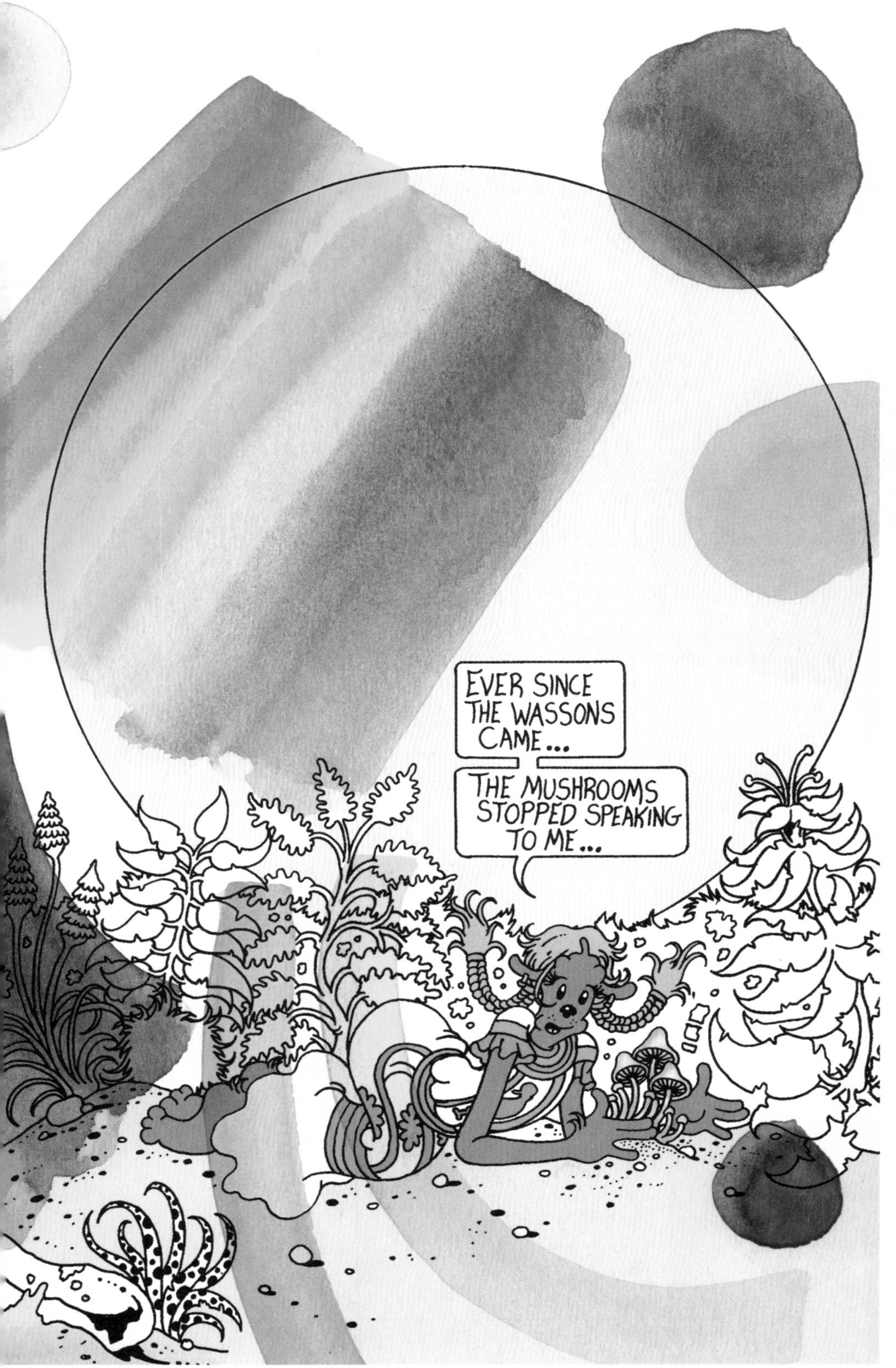
EVER SINCE THE WASSONS CAME...
THE MUSHROOMS STOPPED SPEAKING TO ME...

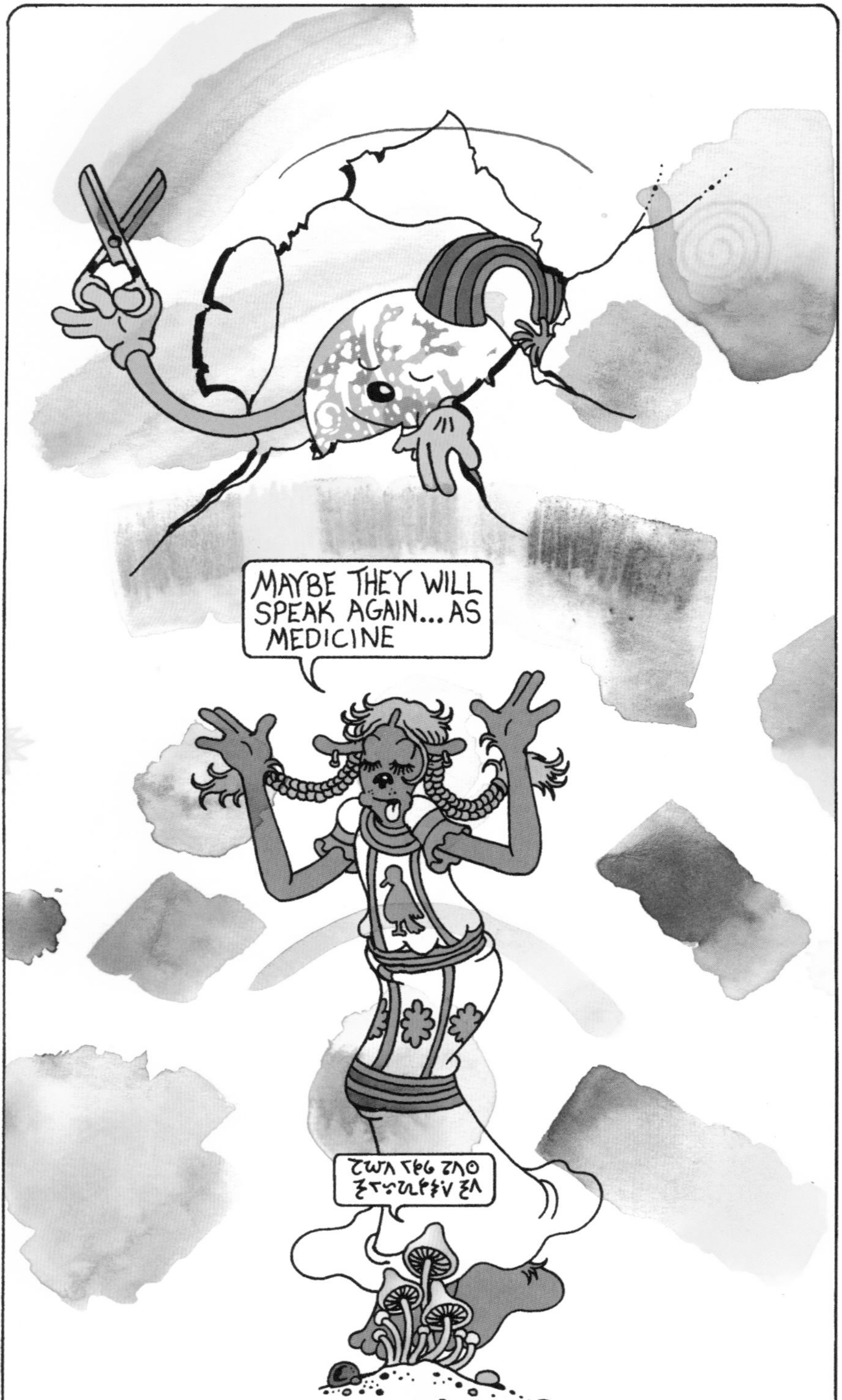
MAYBE THEY WILL SPEAK AGAIN... AS MEDICINE

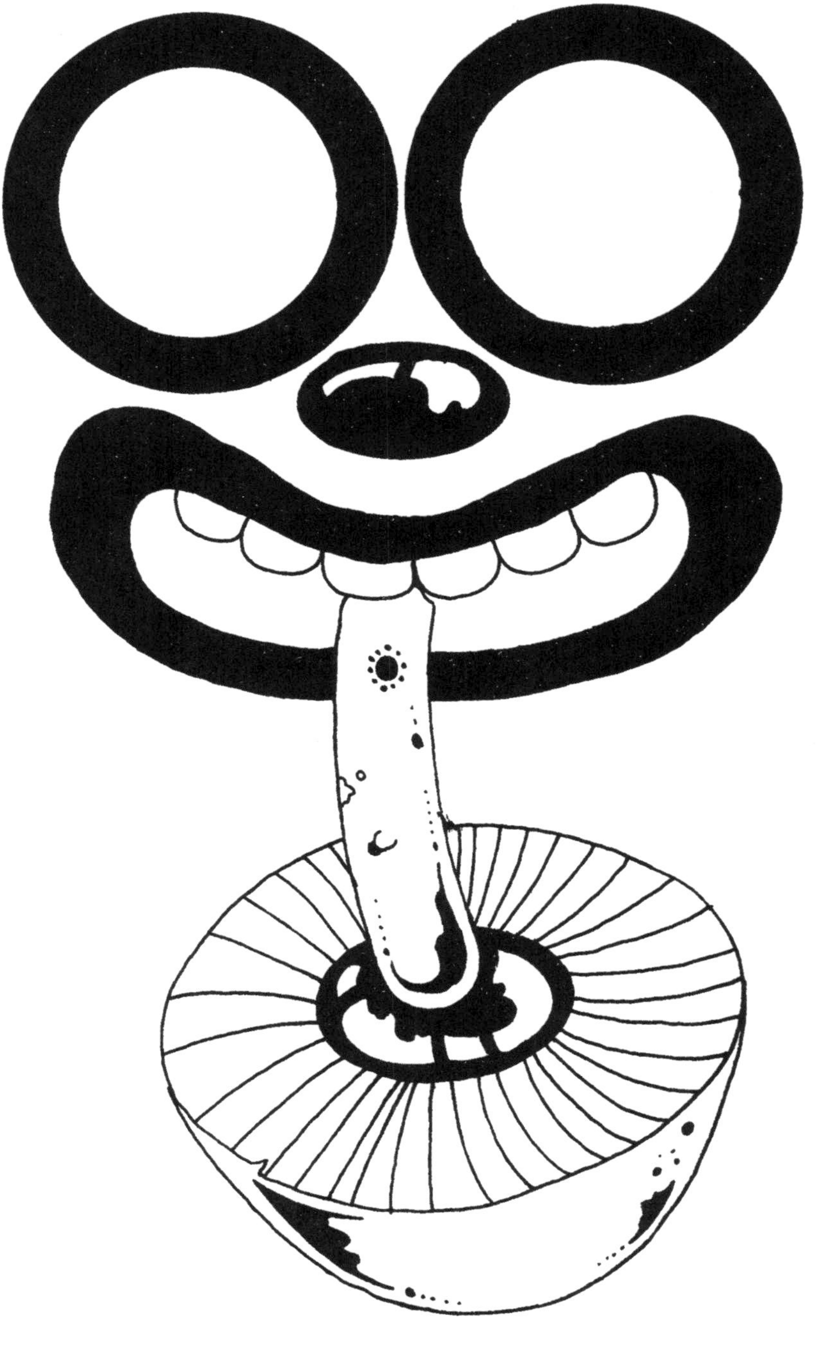

"ENTHEOGENS" IS A NAME
UNVULGARIZED BY HIPPY ABUSE

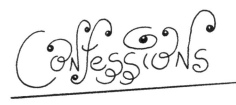

Confessions

IN THE MOST TOXIC PLACE ON EARTH (REACTOR CORE NO. 4 OF THE CHERNOBYL NUCLEAR POWER PLANT) FUNGI IS THRIVING. TERENCE McKENNA DESCRIBED [redacted] PSILOCYBIN MUSHROOMS AS BORSCHT BELT COSMIC COMEDIANS WITH A KNACK FOR SUNBATHING. (I'M BUTCHERING SEVERAL QUOTES HERE BUT STAND BY THE SETIMENT. N)

IN THE SPIRIT OF THE JANITOR STANDING UP AT THE TALENT SHOW AND DELIVERING A JOKE THAT [redacted] [redacted] IS THE FUNNIEST YOU WILL HEAR IN YOUR LIFE (THAT'S MUSHROOMS NOT ME),

I HUMBLY PRESENT YOU... SOME STUFF I SCREWED UP.

ACKNOWLEDGMENTS TO:

VALENTINA AND GORDON WASSON'S MUSHROOMS, RUSSIA, AND HISTORY VOL. I and II

ALSO R. GORDON WASSON'S SUBSEQUENT WORK, THE WONDROUS MUSHROOM: MYCOLATRY IN MESOAMERICA AND SOMA: DIVINE MUSHROOM OF IMMORTALITY

ALSO ACKNOWLEDGING THE SACRED MUSHROOM SEEKER - EDITED BY THOMAS J. RIEDLINGER

AND "THE MYTHOPHILE AND THE MYCOPHILE" BY MICHEL PHARUND

* GRZYBY -

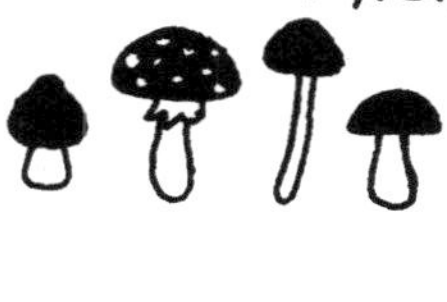

THE #1 PERSON I OMITTED THAT NONE OF THIS WOULD HAVE HAPPENED WITHOUT IS ROGER HEIM, A WORLD-RENOWNED BOTANIST WHO ALSO SUGGESTED MEXICO TO THE WASSONS. HEIM WENT TO MEXICO WITH THE WASSONS SEVERAL TIMES COLLECTING SAMPLES AND █ DOING WATERCOLOR PAINTINGS OF THE SPECIES THEY FOUND. ALL OF THE WATERCOLOR MUSHROOMS IN THIS BOOK ARE BASED ON HIS... IN LIEU OF MAKING HIM A DOG-THING AS TRIBUTE.

MUSHROOMS TO THE MAZATECS WERE A TRUE FAMILY AFFAIR. LIKE CHURCH, PARENTS WORE THEIR SUNDAY BEST AND KIDS SLEPT THROUGH IT. DURING THE WASSONS' ENCOUNTER WITH AURELIO AND HIS ACCESSORIES-- THEY KEPT HAVING TO BREAK TO MOVE A SLEEPING CHILD. THE FIRST TRIP WITH MARÍA SABINA, 25 PEOPLE WERE PRESENT. ← FOR GORDON

½ OF THOSE ARE NON-PARTICIPATING NAPPING CHILDREN. SPEAKING OF KIDS, THE MAZATEC CHILDREN CALLED GORDON "GORDO" WHICH MEANS "FAT" IN SPANISH. MARÍA SABINA SPOKE ▶MAZATEC AND DIDN'T SPEAK SPANISH. ALL CONVERSATION BETWEEN THEM WAS THROUGH AN INTERPRETER. MARÍA'S MUSHROOM VELADA IS FULL OF SONGS ALLUDING TO GOD, THE SAINTS, WHIRLWINDS OF COLOR, AND 13 OPOSSUMS. WASSON RECORDED HER AND YOU CAN HEAR MARÍA'S WORDS VIA FOLKWAYS RECORDS.
IN LIEU OF A LANGUAGE BARRIER... I GAVE THE MUSHROOMS A LANGUAGE... SHOULD YOU YEARN TO SUFFER YOU CAN FIGURE THAT OUT.

THE #2 CHARACTER I OMITTED THAT I WOULD
LIKE TO ACKNOWLEDGE IS MARÍA'S DAUGHTER
POLONIA. I WAS RUNNING OUT OF FACES.

THE WASSONS MADE SEVERAL TRIPS
TO MEXICO... OF WHICH I'VE ONLY SHOWN
YOU SMALL SAMPLES OF TWO. ALBERT HOFMANN
AND ANITA HOFMANN JOINED GORDON IN MEXICO
FOR ONE INVESTIGATION INVOLVING OTHER
PSYCHOTROPIC PLANTS. ALBERT LOOKS DASHING
IN THE ALL-WHITE MAZATEC MEN'S GARB. ANITA
PARTICIPATED IN A RITUAL INVOLVING SALVIA
DIVINORUM WHILE ALBERT WAS SICK FROM FOOD
POISONING. ROGER HEIM IS THE CONNECTION
THAT SENT HOFMANN THE MUSHROOMS.
 Y'KNO WHAT ❓ LEMME DRAW ROGER REAL QUICK
                          (NO ONE ESCAPES)

JAMES MOORE OF THE GESCHICKTER FUND AKA
THE C.I.A. ALSO WENT TO MEXICO WITH GORDON WASSON,
ALBEIT WITH HIS TRUE INTENTIONS DISGUISED.
JAMES IS DESCRIBED AS A REAL WET BLANKET, AND
FAILED TO ISOLATE PSILOCYBIN FROM HIS SAMPLES.

~~ONE LAST DETAIL I LIKED...~~
AS VICE-PRESIDENT OF PUBLIC RELATIONS
AT J.P. MORGAN (I DREW GORDON WORKING
OBVIOUSLY,   IN THE BASEMENT—WOEFULLY
              ~~~~INACCURATE~~~~)
GORDON WAS A TAD CONCERNED ABOUT HOW
HIS CO-WORKERS WOULD REACT TO LEARNING
VIA <u>LIFE</u> MAGAZINE THAT HE WAS
SPENDING HIS VACATION TIME GALLIVANTING
AROUND MEXICO IN SEARCH OF MUSHROOMS.
WITH A LAUGH, GORDON'S BOSS REPLIED
"EVERY MAN HAS TO HAVE A HOBBY BUT
MOST OF US JUST GO SKIING."

I HOPE IT'S NOT LOST ON YOU
DEAR READER THAT THIS IS A TRIUMPH
OF <u>AMATEUR</u> MYCOLOGISTS (WASSONS) WHO
BECAME SO KNOWLEDGEABLE THEY INVENTED
AN ENTIRELY NEW FIELD OF STUDY-
ETHNOMYCOLOGY.
AS FOR POPULARIZING THE MAGIC MUSHROOMS
VIA <u>LIFE</u> MAGAZINE, GORDON DID EXPRESS
REMORSE FOR THE "BEATNIK INVASION"
OF MAZATEC COUNTRY. SOME HAVE
SUGGESTED THAT THIS IS WHY ALL HIS
BOOKS ON THE TOPIC ARE LIMITED EDITION.
NOW IF YOU GO TO HUAUTLA DE JIMÉNEZ
THERE IS A STATUE OF MARÍA SABINA.
SUCH IS LIFE.

AS FOR ME... I'M STILL ALIVE.
I FOUND A BAG OF MUSHROOMS ON
THE CORNER OF BEVERLEY RD. AND
ARGYLE ST. ON APRIL 6TH 2020.
-- ᘛ···

MAYBE I TOOK THEM...
MAYBE I LEFT THEM FOR THE NEXT PERSON.
STILL... AN INTERESTING SIGN
FROM THE UNIVERSE.
AND LIKE THE
HOKEY POKEY
THAT'S WHAT IT'S
ALL ABOUT.

P.S. HOW OFTEN DO YOU GET TO START
WITH ONE BROTHER AND END WITH
THE OTHER?
ENDLESS ACKNOWLEDGMENTS TO
DENNIS McKENNA FOR SUGGESTING
THIS TOPIC. THANKS!

María Sabina, Aurelio Carreras, Valentina
Wasson, R. Gordon Wasson, Masha Wasson
Britten, Peter Wasson, Roger Heim,
Allan Richardson, and Robert Graves.

Slippy, Foxy, Pepper, Pesto, Spiny Maus,
Kate Levitt, Robert and Patricia Blomerth,
Beverly Silver and Richard Levitt,
Allison and Marshall Lamm, Florence Lamm,
Foster Lamm, Paul and Michael Prillaman,
Davey and Mandy, Zach Sokol, Pete Gamlen,
Travis Miller, and of course Jonathan Coward.

Mark Iosifescu, Bryan Cipolla, Casey Whalen,
Jesse Pollock, Keith Abrahamsson, Tom Clapp,
Andres Santo Domingo, Dennis and Terence
McKenna, Anita and Albert Hofmann,
Paul Stamets.

Special thanks to the Heffter Research
Institute and MAPS (Multidisciplinary
Association for Psychedelic Studies). This is
kind of my silly . . . um book with a serious
goal. Look into psychedelic research and
legalization efforts for research and beyond.
Thank you to Johns Hopkins. Last but not
least, thank you to the NY Aquarium sea lion
Bruiser. I will be seeing you shortly.

LEAVE THIS
BOOK OUTSIDE...
A MUSHROOM
MIGHT GROW
FROM THIS
SPOT

↓
●